HPBooks

PRO TECHNIQUES

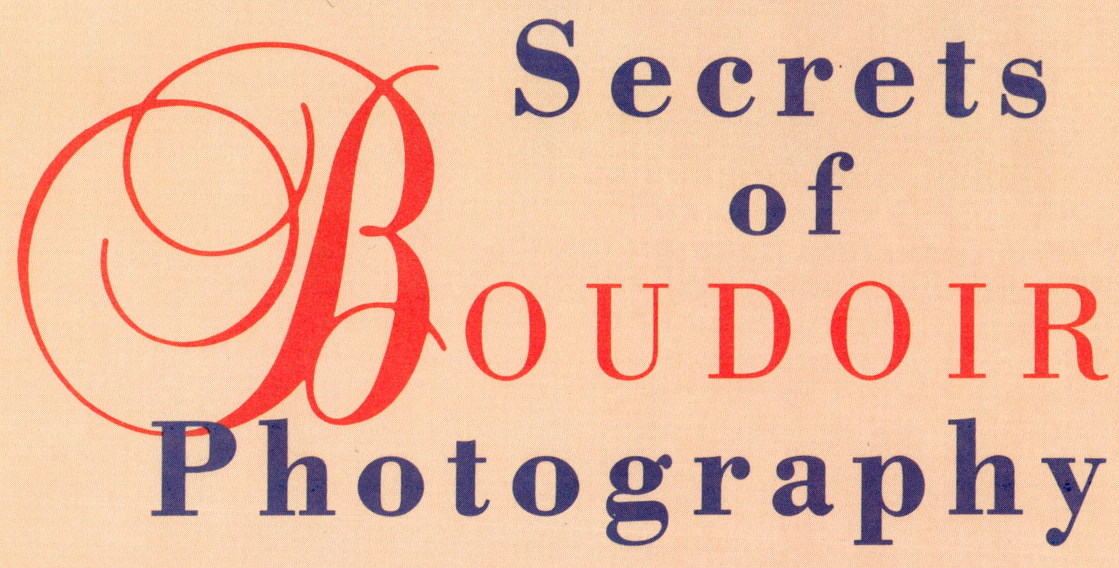

Secrets of Boudoir Photography

By Robert and Sheila Hurth

Published by HPBooks
A Division of Price Stern Sloan, Inc.
360 North La Cienega Boulevard, Los Angeles, California 90048

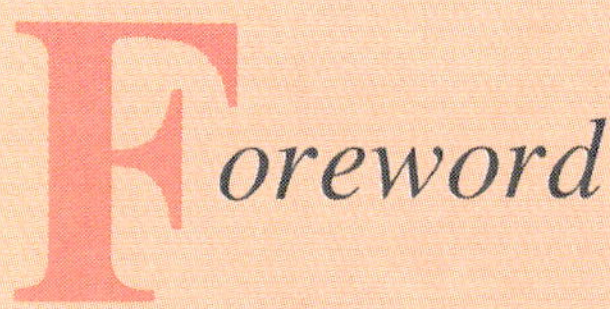

Foreword

Secrets of Boudoir Photography will take you, step by step, into the world of classic romance. Much more than just tips on lighting and descriptions of equipment, this extraordinary book details a whole change of attitude and perception that will enable you to bring out the innate sensuality of your subjects as never before.

But be prepared. In addition to providing clear and concise advice, authors Robert and Sheila Hurth make one clear demand: Do it with style! Every chapter stresses elegance, grace and romance. Every suggestion shows you how to transform a mere photo into a stunningly sensual work of art. Every idea draws you and your subject into the world of classic style.

What does it feel like for a woman to have her special someone see her as undeniably sensually attractive? With you as their photographer, women will soon experience just that sensation.

I highly recommend *Secrets of Boudoir Photography*. For photographers both professional and amateur it is a special window to the visual world of romance. For women who are romantic enough to choose to be photographed in this manner, it represents a chance to truly see their dreams come true.

Langdon Hill

LANGDON HILL, Tucson, Arizona
Mr. Romance; Author of *The Book of Love*;
Editor and Publisher of *The Mr. Romance Newsletter & Catalog*.

Library of Congress Cataloging-in-Publication Data

Hurth, Robert.
Secrets of boudoir photography.

At head of title: Pro techniques.
1. Glamour photography. 2. Photography of women.
3. Photography—Portraits. I. Hurth, Sheila. II. Title.
TR678.H88 1988 778.9'24 88-24277
ISBN 0-89586-733-8

1st Printing
Printed in U.S.A.

Contents

Introduction

Welcome to the Wonderful World of Boudoir Photography! Although it has been around for years, it generally operated behind closed doors. Today, thanks to serious minded, competent photographers, women's equality and awareness, and the craze for health and physical fitness, boudoir imagery has come of age.

The popularity of boudoir photography is nationwide. Not only do the photographs make great gifts for special occasions such as Valentine's Day, Christmas, and anniversaries, but they are in great demand throughout the rest of the year, too. Boudoir images make a special personal statement to that close friend or partner in one's life.

My wife and I have authored an exciting book on the practice and business of wedding photography. In that book, also published by HPBooks, we mentioned how wedding business has played a major part in our studio's growth and how it has led us into developing other areas of photographic business. Although the wedding field has given, and continues to give us, recognition and financial stability, developing the field of boudoir imagery has advanced our reputation as creative photographers and increased our income. It presently constitutes over 30 percent of our nearly $750,000 per-year business.

Although we have been involved in photography for a number of years, boudoir imagery did not cross our path until about four years ago, and then quite by accident. During a simple black and white public relations photo session, a female subject requested a nude photo of herself. Without changing film, lighting, props or sets, we assented to her wishes. The results were disastrous.

Thereafter, other women began to call us with requests for similar photography, not necessarily nude images but sensuous ones. They wanted a unique gift to give to their husbands or boyfriends, something more than just a mere portrait. We tried to accommodate and attempted the photo sessions, but it was obvious that we had neither the knowledge nor the expertise necessary to succeed at this form of photography. The results were consistently poor.

Although it was apparent that a market existed for this type of photography, we weren't sure how large that potential market was. We decided to pursue it, however, thinking that it might be a modest addition to our already growing business. We had no idea that it would lead us into developing a whole new facet of business for our studio.

This was our beginning. We looked high and low for anything written about sensuous, erotic photography. The book market was, and still is, sparse. There were a number of volumes on nude photography, but these were mainly picture books. They taught us little and offered virtually no explanations on how to execute particular shots or what procedures to be aware of.

That was several thousand frames of film ago. Since then, we have experimented with different lighting arrangements, poses, clothing, makeup, sets and props. We have spent a great deal of time, effort and money to learn this area of photography, and we have studied with people who have the knowledge and expertise we were after. It has all been worthwhile.

This book is not just a compilation of pretty pictures. It's a learning adventure into the fabulous field of boudoir photography. It's about having fun and making money at the same time.

Unlike documentary photography, based on reality, boudoir imagery is grounded in illusion. It involves creating sensual images of a woman in the utmost good taste and in a professional manner. These are images that bespeak the sensuous side of a woman without necessarily revealing all to the eye. To take an average looking woman and present a photographic aspect of her that few people realized existed, including perhaps the subject herself, is the delightful challenge to this form of imagery.

We have written this book to offer you insight into this wonderful, highly specialized field of photography, to teach you how to execute this form of imagery competently, and to spare you some growing pains while developing this area of expertise.

Two very special people have played decisive parts in helping to make this fine book reality. They are Tania, our studio manager, and Vernon Gorter, Editorial Director of HPBooks' photo books. We thank them both for their efforts, guidance and understanding.

When you look through the photographs in this book, you might be forgiven for believing you are looking at images that are mainly of professional models. They all look so beautiful. Well, the photos are actually of typical women of all ages, from many walks of life. There are housewives, waitresses, secretaries, business executives, and even an airline pilot.

One of the most important lessons for the beginning boudoir photographer is the realization that every woman has her own, very special and personal beauty. It is the photographer's job and challenge to recognize that beauty and capture it on film. Sometimes, what we record is a true "revelation" even to the woman herself.

We wish you well in your endeavors. May you have much success in producing images that reveal the true beauty and allure of all women—to their loved ones, to the world, and especially to themselves!

CHAPTER 1

What is Boudoir Photography?

The French word *boudoir* means "a woman's private sitting room, dressing room or bedroom." If we took this description at face value, boudoir photography would be nothing more than the photography of a woman in one of these defined areas, but this is far from an accurate description of what we do.

A precise definition of boudoir imagery is somewhat illusive. However, we describe it as creative, intimate, sensitive photography of a woman, in a delicate and soft manner, executed in an alluring, relaxed atmosphere. Such photography seeks to capture, in perfect taste, the enticing, sensual side of all women, a side softly and subtly suggestive but not necessarily revealing.

Let us emphasize that boudoir imagery is not "centerfold" photography, which is usually too revealing to appeal to the average subject. Centerfold photography tends to exploit a woman and her body rather than idealize it.

Origins

Man has always been captivated by the female form. One need only look at the paintings of the old masters for proof of this. However, owning this form of art was often limited to the very few, to the very wealthy.

When camera, film and photographer came upon the scene, the masses were at last able to enjoy owning art themselves. One area that immediately captured the public's interest was photography of women in various positions and states of dress. The French postcard was born.

From about 1900 up to the late 1940s, intimate photos of women sold like hot cakes, but all was very "hush, hush" and "underground." So long as the photo depicted a nude or semi-nude woman, it sold. Most often, the early photographers of this type of picture paid little attention to details such as lighting, props, posing, clothing, backgrounds and the like. Even the size of the print or the physical beauty of the woman did not seem to be of concern. Short, tall, pretty, plain, thin and heavy women were all the province of these early merchandisers. However, the photos did seem to have a common thread among them: the photographic exploitation of woman for money.

Gradually, the serious minded photographer worked his way onto the scene. Attention began to be paid to the types of models selected for such imagery, the models' appearance, the backgrounds being used, the lighting employed, the posing and props, and so on. Such photographers wanted to do this type of photography primarily for the art involved and not for the money. They wanted to extol woman and her form rather than exploit it. Boudoir Photography was coming of age.

Current Popularity

With society's new attitude about sex—both in photos and in the written word—the advent of women's liberation, the craze for health and physical fitness, and women's awareness of their bodies and pride in their figures, boudoir photography has today become socially accepted in most circles of our society, and it is in great demand.

Years ago, the average woman would not have dreamed of equating herself with a magazine model, a person surely very special and out of the ordinary. Today, however, most women have come to the realization that this premise is not true. They know that clothing, makeup, hair styles, and photographic expertise all exist to make them look just as beautiful, sexy, alluring and desirable as most models can be. What's more, the photographic results can be within a price range they can afford. What used to be a dream is now an attainable reality.

Today, through boudoir photography, almost any woman can show the special man in her life or herself that she can be just as alluring, sensuous and lovely as any magazine model.

We tend to worship youth, pretty faces and good figures. At their mid-30s, 40s and 50s some women begin to question whether they are still vivacious, alluring and desirable. Europeans have long known that a woman can be mature and still be very sexually appealing. Fortunately, American women are now starting to recognize this fact, too.

Well executed boudoir photography, handled by a competent photographer, has helped reassure vast numbers of American women that their age need not represent a barrier and that they are, in fact, just as attractive as ever—and sometimes even more so.

A New Art Form—A couple of years ago, we read an article in a national publication which claimed that the days of the old style portrait photographer might be numbered. The article indicated that people today wanted and demanded more from photography than the cliches which had been prevalent in the past. For the portrait photographers who could develop new styles, techniques and markets, the field was wide open, but for those who didn't, professional oblivion was a possibility.

Today, marriage, love, and romance are all back in vogue, and women have never felt more positive about themselves. The modern woman demands a new type of photographic art form in which she can be portrayed more freely, and boudoir imagery fills this need.

Photographers who have been in the business for a number of years know the value of baby photography, child photography, high school and graduation photography, the photography of grandmothers who wish to send portraits as gifts to their grandchildren, and so on. Such photography often produces a high volume of sales. But what about the women who are in between the ages of graduated teenager and grandmother? In the past, such women had professional photos of themselves taken only once or twice over a 10 or 20 year period. They thought there was little reason to be photographed more frequently.

Today, boudoir imagery gives a woman a good reason for memorializing herself on film, year after year. Such images make outstanding and unique gifts for loved ones, for that special occasion or holiday, or just for herself. Each time she is photographed, the woman can be presented in a new manner and dimension, totally unlike the typical portraits of the past. For the professional, such work means not only more challenge and variety, but also more customers and sales.

The potential market is to be found not only with the pretty young woman but with almost any woman, of any age. We have photographed people between 18 and 70 years of age—of various sizes and shapes and from all walks of life: housewives, clerks, doctors, lawyers, accountants, even master plumbers and a female 747 captain. Each of these women has her own special physical assets and attributes for you to work with, and your challenge is to capture these qualities on film in a very special, different and often illusionary way.

Difference Between Glamour and Boudoir Photography

Let's draw some guidelines between the two areas of expertise—glamour and boudoir photography—as they apply to the non-professional subject.

Glamour photography is often done with the subject fully dressed or in a bathing suit. It sometimes involves only head or head-and-shoulders shots. Boudoir imagery, on the other hand, is often executed with the subject scantily dressed in bedroom or similar seductive attire such as a negligee, bra and panties, a teddy, a merry widow, and the like.

Boudoir photography often involves three-quarter and full length shots with emphasis placed both upon the subject's body and body language as well as upon her face. It requires the subject to exhibit an air of sensuality, and it definitely requires her to engage in some form of play acting. In addition, the inclusion of a prop or two or even an entire set often becomes very important.

Boudoir photography has something in common with glamour and fashion photography as well as portraiture, yet it is really none of these. And, boudoir photography is certainly not just a new twist on glamour photography. Its framework is illusion and fantasy, tempered by the bounds of good judgment and taste. It is a new field.

The Bounds of Boudoir Photography

Well executed boudoir photography is not pornographic or obscene. There would be no appeal or market for such photography with the subjects photographed. "Show more" of the subject, and often you'll be reducing the likelihood for referral business as well as reducing the sales from the subject that you were shooting. "Show less," but be suggestive while doing it, and you open the door to a whole new form of business, increased sales, and customers.

Boudoir imagery is not documentary photography, which shows "reality" as it is generally seen, but presents a women as she would like to see herself or have others see her.

Since few women are professional models, most will need some form of assistance in enhancing their body and facial features: proper clothing, makeup, hair styling, directing and reassurance. Without attention to these areas, a photographer would merely record that which was there to be seen. He has to do more: He must introduce illusion and fantasy.

Three Ways of Seeing

A woman can be seen in three different ways, and she can be photographed in each of these ways. She can be photographed as *you*, the photographer, see her. Or, she can be depicted as she appears to *herself*—when looking in a mirror, for example. Both of these examples are documentary photography.

However, you can also photograph the illusive inner person of the subject—perhaps the *femme fatale* the subject would like to look like or thinks she looks like. This is boudoir photography.

A subject may not even realize that she has another facet to herself, a sensuous or alluring side. This fact is part of your challenge: bringing out these facets of the subject and capturing them on film. It will help if you create an illusion for the subject, accentuating the subject's best facial and body features.

Creativity and Good Taste

Seating a half-clad subject upon a posing stool and just snapping away, frame after frame of film, will not get the job done for the usual person that walks into your door for boudoir photography. Not only will you often have to use sets or props to accomplish your goal, but you will also have to have the sitter identify, relate, or interact with the setting—and all in exquisitely good taste.

We cannot overemphasize the importance of producing tasteful boudoir images, not "peep show" photos. The images that you create for a subject must be so tastefully done that the sitter would not hesitate to show these to anyone with pride. To accomplish less than this is to do an injustice to the sitter and to your professionalism.

Boudoir photography is a form of visual expression that will give you tremendous creative freedom. You will be at liberty to let your imagination run rampant: photos of your subject in a bedroom scene, in a bathtub, in a deeply wooded area, at the beach, or at almost any location where the subject would feel comfortable.

Of course, with this much creative license, it becomes necessary to have some tighter guidelines to follow and to offer the subject. Thus, your initial consultation with the subject becomes very important: You must be able to gain some insight into what the subject is looking for, why, and for whom. We shall delve into this aspect in the next chapter.

Sexuality and Sensuality

Dictionary definitions of the words *sexual* and *sensuous* are not enough to help direct a photographer when doing boudoir imagery. A woman can appear sexy and yet not be sensuous and vice-versa. Some women will not openly appear to have the ability to demonstrate either quality. Some women will be able to achieve both a sexy appearance and a sensuous look.

Each subject must be dealt with on an individual basis, and it is part of the photographic challenge to bring forth at least one of these two facets during a successful boudoir photo session. Which of the two facets is the more important? The answer to this question is academic. Which quality can you bring forth? That's the important issue. Of course, being able to have a subject appear both sexual and sensuous before a camera would be ideal.

Shooting Location

Boudoir imagery is not confined to photographs of women in a bedroom scene. You have three major choices for shooting locations—your studio; your home or the subject's; other locations, such as a beach or wooded area.

Although it may seem perfectly logical to engage in boudoir photos using a bedroom as a photo scene, such a setting may not always be appropriate to the particular subject being photographed. The subject may feel much more comfortable or more sensuous doing the photo session in a living room, on an isolated strip of beach, in a bathtub or even on the front seat of a car. And, equally as important, if the final images are intended for someone other than herself, that person might think that the subject is more alluring in a location other than the bedroom.

Any place that the subject or her "special man" would find enticing or alluring is the place that the photo session could take place. The subject's boyfriend or spouse might think that it is extremely sexy to see his loved one scantily dressed while puttering around in a kitchen area, or in a locker area, dressing or undressing for aerobic exercises. Once you know your work boundaries, you can give the subject the variety of settings best suited to her.

The one thing that you should not do is confine yourself to a mold. Don't find one or two "general" outdoor locations or create one or two standard sets in your home or studio and expect all of your subjects to relate to them and photograph at their best. It will not work. Inquire! Find out what she and her special someone likes and relates to, and then use this information as the springboard for your photo session.

If a subject has expressed no open preference for a special look or location, then you must make the decision for her. Choose a variety of different sets, props and articles of clothing and work until you find one or more that presents her well.

Clothing

Some women are much more alluring when attired in a sweatshirt and tight fitting jeans than they are in sleepwear. To put such a woman into a mold and force her into a nightgown to be photographed in a bedroom scene would defeat your purpose. Inquire of the subject as to what she feels she looks best in and use this information as a guideline.

When selecting clothing, make certain that what the subject wears is consistent with the set she is being photographed in. For example, if you are photographing a subject in a barn, it would usually be inappropriate for her to be attired in a very expensive evening gown. It might be great garb for a fashion advertisement but not necessarily for boudoir.

We shall have further discussion about clothing in a later chapter.

Boudoir for Men

Why not! We now live in a very liberated society where sexual discrimination is all but non-existent. Women have boudoir photography done as a special gift for that special man in their life; why not the reverse situation?

Notwithstanding the above and the fact that there are a number of photographers throughout the country who do take male boudoir photographs, we do not—for a number of reasons. First, women happen to dominate our clientele by a resounding 99 percent. Second, women make larger purchases—both as to print sizes and final orders—than their male counterparts.

Women also find it easier to role-play than do most men. Many women can change from a sexy look to a sultry look to a "little girl" look with ease. For the most part, men—unless they happen to be professional models—feel silly when before a camera and tend to want to look "macho." This hardly affords pictorial variety and a chance for increased sales.

Men often tend to approach the concept of boudoir photography with a casual and sometimes flippant attitude. In contrast, females are often eager to follow instructions and do what is required to end up with a stunning photographic result.

Nevertheless, although this book is directed primarily toward boudoir photo sessions of females, a great deal of the same information can be applied if your subject is a male. Of course, most of the basic poses will be quite different.

CHAPTER 2

The Initial Consultation

Most often your first contact with a prospective boudoir subject will be by telephone. This first contact is extremely important since it will establish the ground rules that both you and the subject will ultimately work within, and it will help establish a rapport.

Your primary objective with this initial contact is to get the subject to your studio or home to see samples of your work as it applies to boudoir photography.

Telephone Contact

We cannot overemphasize the importance of the proper use of the telephone as a sales tool. The person who answers your phone must be thoroughly conversant with what you do, how you do it, and what you charge. You want a warm, friendly individual who is anxious to assist a prospective photo subject. The function of this person should not be to merely answer questions with short abrupt answers but to have a genuine interest in the caller's photographic needs.

The boudoir candidate will often be nervous when calling. Usually, it will have taken some courage on her part just to make a telephone call to tell you that she is interested in this form of photography. She will often not know what questions to ask, what the procedures are and whether, indeed, you do this type of work. This is the time for you or the person designated to answer the phone to be helpful, to be very informative, and to assure her that engaging in such photography is a wonderful experience.

***Ask Questions*—**In the first telephone contact, find out from the subject how she got to know about you, why she is interested in this form of photography, whom the photos are to be for, if there is a deadline to meet—such as for an anniversary or birthday—and so on. Also, get some information about the subject herself: color of hair and eyes, height, weight, and so on. Ask questions!

Invite her to see your work and offer to make an appointment, at no obligation to her, to sit with you or one of your staff to discuss the possibilities of her doing a boudoir photo session.

***Answer Unasked Questions*—**Whether she inquires or not, constantly reassure her that your style of boudoir photography is not ever in poor taste but is done instead with the highest standards. Convince her that she will enjoy the experience and have fun doing it and that such imagery will make a fabulous and unique gift for herself, and her boyfriend or husband. Be very open with everything that you say. Leave no questions unanswered.

Don't let the caller feel the least bit suspicious or uneasy about you, your work, where you conduct the sessions, or this form of photography. Advise her that you and your staff know the value of serious boudoir photography and that it is approached and conducted in a totally professional manner.

All of this information and your approach to the caller should leave her with a good feeling about you, your studio and your work even before she has met you. It should motivate her to come to see you in order to learn more.

Personal Contact at Studio

Once the boudoir candidate has come to see you and your work, your next objective is to book the photo session. This often involves some salesmanship on your part since she still may be somewhat nervous and apprehensive or even somewhat embarrassed about engaging in this form of photography. You, or the person designated by you to talk with her, must demonstrate a professional approach, in a warm, friendly and helpful manner. Show her samples of your work and, as you do so, point out how she could easily do something similar.

Have a designated spot in your home or studio for this conference, since you don't want the subject to be embarrassed by strangers looking on as she chats with you and examines your work. Make certain that the area is well lit, bright and friendly. In addition, try not to be interrupted during this conference. It will assuredly distract the subject and may even cause her to cut her consultation short.

At this first face-to-face contact, again inquire whom the intended photos are to be for. Ask if they are for her, for posterity's sake or for a special someone. Display enthusiasm and excitement about her doing a boudoir session.

Inquire if she has a preconceived idea of what she wants. Often a subject will have seen a picture or two in a magazine and will want an image that is similar, if not identical. Assure her that you can do it, plus more.

A number of women will tell you that they are apprehensive about this form of photography for several reasons: They don't photograph well, they are too heavy, their hips are too large, they are fearful that too much will be seen, and so on. Be prepared to deal with these objections sympathetically.

***Putting Subjects at Ease*—**First of all, you can show samples of photos of a subject with large hips or who was overweight. You can explain how you dealt with the problem photographically. You can talk about the magic of lighting and tell the potential client that you will only display as much or as little of her form as she wishes—and all in good taste.

Put her mind at ease. Assure her that she

is not going to be on display during this photo session and that the session will be behind closed doors with a limited number of assistants, at least one of whom will be female.

Assure the subject that it is your intention to minimize any facial or bodily imperfections that she thinks she may have—and every woman that we have encountered has had them—while at the same time capitalizing on all of her better aspects. Let her know that all of this will be accomplished through the careful selection of clothing, poses, sets, props, makeup and lighting.

Ask the subject what she thinks her best features are. Inquire if the special man in her life shows a preference for one or more of her features. Let her know that you care about making her look as attractive and beautiful as possible.

Also, tell the subject that most boudoir subjects are nervous at first but that the tension passes as the session unfolds. Emphasize the friendly, relaxed atmosphere of your shooting area and the refreshments—wine, coffee or soda—that you offer for a subject's comfort.

Spend time with your potential client discussing the length of the session and what she is to wear. Discuss her wardrobe and plan various outfits for her to bring. Assure her that if nothing she brings produces the look that she is after or that you want, you have a few items that she can adorn herself with which will enhance her.

Preparing The Subject Mentally For The Session—You must psychologically and mentally prepare the subject for the photo session. The client's perception of herself—whether she sees herself as pretty or ugly, too thin or too fat, too many inches in one part of her body and not enough in another—is very important to the ultimate success or failure of the session. You must constantly reassure her that you can photographically enhance her face and figure, and at the same time hide all of those features that she may feel insecure about or even dislike.

Preparing her mentally for the session may also involve an advance tour of your shooting area. Most of your subjects will not be professional models, may not have been photographed in years, and may have absolutely no idea of what to expect. This can cause additional anxiety. To help alleviate the problem, allow the subject to tour your facilities and in general tell her what you intend to do, where and how.

People Present During The Session

Some women may openly express concern about the number of people who will be in the shooting area with you at the time of the actual photo session, or they may openly express an intention of not wanting to be in the shoot room area alone with you. Put their mind at ease and discuss your policy. In our studio, for instance, our policy is to have at least two or, ideally, three people present at all times: myself, my wife and one female assistant.

I will be at the camera, my wife will demonstrate and assist the subject with the posing, and the assistant will usually take charge of moving props, adjusting lights, metering, and so on. When assisting the subject with a pose, my wife or the assistant will have all of the physical contact with her. I never touch the subject, and she is assured of this in advance.

Technically, one person could conduct the entire photo session, but having an assistant or two will not only make it easier and faster, but the session will be safer for you and more reassuring to the subject.

In today's society, a doctor would not think of examining a female patient without having his nurse present. This is a form of legal protection for the doctor, in case the patient later claims that he made improper advances or remarks. When you engage in boudoir photography, you are in a situation that is no less sensitive. Having an assistant or two with you at all times will go far in furthering the subject's comfort and sense of security.

Bringing a Friend to the Session—Often, women will inquire if they can bring someone—a husband, boyfriend or girlfriend—with them to the session, to watch as they are being photographed. Most subjects are not professional models and it has been our experience that the average woman cannot emotionally handle the presence of such persons during a boudoir session. The subject's attention span is greatly reduced.

During the entire photo session, the subject will be constantly looking for approval from those present. This disrupts the session, keeping the subject from concentrating on the poses and mood, and extending the time for the session. Also, most onlookers will not sit idly by, watching the events unfold, but will make remarks with each and every pose. They will want to discuss how they liked or did not like the subject in a certain pose, their views about the set, a particular article of clothing, a certain prop, and so on.

Most people—subjects or spectators—don't understand that the camera angle and the lighting that the camera and film "see" are very different from what they see or perceive with their own eyes. By the time you explain this, the damage will have been done: The sitter will have become more nervous and you will have to spend a great deal of time reassuring her and gaining back her confidence.

The best solution, when confronted with the proposition of having someone watch the photo session, is to say "no." Let the subject bring a friend to the session but have the friend wait in some other area of your facilities until you have finished photographing.

Additional Points

At the first face-to-face meeting with the subject, part of your job will be to offer certain other suggestions and recommendations. Cover the following items with the subject in as much detail as you feel is needed.

Makeup and Hair—Inform the subject that it is in her best interest to have her makeup and hair done just before the start of the session—and by a professional. She may go to anyone she chooses, or you can offer a recommendation. The make-over could even be done at your studio if you have the time and space to afford this service, and provided you have makeup and hair people that will travel to your home or studio for a reasonable fee.

Shaving—Advise the subject to shave her legs and under her arms about 12 hours before the photo session. A fresh shave may leave red marks on her body or fresh nicks, scrapes and scratches. These blemishes would be photographically undesirable and would call for additional spotting and retouching on final prints.

Suntan—Instruct the subject not to get a suntan between the time of your meeting and the session. A suntan may leave all or a portion of her body looking blotchy, unevenly tanned, reddened or dry in appearance.

Hose—In virtually all poses, the appearance of a subject's legs will be enhanced if pantyhose are worn. Not all brands will be photographically acceptable, so you will have to instruct the sitter on what to buy, and why. We shall explain this in greater detail in a later chapter.

Marks from Tight-Fitting Garments—A bra, panties or other tight fitting garments can cause the body to become marked or creased. Advise your subjects to wear only loosely fitting clothing on the day of the shoot. Otherwise, all marks or creases will show prominently in the final prints. This, too, would call for additional spotting, retouching, and even tedious art-work on final prints.

Ideally, you should instruct a subject not to wear tight clothing or undergarments at least 24 hours before the photo session. In addition, advise her to apply cocoa-butter to the areas of her body that might have been affected by such garments. This will help to reduce, if not eliminate, the visual effect of any marks.

Duration of Session—Inform the subject that the entire photo session—excluding the time to have her makeup and hair attended to—will be about two hours. This will give her an opportunity to plan her day around the session.

Cost of the Session—At your first consultation, you should be very clear about your pricing structure and so inform the subject. You do not want any surprises for her or misunderstandings at session's end or at the time she places her final order.

Conclusion

If you cover all of the above points carefully, you should be able to book the session with ease. The subject should leave your home or studio feeling very positive and comfortable about doing the session and ideally, be anxious to come back for the actual photography.

CHAPTER 3

How to Direct a Boudoir Session

Boudoir photography demands a great deal of expertise because it requires knowledge and proficiency in many areas of photography and because it usually involves working with non-professional models.

In addition, the ultimate outcome of a successful boudoir photo session is dependent upon a number of factors, not the least of which is the attitude of the subject, and the approach of the photographer and assistants.

During the course of any boudoir sitting, the photographer must be in control and be prepared to totally direct the subject. Photographer and assistants must exhibit an air of professionalism somewhat above the normal requirement for an ordinary portrait sitting. At the same time, they must create a friendly, relaxed atmosphere that causes a subject to relate well to the photographer, the set she is being photographed in, and the mood that has been created for her.

In addition, the subject must be willing to give her total concentration, must want to be photographed in this particular manner, and must have the willingness and cooperation to follow instructions.

The fact that boudoir photography is more than ordinary portraiture or glamour photography places great demands upon the photographer, both in his capacity as technician as well as director. It also places demands upon the untrained, non-schooled, non-professional subject.

Setting the Stage

Photographers who regularly engage in commercial photography are quite accustomed to working with hairstylists and makeup people, stylists, art directors, assistants, sets and props. They are also accustomed to entertaining clients and subjects.

In contrast, such involvement is quite rare and often totally unnecessary for the conventional portrait session. However, the boudoir session must be approached in much the same manner as the commerical shoot.

Makeup and Hair—A boudoir subject must be made to look as attractive as she can possibly be. Having a subject's hair styled and makeup applied by a professional—either in the studio or from an outside source—will go a long way in making the subject feel beautiful. If she feels beautiful, she is likely to photograph beautifully.

Whenever you can, discourage a boudoir subject from applying her own makeup. Most women do not know the difference between everyday, street makeup and makeup that must be used for different types of photography. As a result, your photographic results will suffer.

Dressing Room—Whether you are operating out of your home or from a regular studio, you must provide a boudoir subject with a private dressing room area. Ideally there should be a bathroom facility connected to the dressing area so that she need not leave the dressing room in order to use it.

In addition, the dressing room should have some sort of table top or vanity for her to place her cosmetics and other items, a large, wall-hung makeup mirror—four foot by four foot is an ideal size. The mirror should be surrounded by makeup lights. There should be several wall hangers for hanging up her garments and a full length mirror—about three feet by six feet.

The dressing room and bathroom should be kept spotlessly clean. When a subject finishes using these facitities and before the next subject arrives, make certain that the vanity top is clean and neat, the mirrors are cleaned, the floor is free from clutter and trash, and toilet tissue, paper towels and kleenex are replenished. Make certain that the dressing room is also well stocked with sundry items such as bobby-pins, hair-pins, hair-spray, needle and thread, safety pins and the like. It would also be ideal to have a small ironing board, steam iron, hair curler, and hair dryer available. In other words, you'll want to provide as many creature comforts for a subject as possible.

Clothing—At your initial personal consultation with the subject, you will have discussed the various items of clothing that the subject was to bring to the session. Now, for the first time, you will be able to see exactly what items she has brought.

Help her choose each item that she is to wear very carefully, paying great attention to the cut of the garment and its color. Warn her in advance that, even though she may like a particular item because it looks well on her or flatters her, it may in fact not look well on her when she is put into the various poses that you will be selecting for her.

Music—Having some form of music in your shooting room area is essential. It really helps to relax most subjects. It is immaterial whether you have your music on tape, record or disk provided that you have sufficient variety to cover the musical tastes of most people: Some will prefer jazz, some classical, others vocal, and so on. Don't attempt to use a radio. The commercial interruptions will distract your subject. Keep the volume relatively low. You only want background music and don't want it to break the sitter's concentration on the poses or your instructions.

Refreshments—We have found it absolutely essential to provide our boudoir subjects with some form of liquid refreshment—before and during a session. Having a supply of wine, soda or coffee on hand and periodically offering such to your subject will make her feel special and more relaxed. It helps to make the session more personal and comfortable.

Be cautious about three things: Serve no hard liquor, watch the quantity of wine the subject is consuming, and make sure that she drinks all liquids through a straw in order to preserve her lipstick. If a subject consumes just enough wine or similar spirts to relax her, that's fine. If she overdoes it, however, your job will be made more difficult.

Illumination—When the subject first walks into your shooting room, the level of illumination should be bright. Show the subject that there are no goblins hiding anywhere and there is nothing in your shooting area for her to be alarmed about. Once she has attired herself for the shoot and is on the set awaiting photography, you will be able to lower the level of illumination to your needs without her feeling any apprehension.

Conversation—It is very important to engage a subject in conversation during most of the session. I don't mean frivolous chit-chat about the weather and such, but meaningful conversation about how she looks, how she is reacting, how she is progressing, how the poses look when she executes them, and so on. Such conversation is a great deterrent to nervousness, will serve to bolster her ego, and reinforce her excitement in engaging in this form of photography.

The Security of Clothing

In our society, most people feel very uncomfortable or out of place if not properly attired, let alone scantily dressed. Asking a woman to remove all or part of her clothing is, in effect, asking her to leave a little part of her personality and her security at the sidelines.

Admittedly, we are accustomed and geared to disrobing before others in a number of different situations: When being examined by a doctor, in front of our spouses or loved ones, when at the tailor's or dressmaker's, at the gym and so on. But to ask a woman you don't know, who is an untrained, non-professional model, to disrobe so that she might be photographed in front of strangers, is to make a whole new set of psychological demands upon her. Often such a subject is totally unprepared at the moment to deal with such a situation without sympathetic reassurance.

If you place a female subject in your shooting area and immediately ask her to strip to her bra and pants or dress her in skimpy, transparent attire, often you will have stripped away a great deal of her psychological armor. At this point, the armor must immediately be replaced with an acceptable substitute before you can ever engage in a successful boudoir session.

Our personal recommendation is that all clothing changes should take place in the dressing-room area provided for the subject rather than on the set itself. In addition, however, you will need some clothing substitutes.

A Clothing Substitute—Being nude, semi-clad or scantly attired in front of strangers is not the norm for most of the women you will be photographing. It's not "reality." Thus, allowing a female subject to hold onto something tangible—a string of pearls, a flower, a handheld mirror, or some other prop—or even part of the clothing that she is adorned in—can give her great psychological comfort.

In the early stages of your photo session with any subject, make such items immediately available to her and work them into your photo scene. They can be discreetly entered into the shoot-scene without the subject being made aware of their real purpose—a psychological crutch.

An Additional Security Blanket—Once the actual shooting gets under way, most of your subjects will begin to relax. However, between poses, while you and your assistants are moving lights, stands and props, and even between sets, while the subject has to wait for you and your assistants to set up equipment anew, the subject—being scantily attired—may fall back into a very self-conscious state.

To help avoid this condition, have a cleaned terry-cloth robe available for her to wear. This gesture will go far in giving her confidence in you and what you are attempting to accomplish for her. Initially, the subject will cling to this robe, much like a security blanket, but as the photo session progresses, you will often find that she no longer requires the need of the robe at all between poses. This will be a good indicator to you that she is starting to relax and enjoy herself and that her fears and anxieties are subsiding.

Flatter the Subject—As we've already indicated, without most of her clothing, any woman who is not a professional model is likely to feel a certain measure of insecurity and uneasiness. To compensate for this, you must reassure her constantly. Flatter her, without being dishonest. When she looks good—and, as a competent photographer, you'll make her look good—tell her so.

During the course of the entire photo session, you and your assistants should constantly be flattering the subject and making her feel special by telling her how wonderful she looks and how great the poses are and how natural and glamourous she looks. Such verbalization will go a long way in helping the subject regain and retain her composure and in making her look even better.

Keep the Subject Informed

In most portrait, fashion and glamour sessions that we have done, it has generally been unnecessary to explain the "why" of a particular shot to the subject before executing it. It has only been necessary to convey what we wanted or were looking for.

For example, during the course of a typical portrait sitting of a female subject, you invite her to sit upon a posing stool, tell her to turn her body one way or the other, guide her head into proper position, tell her to assume some form of pleasant look or smile and then take the picture. It is usually this simple.

However, such simplicity does not usually prevail with boudoir imagery. There is too much going on and too many things happening: Each part of the body that is to be photographically seen must be properly illuminated and posed; facial expression and body language must coincide with the setting and mood created; each prop and part of the set that is to be in the photo scene must be properly placed, adjusted and lighted. Most of this cannot totally come about until the subject has assumed a basic pose that is flattering to her.

In other words, with a simple portrait you could literally position your lights before the subject ever comes into your studio. On her arrival, you need simply seat the subject and take her picture. Not so with boudoir. You cannot construct your lighting in advance as you can with simple portraiture. To the contrary, you must pose the subject's face and body and only then build your lighting around these parts, the pose, and the set she is in.

This means that, once the subject has assumed a posed position, you or your assistants will be milling about the shooting area adjusting lights, stands and props. You'll be walking near, around, and even behind the subject to accomplish all of this. This can cause the subject to become extremely nervous and apprehensive about what you are doing, and why. You must constantly reassure her and inform her.

Ease Apprehensions—Before you, or an assistant, makes any movement toward the subject, openly discuss what you are about to do, and why. In our studio, my wife will demonstrate in advance each of the poses that we wish a subject to assume and then assist her into each pose. Our female assistant will be moving and adjusting props, lights, stands, flags and gobos, based upon instructions from my wife or me.

I will usually maintain my position at the camera and have no physical contact with the subject. We leave all of the physical contact up to my wife and the female assistant: adjusting a strap, moving the subject's arm or leg, fixing her clothing, draping her body with material, and so on.

On occasion when I, rather than my wife, meter the lighting, I announce in advance what I intend to do before I ever go toward the subject. This simple gesture goes a long way in reducing her anxiety.

Speak Clearly

Don't whisper. Don't speak in a low, soft voice to your assistants. A subject that is posed, awaiting to be photographed, will conjure up all kinds of thoughts about what you and your assistants are saying about her or are planning to do. Allay this anxiety by talking aloud and discussing the problems and the good points of the shoot openly.

Let the subject know at the start of the session that you and your assistants will be discussing various parts of the shooting as it comes about: the lighting, the pose, the clothing, and so on. Inform her that this discussion does not mean that she has done something wrong; it's done to solve lighting and posing problems that exist with every subject, in every session, in order to obtain the best possible images and photographic results.

Avoid "Cute" Remarks

If you are to engage in boudoir photography as a business, under no circumstance should you approach any session in less than a totally professional manner. In this form of photography, one's reputation and financial future can really be on the line. You must treat boudoir photography more seriously, delicately, and professionally than perhaps any other area of photography. To do otherwise is to do a disservice to your business and to your subjects.

At no time during the course of a session should you or any of your assistants make any remarks or gestures about the subject's body or her physical attributes that could in any way be misconstrued or misinterpreted as a slur or an off-color remark.

For example, during the course of a photo session, if you have to make remarks about the lighting or clothing that is on the upper portion of her body or chest area, refer to it as the upper portion of her body, her chest area, her bust or breast area. Avoid using more descriptive language than this.

By the same token, when making reference to her lower anatomy, terms such as buttocks, derriere, or posterior are acceptable. No other word substitutes should be employed. Even if the subject is somewhat verbally liberal and makes "cute" remarks about the various parts of her body or uses very descriptive language to describe various parts of her body, you should not. The mere fact that the subject is taking license or liberties with her remarks does not give you authority to do the same.

Shoot Discriminately

Even though film is one of the cheapest commodities in photography and even though you may shoot two to six rolls of film per boudoir session, don't waste your time or film taking shots that do not really look correct.

Most subjects can feel intuitively when a pose is right for them. If you take a shot which is obviously not correct for a subject and then verbally reward her with praises, your credibility may suffer. She is likely to sense when the good shots really come about. She may think that you are unable to discern a good pose for her from a bad one.

You should inform a subject in advance that not all of the poses, lighting arrangements, articles of clothing or props you are going to try are necessarily going to work. Some will work well, others not at all. You want her to understand why you change your mind about taking certain shots. Don't give her the chance to speculate that it might be her fault. You want her to understand that not all poses and lightings work well for all people. Without this advance information, she may think that you have not taken the shot because she is too heavy, too awkward, and so forth, and such a negative attitude could affect your photo results.

When you do take a shot, tell the subject how great it looked and how well she did in executing the pose.

Elicit Appropriate Emotions

Most professional models are acutely aware how important it is to role-play when doing a photo session: They must "have their head into the shoot"; they must "project." In a similar manner, so must a non-professional subject who is sitting for a boudoir session. The problem is that the professional model is accustomed to getting herself emotionally and physically involved in the photo session whereas the untrained, non-professional boudoir subject is not.

Almost any person with a camera can photograph a woman in a state of semi-undress. However, the skill—excluding lighting for the moment—lies in being able to direct the subject into projecting her inner warmth and sensitivity and then capturing this on film. To help her achieve this projection, you must directly or indirectly and constantly impress upon the subject to "think pretty." She must think of herself as pretty or beautiful. She must feel good about herself. If she can't do this on her own, you will have to help her by employing laudatory remarks.

Subject's Requests are Important

In a conventional portrait, most subjects want just one thing: to look good. Very seldom will a portrait subject—for a non-commercial photo session—make demands about the type of lighting to be used, the poses, and so on. In contrast you will often have boudoir subjects who have preconceived ideas—from a picture or two that they have seen in a magazine—of what they would like their pictures to look like. If you can't do it, tell this to the subject in advance. If you can—and often you will be able to do a better job with your subject than the magazine photos—tell her this, too.

Pictorially, strive to give her what she is looking for, whether it be a "little girl" look, a seductive look, a "farm girl look" or any combination from a whole host of "looks." To give her something less than this does not spell success.

Most women will not demand that they be made to look like movie stars—although they will not resent it, if you accomplish this result. They do seek images that flatter them. Photograph your subjects in the manner they request first and then do what your judgment tells you is best. They may prefer your ideas and approach over that of the pictures or ideas they had given you to follow. In any event, by doing both, you offer more pictorial variety and an opportunity for increased sales.

Start Slowly and Build

With a typical portrait session, or when shooting with a professional model, it often doesn't matter whether you start with head shots first and then move on to full-length ones or vice-versa. The choice is usually yours. However, in boudoir photography it does make a psychological difference to the subject, even though she may not be consciously aware of it.

If, at the moment the boudoir subject steps into your studio, you instruct her to take off all or most of her clothing or bare a portion of her breasts or derriere, you will often be met with great resistance. Start the subject out slowly, in relatively non-revealing attire—a merry-widow or long robe or dressing gown—and take some tight head shots. Then advance to head-and-shoulders shots, and on to three-quarter length shots. By the time you are ready for full-length shots, which may be a bit more revealing, she'll be better prepared psychologically. She will have become accustomed to you and your assistants; she'll be more comfortable, relaxed and cooperative and not hesitate to become more scantily dressed and to exhibit more of her body.

The Value of Team Effort

Successful boudoir photography requires a team effort. Ideally, the team should consist of one male and one female photographer.

Having my wife and myself photograph all the boudoir sessions together, as a team, gives each subject the benefit of both worlds: the trust and confidence of having another female present during the photo session; a woman's impression and interpretation of each shot and pose to be taken and executed; a man's impression and interpretation of each shot and pose to be taken and executed.

The team effort also allows the team the luxury of developing separate and distinct responsibilities. For example, one can pay strict attention to posing and propping while the other devotes his or her energy to lighting. This gives each person the ability to concentrate upon the area designated to him or her, leading to a more proficient photo session.

Technically, of course, it is possible for one person to conduct a boudoir session. However, lighting, posing, propping and clothing problems are solved much faster and easier when a joint effort is made and especially when the team is a combination of male and female.

We are not saying that a successful session could not be accomplished by two male or two female photographers. It could! What we are saying is that we think that the session can be done more easily and better when that team—regardless of the number of people in the team—is a mixture of male and female. It certainly works best for us.

Establishing the Poses

When shooting a commercial job with a professional model, the photographer has a right to expect the model to know how to execute certain poses that will express the look or mood that he or she wishes to photograph. Even though he or she may expect this, sometimes the photographer may have to demonstrate a pose or two in order to end up with a satisfactory photo result.

With a boudoir session it's different. You will generally have to demonstrate each and every look and pose that you seek, down to its most minute detail. If for no other reason, the inward or outward nervousness of the boudoir subject will prevent her from immediately grasping what you are attempting to convey. Since not all poses will work or flatter all subjects, it becomes necessary for you to have a vast amount of different poses available at your finger tips. You need the ability to flow from one pose to another with ease and minimal delay.

Some poses are designed to flatter certain parts of the body. Some poses look better when executed with a certain type of clothing. Some poses look better when executed in high key over low key. Some poses look better on thinner women than heavier ones. Some poses look better when top lit rather than side lit, and so on. The possibilities are almost endless. It calls for a great deal of experimentation on your part to see which combinations and effects are best.

To cover all possible poses would demand a separate book. Suffice it to say that you should have at least 50 to 60 poses or variations at your command. You'll get lots of ideas by studying the photos in the portfolio section of this book.

CHAPTER 4

The Setting

Having a proper setting for boudoir photography is essential. There are three major areas in which a session could take place: a studio, the subject's home, or on location. However, within these three areas lies an infinite number of potential settings for creating the boudoir sitting. The choices are almost endless since you are restricted only by your imagination and the desires of the subject.

If the subject has instructed you as to where she wishes to be photographed and in which surroundings, you are often initially bound by this dictate. However, if she has placed herself into your hands, then your challenge will be to locate or fashion one or more settings for her that will interpret and capitalize on her inner warmth, beauty and sensuality.

The extensiveness of each sitting will often depend upon how elaborate the settings are. The more elaborate, the more time and equipment you will need to execute the photography but the more versatile will be the end product.

The elaborateness of the setting may be dictated by the quantity of images the subject wishes to ultimately purchase. Some subjects will profess an interest in only purchasing a modest number of small—8x10 or smaller—prints. Some will be interested in purchasing one or more large wall prints—16x20 and larger—along with a number of smaller ones. Others will have no idea what they want to purchase. They will want to wait until after seeing the proofs before making a decision.

You will need to ascertain the needs or desires of the subject at your initial consultation. Do not wait until the photo session. If she is only interested in buying a few small prints, you may decide not to erect an elaborate set. On the other hand, if she has informed you that she is looking for large wall images plus other prints or is unsure of what she wants, then you should speculate and make at least one set elaborate.

You alone will often have to make the initial decision on how versatile, elaborate and extensive you wish to become in creating a setting for a subject. In any case, you should provide a subject with at least two completely different settings for each boudoir session that you do, thus giving her more pictorial variety.

STUDIO

Your greatest pictorial control will come from photo sessions done in the studio, whether a commercial studio or one in your home. You will then have total control over the lighting; all of your equipment will be at your fingertips; you'll know exactly where every item in your studio is located; and you'll know—or should—the exact requirements for producing a high key and low key image, and so on.

Atmosphere

Regardless of where your studio is located, it should look like a professional photography studio and not some makeshift area with just a few pieces of camera equipment scattered about. You also want your studio to look like it's fun to work and be in.

Most people are very impressionable and a subject's first encounter with your studio and its facilities can have a great bearing on how she perceives you, your work and even the outcome of her photos.

Efficient Use of Space

How much information you intended to show in the final photo—both as to the subject's body and the set she is being photographed on—will dictate the amount of space that you will need.

If you intend to do a shot of the subject from the waist up with limited background being pictorially shown, you can afford to work in rather tight quarters. But if you wish a full length shot of the subject and more information of the background set being displayed, you will require more space.

The exact amount of space you will require will often depend upon the choice of lens that you use. This point will be discussed in a later chapter.

Even if you only have one room that you regularly use as a shooting-room area, it should be designed so that you can shoot in at least two different directions. For example, if you normally set up your camera facing the subject and this direction points to the north, have an additional but different set in place to the south. When you finish photographing one scenario on the one side, it will be a simple matter to transfer you, the subject and your lighting over to the other set to obtain a different look.

Creative Permanent Shooting Areas—Whether you work in a home studio or commercial studio, it would be ideal if you had the space to set up a permanent area totally designated for low key photography, another for high key, and three other areas for three different boudoir settings. Then you could shift from one boudoir scenario to another as well as create an additional environment, on the spot, in either the high or low key area with ease and minimal delay.

Lightweight Sets—For many of you, space may be at a premium and you will only have one or two areas that you regularly shoot in, with the balance of your space devoted to the display and assemblage of your work.

In such a situation, it is critical that you have boudoir sets that are extremely mobile, light, easy and fast to assemble and disassemble. From a cost effective standpoint, you cannot afford to take two hours or more to set up one set and then be forced to spend another hour or so tearing it down at session's end.

Effective Use of Time—When space is at a premium and you do not have the luxury of having two, three, or more boudoir sets permanently set up at all times, you will find it more expeditious to schedule boudoir sessions on the same day and one right after the other. This will enable you to take advantage of the one or two settings that you have set up without having to tear them down, immediately after their use, in preparation for the next non-boudoir photo session.

Sets

The setting or *set,* as it is commonly referred to, is an extremely important part of the boudoir scenario. It puts the image in context. It often supplies the mood or theme for the subject: A subject will relate and respond better in a setting that's consistent with her attire, her poses and attitudes.

A photograph of a subject who is scantily attired, seated on a mere posing stool with no other props or settings around her, may produce an image that takes on the character of a model shot. However, if you take that same subject, in the same attire and properly pose her on a bed, in a bedroom setting, the shot could produce a true boudoir image.

Creating a Boudoir Setting—The set can be as modest as a single chair or couch, with an accessory or two, or as elaborate as a fully propped room with drapes, carpeting, windows, doors, lamps, tables, chairs, flowers, mirrors and various items of lingerie scattered about.

A boudoir session is primarily contextual and often involves the blending of two or more of the following to produce that different boudoir image:

1. A proper setting
2. Proper poses
3. Appropriate attire
4. Appropriate accessories
5. Personal props
6. Proper lighting
7. An element of privacy
8. Proper makeup and hair style

Those of you who are operating out of your homes may have a great many areas already available to you for boudoir settings: the kitchen, the bathrooms, the bedroom, and the living room, to name but a few. However, for those that don't have facilities in the home that would readily lend themselves well for a setting, sets must be made.

Number and Variations of Settings—How many different sets you should have at any one given time will depend upon your involvement in boudoir photography. As your business in this area of expertise grows, so should the quantity and variety of your sets.

At the beginning of your career, you should have at least two different sets and they should be very versatile. One should be in the high-key tonality and the other low-key. This will afford a subject two completely different looks.

Change Sets Regularly—Every boudoir subject should not be photographed on the same set. Subjects will tire of it and your business will stagnate. You will be restricting yourself to new clients only rather than getting repeat business from your previous clientele.

A great deal of your boudoir business will come from referrals. A referring subject may not like her friends having the exact same setting as she had, especially if you had previously indicated to her that you were creating a setting uniquely for her.

Major changes may be unnecessary. Without having to throw a set away at the end of its period of use, you could change the color of the walls, carpeting, and so on, and even rearrange the furniture to give the same set a different look.

Make sets versatile. No matter how many sets you have on hand, each set should be capable of producing more than one look; it should have more than one application. In other words, if you create a bedroom set, by changing the type of lighting on the set and on the subject, or color of lighting on the set, or your camera angle, you should be able to generate a different look to the set and the subject in it.

Some sets will not have this versatility: a Christmas boudoir setting is always going to look like a Christmas setting no matter what you do to it; thus it will have very restricted application.

Materials for Sets—If a set is to be permanently placed, it is best to construct any walls that the setting might require from at least 1/2 inch thick plywood or pressboard. But if you require portability, then use 4x8-foot sheets of foamcore board or styrofoam board for your walls. Both materials should be available from your local hardware store.

The foamcore board can be painted or wallpapered. The styrofoam board can be painted or even scored with a hot tacking iron to make a simulated brick effect. You can even make a simulated door from styrofoam board or a simulated window from very thin strips of wood. The final product will look like a real door or window, at about one-fourth of the weight and cost of the real thing, and more importantly, it will photograph well.

Shooting in a Home Studio

A boudoir session is difficult enough to properly execute without the potential psychological barrier of having the subject think that there might be something amiss because your shooting facilites are in your home. She might even get the impression that you are only using photography as a ruse just to get women into your home to see them in various states of undress or to make improper advances.

To guard against this danger, if you regularly use a bedroom as one of your sets, you should make certain that all of your needed equipment is placed in that room prior to the subject's arrival. In addition, make certain that you have at least one female assistant on hand from the moment the subject arrives. Otherwise, the subject might take one look at the bedroom—devoid of equipment and other people—exclaim her displeasure or disbelief in you and your motives, and leave.

Neatness and Organization—Your facilities should be clean, neat and well organized. You don't want a subject to have to step over boxes and other clutter just to get onto the set that you have created. It may affect her attitude toward you and your work and this might affect the pictorial results.

Privacy—No matter where your studio is located, you must constantly bear in mind the sensitive nature of boudoir photography. Most women will be nervous enough without your contributing to the condition by having a number of people—whom the subject has not previously met and who have no bearing on the shooting at hand—walking in and about the shooting room area while the session is underway.

Therefore, once the subject has attired herself for the shooting, maintain a closed-door policy. Close the door of your shooting room and enforce the rule that once the subject is on the set, no one other than you and your assistants will be permitted entrance.

SHOOTING IN THE SUBJECT'S HOME

A boudoir session in your studio—whether it be a regular studio or in your home—will take approximately two hours to complete, excluding set-up and tear down time. Doing a shoot at the subject's home will take you longer: Travel, the loading and unloading of your equipment and working in strange surroundings will all take its toll in terms of time.

Notwithstanding this increased time factor, often you will be able to achieve excellent results from a home sitting, if for no other reason than because of the subject herself: She will be less nervous in her own familiar environment.

Assessing the Scene

It is absolutely essential to visit the subject's home well in advance of the day the session is to take place. You must see—first hand—what areas you will have to work with and in.

To a great extent, boudoir photography consists of solving challenging problems: What set to use; which lighting to use, where and why; what props go with the set. Having a subject describe her home to you, its layout, color and so on, is just not the same thing as actually seeing it. You know what to look for and she doesn't. You know that certain colors look better than others, certain layouts lend themselves better than others, and the like.

Inspecting The Home—Once you have arrived at the subject's home, make sketches and note such items as the color of walls in each room, the size of the rooms you might be working in, including the ceiling height, the location of electrical outlets and whether they are of the old two-prong type or the newer three prong series. Check for the reflectivity of such items as mirrors, paintings, furniture, which rooms have the most natural light coming into them and during what time of the day, and the size, type and arrangement of the furniture.

Once back at your home or studio, you can make your decisions based upon your notes and sketches about the type of lighting you will employ, how you will set it up, which rooms you will work in, and what furniture you will have to move about. When you return to the subject's home for the actual session, everything can be arranged with minimal delay.

Equipment for the Home Shoot

Unlike the photo session in your studio, where you have all of your equipment at your ready disposal, going to a subject's home for a session will require careful planning. It will be essential to make a check list of all of the equipment—lights, reflectors, gobos, cameras and so on—that you intend to bring to the session. You don't want to travel miles away from your studio and unpack all of your gear only to learn that you have left an essential piece of equipment back at your studio. The subject should not be expected to tolerate such delays. Besides, your unpreparedness may be just the excuse they need to cancel the session at the last moment.

Until you become very familiar with this form of photography, take more equipment than you might need. In addition, to minimize leaving important items behind, plan your equipment needs the evening before the session and review the items on the day of the session.

Rearrange Furniture

Most homes are decorated for comfort and arranged for convenience and personal taste. No time or attention will have been paid to whether or not the furniture looks appropriate for seriously executed boudoir photography. This may necessitate moving various pieces of furniture and accessories around, to provide the kind of setting you want.

It's a good idea to bring to the session a large supply of flowers—real or artificial. Once the furniture has been moved about, flowers can be strategically placed to hide or conceal certain defects that might still exist while, at the same time, lending an air of femininity to the scene.

If you have taken careful notes and sketches of the layout of the home and the furniture and accessories in it during your pre-session visit, you should be able to proceed to prop and stage the setting with minimal delay.

SHOOTING ON LOCATION

Most people, when they think of boudoir photography—if they in fact have a preconceived idea of this form of photography—think that such photos must be solely executed in a bedroom. This is a misconception! As previously noted, such photography can take place almost anywhere that the subject or her special someone, might find enticing, sensuous or alluring.

This is not to say that the bedroom scenario should be discounted. However, be prepared to explore other settings as well: a park or beach; a yacht, small private airplane or automobile; perhaps an elevator; and so on.

Scouting Locations

As with a subject's home, it is absolutely essential that you scout various locations well in advance of the actual shooting session. There may be special problems that have to be solved. You don't want to wait for the last minute to handle them.

For example, in our immediate area, in Fort Lauderdale, there is a quaint little wooded spot that is only 50 feet or so away from a main street. It abuts a residential area. The area incorporates a small wooden bridge which spans a small body of water and is enclosed on three sides by dense trees. At first glance it looks perfect for a boudoir scenario, and no obvious problems seem to exist.

However, there is one problem—neighbors. Even though seriously executed boudoir photography is in the best of good taste, there may be neighbors who object to this form of photography being conducted within sight of their homes. Such a neighbor might call the police and complain. This could delay or even cause the cancellation of your shoot in that particular location.

To avoid this danger, when you intend to do a outdoor location session that might be close to an inhabited area, call the police department in that jurisdiction and introduce yourself. Explain that you are doing work for hire or for self-promotion and that you would like to have an officer present when you engage in the shoot. Describe clearly the type of photography you're going to do and assure the officials that it is good, high quality photography, commissioned by a respectable local resident.

There are many areas beyond the boundaries of city limits where you are free to shoot without special permission, provided, of course, no one is caused inconvenience or embarrassment.

If your shooting involves the use of a private plane or yacht, attempt to have the plane moved to an isolated part of the field or have the boat docked in a relatively remote area. This will afford you the needed privacy during the session and make the subject feel more comfortable.

CHAPTER 5

Costumes, Accessories and Personal Props

Just as proper setting and poses are important to the successful outcome of any boudoir photo session, so is the proper selection of costumes, accessories and personal props. Each facet should support the others and, at the same time, make its own statement. At the same time, nothing must be permitted to dominate the primary element—the subject.

COSTUMES

At your initial consultation, you should review with each subject the type of settings that she would like to be photographed in: Bedroom, beach, locker room, gym, and so on. This will then set the parameters for the type of clothing or costume she should bring to the session.

If the subject has no preconceived setting in mind, then you will have to ask her about her likes and dislikes. Is she an outdoor person? Does she feel she relates well in a sports environment? Is she more the evening-gown type? Is she the casual or formal type? The list could go on and on. The more questions you ask, the better prepared you will be to advise her on what clothing to bring and on how to handle the session when it occurs.

Clothing Helps Set the Theme

At a boudoir session, you want to create images that will cause a viewer to instantly identify with the subject and the theme of the photography. A properly chosen costume will help accomplish this.

Police officers look and feel more like people in authority when dressed in a uniform, judges look and feel more like judges when attired in black robes, and nurses look and feel more like nurses when dressed in their uniforms. In the same way, a subject who is dressed in boudoir-type fashion will become caught up in the spirit of the attire and relate better during the session than if she were clad in simple street attire.

What is a Boudoir Costume?

There is no exact definition of, or formula for, a boudoir costume. It may be something as simple as a lacy, matching set of bra and panties or a black see-through dressing gown. It could be a teddy, a nightgown, a short mini skirt with a tank top, or even just a few yards of lacy material. The main consideration is that the garment must look sexy on the subject and enhance the subject's figure. If those needs are not met, you will have defeated your purpose in your photography.

In addition, the costume should, by its own accord or through fitting or rearranging of a portion of its material, allow a viewer to subtly see one or more portions of the subject's body that might otherwise be covered.

The shooting location and the costume are inextricably linked. For example, a simple bathing suit is not generally thought of as a proper boudoir costume. However, if you place your subject in a locker room, using proper lighting and props and accessories, and have her dressed in an alluring bathing suit, with the subject posed to suggest she is about to bare a portion of her anatomy that the suit was concealing, you may create a very effective boudoir image.

Picking the Appropriate Costume—Not only will the appropriate costume help the subject get into the mood or spirit of the photo session, it will also serve other purposes: to hide, to suggest, or to enhance.

For example, very few of the subjects you photograph will have a perfect figure. Most woman will have one or more areas of their bodies that they are less than proud of. Photographically, they want those parts to be understated or even hidden. An appropriately selected costume, worn in the right manner, can serve this purpose.

Suggestive Apparel—The appropriate choice of costume can also enhance a subject's sexy or sensual look when it is placed into context with the other elements, such as a proper setting, pose, and lighting. For example, a man's sweatshirt can be an ideal costume for a subject who is wearing nothing else and is in an appropriate setting.

Not only is *what* the subject wears important but also *how* she wears it. Once attired, in whatever garment you or she has selected, she must move and think sexy while wearing it. She must role-play and get into the spirit of the costume and setting.

What the Subject Should Bring

At your initial consulation, you should review with the subject each item that she owns that may be of a sexy or sensuous nature. Her special someone may like to see her in a plain T-shirt or a special piece of lingerie that he purchased for her. She may already own various nightgowns or other pieces of lingerie that look very well on her.

Encourage her to bring as many of these items to the session as she can. Once at the session, you can review her wardrobe and help her choose those items you consider photographically most appropriate. Caution the subject that whatever she brings must look good, be neat and fresh, and not appear worn or tattered.

In the event that she has little or nothing to bring, advise her to purchase some well-chosen items and, if necessary, supplement these items with a few items that you have in your studio.

You might suggest that your subject purchase one or more of the following:

1. A teddy

2. A merry-widow corset

3. Matching bra and panties: They should be lacy and the bra should be of the uplift variety.

4. Negligee

5. Garter belt with black mesh hose

6. Baby-doll

7. Short shorts

8. Form-fitting designer jeans

9. Aerobics outfit

Where To Buy Costumes—Often you will have subjects inquire where to buy various and sundry items that are proper for the session. Normally, your local department stores will not carry a wide variety of sexy or sensual underwear and sleepwear and a specialty shop will have to be visited.

Before you refer your subjects to such shops, visit them first yourself. Make certain that they are quality stores. If the subject were to be directed to a low-quality shop, not only would she not get the kind of attire she should have, she might also get the wrong impression of you, your work and your motives.

If time permits, from your initial consultation to the time of the actual session, a subject could order various items from a catalog house such as *Fredericks of Hollywood* or *Victoria's Secret*. They have a wide variety of garments that would lend themselves ideally to a boudoir session.

Shoes—Don't forget to mention shoes. Have the subject bring at least two pairs, one white and one black, the plainer the better. The viewer's attention should not be drawn unduly to the foot area. Ideally, the shoes should be brand new because an unworn, new sole looks much better in a photograph than a worn one.

The shoes should be high-heeled, preferably with open backs. Even if the shoes are not shown in a picture, the high heels will cause the legs of a standing subject to look and photograph better.

Selecting the Right Colors

If a subject has less than a perfect figure, you may wish to have her purchase items in relatively dark tones: black, wine, dark-green or dark-blue. The darker colors will draw less visual attention to the area that is clothed, especially if the subject is being photographed in a low key setting. If the subject's figure is good enough to permit it, you can have her wear lighter and brighter colors: white, soft-pink, or red.

A word of caution: The body will photograph larger when it is clothed in lighter colors and tones than when in darker ones. Choose your colors carefully in accordance with a subject's figure as well as in harmony with the setting.

The color of the item selected should also match or compliment the subject's hair and skin tone. A blonde woman with light complexion may look very well in black or wine-colored garments and terrible in blue or brown tones, while a red-haired woman may look outstanding in emerald-green but terrible in black or dark-blue.

Fitting the Garment

Most sleepwear, if not in fact most clothing, seems to be designed for one position—standing. Once a subject sits or assumes a position other than standing, the garment wrinkles, bulges, creases and reveals other imperfections of fit. Paying attention to conditions such as these is essential in any professionally executed boudoir session.

Each time the subject changes poses, be prepared to play seamstress and to make on-the-spot alterations where needed. Keep a stock of clothes pins, safety pins, straight pins, adhesive tape and clamps on hand to accomplish any of the clothing adjustments.

Your Own Costume Inventory

It would be impractical, if not in fact financially prohibitive, for you to maintain boudoir costumes for your subjects to wear. Because you would have to have such a large variety of colors, sizes, styles and types on hand to accommodate all of the subjects that you are going to photograph, you are much better off requiring the subjects to bring their own garments.

Nevertheless, you should keep a few items on hand that you know will work well with most people: a black negligee, a black teddy, a length of lacy material, a white and black feather boa, and the like. The garments, such as the negligee and teddy can be purchased in a one-size-fits-all variety and can be used by the subject in case everything that she brings looks poor or inappropriate on her.

As with anything else in photography, make certain that you do a test shoot of any garment that you buy in advance of a subject's session. The dyes in some materials, under certain types of illumination, reproduce a little differently on film from the way they appear to the eye. You don't want to experiment at a subject's expense.

ACCESSORIES AND PERSONAL PROPS

Accessories and personal props are not main items to a boudoir sitting. They are supporting elements and help round out a photo scene. Nevertheless, such items are important and should be incorporated into the photo scene whenever you can. This is especially true if an accessory or personal prop has some special significance to the subject. Such items will provide a special personal touch and help a subject relate to the final image.

Encourage all of your subjects to bring as many accessories with them to the session as they wish. Items such as jewelry—whether real or costume—scarves, hats, gloves and the like can add a very nice touch.

Make certain that you have a few accessories of your own to supply, in case you wish to supplement what the subject brings. A strand or two of pearls are always good items to have on hand and can be used very effectively to augment a subject's figure. In the same vein, flowers, carefully placed, can add an air of femininity to the entire scene.

SPECIAL OCCASIONS

For those who engage in boudoir photography on a regular basis, it's advisable to have sets and props for special events. For example, think of having a large Valentine's Day heart—five or six feet tall—or a Christmas tree with a sleigh, together with a suitably sensuous Santa outfit for the subject. Such sets and props are usable only once each year—but that one occasion can prove a very profitable one for a boudoir photographer. Birthdays and anniversaries also lend themselves to special props and sets.

Boudoir Calendar

A particularly attractive idea for the boudoir photographer is the production of a boudoir calendar. You can shoot it any time of the year, in readiness for the coming year. Shoot a picture that's appropriate for each month. This assures you of 12 definite sales. Then make the series of photos into an attractive calendar. In addition to being profitable, shooting this kind of series can be great fun for both photographer and subject.

CHAPTER 6

Makeup and Hair

To ensure success in a boudoir session, you must pay strict attention to a subject's makeup and hair. It's a necessity!

The purpose of this chapter is not to make you an expert in the field of makeup and hair styling. That would take much training and practice. What we do hope to accomplish is to give you a better understanding of makeup and hair as they apply to your subject.

These two elements—makeup and hair—are just as important to a successful boudoir session as are a proper setting, lighting, pose, costume and the like, and they cannot be overlooked nor minimized.

If a subject looks good, she'll feel good about herself—she'll feel more confident—and this feeling will be captured in your photographs. In addition, having her makeup and hair attended to is a part of making her feel very special and catered to. This enhances the subject's positive attitude.

Most of the subjects you'll photograph will have little knowledge about photography. They will not know if a setting, lighting, pose or exposure are correct or not. They look at the total photographic results and decide if they like them, and one of the first things that subjects look at is their makeup and hair.

MOST SUBJECTS NEED A PROFESSIONAL

Most of your subjects will not have the faintest idea how to properly apply their own makeup or fix their own hair so that both will present at their best for *photography*. Applying makeup and fixing hair properly for photography is completely different from simple street makeup and hair preparation and requires special knowledge. To do the job correctly and well is truly an art.

Not only is information of the proper makeup types, quantity and colors important to know and understand, but one must also know how and why to apply each type and form of makeup. Clearly, this job is not one for an amateur; it requires the talents of a trained professional.

MAKEUP

At your initial consultation, after discussing makeup and hair styling in general, find out whether the subject will be having her makeup and hair attended to by someone she knows and has used in the past or whether she wishes you to make the arrangements.

Subject's Personal Makeup Artist

If a subject intends to use a makeup artist that she has selected, whether or not you are familiar with the person's work, you should plan to call him in advance of the photo session so that you can discuss the look you are after. Let the makeup artist know the theme of the shoot, the specific makeup requirements for the film and lighting you're going to use, and the approximate colors of outfits to be worn by the subject.

Inexperienced Artists—Often, subjects will choose makeup artists who have absolutely no knowledge of the required type, quantity or color of makeup needed for photography. Having prior contact with such an artist will often help alert you to their knowledge and ability.

If you know the work of the makeup artist in question to be inadequate for photography purposes, do not hesitate to steer the subject away from such a person. Because your photographic results depend a great deal on the subject's makeup, using the wrong makeup artist could result in the need for an expensive and time-consuming reshoot.

Personal Supervision—Have the makeup done where you're shooting. When the subject has chosen her own artist, encourage her to have the make-over session done in your studio or at the location site just prior to the sitting. This will allow you to keep an eye on the makeup application, step-by-step, and to make recommendations, if the situation calls for it.

When You Select The Makeup Artist

You can choose a makeup artist in a number of different ways: Recommendations from others, calling local beauty colleges or beauty shops and seeing evidence of their work or contacting the cosmetic department of local department stores. You can also call local modeling agencies and find out whom they use on a freelance basis.

Always remember that the work of the makeup artist will be either an asset or a liability to your photographic results. You cannot afford to select someone just because he or she is convenient, accommodating or cheap. You need a true expert.

The Cost—Even though the subject is paying for it, bear the cost of the artist in mind. Most will charge more for coming to your studio or going on location than if the subject went to their shop. However, if the subject goes to a shop, you will not have control over what is happening. Get prices for both situations so that you can offer your subject a choice. Explain to your subject why you consider it preferable for the makeup to be done in your presence.

You should have at least two or three makeup artists at your disposal. Prices will vary among them, and you should be able to offer your subject a choice. In our area of southern Florida, having an artist come to our studio to do a subject's makeup can cost between $25 and $60.

Makeup Pointers

There are a number of items to keep in mind when dealing with makeup for a boudoir session:

1. Makeup should be different for electronic flash than for tungsten lighting. Lighting affects the way film sees color. If the makeup selected is not compatible with the illumination, less than flattering skin tones can result.
2. Certain diffusion filters can alter the coloration of some makeup, so it's wise to test your filters against various makeup types.
3. Makeup for a boudoir session should be applied much more heavily than the subject's everyday or evening makeup. Although, to the eye, it may appear to be too heavily applied, the makeup will photograph less intense than the human eye perceives.
4. The makeup artist should use the more expensive, high-quality, makeup brands. Often, cheap makeup results not only in a poor appearance but also in a poor photographic result.
5. The artist should have a makeup kit that contains a large variety of materials and colors to choose from.
6. Using a water-based moisturizer helps the makeup application to last longer.
7. A subject's foundation makeup is critical. It should be unaffected by ultraviolet radiation—which is recorded on film, even though you can't see it—and its color should match or be slightly darker than the subject's facial skin tone. The foundation must give the subject's face a good, even tonality. Any one of the following brands would be a good choice: Max Factor, Joe Blasco, Willim Tuttle and Elizabeth Arden.
8. Rouge helps to contour a subject's face. The artist should have at least the following colors to choose from: mauve, pink, coral, plum, brown and rose.
9. The powder used should be of the translucent variety and the same color as the foundation makeup. The makeup should be freshened, and powder reapplied, as needed throughout the session, to keep the subject's face looking fresh.
10. The artist should have lip liners in at least five different colors: red, plum, brown, coral and tawny. There should also be a selection of 15 to 20 different colors of lip sticks or pots that can be mixed or blended to suit a wide variety of needs. The lip liner—which is used to line the outer edges of the lips—should match or be slightly darker than the lipstick used.
11. Cover sticks or concealers in clown-white or of a very light color can be used under eyes, under the bottom lip, under cheek bones or on facial expression lines to help minimize or conceal defects.
12. Eye shadow should be used to accentuate the color and shape of the subject's eyes. It's generally best to use darker colors to define the outer half of the eye lid. The eye shadow should be matte and not iridescent. Eye liner will further define and shape the eye.

HAIR

Many boudoir photographs are ruined simply because a subject's hair did not look correct. The eye and the camera lens see things very differently. What might look very acceptable in life can sometimes look terrible in a photographic print.

You can hardly be over-critical when it comes to a subject's hair. Make certain everything is in place and neat. Pay attention to detail. If a subject's makeup is less than perfect, you can resort to negative or print retouching and enhancement, but if the hair style isn't right, there's little you can do with the final images.

Instruct the subject to have her hair done within hours of the sitting and in the style you are looking for to ensure a proper look. However, don't let her have her hair cut. More sessions are canceled or postponed than you might think, simply because a subject decided to have her hair cut and then didn't like the results.

The Final Responsibility is Yours

Ultimately—just like the captain of a ship—you and you alone are responsible for the work produced by you and your staff or helpers. That includes hair style and makeup—even though you don't actually do these things.

This does not mean that you should take bold steps such as asking a blonde subject to have her hair dyed black. This would be met with understandable resistance. It does mean that if you want a hair style and makeup that give a sophisticated look, a little-girl appearance or create a trampy impression, you must inform the makeup artist and hair stylist as to what exactly you are looking for. Don't leave anything to chance.

Conclusion

One of the goals in boudoir photography is to present a subject in a manner that is different from her everyday look. This means changing the subject's usual appearance, at least to some extent. One of the ways to create this change is through proper hair styling and use of makeup. Take advantage of this and have the experts be as creative as they can, all within the bounds of your own good taste and judgment.

CHAPTER 7

Basic Equipment

Since boudoir photography involves creative photography, equipment should be as simple or as elaborate as each situation requires and dictates. In this chapter, we give you some guidance on general equipment. In the next chapter, we'll discuss lighting technique and the equipment required to achieve the lighting effects you want.

ESSENTIAL EQUIPMENT

Keep the quantity of equipment limited to your needs and as simple as possible. Since most of you will be working with non-professional models, charging only a modest sitting fee, and having only a few hours in which to take your shots, you should use equipment that is very familiar to you, and also is easy and fast to set up, tear down, and manipulate.

Where the session is to take place—the subject's home, your studio or on location—will also help set parameters on the amount and type of equipment needed. Notwithstanding, there are a couple of items that you must use no matter where the session takes place: You need a camera and film.

Camera

Boudoir photography is open to all camera formats: 35mm, 2-1/4-inch-square, 4x5, and up to 8x10 view cameras. Although we do most of our boudoir photography with cameras using the 2-1/4-inch-square format, today's lenses are so excellent that there is little reason not to use 35mm cameras and get truly excellent results.

Lens

For about 80 percent of our boudoir work, we use a medium telephoto portrait lens. It's an excellent lens for providing a flattering, undistorted image of a subject's face and figure. It also affords good selective control over depth of field. When we're not using this lens, we use either a standard or slight wide-angle lens. The wide-angle lens is ideal when doing full length shots indoors where space is limited. It's also an ideal lens to use outdoors when you want to emphasis the surroundings as well as the subject herself. However, to avoid unflattering distortion, all tight head shots and head-and-shoulder shots should be done with a medium telephoto lens.

Film

Most of the subjects you'll photograph will want prints rather than slides. This means using color negative film. Because your main purpose is to produce flattering images of people, select a film that yields skin tones well. The film's contrast should give just the right amount of snap to the final image. When you first start boudoir photography, experiment with different negative films and compare the results. See which film you prefer under your specific lighting conditions and then consistently use such film under those conditions.

EQUIPMENT FOR OUTDOORS

Boudoir images made solely by natural daylight can be stunning. These are also the easiest and fastest conditions in which to shoot. Other than a camera, film, tripod and a couple of lenses, the only other equipment you'll often need is a couple of reflectors, which you can easily make yourself. You can also buy them ready-made. You may also need a light panel, which is discussed in the next chapter.

Reflectors

Silver, gold or white reflectors can be used to highlight all or parts of a subject's body and parts of the setting. They are also useful for accenting props.

In some situations, reflectors can play the part of main light, while the sun—from behind or to the side of the subject—acts as rim or edge light.

You should have at least two reflectors. One should be white on one side and silver on the other; the other should be white on one side and gold on the other. Each should be about 4x8 feet in size and should be capable of being folded for portability. White foamcore boards, cut into sections and then taped back together, with aluminum foil taped on one entire side of one unit and gold mylar on one entire side of the other unit, make ideal and inexpensive reflectors.

Mirrors—If you require light reflection of the highest efficiency, a mirror can be the answer. Mirrors are ideal to use for adding a strong highlight to a particular area of a subject's body, a prop or even a setting.

Glass mirrors are heavy. A viable substitute would be a plastic mirror. They come in 4x8-foot sheets, usually 1/8 to 1/4 inch thick. They can be cut into any size or shape you wish and are lightweight and easily transportable. Although, at about $50 per 4x8-foot sheet, they are somewhat expensive, they have the advantage of reflecting almost 100 percent of the light striking them. Any sign company in your area should be able to guide you to an appropriate dealer of plastic materials.

Gobos

Anything that you put in front of a source of light to block all or a portion of the light from spilling onto a subject, your lens or a portion of the scene, is called a *gobo*. You should have at least one of these for your studio and for location shooting. Ideally, a gobo should be black. Gobos, too, can be purchased ready-made, or you can buy a 4x8-foot white foamcore board, cut it into sections, tape the sections back together, and either spray it with a matte, black spray paint or tape black background paper on top of it.

Black Flags

These are like gobos but smaller and serve the same purpose, but over smaller areas. The ones we use are sold by Matthews Studio Equipment, Inc., of Los Angeles, Chicago, and New York. They come in a variety of sizes and shapes and are easily attached to stands. We most frequently use the 18x24-inch size.

Flash

If you elect to use flash as a main or fill-light source when on location, you should buy one that is very portable, reliable and easy to use. It should put out adequate power for your needs and should be equipped with a modeling light. The one we like to use is made by Multiblitz. It is capable of both AC and DC use.

Filters

In most outdoor work, you will find that using a warming filter such as a Wratten 81 or a 1A Skylight filter on the lens will dramatically improve the color rendition in your final images. A lot of unwanted blue, generally unflattering to skin tones, will be eliminated.

We also recommend the use of a soft-focus attachment on the lens most of the time. For tight head shots, we like to use a medium to heavy soft focus filter; for full length shots, lesser soft focus is often the better choice. Tiffen makes an excellent series of soft focus filters under the name *Softnet*. Use the #2 for full length shots and the #4 for tight head shots. Whichever filters you use, don't go for the cheapest in price. Buy good quality. It makes no sense to buy an expensive camera lens and then put a cheap filter on it.

EQUIPMENT FOR INDOORS

With the exception of the portable flash unit mentioned above, all of the above equipment is also appropriate for indoor shoots. However, you'll also need a few more items. With the exception of lighting equipment, which is discussed in the next chapter, your basic boudoir equipment should include the following:

- Two or more century stands
- A flash power pack with two or more flash heads
- A reliable flash meter
- Assorted colored gels

Here's some brief guidance on each of the above items.

Century Stands

These stands, generally known as C-stands, are very useful in the studio and can be used on location, too. Even though they are very portable, they are strong and sturdy and can hold almost anything: lights, flags, gobos, and so on. Sometimes they are useful in helping support an entire set. Although the stands come in a variety of different sizes, the ones we use the most are the 30- and 40-inch stands. They extend to approximately 8 feet in height.

Power Packs

We favor Balcar, Norman and Dynalite power packs. Buy a power pack that has a maximum output of at least 1000 watt-seconds and recycles quickly between shots. You'll need all the power you can get, especially when you're lighting through a diffusing sheet and want to use a small lens aperture for maximum depth of field.

Another reason for using a power pack that gives a lot of light is that you'll generally want to use more than one flash head. The total power available has to be divided among the number of flash heads you use. We use 1000, 1250 and 2000 watt-second power packs.

Light Meter

It is very important to have a reliable, accurate light meter. You will be lighting a number of different items—the subject, various props, the set, and so on—and will want to control the light on each of those areas. The meters we favor are the Minolta Auto Flash III and IV. They can be used with flash and continuous illumination, in incident-light or reflected-light mode.

Color Gels

Gels are large colored filters, normally used over light sources. You'll use them for accenting a portion of the subject's body or a prop, or for affecting an entire set. Although there are a number of different brands on the market, the ones by Rosco have served us well. The colors we use most are amber and deep blue. When we want red, we use rubilith sheets. Don't attempt to use a colored gel for a subject's face in a boudoir session. It is rarely flattering to a subject's face.

Conclusion

Don't overburden yourself with equipment. Remember that it isn't equipment that's responsible for good photos; it takes a photographer's skill and imagination. Any piece of equipment is but a tool and should be purchased only if it is going to accomplish a specific result or solve a specific need, making your work both better and easier.

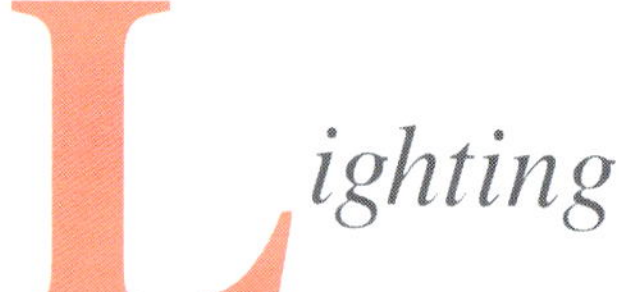

Lighting

Proper lighting is critical to the success of any boudoir session. You must pay strict attention to the type and quality of lighting you use for each session.

Just as all poses, costumes and sets will not work with every person, so it is with lighting. Lighting must be fashioned to the subject, setting, props, theme, and mood of each of your shots.

In establishing the lighting for a boudoir session, you must make several decisions: What type of light source should be used; what should be the quality of the illumination; what power setting should be used; how far should the light source be from the subject; what angle should the light source be in relationship to the subject-camera axis; what color should the light source be? The possible variations are almost endless. While there may be a lot of wrong ways to light a boudoir subject and scene, there is no one correct way. There are many possibilities.

The purpose of this chapter is to give you some lighting and lighting-equipment guidelines to follow.

QUANTITY AND QUALITY OF LIGHT

Quantity of light refers to the power of a light and has nothing to do with the quality of light coming from a source. The quality of light from a light source refers only to the hardness or softness of the light and has nothing to do with a light's power output.

Quantity

The power output of any light affects only depth of field. In other words, the more power a light has, the higher an *f*-stop setting you can use on your camera. The higher the *f*-stop on your camera, the greater the depth of field.

If you had two identical lights, connected to two identical power sources, and you put both lights 10 feet from a subject and adjusted one of the lights to emit one half the power of the other, only your depth of field would be affected. The quality of light would be the same no matter which light you used.

Quality

In order to have a better understanding of quality of lighting, some additional terms need to be reviewed: light housings, hard light, and soft light.

Light Housings

Anything that you put a light into, to hold it and to redirect or diffuse its light, is called a *light housing*. A softbox, a pan or bowl reflector and an umbrella are all examples of light-housings.

Hard and Soft Light—This generally refers to the line of demarcation, between the highlight side and the shadow side, that is created by a light source and falls onto a subject. If this line appears very sharp edged, usually a hard light source will have been used to create it. If the line appears very soft or almost nondiscernible, a soft light source will probably have been used.

For most boudoir photography, soft lighting is what you'll want to strive for since it is flattering light for both the face and figure of a woman. It helps reduce or minimize facial and body defects. Hard light does the opposite, tending to emphasize texture and bring out detail. It may often highlight a defect that you should really subdue.

Changing Light Quality—There are many variables that can affect the quality of light:

- The size of the light source
- The angle of a light in relation to the subject-camera axis
- The distance of the light source to the subject
- The type of material a light has to travel through
- The color of the housing that the light source is in

Take any light and change any one, or any combination, of these five conditions, and you will have changed the quality of light emitted from it. The possible lighting variables are almost endless.

Size of Light Source—As a general rule, the smaller the light source the harder the light it produces. The larger the light source, the softer the light. A small, portable flash unit, such as our Vivitar Model 283, emits a hard light compared to a light that is housed in a 4-foot softbox.

Angle of Lighting—The closer a light is to camera-subject axis, the softer the illumination will appear. The farther the light is from camera-subject axis—such as 70 to 110 degrees to the right or left of that axis—the harder the light.

Distance of Light Source—Quality of lighting is also affected by the distance a light is from a subject. As a general rule, the closer a light is to the subject the softer the light will be falling onto the subject. Conversely, the farther a light is from the subject the harder will be the light. That's because the apparent size of the source is dependent on its distance from the subject. As a source is brought closer to a subject, it becomes *apparently* larger.

No matter what the power settings of any two similar lights of identical sizes may be, the one that is closest to a subject will always emit a softer light than the one that is farther away.

Types of Materials—Having light pass through material—translucent plastic, clear plastic, rip-stop nylon, bedsheeting and the like—before it reaches a subject can affect the quality of the light. The more translucent material you put in front of the light, the more diffused and softer the light will become. When you use more diffusing material, you'll also need more power to maintain any given *f*-stop.

For example, take any light in any housing and put it 10 feet from a subject. Adjust its power to emit 400 watt-seconds of light. Take a meter reading. Now place one thickness of bedsheeting material in front of the light. If you took another meter reading with the light at the same distance as before, you would note that the light is now less intense. To increase the intensity of the light to the same level as it was without the sheet, the power would have to be increased to about double. In other words, about 800 watt-seconds would now give you the same meter reading as before.

Putting anything translucent in front of a light source will not only affect the light's quality but also its brightness. If you can't compensate by changing the power setting or the lamp-to-subject distance, this will affect the ultimate *f*-stop range you have to work with.

No diffusing material is necessarily *better* than another. White milky plastic, rip-stop nylon, bedsheeting, and so on, all have their own advantages and drawbacks. The important question is which material do you *prefer* to use? Which will give you the results that you like for any given situation? We may prefer to use a bedsheet 80 percent of the time. You may prefer the rip-stop nylon. Experiment, and decide for yourself.

Surface Texture Affects Light Quality—A matte white reflector of any kind will always yield a softer light than a specularly reflective gold or silver metal reflector. Matte white will also reflect light less efficiently than its gold or silver counterpart.

For most boudoir photography, a large, diffused light source, 4x4 feet or larger, used close to the subject, is an ideal choice as a main source of illumination.

SELECT LIGHTING EQUIPMENT WISELY

As a result of all of the possible lighting combinations that one can achieve, proper selection of equipment becomes very important when preparing to buy lighting for boudoir or any other type of photography. Start slowly and build your arsenal gradually. Make certain that whatever you buy you can easily modify and build upon without having to throw out your old equipment.

For example, if you want to start out with a 200-watt-second power pack and three lamp heads, make sure that you can later buy a more powerful power pack and still use the same lamp heads.

BASIC LIGHTING SETUPS

Before you can determine the lighting technique to be used, you must visualize in your mind the shot you plan to take. Determine what set you want to use, where you want to place the subject, and where you want various props. When you have done this, you can set up the shot.

Next comes the lighting of subject and scene. Follow this basic rule: If you want to show or reveal something, light it; if you don't, don't! The more aspects of subject and set you want to reveal or highlight, the more lights you'll need. Build your lights—and reflectors—up, one at a time.

To help you get started, we suggest the following equipment:

- A five-light setup for studio and indoor locations
- A two-light portable setup for outdoor locations
- A light table
- Softboxes and diffusing umbrellas
- A light panel

Each of the above is discussed in more detail below.

Five-Light Setup

Having equipment that enables you to employ a five-light setup in your studio or the subject's home give you a good basis for creative photography. You can add or subtract lights, reflectors, gobos and other lighting devices as your needs, taste and style dictate. Here's the basic five-light setup for a boudoir subject:

Main Light—A large, soft, light source should be used. This can be an actual light placed in a large housing or a large white reflector with adequate light reflected from it.

Fill Light—As with the main light, it can be an actual light source or a large, stand-alone, white, silver or gold reflector.

Back Light—This light is often used directly behind a subject, to rim light the area of her buttocks or the small of her back. Its purpose is to outline the body and separate the subject from the background. We generally have this light in a small, silver-lined pan or bowl reflector that provides fairly directional illumination.

Top or Hair Light—This light is generally on a boom stand, above and slightly behind the subject and directed toward her head. Its purpose is to accent the hair and outline the shoulders. Like the back light, it's often used in a small, silver-lined pan or bowl reflector.

The Fifth Light—This light, which can be an actual light source or a stand-alone reflector, generally serves as an accent light to accentuate a portion of a subject's body, a prop or set. If it is an actual light, in a bowl reflector, it could also be used as a source for illuminating a light table, discussed shortly.

Of course, depending on the size and nature of the set, more lights may be needed to illuminate the entire scene satisfactorily.

Two-Light Setup

When doing boudoir photography outdoors on location, where no household current is available, you have several lighting alternatives. Your main light can be indirect sunlight, reflected onto the subject from a large white reflector. A second, silvered reflector can provide fill light for the shadows. Strips of plastic mirror can be situated behind and to the side of the subject and used as accent lights.

As an alternative main-light source, you can use a portable electronic flash unit such as the battery-operated Profilite by Multiblitz. Aim the flash through a diffusing panel, to obtain a soft light. A second Profilite, activated by a slave unit, can be used behind the subject's back to separate her from the background. A large, white reflector can serve as fill light.

Light Table

To do tight head shots with glamour lighting in the studio, you can create a setup using a light table. To create such a light table, support a 4x4-foot piece of milky-white plastic, 1/8 or 1/4 inch thick, on two saw horses. Put one 4x8-foot foam-core reflector board next to each side of the table and place one of your lights under the table so its light shines through the plastic, onto the lower portion of the subject's face. This light's power should be adjusted to emit one *f*-stop less light than the main lights.

You'll need two soft main lights—one to each side of the camera. Add a top light on a boom stand. You may also need a back or background light.

Softboxes and Diffused Umbrellas

To vary the quality of the lighting, and thus the appearance of the subject, in three-quarter or full-length shots, we use a variety of different light sources during a session. Among these are the 6-foot Starfish by Larson, 4-foot and larger Chimera softboxes, a 42-inch white-lined umbrella, with a plastic diffuser cap by Balcar, or a light panel. Each source yields a different feel or quality of light. Which is best? That's largely a matter of personal preference.

If a subject has a number of facial or body lines that need to be minimized, lighting from a light panel or Starfish is a good solution. When a subject has less lines to hide, you can afford to use a crisper main light, such as is produced by the Chimera softboxes.

When we limit the lighting to a single source, such as for a tight head or head-and-shoulders shot, either the Starfish or the Balcar umbrella with its plastic diffuser cap is an excellent choice. The light quality is very soft, engulfing a subject's face, bathing it in light, and minimizing facial lines.

Light Panel

One of our favorite sources of illumination is the light panel. You can buy one ready-made or you can easily make one yourself. We use a 4x7-foot panel a great deal.

Construct a frame of the appropriate size, using 1-inch PVC plastic pipe. You can stretch any one of a wide variety of materials over the frame: Rip-stop nylon, available from any yard-goods store, parachute material, and a common white bedsheet are but a few examples.

White Bedsheet—A light panel with common white bedsheeting on it will give an excellent, soft quality of light. You can use the panel instead of a softbox or any of the other large, soft-light housings we have mentioned. We like to use bedsheets because they are readily available almost anywhere and are inexpensive.

A new white sheet will give off a colder or more blue light than an older sheet will. The older the sheet, the warmer the color of the light that will come through. By selecting older or newer sheets to place over the frame, you can vary somewhat the color quality of the light.

Instead of putting the sheet onto a light panel, you can simply secure it using two century stands.

CHAPTER 9

Accentuate the Positive; Eliminate the Negative

This chapter is a guide to help you to maximize a subject's positive physical attributes and minimize her less desirable features.

Your aim is to glamourize or idealize the ordinary, average subject. To achieve this, you must photographically enhance her best features while hiding or toning down her less photogenic characteristics. In other words, you must get the very best from the subject. This means seeing the finer physical qualities in a subject—and each one has them!

Even a less-than-perfect image of a baby or portrait of an adult will generally have some appeal. However, the whole basis of boudoir photography is beauty, glamour and allure. If your subject doesn't appear beautiful, glamorous and alluring, you've failed in your job as boudoir photographer. You must see the beauty in every woman—even if she happens to be a little overweight, doesn't have a perfect complexion, or perfectly shaped legs.

One of your main assets is the realization that every woman is beautiful. It's up to your sensitivities to see that beauty, and to your photographic skills to depict it.

It's not difficult to create stunning boudoir images when the subject has a gorgeous face and a sensational figure. It's not so easy to take a woman with less than perfect characteristics, and mold her into the image that is in the mind's eye of those who love her. With the proper use of sets, costumes, poses and lighting you can do it. You do it, in the words of an old song, by "accentuating the positive and eliminating the negative."

THE IMPORTANCE OF EVALUATION AND PREPARATION

Just as you should not go on a location shoot without having previously scouted the area to see what photographic problems there might be, so should you not attempt to do a boudoir session without having first evaluated the subject. You must know, in advance, what problems there might be in photographing each subject so that you can mentally devote time to thinking out solutions on how to light, costume, and pose a subject and so on. You cannot wait until a subject is on the set to start these mental gymnastics. The subject may lose patience while you attempt to solve any major problems that are before you.

Of course, in your initial interview with a potential subject you won't see her as your camera will see her. She will be fully clothed. However, you should assess her general physical attributes as best you can. Listen carefully to what she tells you. Evaluate her general attitude toward sitting for boudoir photographs.

Subject's Self Image

When booking any boudoir session, you must ascertain from the subject what features she or her special someone think are her strongest ones. You may not agree with her selection, but that's not important. What is important is what she thinks about herself. She may think she has attractive hair or expressive eyes or shapely legs. Take notes on which parts of her face and figure she is proud of. You will have to photographically capitalize on these features during your photo session to ensure a successful sitting.

Your Evaluation

At the same time, make notes about areas of her face and figure which you think are her positive attributes. These areas may or may not agree with her evaluation, but they should be capitalized upon as well. You must also make notes of those less-than-perfect parts of her face and body which might require special photographic attention and problem solving, such as cellulite on thighs, blemished complexion, or a thick waist.

Be Prepared

After your initial conference, you should have some idea what problems you may need to deal with at the shoot. You can be prepared with appropriate lightings, sets, poses and costumes. You'll know what to avoid.

When you enter the studio or shooting location, you should have a general idea of what you intend to do. You should work confidently, decisively and as quickly as possible. Make minor changes to the sets, props, costumes, and the like, as the situation dictates.

PHOTOGRAPHIC CONTROL

In earlier chapters, we discussed the importance of having proper lighting, sets, poses, and props. At this point it becomes necessary to focus attention upon some of these areas, as well as others, again and discuss how they can be used to achieve the ideal photographic result: maximizing a subject's positive physical attributes while minimizing or eliminating her less desirable features.

To achieve this goal, a photographer has a number of items and controls—which we like to call *helpmates*—at his or her disposal. No single one is more important than another. You may have to employ a host of different helpmate combinations to ensure a successful session. What will work for one person may not work for another.

Listed below are some typical helpmates that can aid you in attaining the desired result of maximizing a subject's positive physical attributes while minimizing her less than perfect ones. Each helpmate is then discussed more fully.

1. Appropriate poses
2. Appropriate hair style
3. Proper makeup
4. Wise lens selection
5. Selective focus
6. Good lighting technique and control
7. Use of shadows
8. Wise use of costumes, drapes and props
9. Accentuating special features such as legs, eyes, hair, and bust
10. Use of soft focus
11. Use of pantyhose

Poses

Not all poses will work or be appropriate with all subjects. Therefore, don't belabor any pose. Once a subject is placed into position, you will know almost immediately whether or not it is visually appealing and flattering to the subject's figure. Slight modifications can certainly be made, but don't push to make the pose work just because you like it conceptually. The subject will tire and lose confidence in herself, and possibly in you, too.

Poses can be used to emphasize and flatter or, if necessary, to subdue or conceal. A pose should also be part of a pleasing composition, taking into account other image elements, such as the set and props.

Specific Posing Situations—In addition to helping you accentute or eliminate, poses should be appropriate for the costume the subject is wearing, the setting she is placed in, the subject's figure and even her age.

For example, a pose that might look very attractive for a woman in her late 20s or early 30s may be totally inappropriate for a woman in her late 50s or early 60s. A pose that might look very well when the subject is standing may look terrible when she is seated because of the particular costume she is wearing.

If a subject has a thick waist line, many seated poses, which tend to compress the body, may not work well. In such a case, a subject should be placed into a pose which stretches the body, thereby de-emphasizing the stomach area.

If a subject has less than flattering legs—either too heavy or too thin—you will often find that putting the legs into a different plane of focus than the rest of the body will help. For example, if the subject is seated, place her legs so that they are positioned to one side of her body and directed toward the rear of the photo scene. Use a relatively long lens and large lens aperture to limit depth of field. Focus on the subject's face and upper portion of her body, allowing the legs to go slightly out of focus. This will help to detract viewer attention from the legs.

The posing possibilities are almost endless. You will find many more examples in our Portfolio section of this book.

Hair Style

A subject's hair should be styled in a fashion not only to complement her face and flatter her overall appearance but also to help conceal features or characteristics that may not be appealing. For example, if a subject is heavy and full-faced, it will usually be inappropriate to have her hair slicked tightly back against her head because this would cause her face to appear even fuller. If the hair is styled so that it softly drapes close to the sides of the face, the face will appear thinner.

If one side of a subject's face appears fuller than the other, having the hair styled so that the fuller side of the face is framed by the hair will often create the illusion that both sides of the face are equal.

If a subject is very thin, avoid having the hair styled close to the head. Instead, you should consider having the hair teased so that the hairdo is bouffant and full. This will make the face appear fuller.

A subject may have a very prominent forehead. In such a case, consider using a hair style with bangs which cover most of the forehead.

Sometimes you'll be confronted with a subject having limp or lifeless looking hair, or the color may be rather bland. She may need conditioner applied to the hair before styling. It may be advisable to have her hair waved or curled. She may even have a color rinse added.

During your evaluation of the subject, discuss possible hair and facial problems. Your goal is not to criticize but to offer constructive advice to ensure great images. Make certain that you also speak with the subject's hair stylist in advance of the session. Let that person know what problems you have observed and what you want to achieve, and get his or her advice on the proper solution.

Makeup

The proper use of makeup can work wonders in either concealing blemishes and other undesirable aspects or, on the other hand, for maximizing the most attractive features. This is another good reason for leaving the application of makeup to a true professional who knows—or should know—exactly what to do in each individual situation.

For example, a subject's lips may be very large or too small. The upper lip may be smaller than her lower one. One eye may be larger than the other. The face may be blemished or pock-marked, the nose too wide or too narrow, the eyebrows too heavy or too thin, the jaw line too narrow or too broad.

All of these features must be noted and discussed with the makeup artist in advance of the session to ensure that you get the desired photographic results.

The eyes—the windows to the soul—are often the most powerful and appealing features in a woman's face. They should be emphasized, when at all possible.

Lens Selection

Even though we shoot most of our boudoir images with a medium-telephoto portrait lens, there are cases when it is preferable to use a different lens.

Head-and-Shoulder Shots—Since our main objective is to flatter our subjects, we would not consider using a lens of a focal length much shorter than twice that of a standard lens for tight head or head-and-shoulders shots. When shooting with a 35mm camera, whose standard lens has a focal length of 50mm, you should use a lens of about 100mm focal length.

Shooting with a shorter lens would require you to work too close to the subject to get a frame-filling image. This closeness would lead to unflattering facial distortion in the image. A secondary disadvantage of the shorter lens is the fact that bringing a camera too close to a subject can make her feel uncomfortable and this can lead to less than ideal expressions in the photographs.

Although a 100mm or 135mm lens is ideal for head or head-and-shoulders photography, nothing prevents you from using a 200mm, 300mm or even 500mm lens if space permits. The longer the lens, the farther you have to move the camera from the subject.

A long telephoto lens creates some special effects of its own. First, it causes an extreme limitation of depth of field. Second, it makes the background appear relatively larger and closer to the subject. When those are the effects you're after, select a long lens.

Three-Quarter and Full-Length Shots—Not only is a medium telephoto lens ideal for head or head-and-shoulders photography, it is also a very flattering lens to use when doing three-quarter and full-length shots. The body proportions are rendered natural in appearance, without unpleasant distortion. However, as you want to include more of the subject, you will have to move the camera back more. This means you'll need even more working space than you would with a standard or slight wide-angle lens.

***Long Distance Shots*—**If, because your subject is not sufficiently spectacular to hold viewer attention alone, you want to include more of the environment in a shot, a standard or even slight wide-angle lens might be best.

Selective Focus

As stated earlier, a very useful technique for de-emphasizing a subject part is to throw it out of focus. This is done by selecting a lens that's long enough and an *f*-stop that's large enough to limit depth of field and then to focus selectively. Focus to get sharp those parts you want to emphasize in the image and render out of focus those parts you want subdued.

***Depth of Field*—**Basically, depth of field is affected by three factors: the focal length of the lens, the *f*-stop used, and the camera-to-subject distance. The closer you are to your subject, the less the depth of field you will have at any *f*-stop and with any lens. The larger the lens aperture—which means the lower the *f*-number—the less depth of field you'll have. The longer the focal length of the lens, the less the depth of field you'll have at any set subject distance and lens aperture.

When you use a long lens at a large lens aperture, close to the subject, you'll get the most limited depth of field. Major visual emphasis is then on the main focal point in the image. All other areas will be rendered more or less "softly."

Lighting Technique and Control

Lighting constitutes one of the most important and effective helpmates a photographer can have. Whether it be tungsten light, electronic flash or natural daylight, knowledge of how to use and control that light to flatter a subject's positive physical attributes or de-emphasize other portions of the face or figure is essential.

We can't overemphasize the fact that it's not the brand of equipment that one uses that's important, but how it is used. A photographer must be so adept at the craft of photographic lighting that he or she can literally "draw" a subject with light—much as a painter does with a brush—so that the subject's physical attributes are maximized. This means falling back upon a previously stated, basic rule: If you want to see it, light it; if you don't, don't!

Use of Shadows

A viewer's eye will generally be directed toward the brightest or lightest part of a photographic image. Therefore, shadows play a dual purpose. First, they give emphasis to those areas that remain highlighted. Second, when deep enough, shadows can conceal areas you don't want to reveal to the viewer.

Here's just one example: If a woman is heavy, place her in a dark, low-key setting, using a single main-light source at an angle of 30 to 50 degrees from the camera-subject axis. This will have a remarkably thinning effect on the figure. The light will emphasize the part of the body that is illuminated while the shadow area will conceal the remainder of the body from undue scrutiny.

At the other end of the scale, the wise use of light and shadow can also add the appearance of size to a woman's body. We have photographed numerous small-busted women and given them the appearance, in their photos, of being "busty." This can be done quite easily. If the main light is directed into the bust area frontally, it will tend to reduce the apparent size and contour of the bust. If the main light is allowed to skim across the bust line at an oblique angle in relationship to the camera-subject axis, the light will emphasize the contours of the breasts and make them appear larger.

Costumes, Drapes and Props

A boudoir subject's costume or attire must serve one or more of the following purposes: It should flatter the subject and her figure, it should conceal the less-than-desirable parts of her figure, and it should evoke a feeling of mystery.

If you cannot hide a particular portion of the subject's body in shadow or if you don't want less light but still need to subdue or suppress an area of the subject's body from the viewer's attention, then drape it with clothing, an accessory, or anything that will down-play its presence. A feather-boa—available from most costume supply stores in a variety of colors—is a great accessory to have on hand. It can conceal portions of a thigh or waistline and, at the same time, produce an air of femininity consistent with a boudoir image.

People are curious. They are most interested to know about those things that are hidden from them. By allowing a costume, drape or other piece of material to conceal selected portions of a subject's anatomy, you force a viewer to think about and imagine what lies hidden. Often this suggestive image is stronger and more effective than a view of the real thing.

Accentuating Special Features

It will be obvious to you by now that it is a misconception to think of boudoir photography as consisting only of images that blatantly reveal a woman's entire body. In fact, every session should include a few shots of selected parts of the subject's face or figure. This may mean close up shots of her lips, eyes, breasts or legs. At our studio, we have been very successful with closely cropped leg shots. When such images are made in addition to the other images, which show more of the subject, they make a considerable contribution to the total pictorial "package" offered to the subject.

Somewhat related to the deliberate use of shadows in an image is the total silhouette. Although the entire body of the subject is displayed, no detail other than the outline is shown.

When shooting silhouettes, the posing is very critical. There must be no ambiguity in what you reveal. An arm must not cover a breast, a chin must not merge with a shoulder, and two shapely legs must not appear like one extremely heavy leg. The outline, which is the *only* message provided by the image, must be totally explicit.

High-contrast silhouette images can make great additions to a subject's boudoir book.

A wonderful and effective way to accentuate a subject's best features is to use special "kicker" lights to highlight those parts. For added drama, you may want to use colored gels over those lights. For example, by allowing one kicker light—gelled with amber—to be directed onto the subject's breast or buttocks area, this area will be given special prominence.

Examples of all of the above are shown and described in detail in the Portfolio section of this book.

Soft Focus

With today's incredibly—almost unforgivingly—sharp camera lenses, regardless of which camera format is used, it would be a serious mistake to take all boudoir images without some form of soft-focus attachment. In fact, we use such an attachment more often than not. Without it, the resulting images would be too sharp, too literal, too unflattering and too unromantic. A viewer would be able to perceive too much: He would see in sharp detail every wrinkle, every line and every imperfection in a subject's face or figure.

A soft-focus attachment helps to take the "cutting edge" off the sharpness of an image, smoothing out lines and wrinkles and softening the overall image, as is consistent with the basic intent of boudoir photography.

How much diffusion you use, and which type of attachment, is a matter of style and taste, as well as being dependent on the subject matter. For our full length shots, we use a Softar 1 on our Hasselblad camera or a Tiffen Soft Net 1 or 2 when we use 35mm SLRs. For tight head shots we normally use heavier diffusion: the Softar 2 or 3 for the Hasselblad and the Tiffen Soft Net 3 or 4 with 35mm cameras.

Pantyhose

Pantyhose can work wonders in enhancing and flattering a subject's legs. They will firm and smoothen the legs and usually make them look just wonderful. In addition, if the legs have minor scars or bruises, the pantyhose will help conceal these. However, you should be warned that not all brands of pantyhose will work. Some brands on the market have too much sheen—a sure giveaway that they were worn during the shooting. Ideally, you want the legs to look perfect without revealing that pantyhose helped to give them that appearance.

While there may be other brands on the market that would serve as well as the brand we use, to date we have not found them. We try to insist on the *No Nonsense* brand, available at most drugstores. For obvious reasons, the color should be "nude" and the hose should be sheer from toe to waist. We're sure you'll be delighted with the photographic results, just as we have been.

CHAPTER 10

Picture Presentation

Once a photo session has been concluded, your subject will be very anxious to see the results. You will have paid very special attention to her, the poses, lightings and so on, and she will have worked hard to attain the photographic goal that both you and she sought—dynamic boudoir images.

To enable the subject to make her picture selection, you must submit proofs. The way in which you do this will have a great bearing on maintaining her enthusiasm and on the size of the order she ultimately places with you.

HOW TO SUBMIT PROOFS

During a typical boudoir session, we usually use two or three different sets, make major changes in our lighting several times, have the subject wear three to five different outfits and shoot between 48 and 72 frames of film, rarely shooting the same image twice without some modification. This gives the subject a great pictorial variety to choose from, but it also often makes her decision of which images to choose difficult.

Up to the time of placing the final order for prints, most subjects will not have the faintest idea of how many photos they want to buy or even what sizes they want. They will often look to you for guidance.

Turnaround Time

It has been our experience—except when dealing with commercial, corporate clients—that most photographic purchases involve a great deal of emotion. Reduce or eliminate the emotional impact of your work and you will have considerably reduced the potential of your ultimate sale.

For example, if you were to submit wedding photography proofs to the bride and groom eight weeks after the wedding, their interest and purchase of prints is likely to be considerably less than if you had presented them with proofs two weeks after the wedding. The impact of the wedding day will have been reduced if not lost.

In a similar manner, once a subject has made up her mind to experience a boudoir photo session and has actually gone through with it, she waits with excitement to see the results. If you delay the time of showing the results of your mutual efforts, you will have lost a great selling advantage. Accordingly, make a point to have proofs available within five to seven days from the photo sitting. The faster you can have something for them to see, the larger will be the order.

Make an Appointment

When we have proofs ready for a subject to see, she is called and an appointment is made for her to come into our studio to view them. By making an appointment, we insure that at least one of us will be available to spend time and devote attention only to her and her images. This is quality time, time reserved for her only. As in the photo session itself, a subject needs to feel special, to think that you are spending time and effort only on her. The size of the order often seems to express a subject's gratitude for this consideration.

The Proof Room

We think that it is absolutely essential to have a specific area in your studio set aside for showing boudoir proofs. It should not be in the mainstream of your traffic area. Some subjects may not want others to see the images. They may be embarrassed or have a host of other reasons, especially if there is to be discussion about retouching or art-work on certain portions of their body. Strangers milling about will deter such conversation and can stifle a sale.

The proof-room area, like the rest of your studio, should be a comfortable room with a relaxed atmosphere. Offer refreshments. Make the subject want to stay, see the images, and listen to what you have to say about each photo. Once the subject has entered the proof room, tolerate no interruptions. Up to this point, you've made every effort to make the subject feel special. Don't spoil the atmosphere, and the impression she has of you and your methods, at this late point.

Allocate Sufficient Time

When you show a subject her proofs, plan to spend at least one hour with her. You will need this time to adequately review all of the prints, discuss spotting, retouching, quantity, and sizes. You don't want the subject to feel rushed.

Form of the Proofs

Because of the different sets employed during a session, the different costumes a subject wears, the amount of time and film expended on each session, and the pictorial variety you will be offering, you will want to have available a number of prints in various sizes.

At our studio, once the film has been developed, we make contact sheets. Each contact sheet is closely examined through a magnifying glass to ascertain which ones we like. Each of these is marked with a red grease pencil. We then make 8x10 inch proofs of each image marked and often—based purely upon speculation and our experience—choose one of these images to make a 16x20 or larger print. We work by this simple philosophy: If you show it, you can sell it; and if you don't, you can't.

When the subject arrives at our studio she is escorted to the proof room and shown the contact sheets first. Then, one at a time and with the care one takes with fine crystal, she is shown the 8x10 enlargements. We allow her to spend as much time as needed with each image so that she can study each one carefully. Finally, she is shown the 16x20 print of the specially selected image. We also direct her attention to other samples of various sizes—11x14, 20x24, 24x30 and even larger—displayed on our walls.

Boudoir images should not be presented in small sizes such as 4x5, 5x7, or even wallet-size. If you show small sizes, you'll sell small sizes. Good boudoir images demand enlargement to be truly effective, and 8x10 is the smallest size we present.

Using an Optyliser

All of the images that we did not enlarge are shown to the subject on our Optyliser. The Optyliser—which is an electronic film viewer made by the Lucht Engineering Corporation of Bloomington, Minnesota—allows us the luxury of taking a negative and having it instantaneously viewed as a positive on a 20-inch color television monitor.

Although the resolution of each image on the monitor is not as good as on an 8x10 print, it does give a subject an extremely good idea of what each image looks like and aids her in the decision-making process.

In the beginning of your career you may not have the luxury of having such a machine, since the cost is several thousands of dollars. Accordingly, speculate and have your lab make 8x10 proofs of the images that you think are the strongest ones from the session. If you don't sell them all, you at least will be able to use one or more in your own sales portfolio.

Explain Cropping and Retouching

Even though we have 8x10-inch proofs made for a subject's review, none of these is spotted, retouched, or sprayed. That would involve too much time and expense. At this proof-review session, time is devoted to explaining spotting, retouching, and cropping. For example, we will explain to a subject how some facial lines, which she may find objectionable in the proofs, will be softened, reduced, or eliminated in the final print. Do not assume that any subject knows or understands anything about these matters or how these procedures will apply to her prints; you must explain them to her.

Sizes, Finishes, Frames and Books

Once all of the proofs have been reviewed with a subject, it will be necessary to give her some further information to aid in the placing of her order. It is necessary to have various print sizes in and about your studio so that you can make visual reference to an 11x14, a 20x24, and so on. If you offer more than one surface finish and texture—and you should—you should have examples of prints with such different finishes for her to see. In addition to prints with a standard finish, you might have prints on canvas, prints on canvas with brush strokes applied, and so on.

This is also a perfect time to discuss frames for any of the larger prints that she has selected. You should have a variety of frames for her to choose from that will match or harmonize with the tone or color of the prints selected.

For those images that she does not want framed—generally the smaller ones, such as the 8x10s—you might offer a boudoir book, as we do. This book can hold a large number of images. Our standard book contains 12 8x10-inch images and can be monogrammed on the front cover with almost any inscription the subject would like: "To My Love," "From Marie To Tom," and so on. The book can, of course, be ordered to include enough pages for boudoir images to be taken in the future to be added.

There are many fine photo album companies, but the one we use for our boudoir books is Leather Craftsman of Farmingdale, New York. Most of our boudoir subjects want the quality look and feel of a fine leather album for their boudoir prints, and Leather Craftsman has it.

CHAPTER 11

How to Enter the Business of Boudoir Photography

Any business requires a certain investment to help insure success and the photography business is no exception. A successful boudoir photographer is one who has made an investment in time, education, effort, energy, emotion, and money. A little talent and luck don't hurt either.

The purpose of this chapter is to pass on to you some business hints that might make your journey into this field of photography a little easier.

Some fields of photography require less investment in equipment, studio space, sets and props than does boudoir photography. Professional boudoir photography, by its very nature, demands relatively elaborate "staging," if it is to be a success.

Boudoir photography is too sensitive an area to be treated casually. You, your equipment, your studio—whether it be in your home or elsewhere—and your total personal attitude and business environment must reflect total professionalism at all times.

Of course, to become and remain successful, you must be able to produce dynamic photographic images, and do so consistently. But that's not what this chapter is about. In this chapter, we'll tell you how to go about attracting clients, how to get people to understand what you do, how to project the right attitude and provide an appropriate atmosphere.

BUILD A PORTFOLIO

You cannot get subjects to hire you for boudoir photography without having a number of different boudoir images—a portfolio—to show them, and you can't have images to show until you have subjects to photograph. At first, this can appear to be an insurmountable problem. However, there is an easy solution: You can ask your wife, girl friend, female relatives, or the wives or girl friends of your friends to sit for you in exchange for free prints.

Try a variety of lighting setups, poses, costumes, sets and props with these non-paying subjects. Learn what works and what does not. Keep experimenting until you are satisfied that you have truly dynamic prints to show to prospective clients. You'll gain a wealth of experience through this initial work.

Once you have amassed a number of prints—a dozen or two 8x10 enlargements of your best shots should be adequate for a start—put them into the most expensive leather-bound book you can afford. Make certain that all of the prints are cropped, spotted, retouched and sprayed to your satisfaction so that they make an attractive presentation. Now you are ready for business.

HOW TO GET BUSINESS

There are no hard and fast rules for getting business or becoming successful but the following basic guidance may help you on your way.

Talk Boudoir

Wherever you go—the grocery store, beauty shop, barber shop, non-photographic meetings, the gym, and so on—let people know what it is you do. Display enthusiasm for your profession and in the type of photography you do. It's contagious and people will remember you, if for no other reason than for your enthusiastic attitude.

Not only should you tell people that you are a photographer, tell them that you do boudoir photography. Most people will not know exactly what this means, and this gives you an excellent opportunity to explain more about yourself, your talents, your studio, your set-up and what boudoir photography is. Tell them how much fun it is to engage in this form of photography—both from your standpoint as well as a subject's—and what great and unique gift items boudoir images make. You'll often have a very interested audience, so capitalize on it.

Ask for Business

Once you have people's attention, give them a business card and invite them to your home or studio to see your work—your portfolio. Assure them that such photography is handled in the utmost good taste. A number of women are initially put off by the fear that this form of photography is undertaken by less than reputable people, in undesirable surroundings. Make certain that you set their minds at ease.

Maintain a Professional Approach

Never make dubious jokes about this form of photography. The subject is too sensitive and, as yet, too new. You're likely to be misunderstood. Once you gain the reputation of being frivolous about this form of photography—and this can happen very quickly—you'll have done yourself and your chance of developing a successful business irreparable harm.

Contact Your Previous Clients

If you already have a list of photographic clients—from weddings and portraits, for example—show them your boudoir portfolio and suggest that they might enjoy being photographed in this manner. We suggest that, initially, you don't charge a sitting fee but simply charge for prints that you sell. You will get more responses to your request by initially using this approach.

If your work is good, the subjects will buy prints and, more importantly, they will spread the word about you and your work.

Although word-of-mouth advertising is the slowest method for getting new business, we think that it is the best and strongest form in the long run. What better advertising can you have than the praises of a previous customer who is thoroughly satisfied with you and your photographic results?

Other Ways of Attracting Business

There are many other ways of getting business, whether it be for boudoir or your other photographic services. However, what may work for us, in our area, may not for you. Here are some suggestions that you may want to try:

- Advertising in the Yellow Pages
- Direct-mail advertising
- Newspaper advertising
- Public displays
- Slide-show presentations
- Radio or TV talk shows

Advertising in the Yellow Pages—Although the Yellow Pages have not been a great source of business for our other photographic services, we do get about five percent of our boudoir subjects from this form of advertising. Boudoir photography has become very popular and has become a common subject of discussion on television shows and in magazines and newspapers. After hearing or seeing such material, people are stimulated to find out more. They often refer to the Yellow Pages to find out who, in their area, does this kind of photography.

Advertising in the Yellow Pages also helps to keep your name before the public.

Direct-Mail Advertising—This has been an excellent form of advertising for us in the boudoir business. You should prepare a colorful brochure, consisting of one to four tastefully done boudoir images, with appropriate accompanying text, and mail a copy out to all of your past female photographic clients.

In addition, you should consider buying a mailing list from one of the better mail-list houses in your area. They will have names and addresses of women in your area whose incomes are over a certain dollar amount, who are professionals, who are between certain ages, and so on. Such a list can yield a number of women who are potential candidates for such photography.

Newspaper Advertising—This form of advertising has been very good for us. Every time we run an ad announcing that we do boudoir photography, we get new business. And the business we get from the ad leads to further business—because these customers recommend us to their friends.

The unfortunate part about this form of advertising is the cost. We have found small ads to be relatively ineffective. However, every time we place a half-page or full page ad, we get considerable business.

We have found that relatively small, local newspapers, will often run an editorial story about you and your business if you purchase a sizeable ad. That is, of course, largely because boudoir photography is such a topical and popular subject today. In any event, such an editorial story means additional, valuable—and free—advertising for you.

Public Displays—Displaying 16x20 and larger prints of our work in selected places such as fine restaurants, banks, local city halls, shopping malls, and so on, is a great business generator for all of our photographic services—with the exception of boudoir photography! People in charge of granting permission to erect displays are often hesitant to allow boudoir images to be displayed. Even though the images are in good taste, they fear offending some of their important customers.

Accordingly, displays have played no part in generating boudoir business with one exception—better lingerie shops. Every time we display in such shops, new clients come to us.

On the gallery walls in our studio, we display boudoir images with pride, alongside wedding photographs, family portraits and photographs of children. Don't ever hide or conceal the fact that you do boudoir photography. There is nothing to be ashamed of. It is a legitimate art form.

Slide-Show Presentations—This form of advertising is relatively new for us, but we know that is works. We have put together a complex multi-projector show of our boudoir work. We use four projectors, an 8-foot screen and about 300 strong boudoir images to create a 20-minute slide show, accompanied by appropriate background music in stereo. We present the show at any function we can get ourselves invited to, such as businessmen's luncheons and women's-club activities. Such a presentation can make you and your work a great topic of conversation and generate a large amount of business.

Although our slide show and the related equipment are elaborate and expensive, there is nothing to prevent you from starting out slowly, building from a single slide projector and an audiocassette player.

Radio and TV Talk Shows—If you are not faint of heart, call a number of local radio stations in your area and ask for the person in charge of producing their talk shows. You will be amazed how well you and your work will be received. Photography is topical, and many of the radio stations will love the idea of having a competent photographer on their show to inform their listeners about photography in general and boudoir in particular. Such shows have been a great business vehicle for us, and the best part of it is that it's free! And don't forget TV shows, either. We have appeared on numerous such talk shows, explaining our work and showing our images.

SPACE, FACILITIES, PROPS AND EQUIPMENT

Our studio is elaborate and handles a lot of work. Accordingly, our equipment is extensive. However, we must emphasize that you can take excellent boudoir photographs with relatively modest equipment. What you need most is the true desire to engage in this form of photography. You also need the determination to develop a high level of skill—which comes through practice, practice and more practice—and a positive attitude toward your clients.

Space

Although we use elaborate sets in an ample studio area, you can do fine boudoir photography in modest surroundings. Even the rooms in your own home will do the job. Of course, it would be great if you had 5,000 square feet or more of shooting area that could be totally devoted just to boudoir imagery—but you don't need it. In the beginning, you can do very well even in a 12x15-foot room.

If you don't have even this much space, you could do all of your sittings in the subject's home or even outdoors at a park or beach.

Props and Costumes—As with equipment, it's nice to have 30 or 40 props and 12 or so costumes at your disposal but, in the beginning, it's not necessary. Go to a thrift shop or second-hand store and buy three or four props and two or three costumes and learn to work with these first. You can always expand your prop and costume collection as the demand increases.

BASIC ADVICE

If you're planning to enter boudoir photography as a business, some of the following suggestions should be helpful to you.

Printed Material

Have a printed brochure describing your boudoir photography and also have a printed price list. In the brochure, describe and illustrate the nature of your service, your operating facility and your basic working philosophy. This will help to familiarize potential clients with a relatively new form of photography and, as a result, make them more at ease discussing it and may eventually persuade them to use your services.

Letters of Recommendation

As your boudoir business begins to increase, never hesitate to ask a satisfied subject to write you a letter of recommendation. She can address it to you or to whom it may concern. It does not have to be lengthy. The important thing is that she writes or types it in her own words, setting forth how she liked the experience of being photographed by you in this style of photography, and how impressed she was with the results. Such letters can be very persuasive in attracting other prospective boudoir subjects.

Your Fee

People go into the photography business for two major reasons: To do the type of work they love doing and to make a living at it.

It is advisable to never reduce your set and agreed fee. Boudoir photography demands more time, energy, space, money, equipment, not to mention sheer artistry, than most other fields of photography. If your work is good and strong, don't work at discount prices.

If, for any special reason, you sometimes want to provide a free service, that's OK, but never compromise your fee.

Regarding the amount you should charge a client, you must be guided by the area that you are in. If you are in an affluent area, you may be able to charge more for the same service than another photographer who is situated in a less affluent area. The cost of many of the items needed for your work will also vary from one region of the country to another. This should be reflected in the fee you charge.

Visit as many of the photography studios in your area as you can. Find out how much they charge for their boudoir work, including sitting fee and print prices. Use this as your starting guide. You can always increase your prices as your work becomes stronger and in greater demand.

Portfolio

BEDROOM SET

Most people associate boudoir photography with the bedroom and, therefore, a sitting should include several shots in this setting. If lighting and staging are properly arranged, this setting can afford great variety and versatility.

For a sitting in your or the subject's home, you may only need to arrange the furniture to suit your taste and add a few props and accessories to otherwise complete the setting. However, if you are doing the session in your studio, a bedroom setting will have to be constructed.

In our bedroom set, the walls are 4x8-foot sheets of foamcore board. The window and door are made of 1x1-inch strips of wood hot-glued together and the bed is constructed from 1-inch PVC plastic pipe with a 3/4-inch piece of plywood on top of the bed frame. A 1-inch piece of foam is put on top of the plywood for the subject's comfort and to make the bed appear realistic.

Sheer white drapes are hung over the window and door area to add a feminine touch. Two panels of white, fur-like material are used as the floor covering. The two 48-inch-wide panels are sewn together. A vanity table, an end table with a lamp, a frilly bedspread, pillows, and a rocking chair complete the bedroom set.

A bedroom set should have a distinctly feminine atmosphere. This can be achieved with color, such as white or pink, or with props and accessories, such as flowers and delicate feminine clothing, appropriately placed about the scene.

PORTFOLIO 1

In this shot, our subject was directed to look away from the camera in order to enhance the feeling that she was unaware of the camera's, or viewer's, presence in a very private moment.

The lighting for this photo—see diagram—was adjusted and placed to produce an airy feeling to the overall image.

The main light, 2000-watt-second flash in a 6-inch bowl reflector, was to the far side of the subject, positioned high on a boom stand. This hard light source outlined the body and backlit the subject.

A light panel and a 3x4-foot softbox served as fill lights. Each had a 1200-watt-second flash behind it, adjusted to emit half the power of the main light.

Two accent lights—one for the door and the other for the window—each in a 6-inch bowl reflector, were set to emit one full *f*-stop more light than the main light. Both the door and the window were covered with architectual velum so that the light, coming from the respective accent lights, would be more evenly distributed.

You can easily produce different pictorial looks, especially when several costume changes are also made, by making the main light an accent light and allowing the light panel to become the main light.

In the following 11 bedroom-set images, we will show you how simply you can achieve a different look and pictorial result with only minimal changes to this basic overall set up.

This photo was taken with a medium telephoto lens, at an exposure of *f*-11. A Softar 1 soft-focus filter was used to achieve a slightly soft effect.

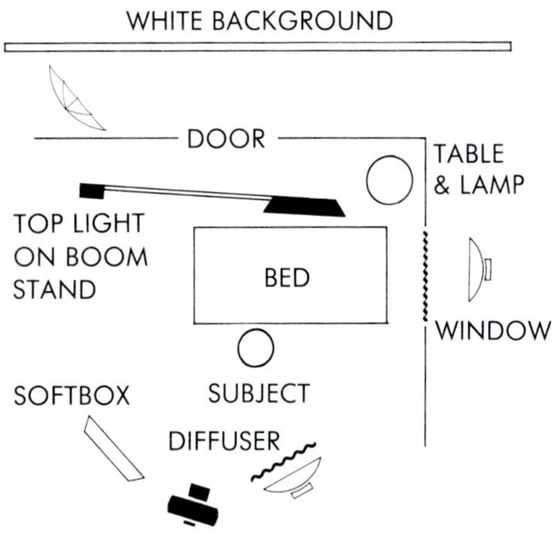

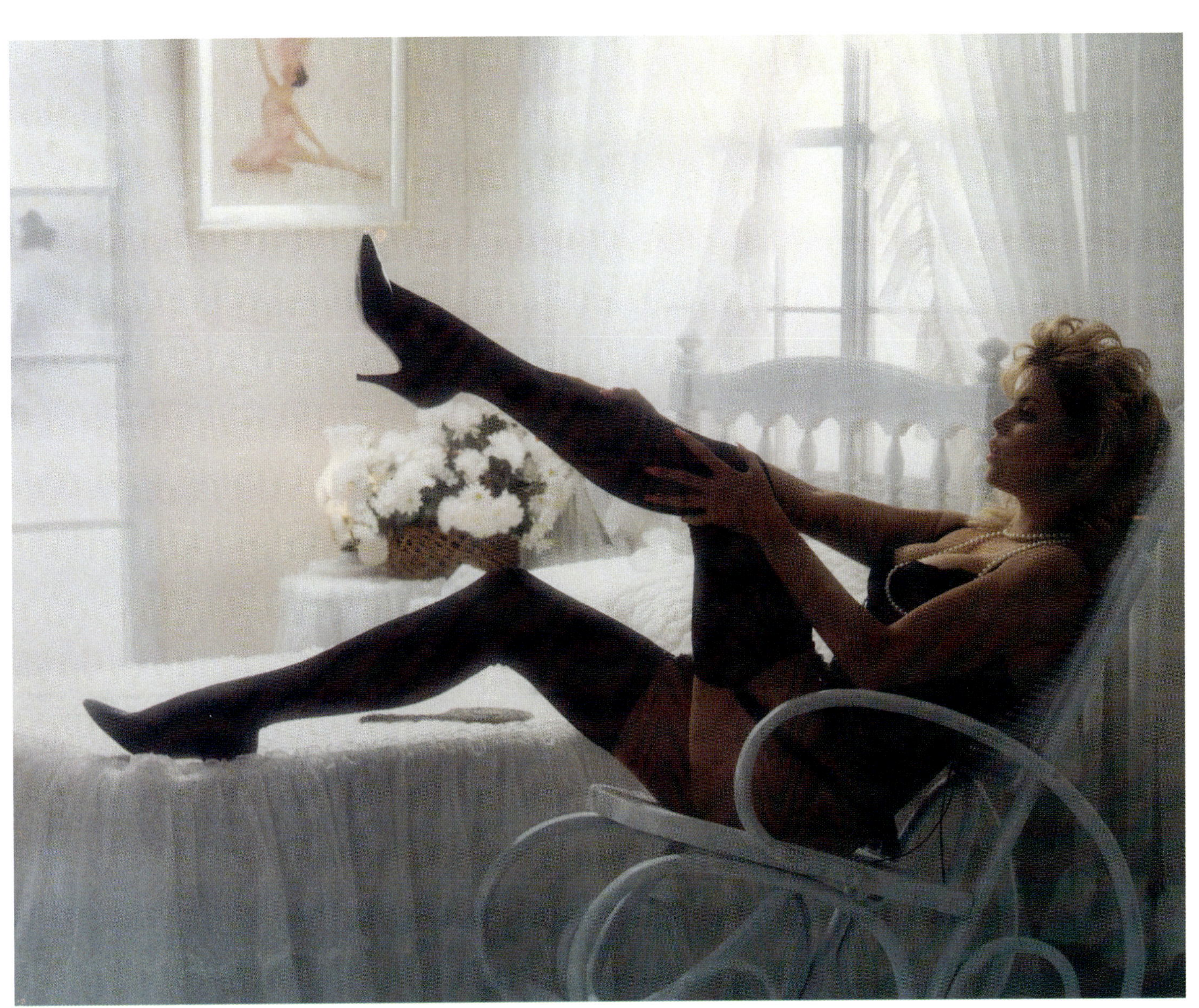

PORTFOLIO 2

This is a typical example of how the bedroom set, with complex lighting, can be given a different look with only slight effort and minimal changes.

The same lighting and exposure were used as for Photo 1, but two other items were added: A warming filter was placed over the camera lens and a 6-foot pink venetian blind was placed approximately 5 feet in front of the subject. The point of focus was on the subject, allowing the blinds to be rendered slightly soft.

The use of the pink blinds, the warming filter, and the highlight from behind the subject gave the image a totally different look.

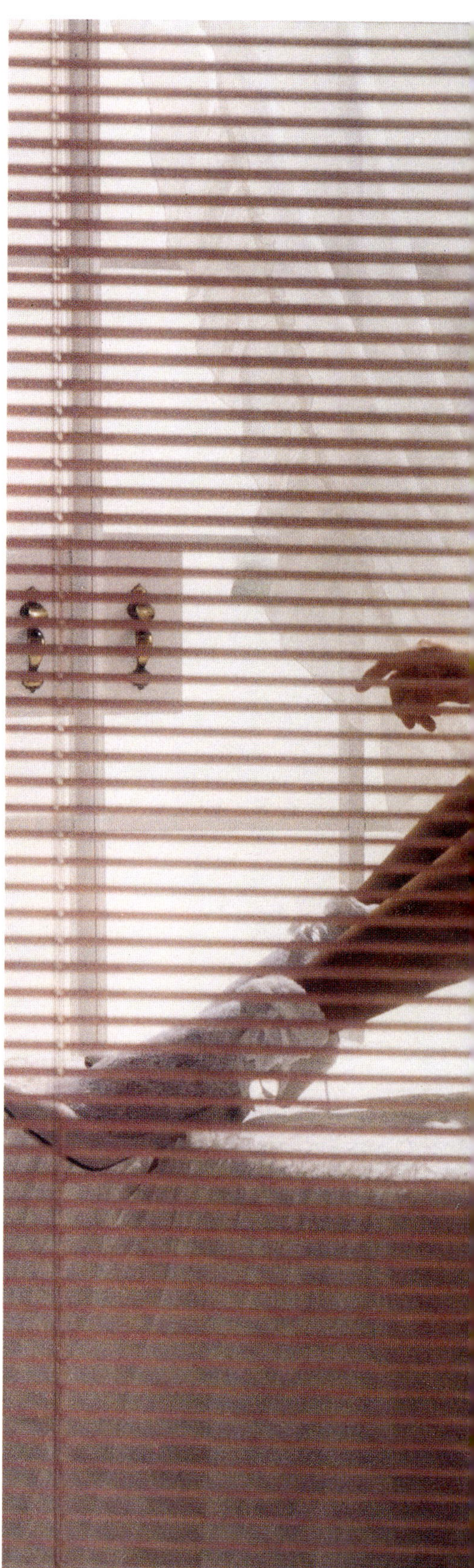

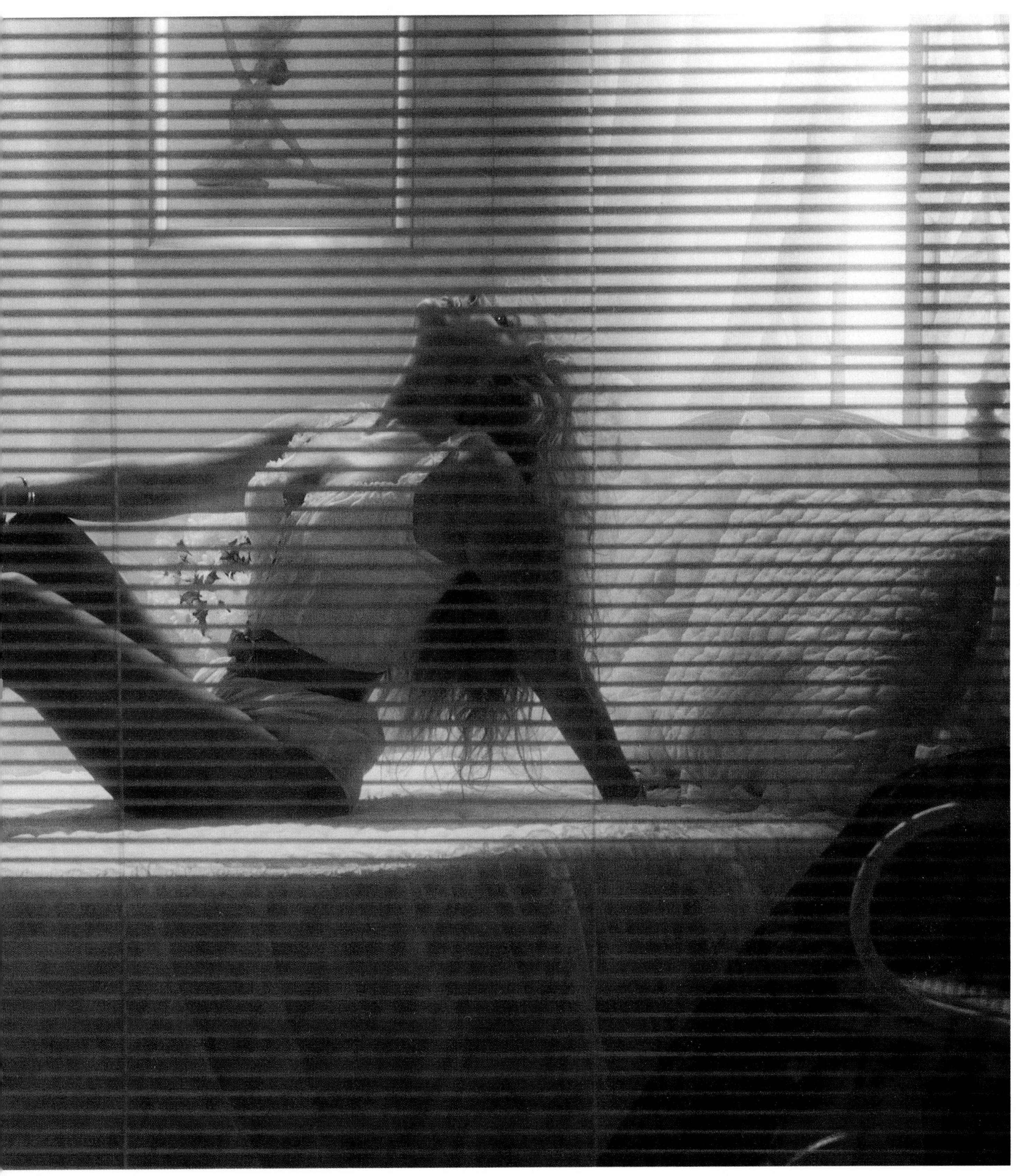

PORTFOLIO 3

This is another example of how easy it is to give a different look to the same set while making only minimal changes.

The light that was used as main light in Photo 1 was made another accent light for this image, along with the window light and door light. The subject was positioned next to the folding screen. A Balcar Opalite, with a 20-degree grid spot and opaque diffuser cap, which was substituted for the light panel, was brought in close to the subject—about 6 feet away—and made the main light. An additional accent light, in a 6-inch bowl reflector, placed behind and to the left of the subject, was directed onto the subject's back and hair for additional separation. A 3x4-foot softbox, placed to the left of camera-subject axis, was used as fill light.

With the exception of the main and fill lights, all lights were gelled with a pink gel. The accent lights were adjusted to the same power output as the main light, and the fill light was set to emit one-half the power of the main light.

The subject was asked to avoid looking directly at the camera. This helped to create an intimate impression.

A medium telephoto lens was used to take this photo, with a Softar 1 filter. Exposure was at *f*-11.

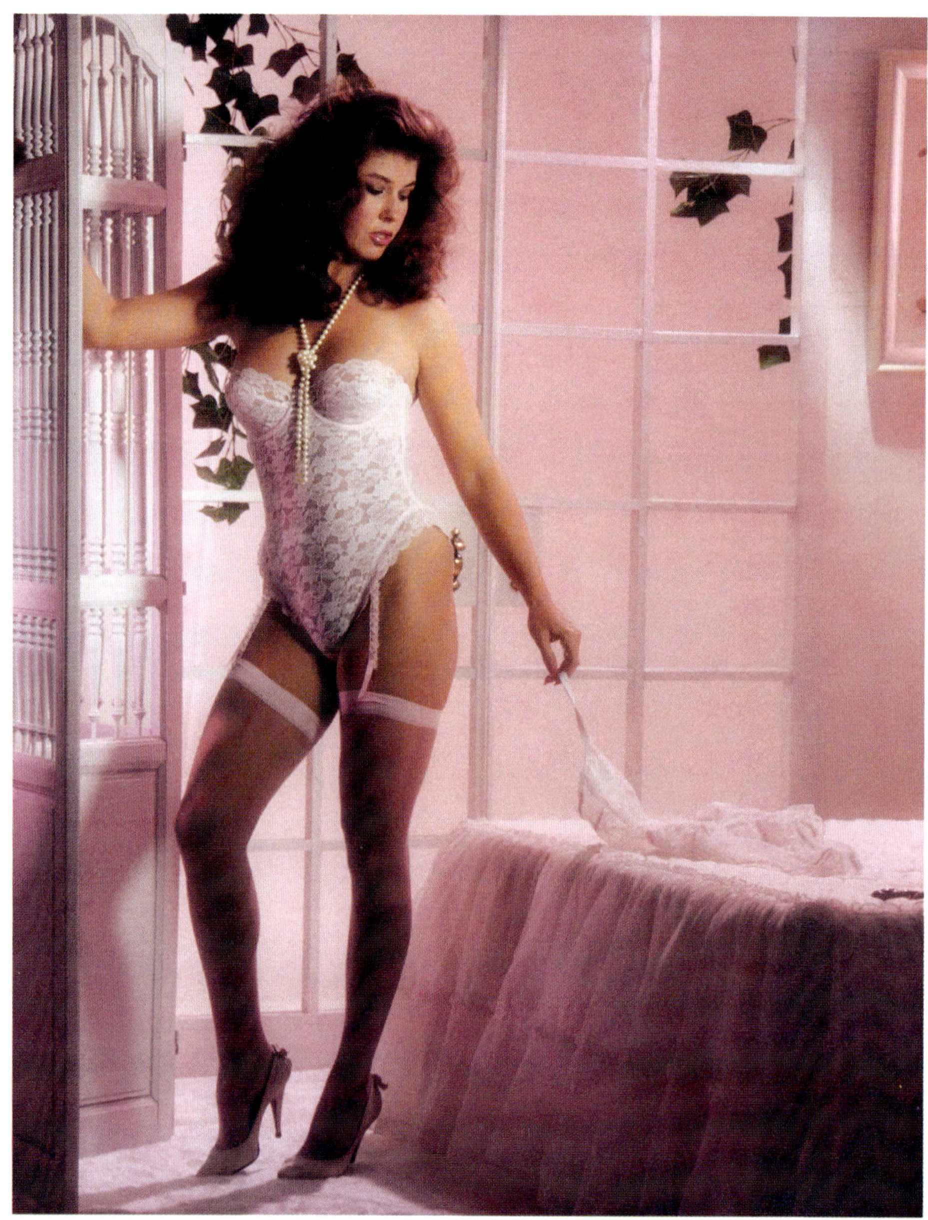

PORTFOLIO 4

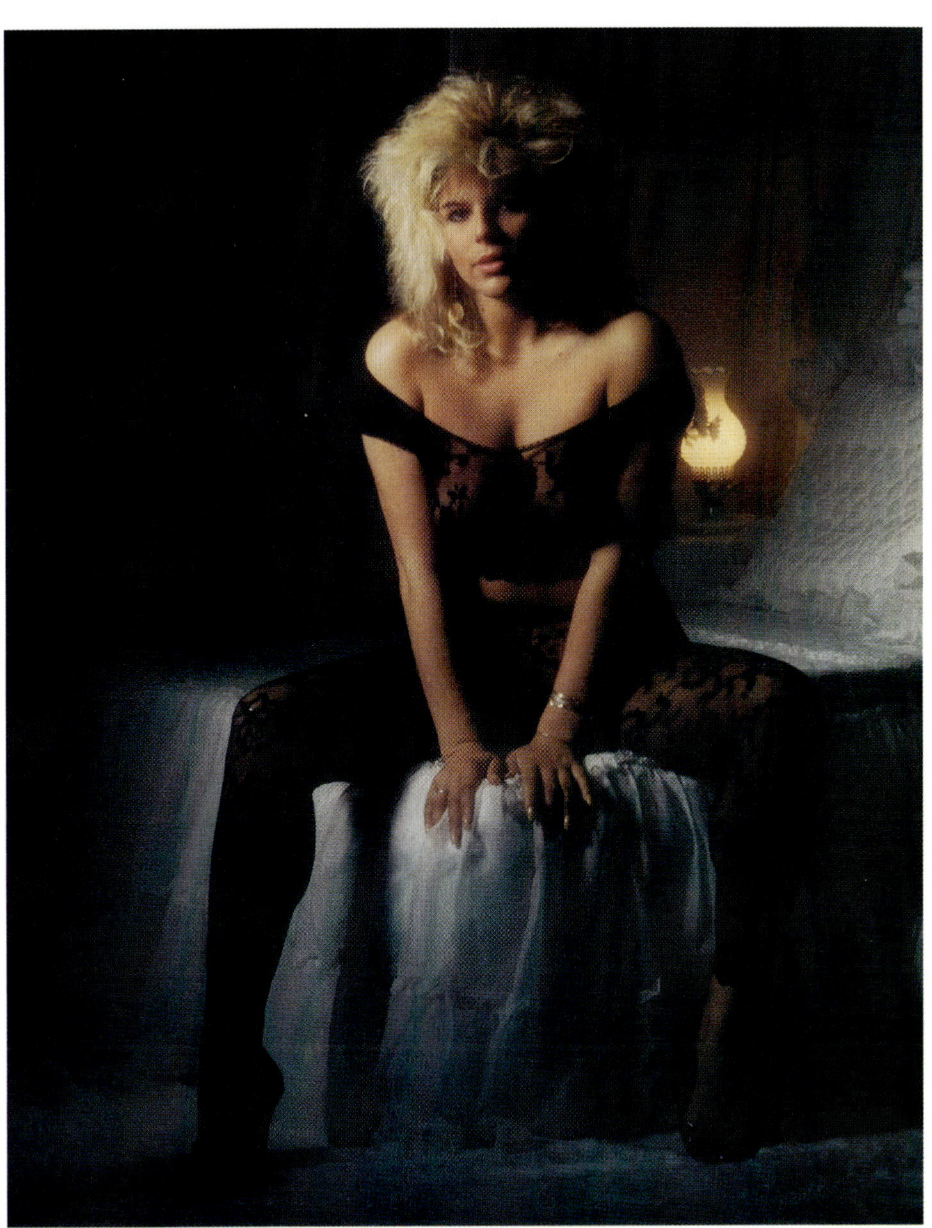

In this image, a dramatic effect was obtained by using only one flash—the Balcar Opalite, with a 20-degree grid spot and plastic diffuser cap. This light was positioned to the left of camera axis so that its light skimmed across the subject's body, enhancing the contour of her bosom. All other lights were turned off, with the exception of the table lamp.

The shutter speed was sufficiently slow to enable the illumination from the table lamp to be recorded. Although the table lamp gave no illumination on the subject, it aided in separating the subject from the background and added to the mood of the image.

A medium telephoto lens and a Softar 1 filter were used. Exposure was 1/15 second at *f*-8.

PORTFOLIO 5

This image differs only slightly from Photo 4. The Opalite was again used as main light, to the left of the camera. A white, 4x8-foot reflector was placed close to the subject, to the right side of the camera, to open up the shadow area. Two accent lights—one behind the window and the other high and behind the subject, each in a 6-inch reflector and with a blue gel—were adjusted to emit one *f*-stop more light than the main.

The subject's pose and hair were altered slightly to make this image a little different from the preceding one.

A subject sometimes shows concern that some part of her body may look less than pleasing. If costume, prop or lighting does not cure the problem, altering the pose may help.

In this instance, the subject was concerned about her waist area. To block a portion of her tummy from view, we had her strike this pose and raise her right leg slightly higher than normal.

The lens, exposure and filtration used for this photo were the same as for the preceding image.

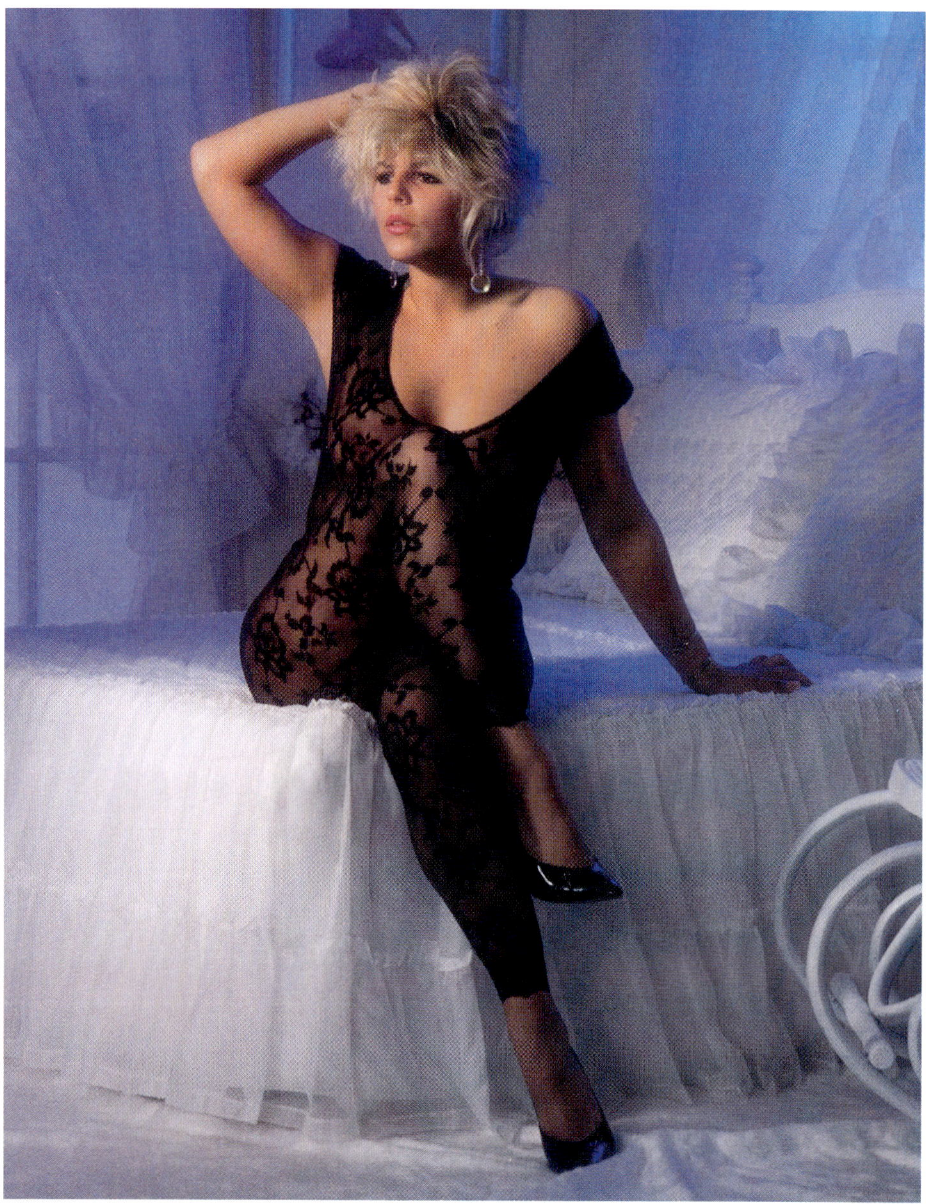

PORTFOLIO 6

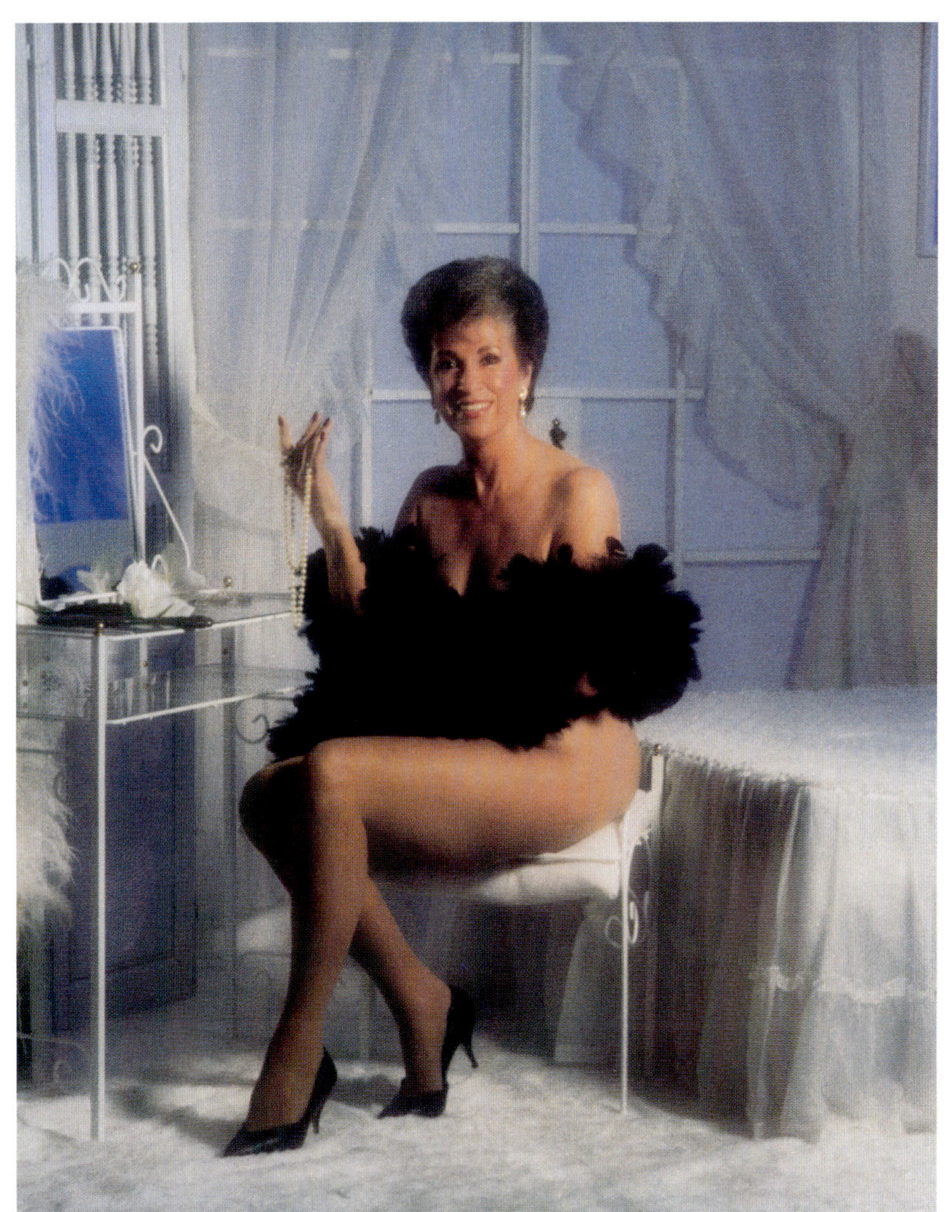

The Opalite was used as the main light, to the right of camera axis, with a white foamcore reflector to the camera's left as a fill. The vanity table was turned slightly toward the camera to capture the reflection of the blue-gelled window accent light.

By changing a subject's locale—from the bed to some other area within the bedroom setting—and changing her costume, you can achieve a totally different image.

This photo, of a woman over 50 years old, shows very convincingly that a woman need not be in her twenties to be a good, sensuous boudoir subject.

Initially, this subject was hesitant about engaging in boudoir photography. She thought that she had neither the face nor the figure to support such imagery. This image, and the others we took for her, clearly demonstrated that she was wrong. When she showed her photos to her friends and peers, even they were amazed. They saw an aspect of her that they had never known existed. In her immediate neighborhood, she is now referred to as "the model."

PORTFOLIO 7

This photo is one of our favorites. The subject is a wife and career woman who wanted a very unique gift for her husband—and she got it! Since her skin is almost alabaster white, we decided to keep the lighting as soft as possible and the tone high key.

We used the basic bedroom set, with some minor variations: Instead of a small light panel, a large, transilluminated bedsheet was used as main light source. It was placed very close to the subject—approximately 4 or 5 feet away—to produce extremely soft lighting. The pose was chosen to emphasize the subject's beautiful figure.

The bedsheet had a 1200-watt-second flash head behind it. A 3x4-foot softbox, placed to the left of camera-subject axis, was used as fill light. Its power was adjusted to emit one-half the power of the main light. Three accent lights, each in a 6-inch bowl reflector, were also used. One was directly behind and above the subject, one behind the door on the left side, and a third behind the window. Each accent light was adjusted to emit one *f*-stop more power than the main light.

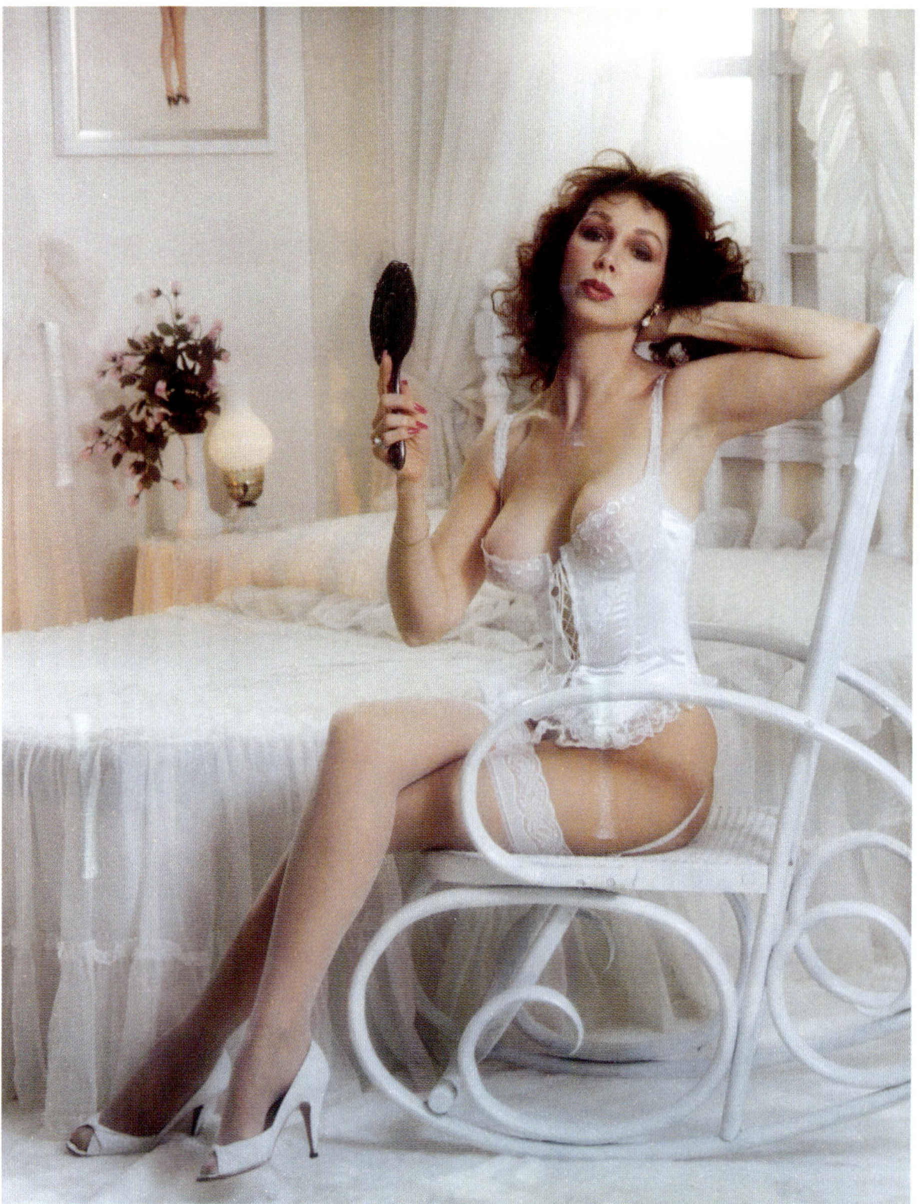

PORTFOLIO 8

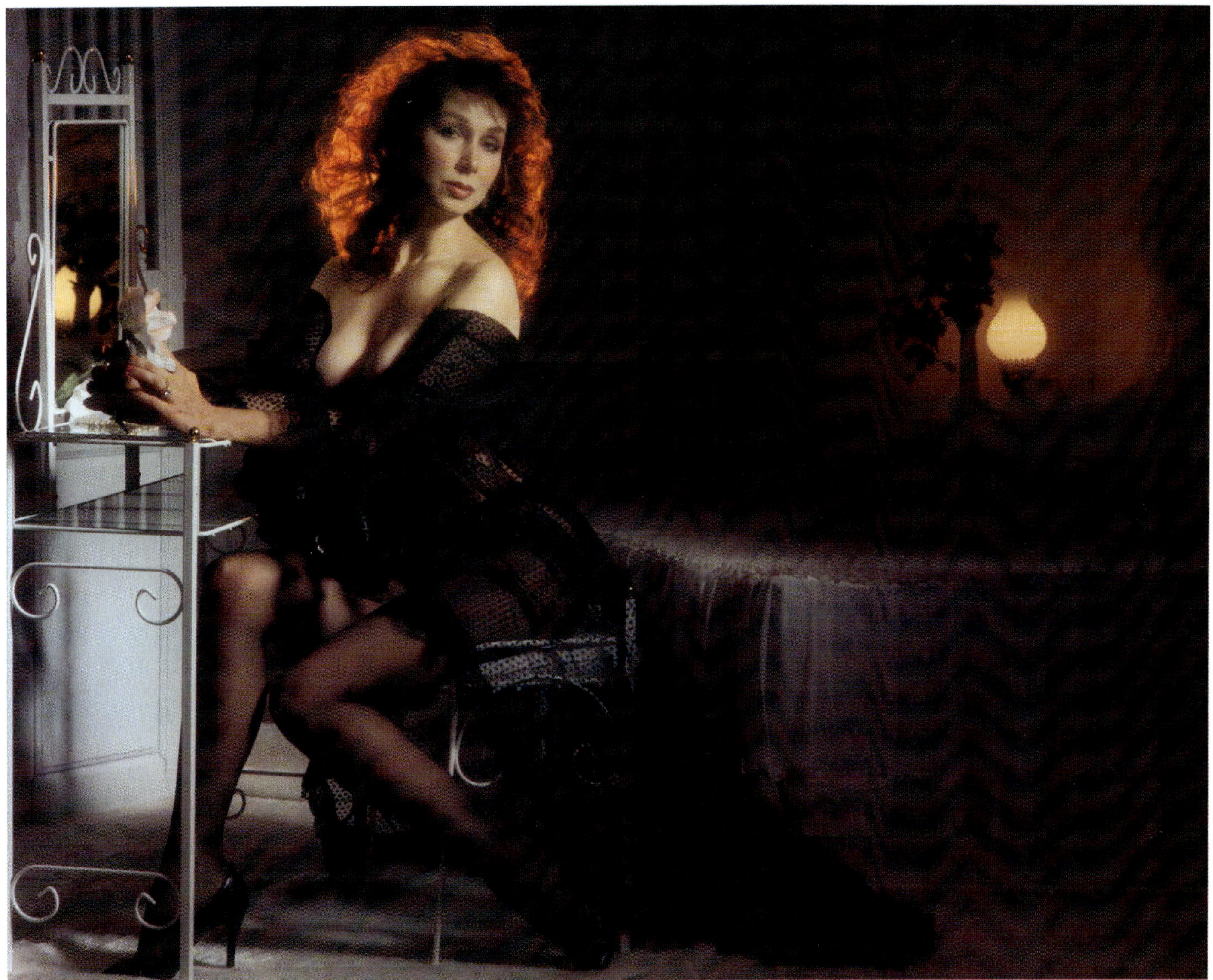

To achieve a totally different appearance, we changed the subject's costume and pose and altered the lighting. Because our basic bedroom set and the lighting are so versatile, changing the mood of an image can take place in a matter of just a few minutes.

The snooted back light behind the subject's head could have been set at a power setting from one-fourth the power of the main light to two *f*-stops more power than the main light, with each setting yielding a different pictorial result. For maximum emphasis, we set it at two *f*-stops more power, and used an amber gel. This helps to keep the viewer's eye riveted on the subject. A shutter speed was chosen that was long enough to record the glow of the table lamp.

Other than the main light—which was a Balcar Opalite with a 20-degree grid spot and plastic diffuser cap—and the back light, no other flashes were used. We wanted to keep the scene as dark as possible in order to add an air of mystery.

A medium telephoto lens was used, together with a Softar 1 filter. Exposure was 1/15 second at *f*-11.

9 PORTFOLIO

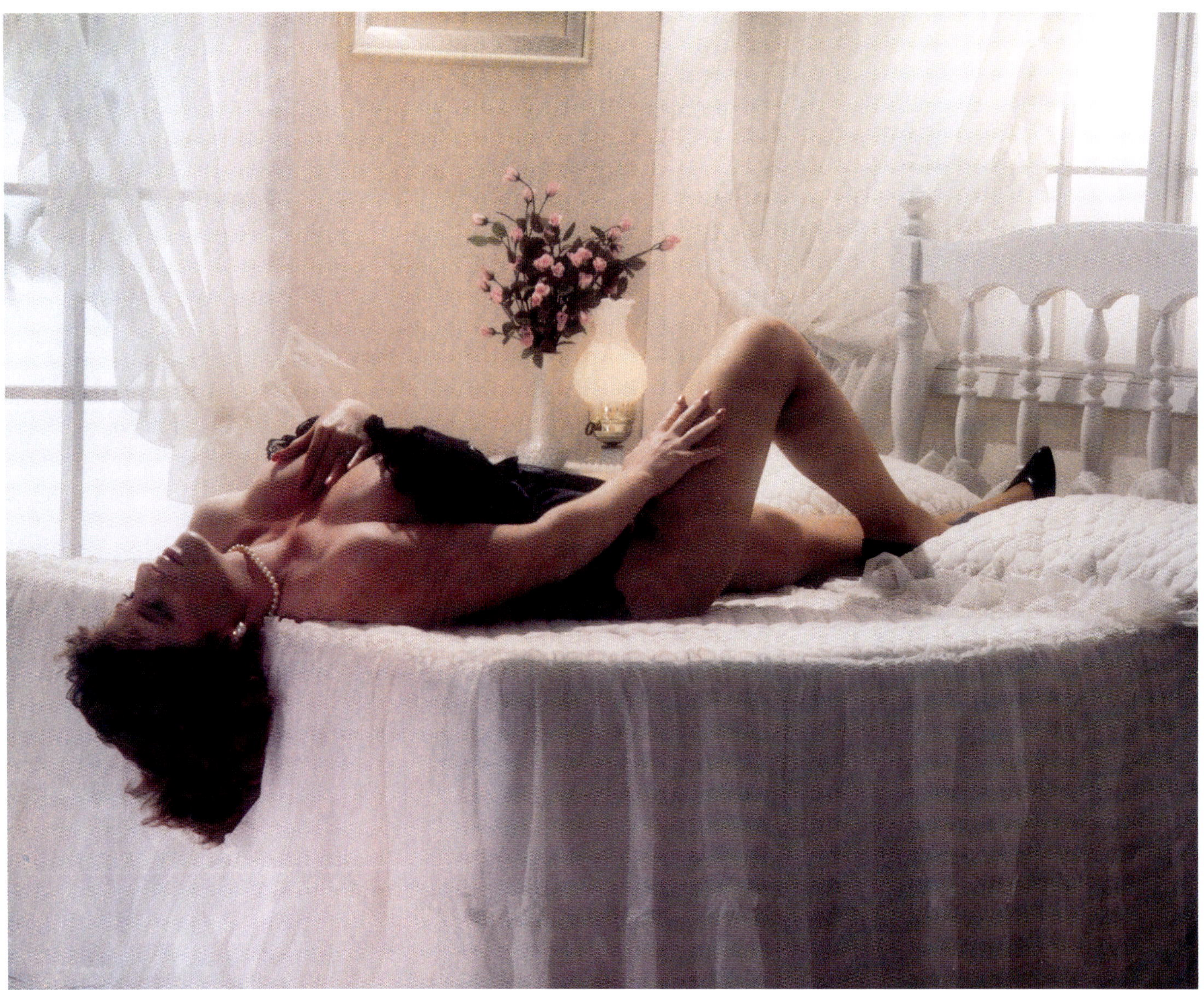

Technically, this photo is similar to the first photo in this portfolio in camera angle, lens employed, filtration, and lighting.

A woman does not need to have a model's tall, slender figure in order to be feminine and sensuous. In fact, this subject was several months pregnant when she had this photo taken for her husband.

We chose this pose for this very attractive subject. It tends to stretch the body to give her a slender appearance. The impression of slimness was further enhanced by putting the right side of the subject in shadow.

When you photograph a woman who is a little overweight, or one who is concerned about certain areas of her body such as her stomach or hips, a stretching pose can help to make the subject appear thinner.

PORTFOLIO 10

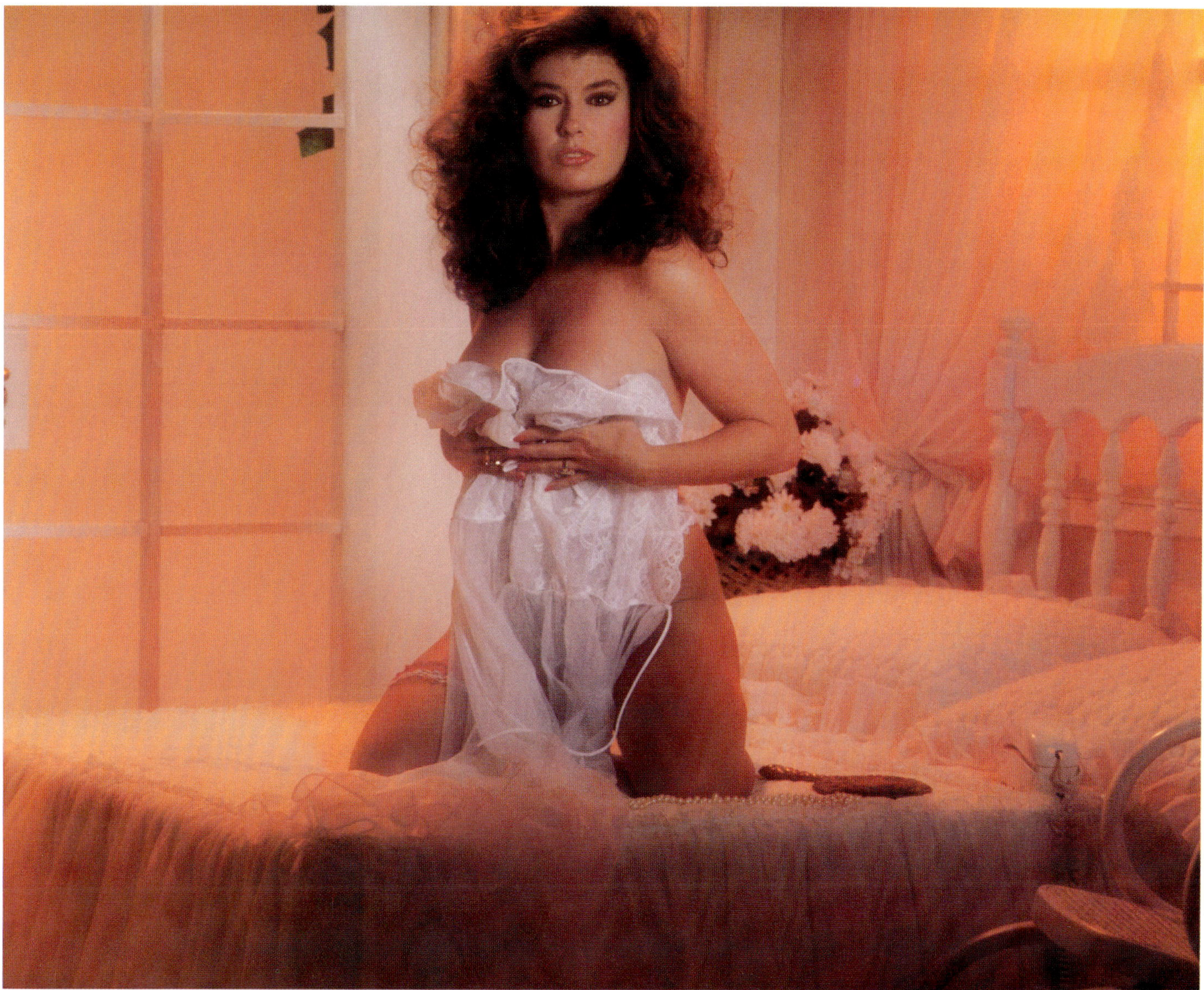

The main light for this image was a light panel with a 1200-watt-second lamp behind it. The fill light, which was a 3x4-foot softbox, was placed on the opposite side from the main light and its power was adjusted to emit one-half the power of the main light.

Three accent lights—each in a 6-inch bowl reflector and covered with an amber gel—were placed behind the subject. One was behind the window, one behind the door, and one high on a boom stand. The power of the accent lights was adjusted to equal that of the main light. This lighting gave the set a totally different feeling.

Allowing a subject to hold a garment in her hands—as we did here—can accomplish a number of purposes: It can make the subject feel more at ease as well as hide body parts that you or she may feel need to be de-emphasized. Not revealing everything also heightens the allure: Subtle and tasteful suggestiveness is a keynote in boudoir photography.

A medium telephoto lens was used, with a Softar 1 filter. Exposure was at *f*-11.

PORTFOLIO 11

The addition of a small white stepladder to the set, a sultry pose, and carefully positioned lighting netted this seductive image of our subject.

A light panel, with a 1200-watt-second lamp behind it, was used as main light. It was placed about 45 degrees to the right of camera-subject axis. A 3x4-foot softbox was placed on the opposite side of camera-subject axis to act as fill light. Its power was set to one-fourth the power of the main light. No other flash illumination was used. This produced a more dramatic result than if the set had been illuminated uniformly.

A medium telephoto lens was used, and a Softar 2 filter. Exposure was at *f*-8.

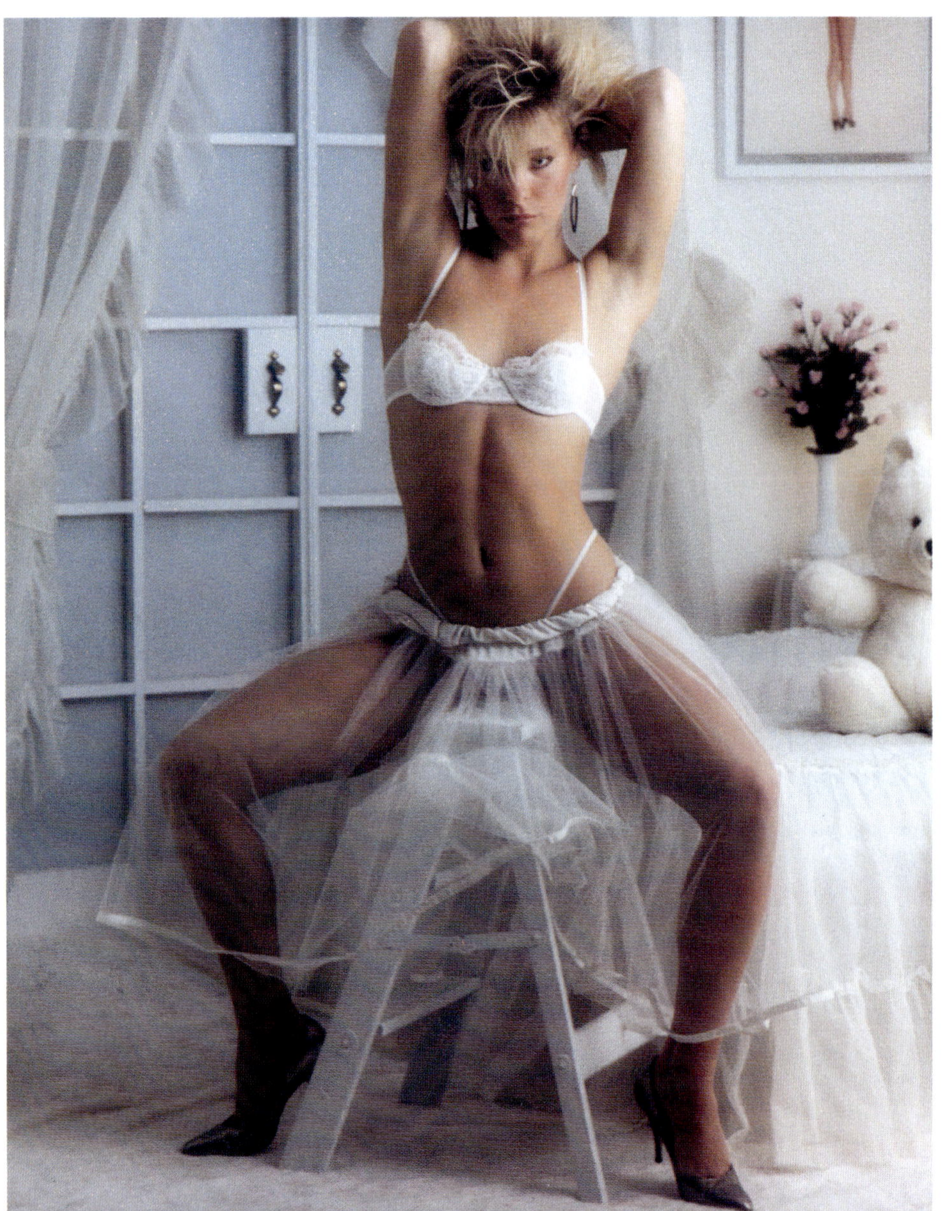

PORTFOLIO 12

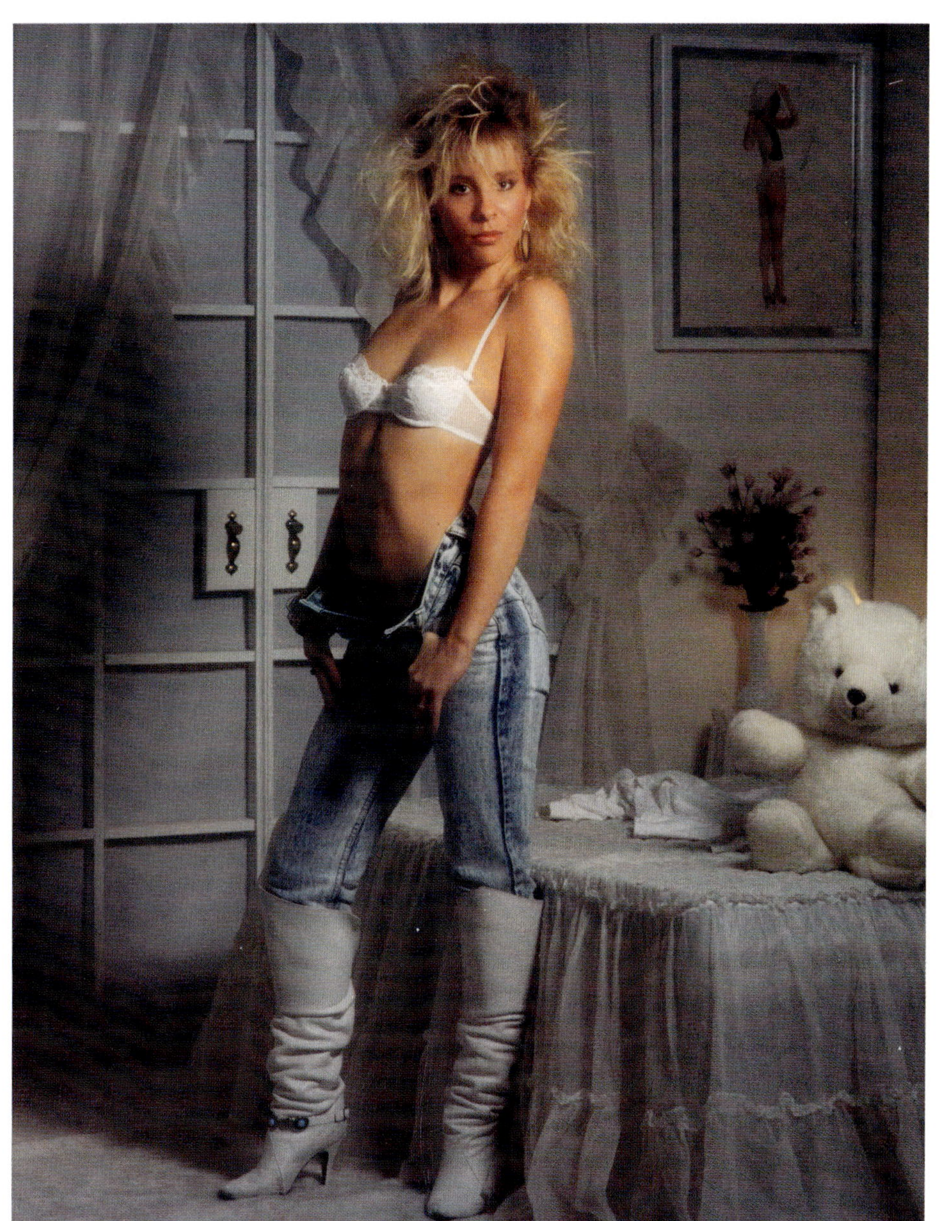

It has long been recognized that woman can acquire the skill of undressing in a very sensual manner. Although not all boudoir subjects are able to playact this scenario well, you should attempt to capture a few images of your subject in this process. If you are successful, the results can be stunning.

The more brightly you illuminate the subject and set, the more you will lose the mystery to the act of disrobing. To enhance the seductive mood, we chose a Balcar Opalite, with a 20-degree grid spot and plastic diffuser cap, as main light. It produced soft but confined illumination. A white 4x7-foot reflector was placed close to the subject's right side. Other than a table lamp behind the bear's head, no other illumination was employed.

A medium telephoto lens was used, with a Softar 1 filter. Exposure was 1/15 second at *f*-8.

BATHROOM SET

If the first setting that comes to mind when a woman thinks of boudoir photography is the bedroom, a close second would be a bathroom setting. Accordingly, we built one in our studio.

Colors for the set had to be selected carefully. We chose black as the theme color: black walls, constructed of 4x8-foot foamcore boards, black tub, and black columns and vinyl floor. We wanted an elegant and dramatic look that would flatter most subjects. The red accents—both in props and lighting—against the black of the set helped accomplish this goal.

Since the lighting that we use for our bathroom set is complex and would be time-consuming to set up and tear down, our lights are set up permanently. However, once a set of this kind is constructed and in place, it offers a number of pictorial possibilities. With only minimal changes in lighting or of lens, one can quickly move from one pose to another with very little effort and delay.

The bathroom set and the lighting for it are excellent examples of our previously stated rule: If you want to see something, light it; if you don't, don't! Because of the black color of the tub, the walls and vinyl steps, each facet of the set that is to be clearly seen must be lit separately from the subject. At the same time, however, care must be taken not to overlight the set, since the richness of colors would otherwise be lost.

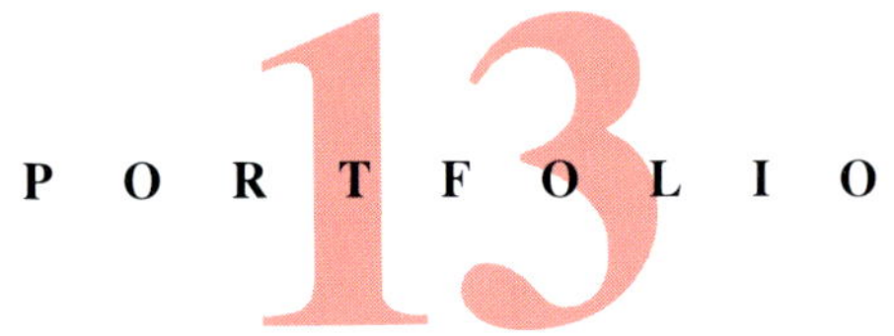

PORTFOLIO 13

The main light for this photo, and the bathroom shots that follow, had to be chosen carefully. We wanted the subject only to receive illumination from this source, with no other part of the set being affected to any great extent. We chose a Balcar Opalite, with a 10-degree grid spot and plastic diffuser cap, as main light. It was placed a little to the right of the camera. This gave soft but directional lighting. The light was connected to a 2400-watt-second power pack.

The secondary lighting also had to be selected with care. If the lighting were too soft, the set would lose its visual impact. If it were too hard, emphasis could have been taken away from the subject.

A light panel was used as fill light. It was placed to the left of camera-subject axis and about 12 feet away from the subject. The panel was backlit by a 1000-watt-second light. The light had its power adjusted to give one-fourth the light of the main light.

The background behind the window was black seamless paper, illuminated by a light in a 6-inch bowl reflector. This light, covered with a red gel, was placed close to the floor and behind the subject and window. It had its power adjusted to one full *f*-stop less than the main light.

Another light, in a 6-inch bowl reflector, was put above and behind the subject and directed onto the subject's back and top of her head. This light helped to further separate the subject from the background, illuminate her hair, and rimlight her body. This top light had its power adjusted to equal that of the main light.

A kicker light, with a 5-inch snoot, was placed about four feet above the floor, behind the set and to the right of camera-subject axis. Its light was directed through the window of the set, onto the wall that is to the left of this axis. Its function was to create a light pattern of the window on the black wall. Its power was set to emit one *f*-stop more light than the main light.

The pose in this photo is a difficult one for most subjects. It calls for some acting ability and a lot of concentration. The overall image is strengthened by the subject's body being in a diagonal position.

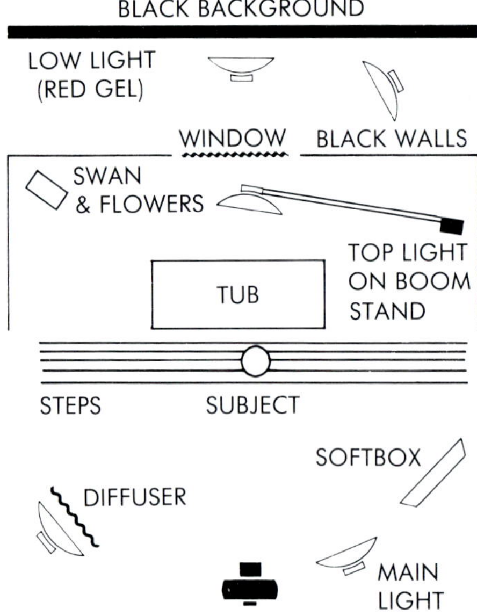

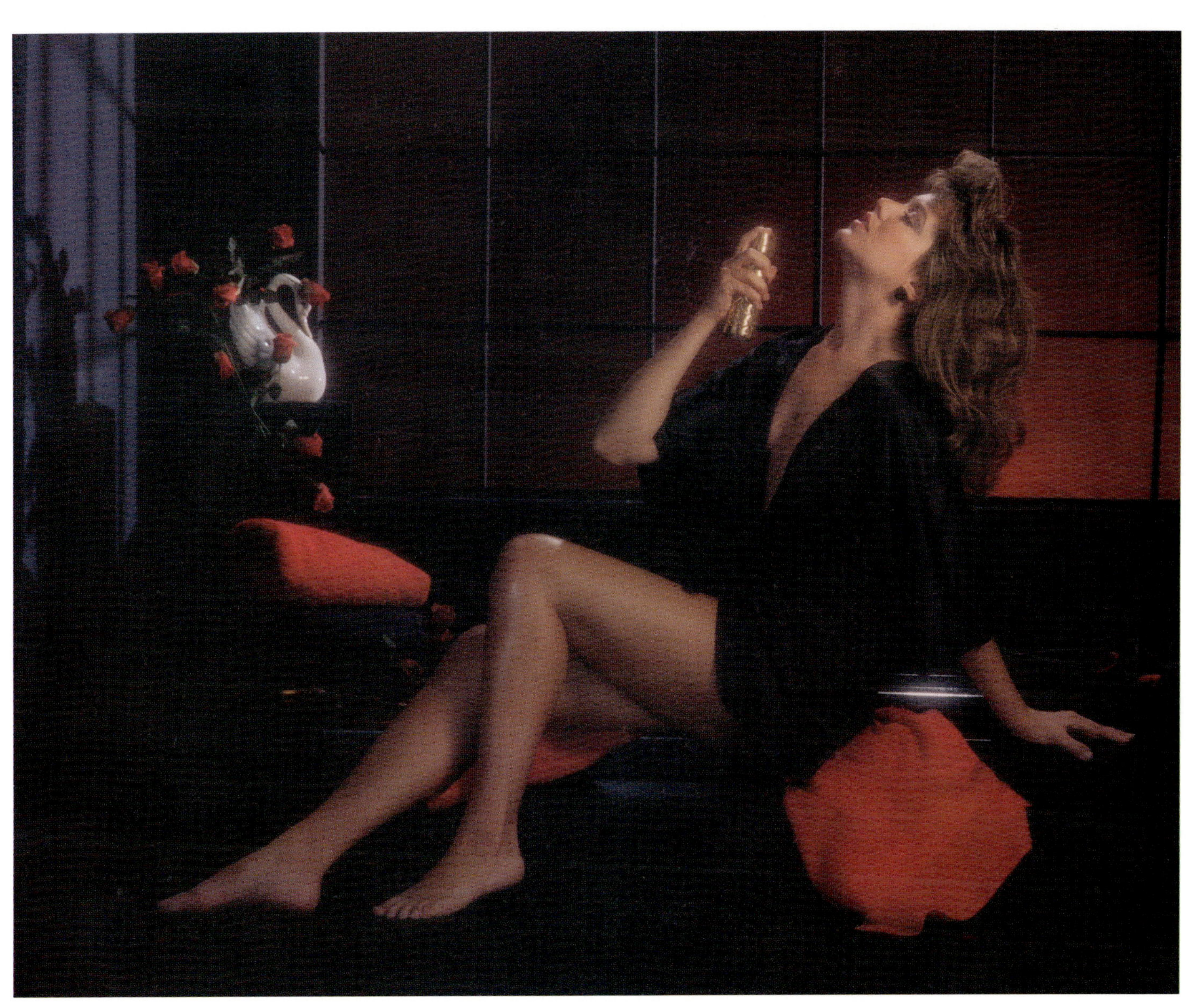

PORTFOLIO 14

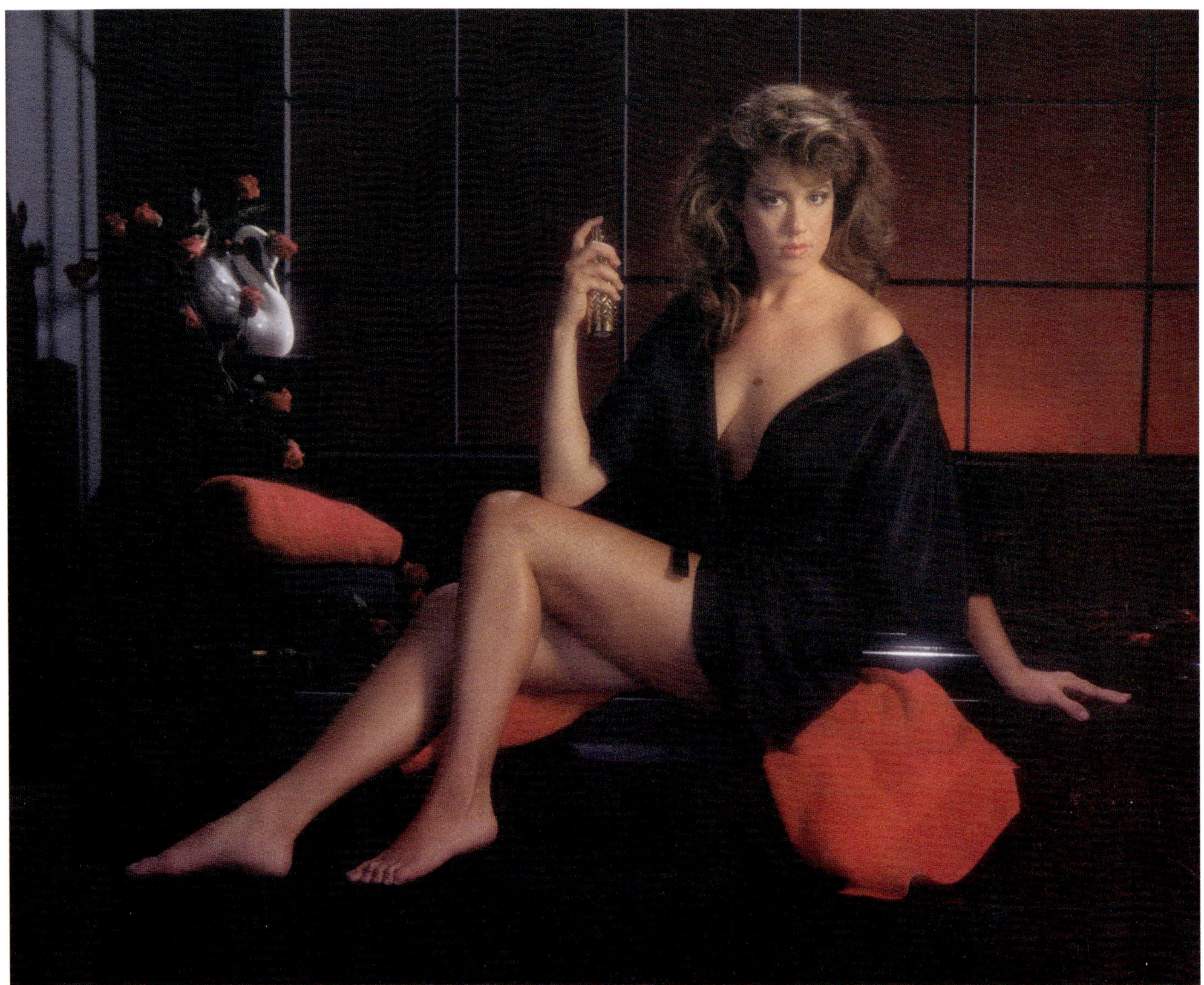

This is an exact duplication of the preceding photo in camera technique, lens employed, and lighting used. Only the subject's pose was changed.

The subject's head was turned toward the camera to allow eye contact with the viewer. Her shoulder was turned slightly so that more of the main light would be trapped in her chest area, thereby accentuating the bust. The robe was draped off her left shoulder to add to the allure of the image.

When working with boudoir poses, great attention must be paid to the most minute details: the placement of the subject's hands, the tilt of her head, the position and separation of her legs, the drape of her robe or costume, and so on. Once the shutter is snapped and a print made, undesirable factors that were previously unnoticed will seem larger than life: things such as hair that is out of place or a foot that is bent in an awkward way.

PORTFOLIO 15

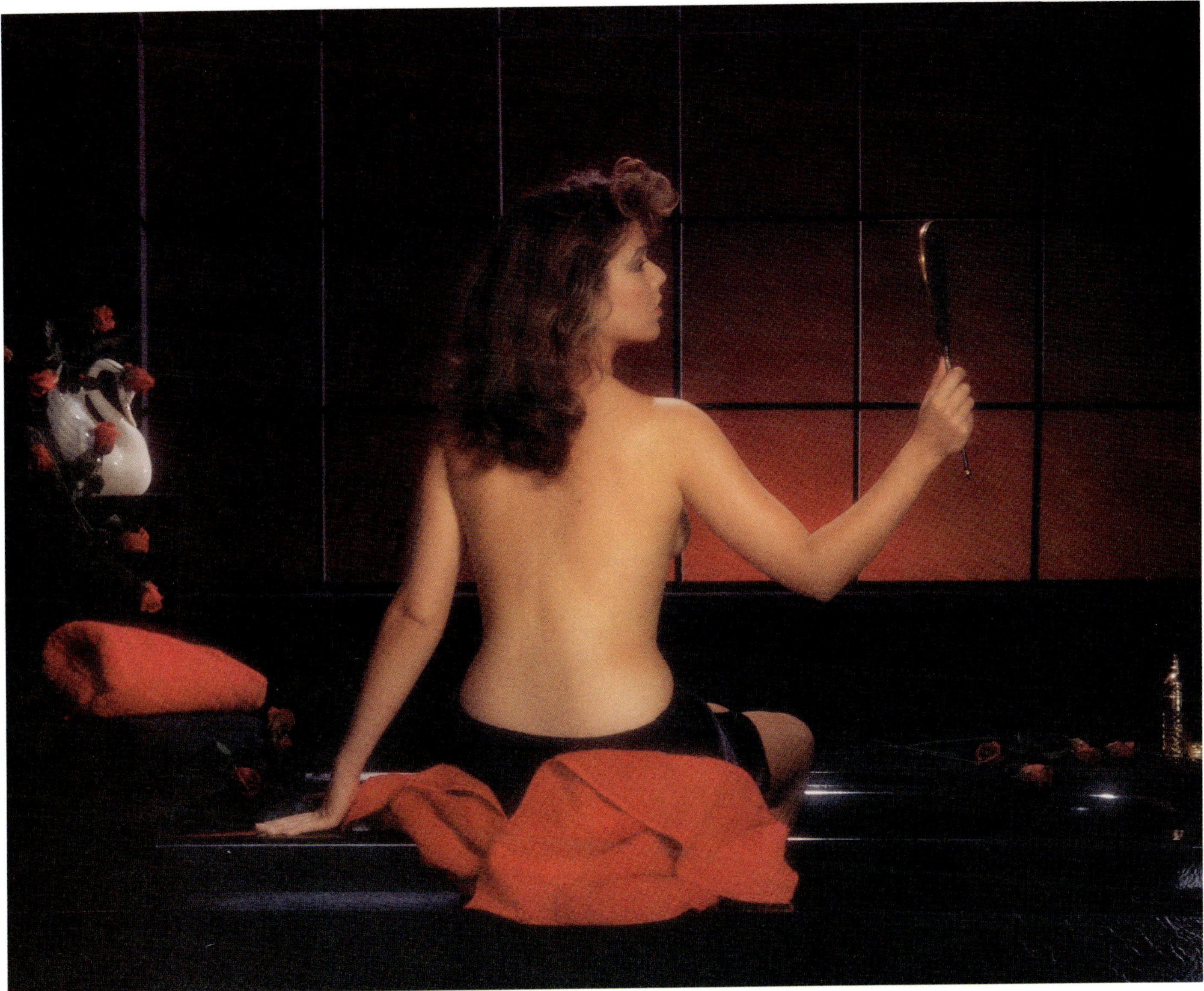

Depending on the modesty and personal preferences of your subject, a back shot, such as this one, can make for a beautiful image.

For this photo we decided to keep the subject lightly clad. We instructed her to drop the black robe to below her waist and turn her body slightly so that only a hint of breast could be seen. A suggestion of nakedness in a photo can often create greater viewer impact than a totally nude image.

For this shot the Opalite, with a 10-degree grid spot and plastic diffuser cap, was again used as main light. It was placed about 45 degrees to the right of camera-subject axis. A more dramatic effect could have been achieved by having the main light at 80 to 90 degrees from camera-subject axis, but this would have required more time to set up. When a subject is feeling awkward about her body being exposed, your chief concern must be for the subject and her feelings and this may sometimes require you to work fast.

Other than moving the main light farther from the camera-subject axis, the placement and power settings of all the other lights were the same as for Photo 13.

PORTFOLIO 16

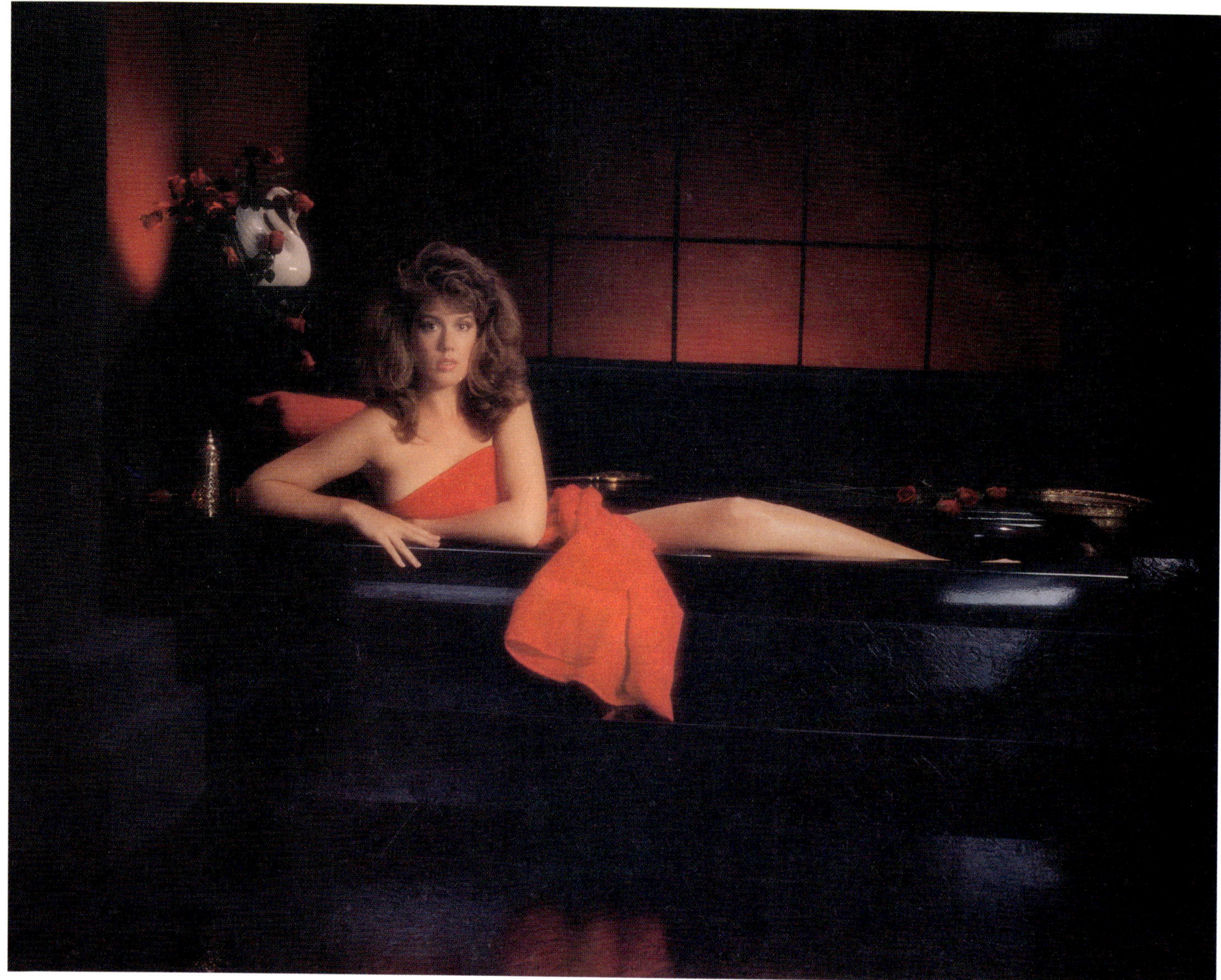

To achieve good boudoir photographs, professionalism must be a keynote. Subjects will often feel modest and a little self-conscious when being prepared and posed for images like this one and several others in this portfolio.

If you are a male photographer dealing with non-professional boudoir subjects, it is a good idea to have one or two female assistants on hand. They can set up the pose that you want and arrange a subject's clothing or drape, while you turn your back or momentarily step out of the shooting room. We followed such a procedure when making this photo. The tactic helped to give our subject confidence in us and our motives.

We used the same main light, fill light, top light and red-gelled background light as in Photo 13, and at the same power settings. The kicker light, used in Photo 13 to create a light pattern of the window on the wall, was turned off. Another 5-inch snooted light, connected to a 1000-watt-second power pack, was placed behind the white swan and covered with a red gel. Its power was adjusted to one full *f*-stop less light than the main light.

To achieve a different perspective and get more information of the scene into the final print, a standard lens was used. We also used a Softar 2 filter. Exposure was at *f*-11.

PORTFOLIO 17

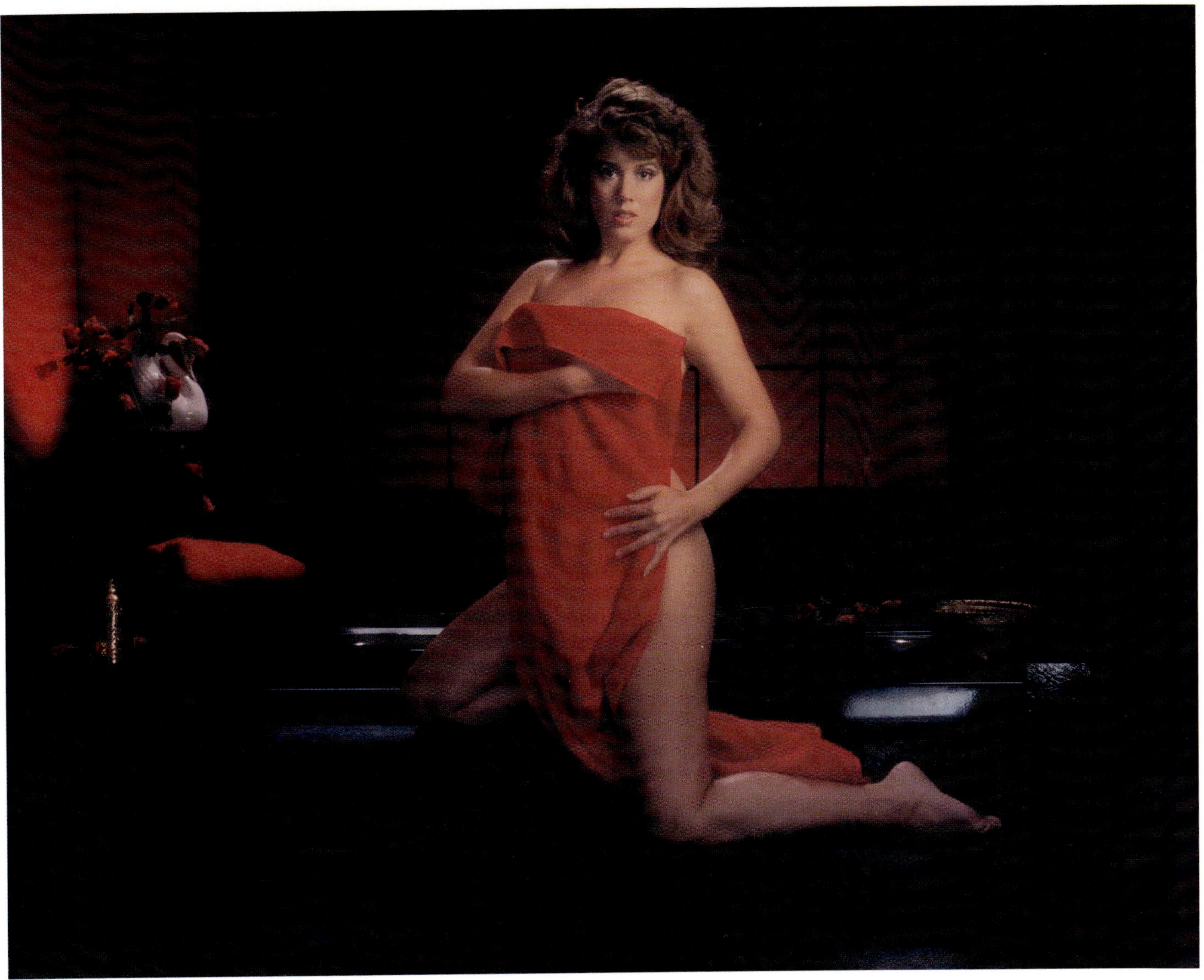

Although the subject is covered by the towel, the look of innocence on her face and the body position render this image a sensuous and suggestive one.

The use of a prop, such as a towel, can offer a subject a feeling of great security when posing for shots of this type. It can also be used effectively to add to the overall design of the image.

A number of shots can be taken with the same prop by having the subject assume different poses. However, care should be exercised not to take too many shots with the same prop. Generally, you can use a prop more often if, at the same time, you make appreciable changes in lighting or you move to a different set.

This image was shot with the same lights, light placement and power settings as Photo 16. The only exception was the lens and filter. For this photo, a medium telephoto lens was used, with a Softar 1 filter. Exposure was at *f*-11.

18 PORTFOLIO

This subject was photographed approximately one week before her marriage. She wanted a unique gift to give to her husband-to-be on their wedding day. She got it! This is only one of numerous stunning images we took of her.

Seriously executed boudoir photography involves a number of different factors, not the least of which is the subject herself. A photographer can have all of the proper "tools" at his or her disposal, full knowledge of what, basically, needs to be done, and still not get the desired photos—all because of the subject herself.

Successful boudoir photography requires a subject to have a positive attitude and to be cooperative and motivated. This subject had it all and, consequently, our shooting session was highly successful.

The tilt of the subject's head, the placement of arms and hands, the angle of the body, and the leg positioning all worked together to produce this very sensuous image. The towel contributed an element of design and offered some security for the subject while helping to create a suggestion of nudity.

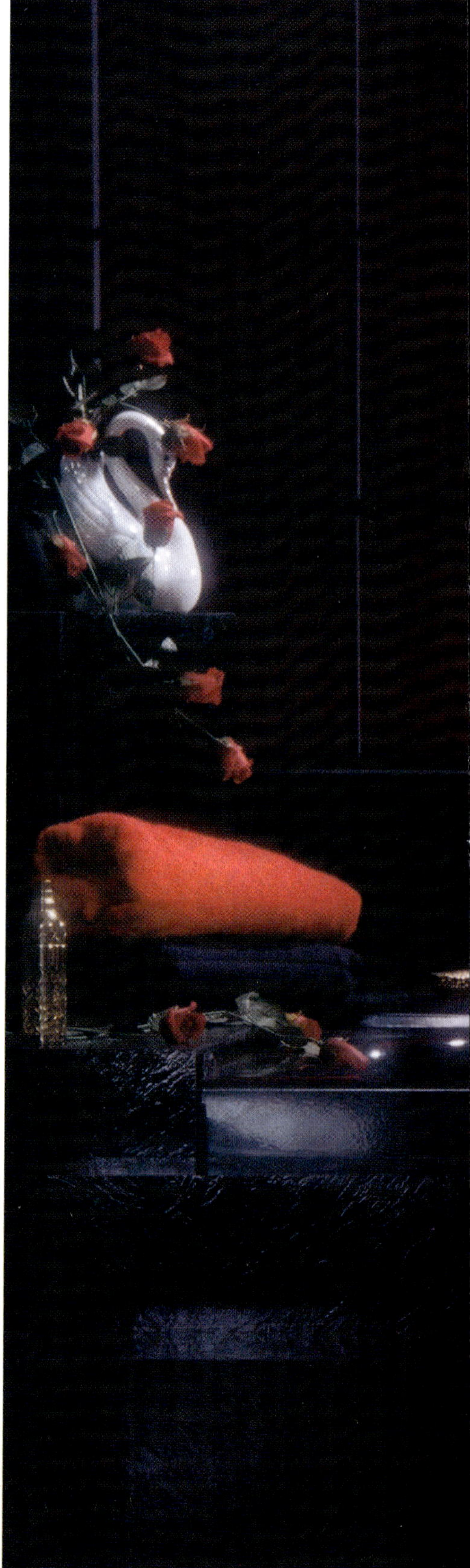

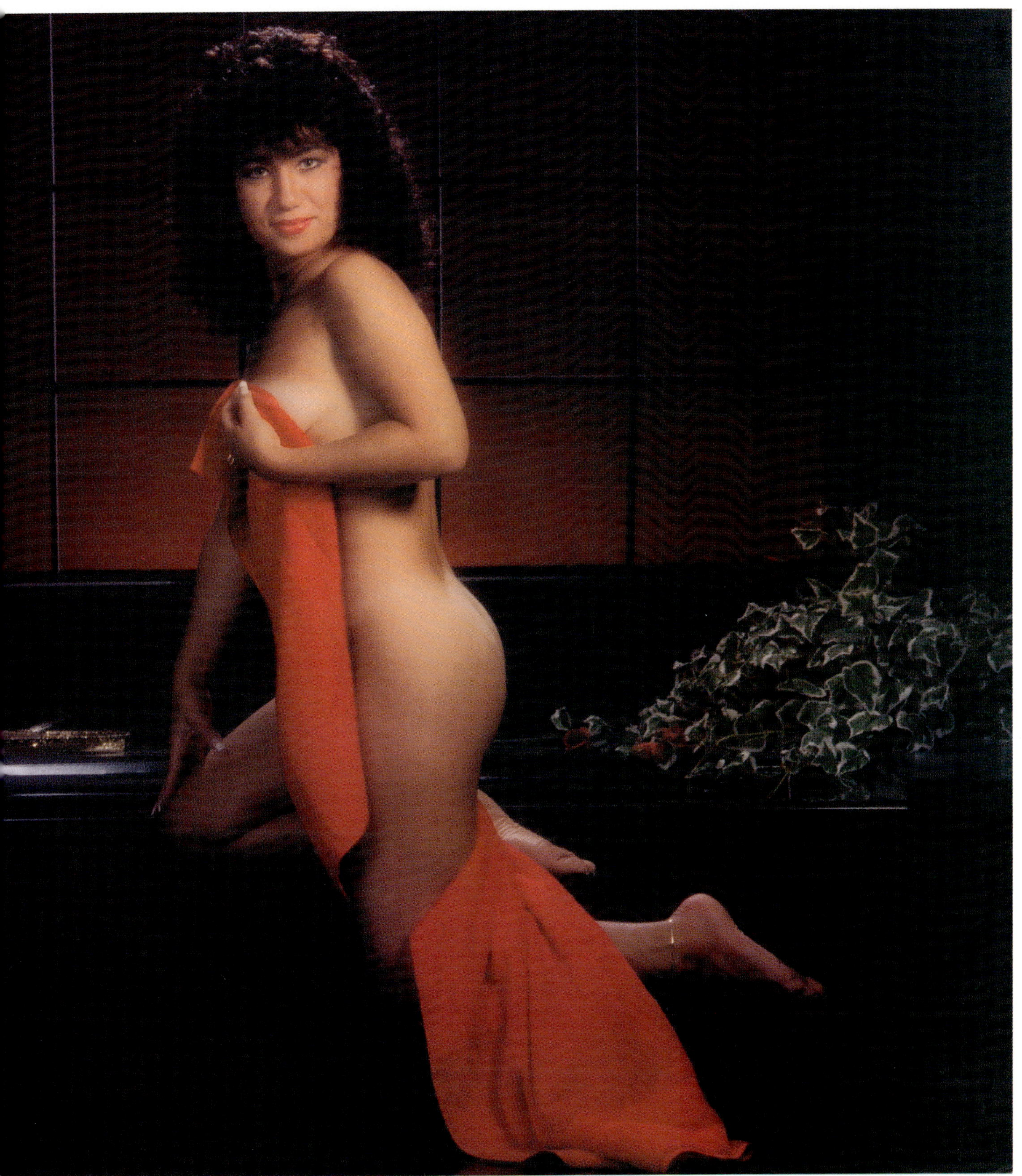

SHOOTING AT A SUBJECT'S HOME

Shooting at a subject's home offers new and exciting challenges, allowing you to work in a totally different environment. Of course, this presents you with new photographic problems to solve, too.

Although a session in a subject's home can be very rewarding and can produce some very stunning and dramatic images, there are several important factors to remember when working in an unfamiliar location.

Scout the home well in advance, seeking out all potential places to conduct the photography. Then, on the day of the actual photo session, you'll be able to move all of your equipment into position with minimal delay.

Since it takes time to set up and tear down equipment, don't attempt to photograph in too many different areas of the home during one photo session. It will be a better shoot if you limit yourself to two or three areas—by the pool, in the den and in the bathroom, for example—rather than trying to use more areas, with less time spent in each.

A subject likes her home. That is why she lives there and wants you to photograph in it. Take advantage of as much of the environment as possible and include as many of the subject's personal effects as you can. Most of her effects will have some definite meaning to her or her "special someone."

During the course of a session, you will often find that you will have to move items about—chairs, lamps, furniture and other accessories—in order to have your photo scene look compositionally correct. Never assume, however, that you automatically have permission to rearrange things. Ask first.

A subject will initially feel much more comfortable in her own environment than she would in your studio or elsewhere on location. This often means that you will be able to elicit poses from her more easily and quickly.

The following 22 photos will give you some idea of what you can do when shooting on location in a subject's home.

PORTFOLIO 19

The main light used to create this photo was overcast daylight. It was coming into the room through sliding glass doors to the left of camera-subject axis and about 10 feet away from the subject. The light was totally diffused, which accounts for the overall softness of this image.

To keep the shadow area from becoming too dark, a 2x4-foot plastic mirror was placed to the right of camera-subject axis to reflect some light back onto the subject.

A pool table in a den can provide a very natural setting for boudoir photography. The setting can lend itself to a number of different-looking images, especially if costume and lighting changes are made.

The pool cue was brought into the scene to help the viewer identify the location and to give the subject a prop to lean on. The cue was placed at a slight angle, to add strength to the composition.

This pose, and the way in which the subject's costume is draped, is a good starting point. The pose and the costume are not revealing and this makes the subject feel comfortable. As a session progresses and a subject gains more confidence in herself and in you, the poses and costumes can become more bold and revealing.

For this photo, we used a medium telephoto lens and two filters—a warming filter and a Softar 1. Exposure was 1/15 second at *f*-8.

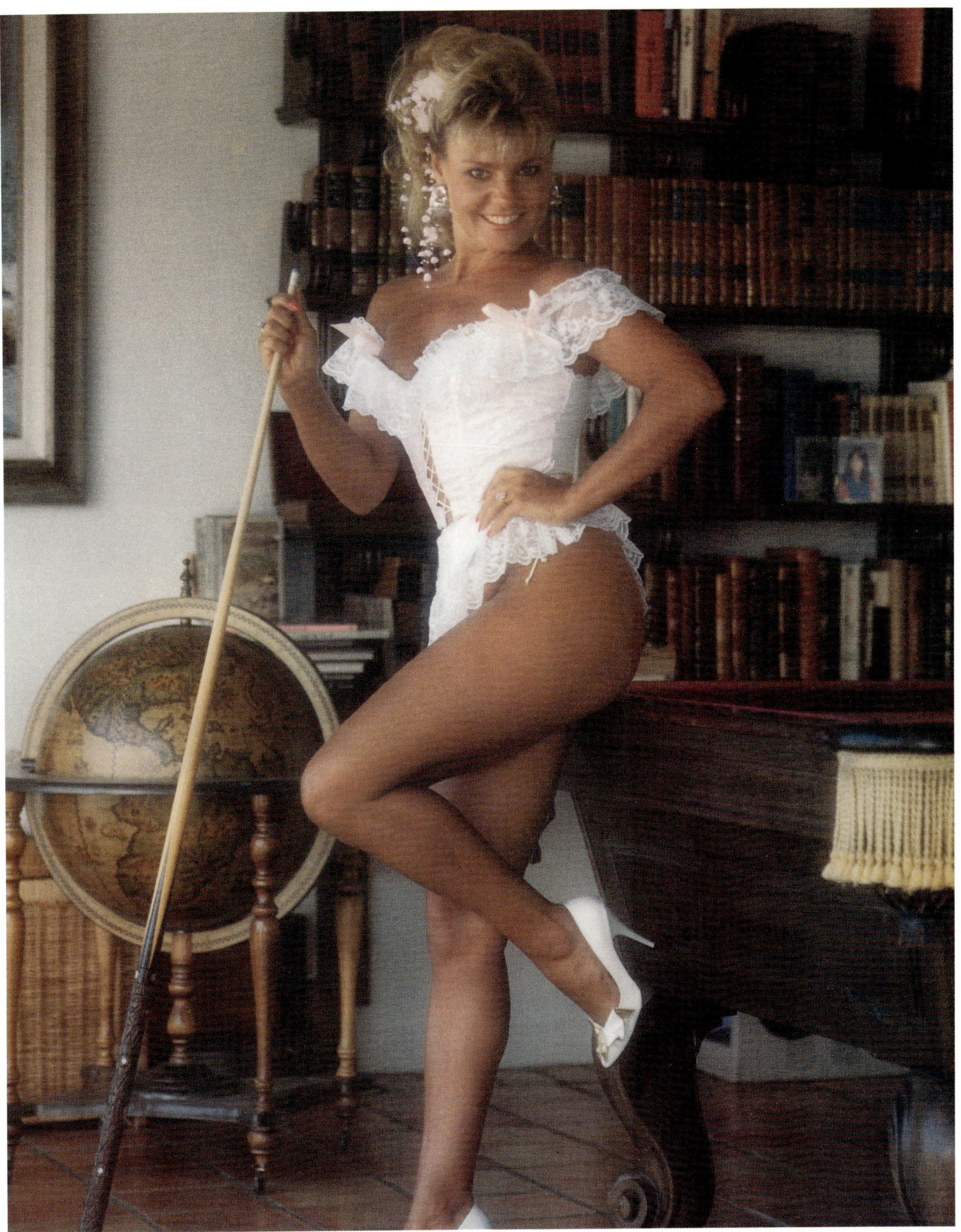

PORTFOLIO 20

In Photo 19, the main light was totally diffused daylight. This condition often leads to prints that lack sparkle and contrast. For the photo reproduced here—which was taken seconds after the preceding one—flash was used to add snap to the image.

The main light was a light panel, placed in front of the sliding glass doors to the left of camera-subject axis. The panel was backlit by a light in a 5-inch bowl reflector, connected to a 1000-watt-second power pack. The daylight was used for additional illumination. A 3x4-foot plastic mirror was placed to the right of camera-subject axis to reflect some of the main light back into the shadow side of the subject.

By having the subject assume a bent position and having her buttocks and legs closer to the main light than other parts of her body, prominence was given to these areas.

The pool cue, used as a crutch for the subject, was placed at an oblique angle to give the composition a feeling of vitality.

If you have never photographed in a subject's home before, be very sensitive to minute detail. When shooting in a den, family room or library, numerous, small, personal effects will often abound. An otherwise beautiful image can be spoiled by allowing an inappropriate item to remain in the photo scene.

A medium telephoto lens was used to make this photo, together with a warming and Softar 1 filter. Exposure was 1/60 second at *f*-11.

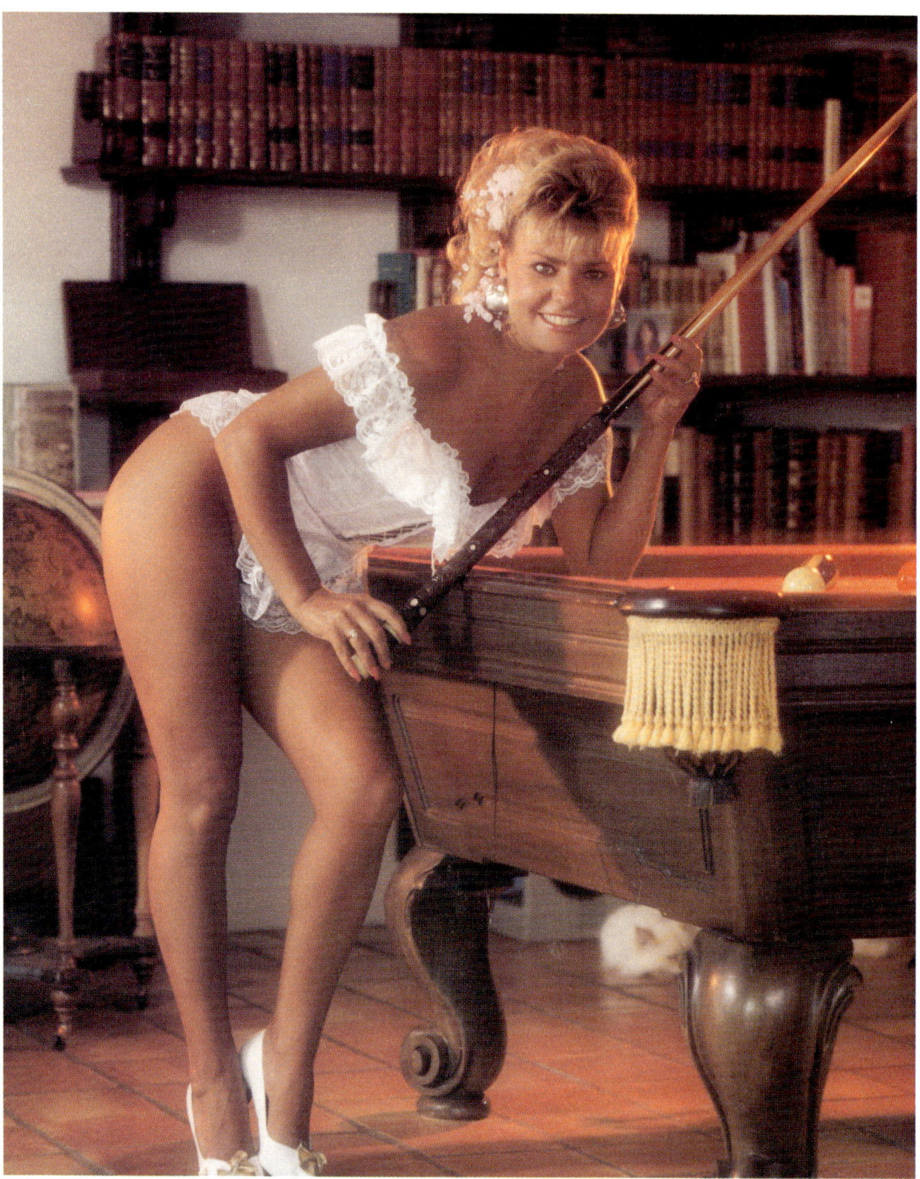

PORTFOLIO 21

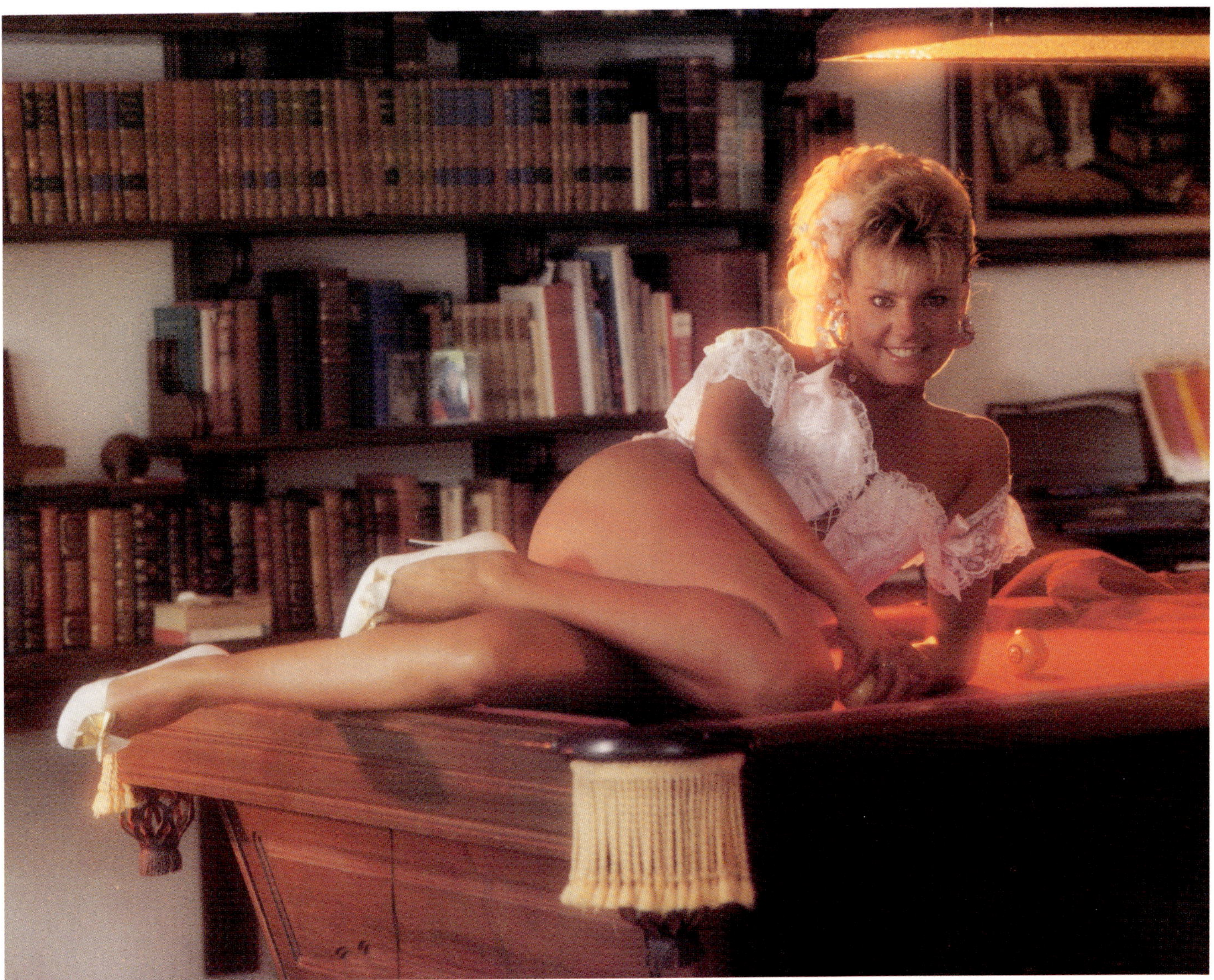

This is almost an exact duplication of Photo 20 in camera technique, lens employed and lighting used. However, a back light was added. This light, in a 5-inch bowl reflector and connected to a 1000-watt-second power pack, was placed low, right behind the subject and directed toward the back of her head. The light was adjusted to emit one *f*-stop more light than the main light. This increase in power, in relationship to the main light, caused the back of the subject's hair to become intentionally overstated.

Although this pose is very guarded and reveals little about the subject's body, the reclining pose can be a very sensous and suggestive one.

The pose can also produce some problems. When you're photographing a subject in a reclining pose, lens and camera angle should be carefully chosen. If the lens is too short in focal length or the camera angle too low or too high, some degree of body distortion will appear and the resulting photos may be unacceptable.

Unlike many commercial model shots, where body parts of a subject are often intentionally distorted to gain viewer interest, boudoir photography demands that a subject's body be flattered. Distorting a body part may be considered by some as "artistic" but it is seldom flattering.

PORTFOLIO 22

Both the subject and the photographer should be involved in the selection of appropriate shooting locations in a subject's home. A subject may have a specific locale in mind, for example by a piano, at the bar, or by the pool. Her preferences should not be ignored.

For those who have no preference, spend time looking for the obvious and not-so-obvious spots and make your recommendations. If she disagrees about an area or prop you have chosen, move on to another. If you were to force the issue, the resulting images would not be likely to appeal to the subject, even if they appear stunning to you.

An open staircase can be a great prop to work with and can lead to many creative photos.

The lighting for this photo was very simple. A light panel, close to the subject, was used as main light. It was backlit by a flash in a 5-inch bowl reflector, connected to a 1000-watt-second power pack. The light was placed to the left of camera-subject axis. No fill light was needed.

Another lamp head was placed beneath the stairs, to illuminate the background. Its power was adjusted to emit one *f*-stop more light than the main light.

By instructing the subject to turn at the waist toward the camera and arch her back, the roundness of her chest area is enhanced.

A medium telephoto lens was used, and a warming filter and Softar 1 filter. Exposure was at *f*-8.

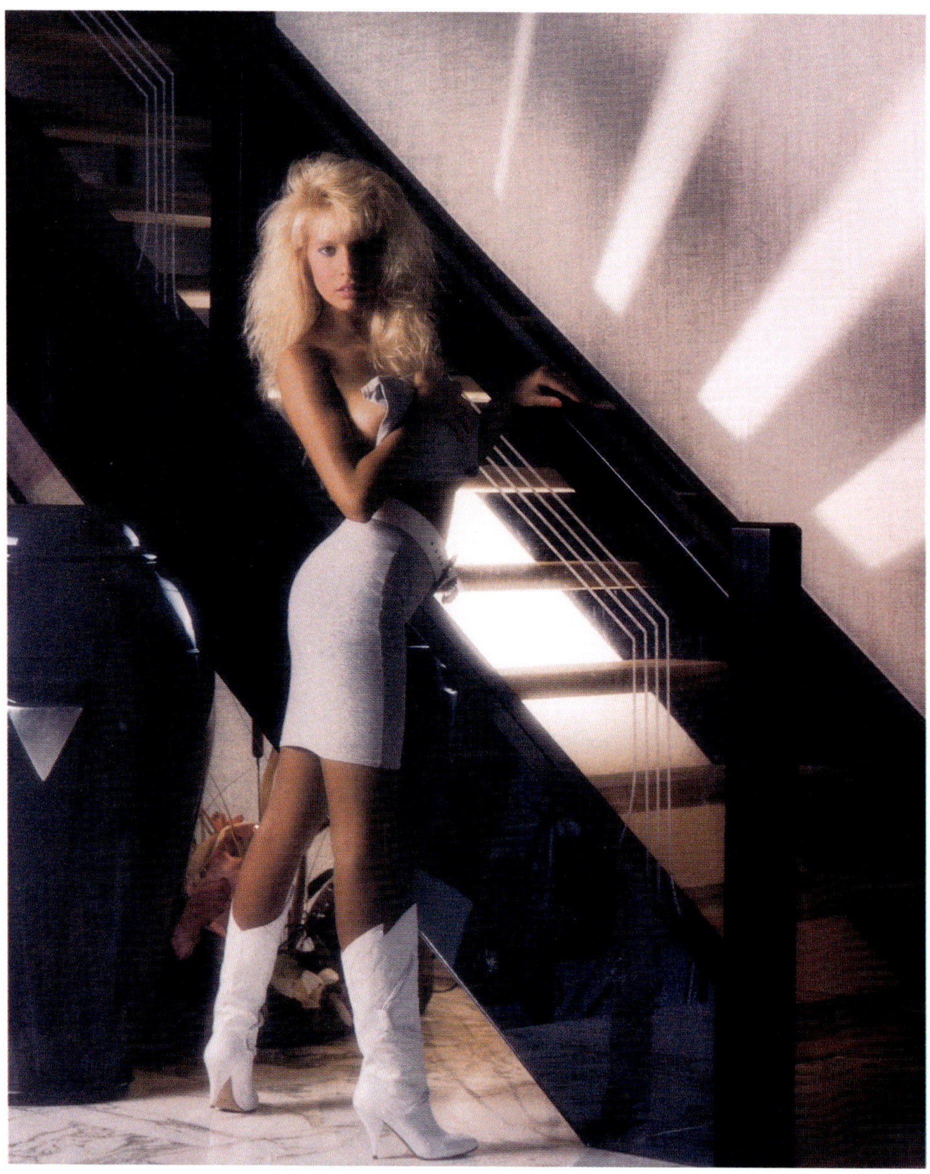

PORTFOLIO 23

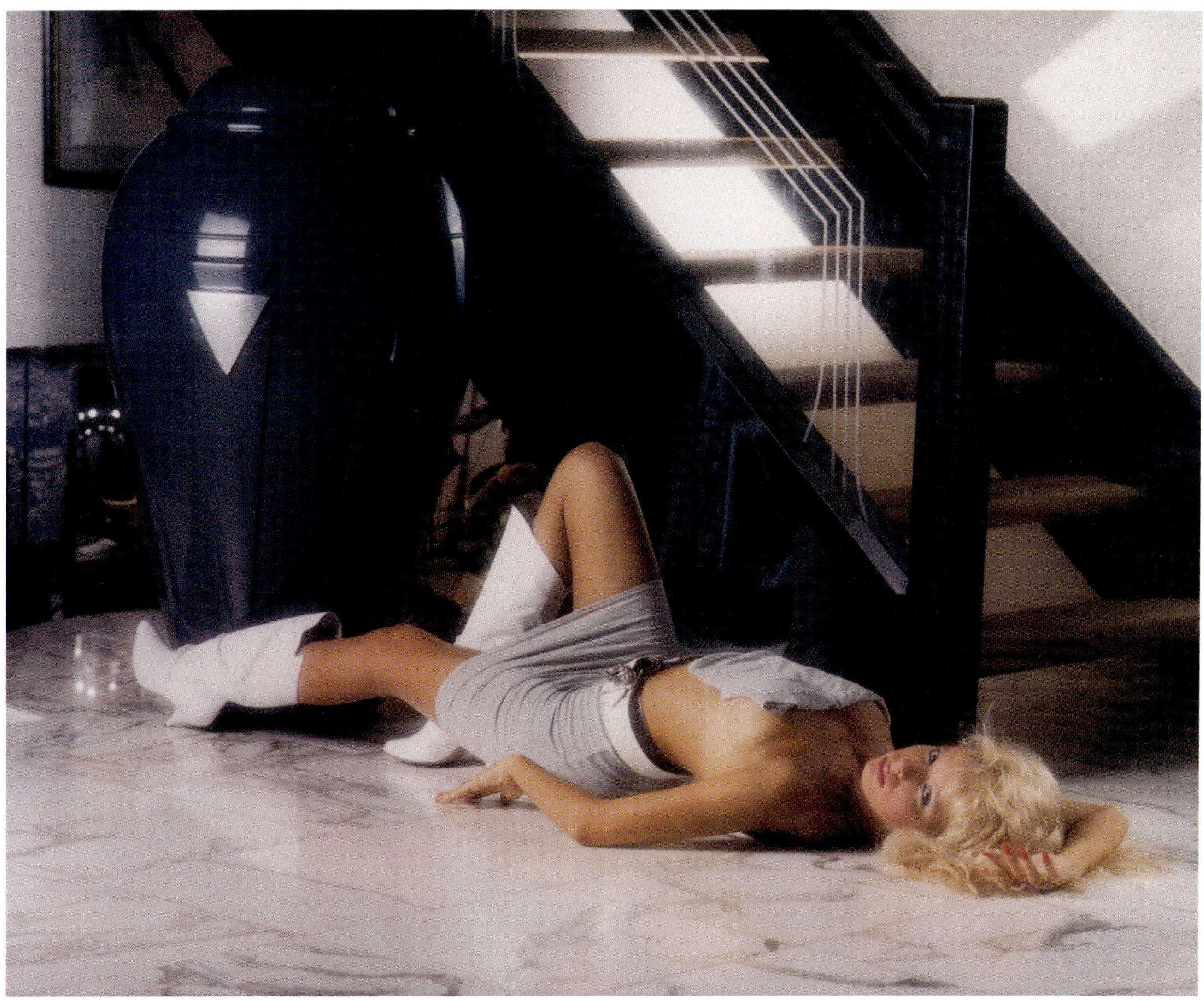

This photo is similar to the preceding one in camera technique, lens employed and lighting used. However, the pose is very different.

A setting—whether in your or a subject's home, a regular studio, or elsewhere on location—should be versatile. It should allow you to photograph a subject in several different poses and get different looks, even with the same costume and lighting. If the setting is not strong enough to support more than one pose, it should be abandoned and your efforts directed elsewhere where you can be more productive.

This photo and the preceding one are good examples of how you can produce very different images, even when the subject is wearing the same costume and is lit in the same manner.

This pose was chosen to make the image more suggestive. We had the subject separate her legs, putting tension on her skirt. We then had her place her arm behind her head to make the pose appear less guarded. She was instructed to arch her back, forcing her chest up to make her bust appear larger.

PORTFOLIO 24

This image was illuminated a little differently than the previous two photos.

The light panel was again used as main light. It was backlit by a flash in a 5-inch bowl reflector, powered by a 1000-watt-second power pack.

The background light was also in a 5-inch bowl reflector and its power was adjusted to emit one *f*-stop less light than the main light. A stronger light on the wall would have been distracting. It would also have caused the lower portion of the subject's body and legs to become too overstated.

A hair light was put at the top of the stairs and directed onto the back of the subject. This light was in a 6-inch bowl reflector and its power was adjusted to emit one *f*-stop less light than the main light.

Instructing the subject to lean on the railing forced her to arch her back. This emphasized her bustline. The subject's legs were intentionally given less light than the upper half of her body.

A medium telephoto lens was used, and two filters—a warming filter and a Softar 2. Exposure was at *f*-8.

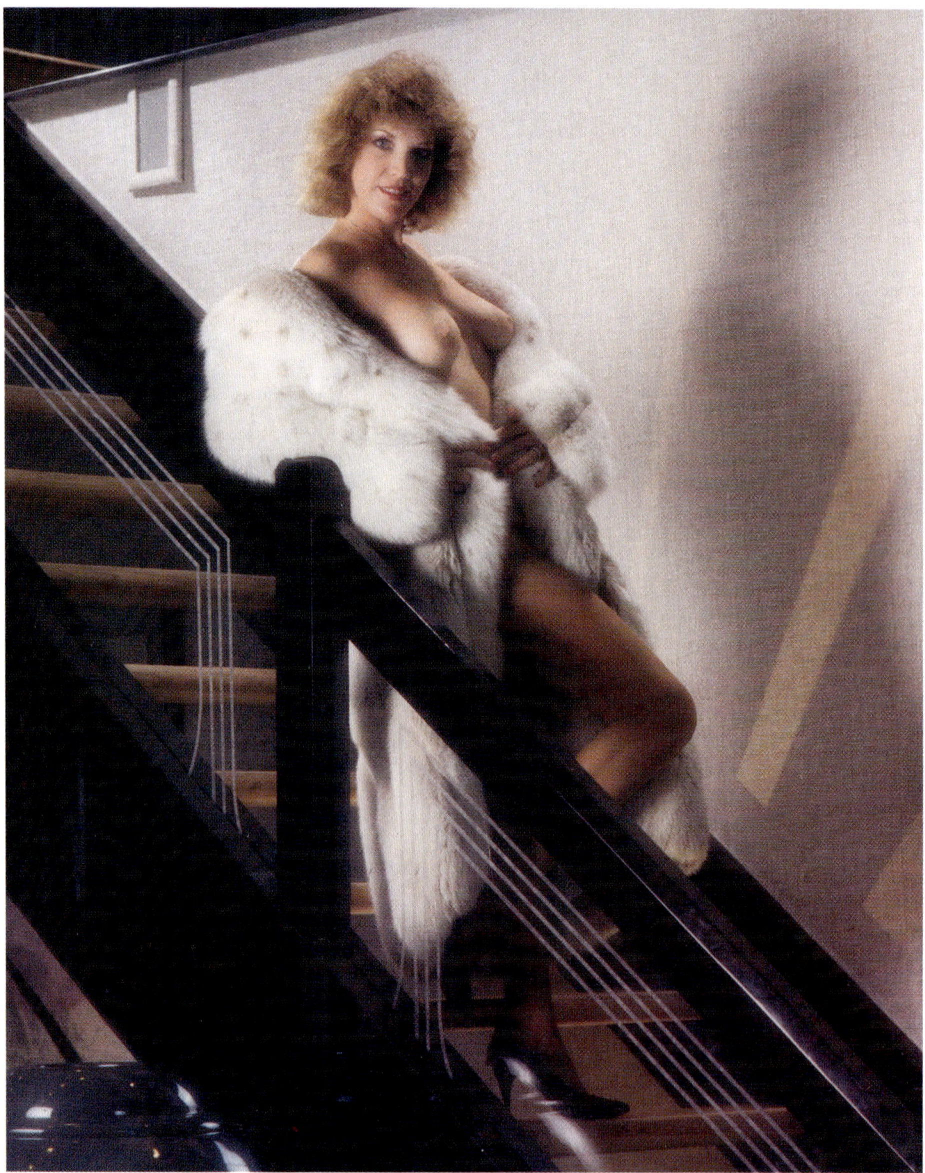

PORTFOLIO 25

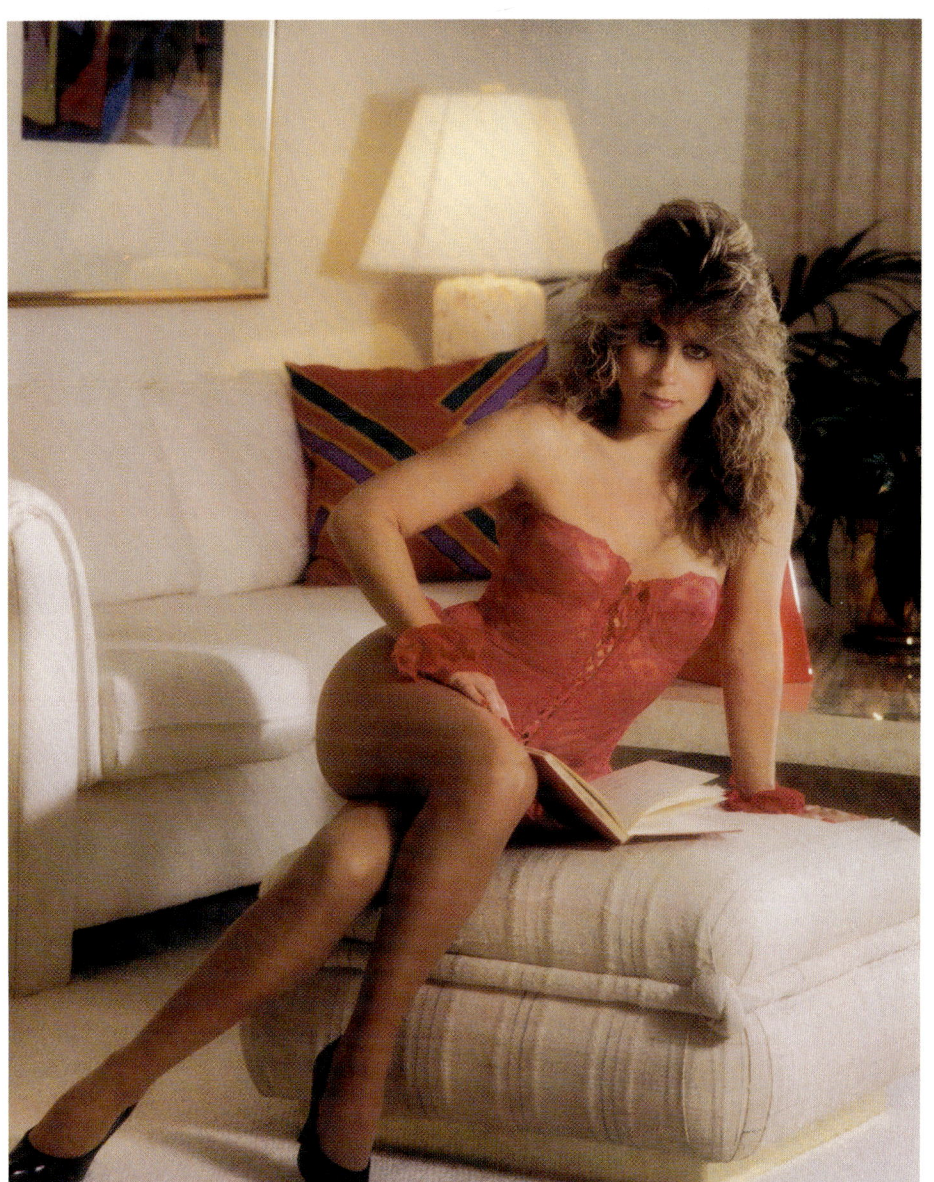

For this image, only one electronic flash was used. The light was in a 5-inch bowl reflector, placed behind a light panel, and positioned to the right of camera-subject axis. It was connected to a 1000-watt-second power pack.

A large window was also to the right of the camera-subject axis. It helped to light the remainder of the room.

The shutter speed was adjusted so that the ambient light and the light from the table lamp was one *f*-stop less than the main light.

The stretching pose was chosen for the subject for a number of reasons. It minimized wrinkles and bulges in the garment she wore, gave her body a sense of motion, and elongated her body. The pose gives the viewer an impression that the subject is really taller than she is.

A medium telephoto lens was used, with a warming and Softar 1 filter. Exposure was 1/15 second at *f*-8.

PORTFOLIO 26

This pose draws viewer attention to the subject's buttocks.

Most clothing is designed with a standing position in mind. Once you have a subject assume a pose, adjustments will often have to be made in the pose, the garment, or both, to make the garment look correct.

With the subject in this pose, her costume did not fit well. It bulged in the front. To cure this easily and effectively, we had her bring her right arm down low and place her hand onto the keyboard. This visually blocked the problem area.

The main light was a light panel, backlit by a flash in a 5-inch bowl reflector. It was powered by a 1000-watt-second power pack. The main light was placed to the right of camera-subject axis.

A second light, also in a 5-inch bowl reflector, was placed to the left of camera-subject axis and directed onto the subject's buttocks. Its power was adjusted to equal the main light.

The ambient light from the background was allowed to be recorded in some detail, giving the image a feeling of depth.

Exposure was 1/30 second at *f*-11.

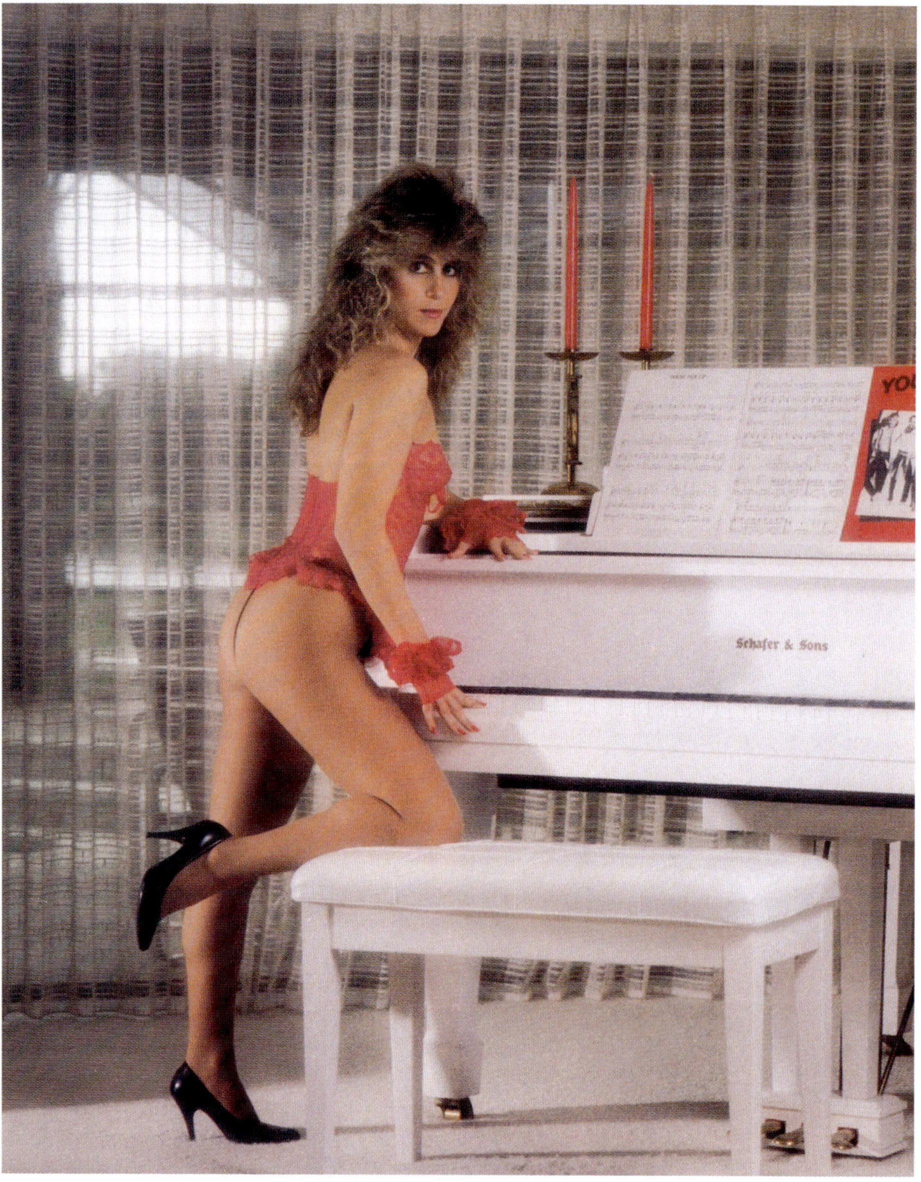

PORTFOLIO 27

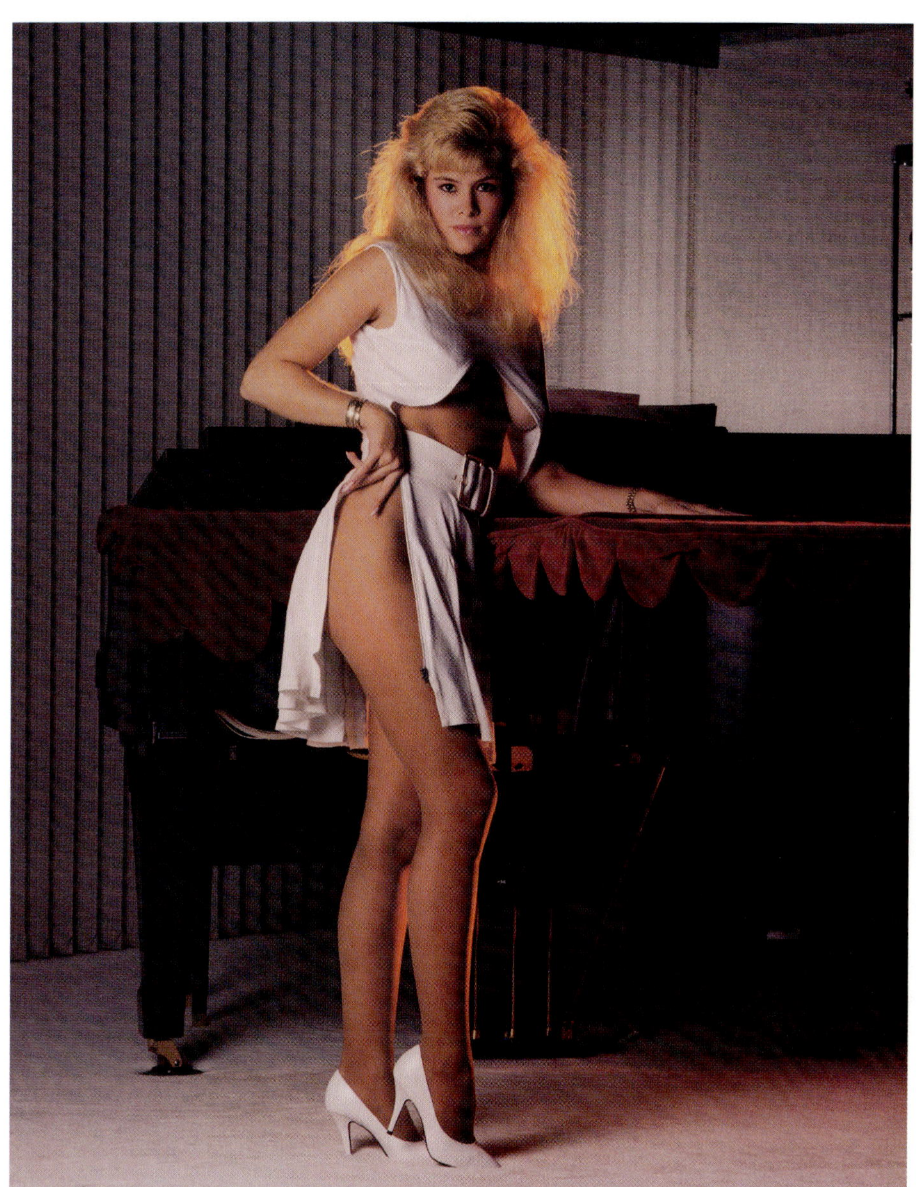

For this photo, only flash illumination was used. The ambient light was not recorded.

The main light was positioned about 30 degrees to the left of camera-subject axis. It was a small light panel, backlit by a light in a 5-inch bowl reflector and powered by a 1000-watt-second power pack.

A second light—also in a 5-inch bowl and covered with an amber gel—was positioned directly behind the subject's head. It was adjusted to emit one *f*-stop more light than the main light. Its function was to outline the hair and shoulders, separating the subject from the background.

Two more lights were used, each in a 5-inch bowl reflector, with their power adjusted to one *f*-stop less light than the main light. One was positioned in the far corner of the room, to add more separation and give an increased sense of depth. The other was positioned low, underneath the piano and to the right of the camera-subject axis. It was used to rim-light and outline the subject's legs.

A 2x4-foot plastic mirror was also positioned to the right of the camera-subject axis, to reflect some of the main light back onto the subject to fill in the shadows.

To keep the pose from being too static, the subject's arms were positioned in the manner shown. We also instructed her to bend her right leg, to give the pose a sense of motion. Her body was turned, to accent her legs and emphasize her bust.

A medium telephoto lens was used, and a warming and Softar 1 filter. Exposure was at *f*-11.

PORTFOLIO 28

This is an exact duplication of Photo 27 in camera technique, lens employed and lighting used. Only the pose was changed slightly.

Once you have established a workable pose for a subject and have taken a shot or two, see if the pose can be modified to create new and different images before moving on to others.

When dealing with non-professional subjects, it often takes considerable time to instruct, demonstrate and place a subject into a specific pose. If the basic pose can be easily modified—with minimal effort and delay on the part of the subject and with no lighting changes—you'll be able to offer your subject greater pictorial variety with each scenario.

In this photo, we had the subject separate and straighten her legs, creating a solid, triangular base for her. By having her fold her arms across her chest, her breasts were pushed together to form a distinct cleavage.

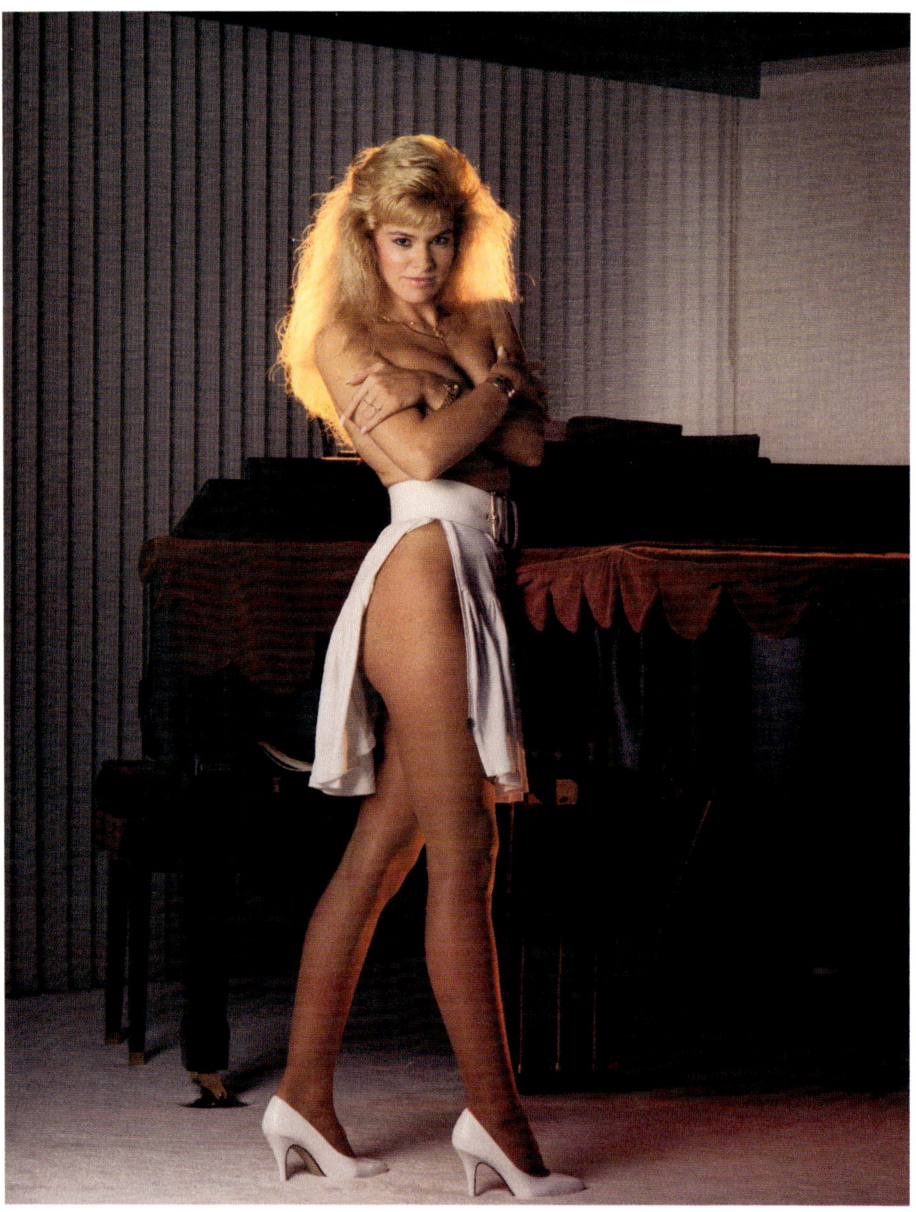

PORTFOLIO 29

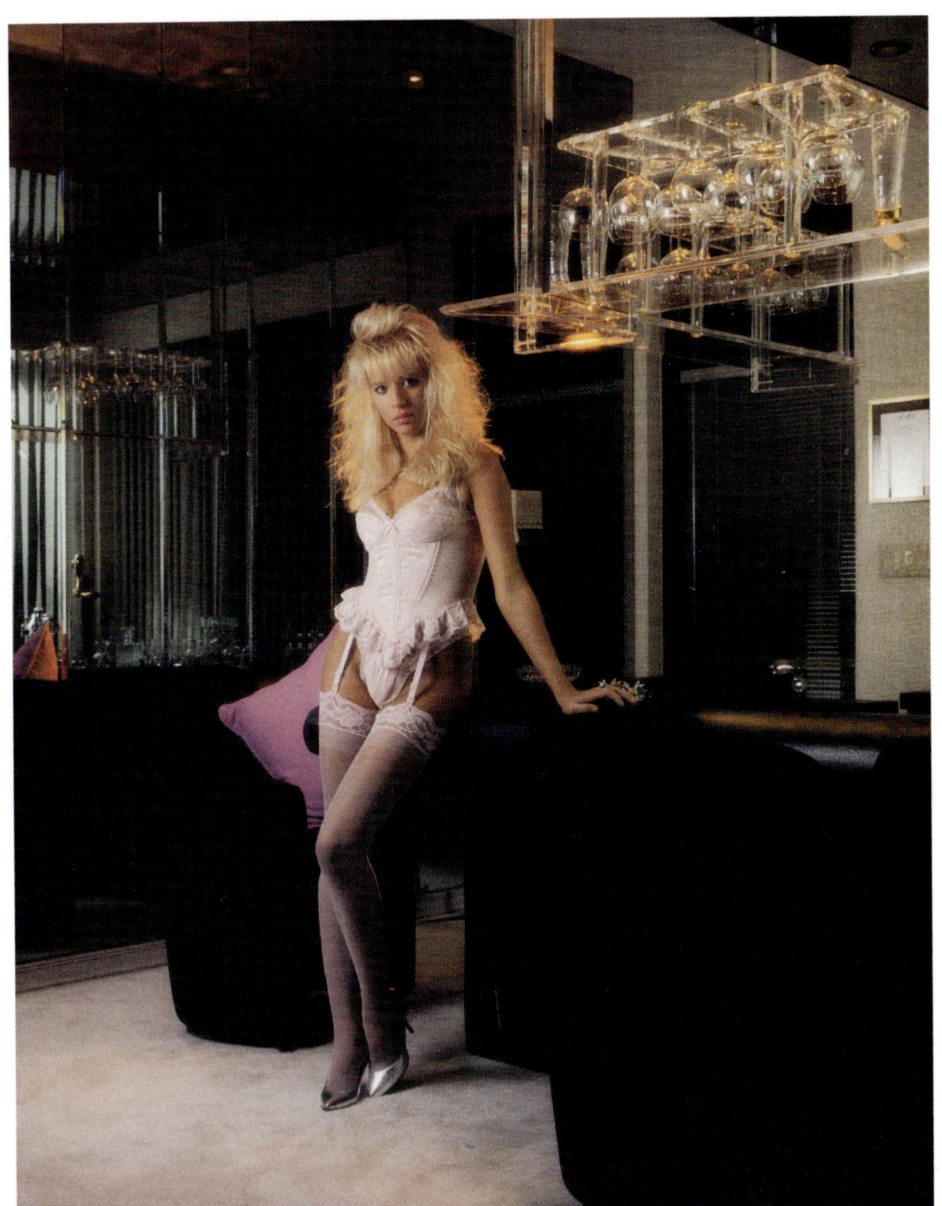

All boudoir photography involves photographic problem solving. Some problems can be solved easily and quickly while others consume more thought and time. This photo, and the two that follow, took some extra thought and time.

The bar area in this lavish home was surrounded by mirrors and windows. The reflections and the light coming through the windows caused lighting problems.

Our lights and wiring had to be well concealed so that they would not cause unwanted mirror reflections. The photo session was held in the afternoon, with bright sunlight streaming into the room. This was inconsistent with the low-key mood we wanted to create.

A meter reading taken at the windows indicated an exposure of 1/60 second at *f*-8. To reduce the effect of this light on the room, all of the blinds, with the exception of one set, were shut to almost their fully closed position. The one set that was left partially open—to create a greater sense of depth—was the one that caused a direct reflection to appear in the mirror.

To get soft lighting on the subject, a light panel was used as main light. It was backlit by a light in a 5-inch bowl reflector and powered by a 1000-watt-second power pack. It was placed to the left of camera-subject axis.

To enhance the separation of subject from background, an additional light, in a 5-inch bowl reflector, was used. It was covered with an amber gel and placed low, behind the bar. It was directed onto the back of the subject's head and the hanging glassware. Its power was adjusted to emit one *f*-stop less light than the main light.

The pose was designed to yield a seductive and sensuous low-key image. Exposure was 1/125 second at *f*-11.

PORTFOLIO 30

For this photo, the same lighting and lens were used as for the preceding one. The camera viewpoint and pose were changed.

The camera was placed at an angle that enables the viewer to see the back of the subject reflected in the mirror.

The subject was instructed to turn her body slightly away from the main light so that its light could skim across her body, making her waist appear smaller and her bust larger.

We had the subject assume a rather coy facial expression. We instructed her to place her right leg in the position depicted, to conceal part of her body from view. The image would have taken on a completely different look if she had straightened out her right leg. More of her body would have become visible to the viewer and she would have taken on a more aggressive, provocative look.

Generally, boudoir images are more successful when a subject projects a sensuous but gentle look rather than an unabashed provocative one.

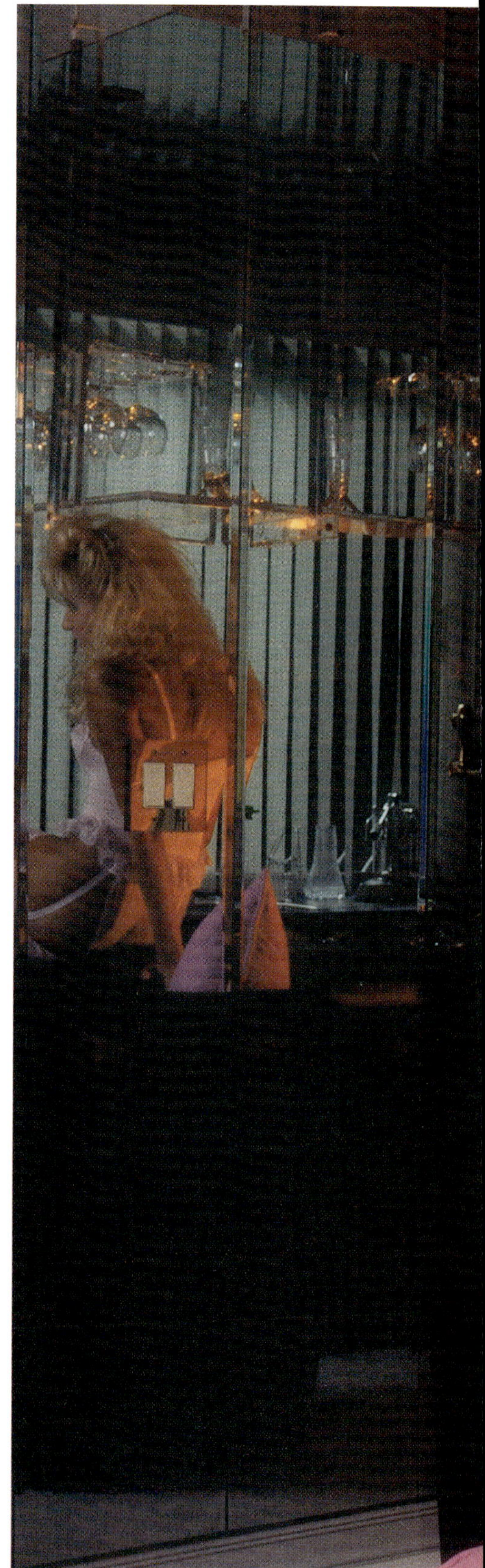

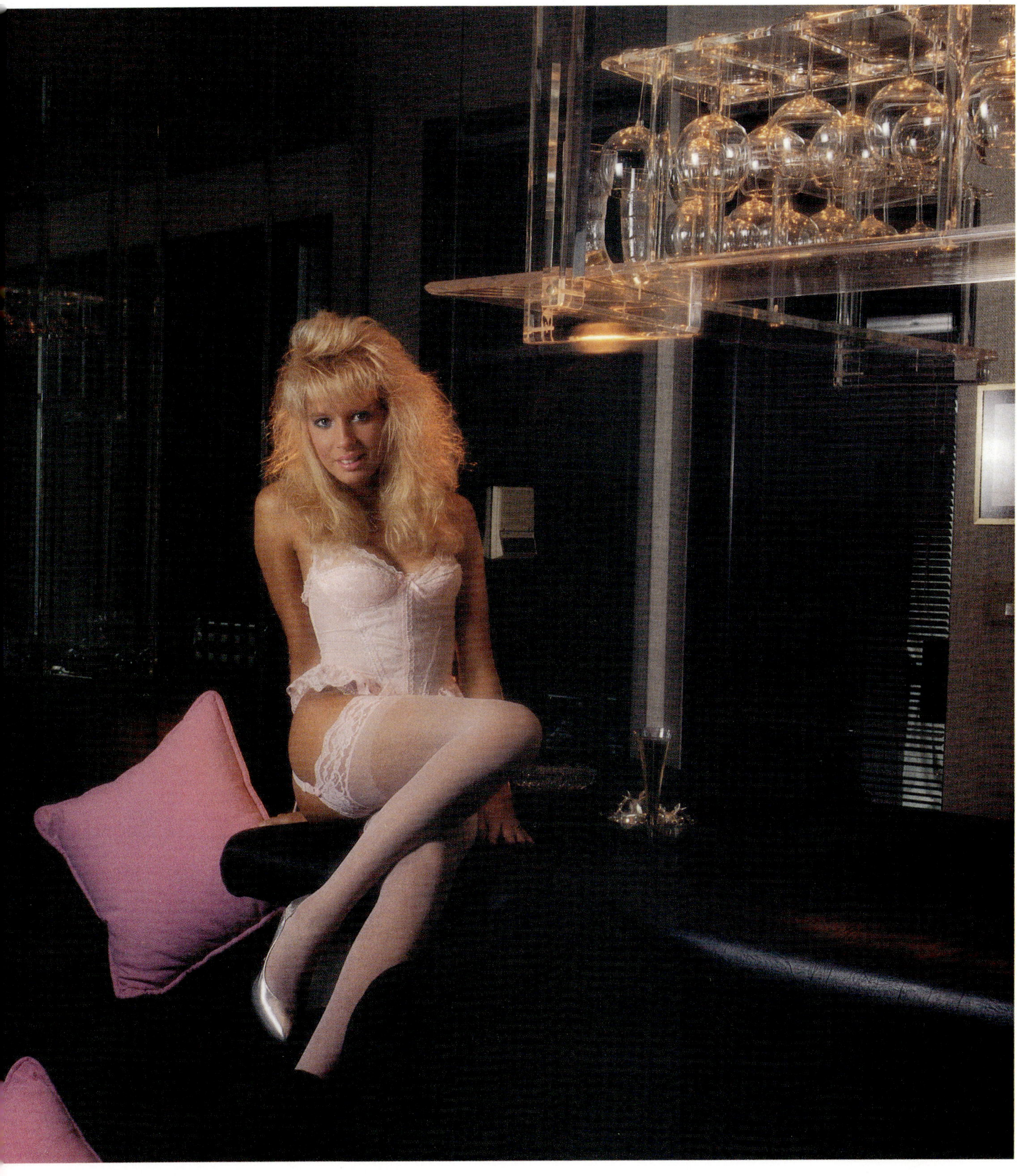

PORTFOLIO 31

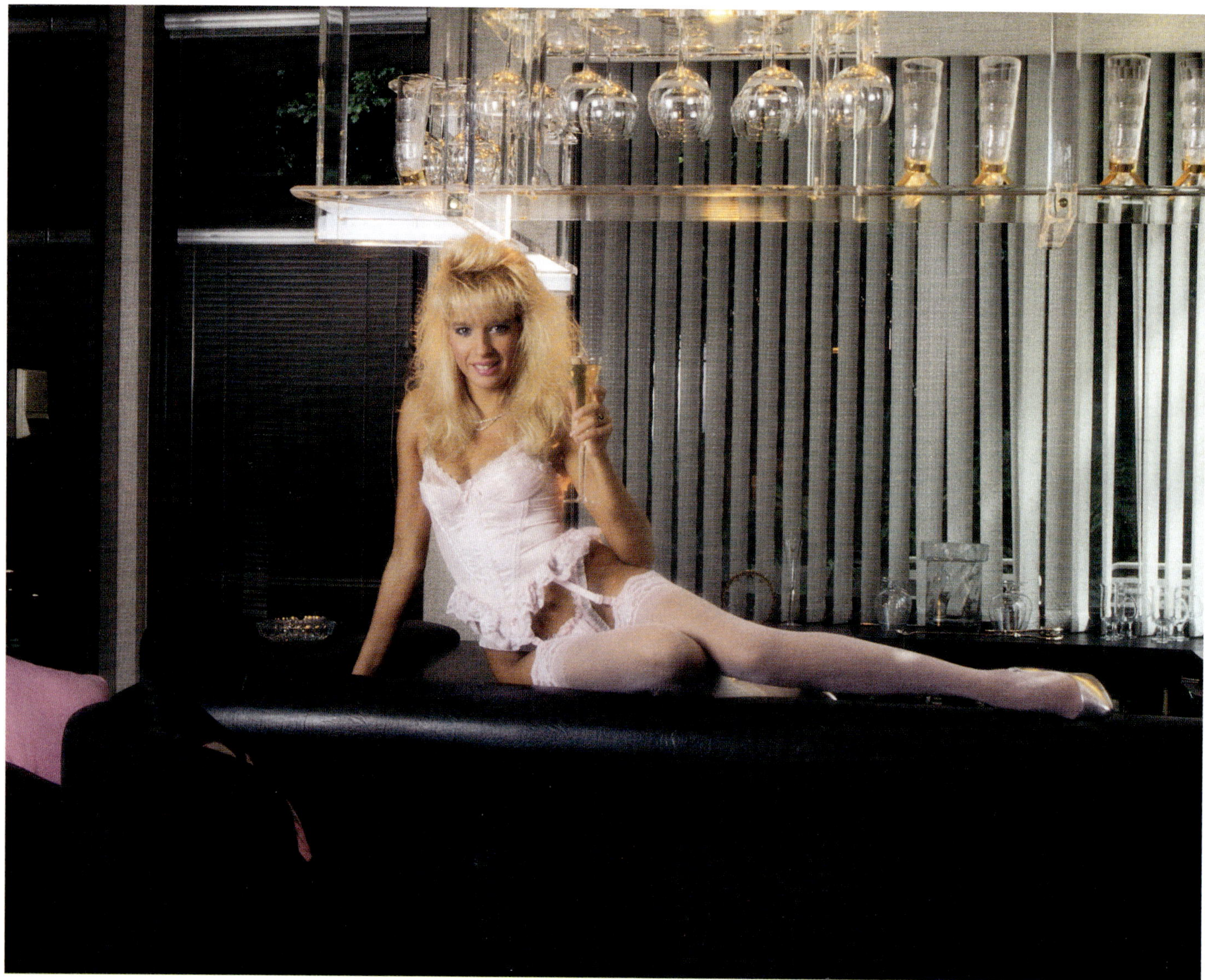

This photo is similar to the previous one in camera technique, lens employed and lighting used. The subject was directed into a modified stretch pose to accent the length of the leg that is extended. She was turned toward the main light, causing more illumination on the front of her body. More of the subject is now discernible.

A slim subject lends herself to greater lighting variety than a heavier subject. Frontal illumination, as used here, or even high-key lighting, is OK. A heavy subject, or one with a less than flattering body, requires more careful placement of light and shadow.

A full reclining pose, or a modified variation of it, such as in this image, is often very seductive and flattering and should be used in each boudoir session, if possible.

PORTFOLIO 32

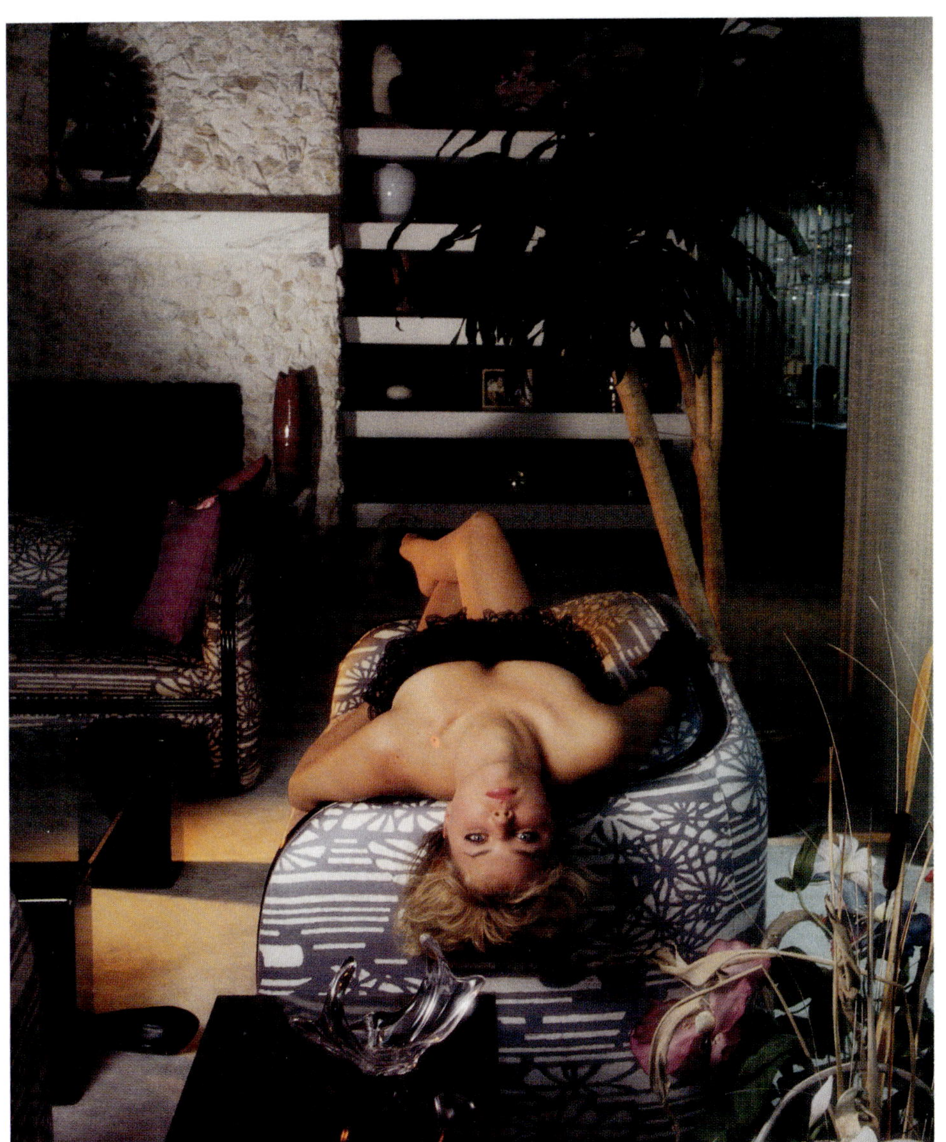

When we created this photo, we were faced with several problems. The possible solutions were equally numerous. We elected to use a simple solution.

To the right of camera-subject's axis, about 6 feet away, were large, sliding glass doors. To the eye, there appeared to be ample and even illumination throughout the entire room and on the subject's body. However, various meter readings indicated the contrary.

The light falloff on the subject's body, and from one point in the room to another, was great. There was approximately a two *f*-stop difference between the light striking the subject's right arm and left arm and a four *f*-stop difference between the light on her right arm and the light falling onto the back bookcase wall. Accordingly, we chose flash as the primary source of illumination.

We had just finished shooting in one area of the home and were en route to another when the subject sat down on the couch to relax. She looked so attractive that we wanted to capture a few images on film before moving on, so a very simple lighting arrangement was fashioned.

A light panel, placed about 30 degrees to the left of camera-subject axis, acted as main light. It was backlit by a light in a 5-inch bowl reflector and was powered by a 1000-watt-second power pack. Daylight acted as fill light.

Another light, with a 4-inch snoot and covered with an amber gel, was placed approximately 90 degrees to the left of camera-subject axis. A third light, also in a 5-inch bowl reflector, was directed onto the back bookcase wall. Both of these auxiliary lights had their power adjusted to emit one *f*-stop less light than the main light.

A standard lens was used, together with a warming filter and a Softar 1. Exposure was 1/30 second at *f*-8.

PORTFOLIO 33

Because the daylight in this room was dull and flat, we decided to take this photo and the next one with flash as the sole source of illumination.

A light panel—backlit with a light in a 5-inch bowl reflector and powered by a 1000-watt-second power pack—was used as main light. It was placed about 30 degrees to the right of camera-subject axis. Another light was put into a 5-inch bowl reflector and directed at the bottom of the counter and the lower part of the subject. It was placed on the floor, to the right of camera-subject axis. This light was covered with an amber gel and its power set to one *f*-stop less than the main light.

A third light—a back light in a 5-inch bowl reflector with barn doors—was positioned immediately behind the subject. Its power was adjusted to emit two *f*-stops less light than the main light.

The subject was asked to assume a standing position, with a wide stance, to make her legs appear more firm and the overall image more sensuous. We had her position her right arm at her waist area for two reasons. It covered the waistband of her pantyhose and it covered a crease in her side, caused by the turning pose.

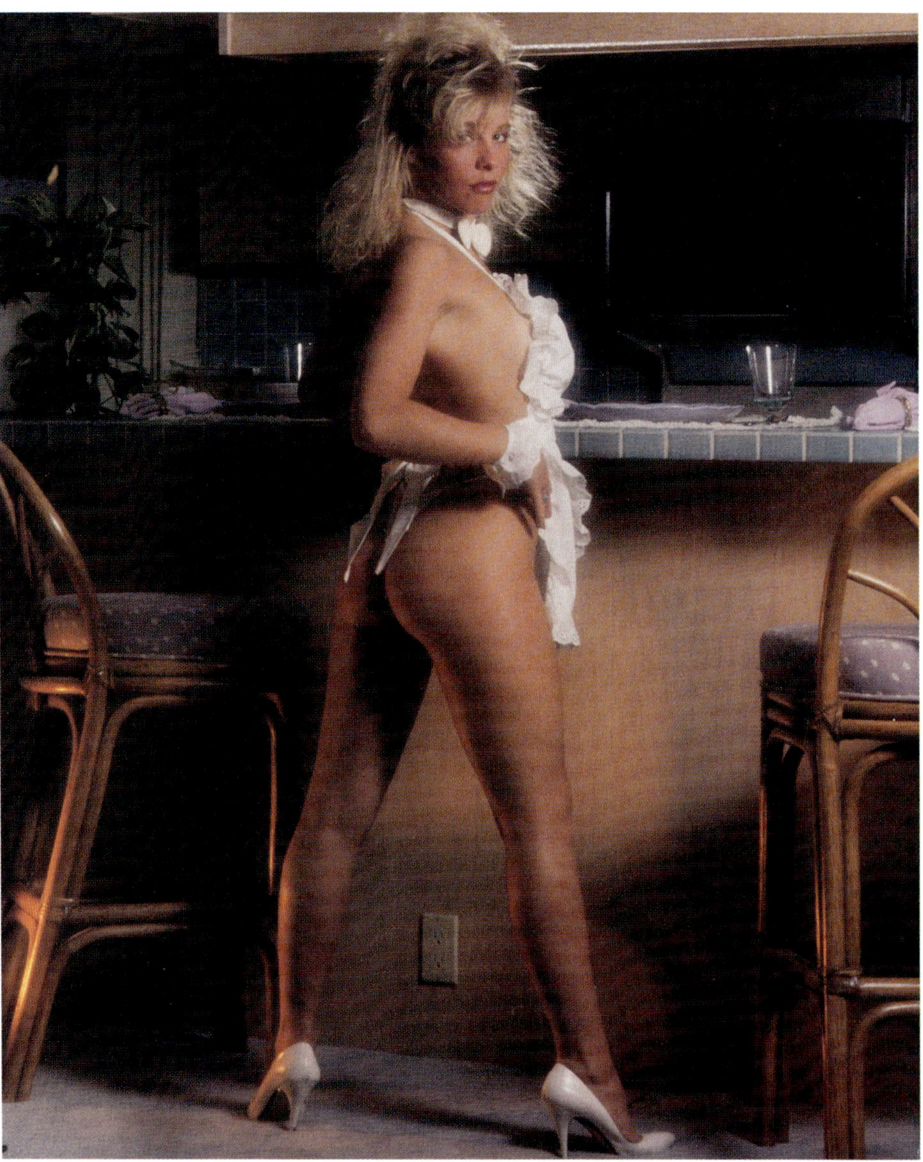

PORTFOLIO 34

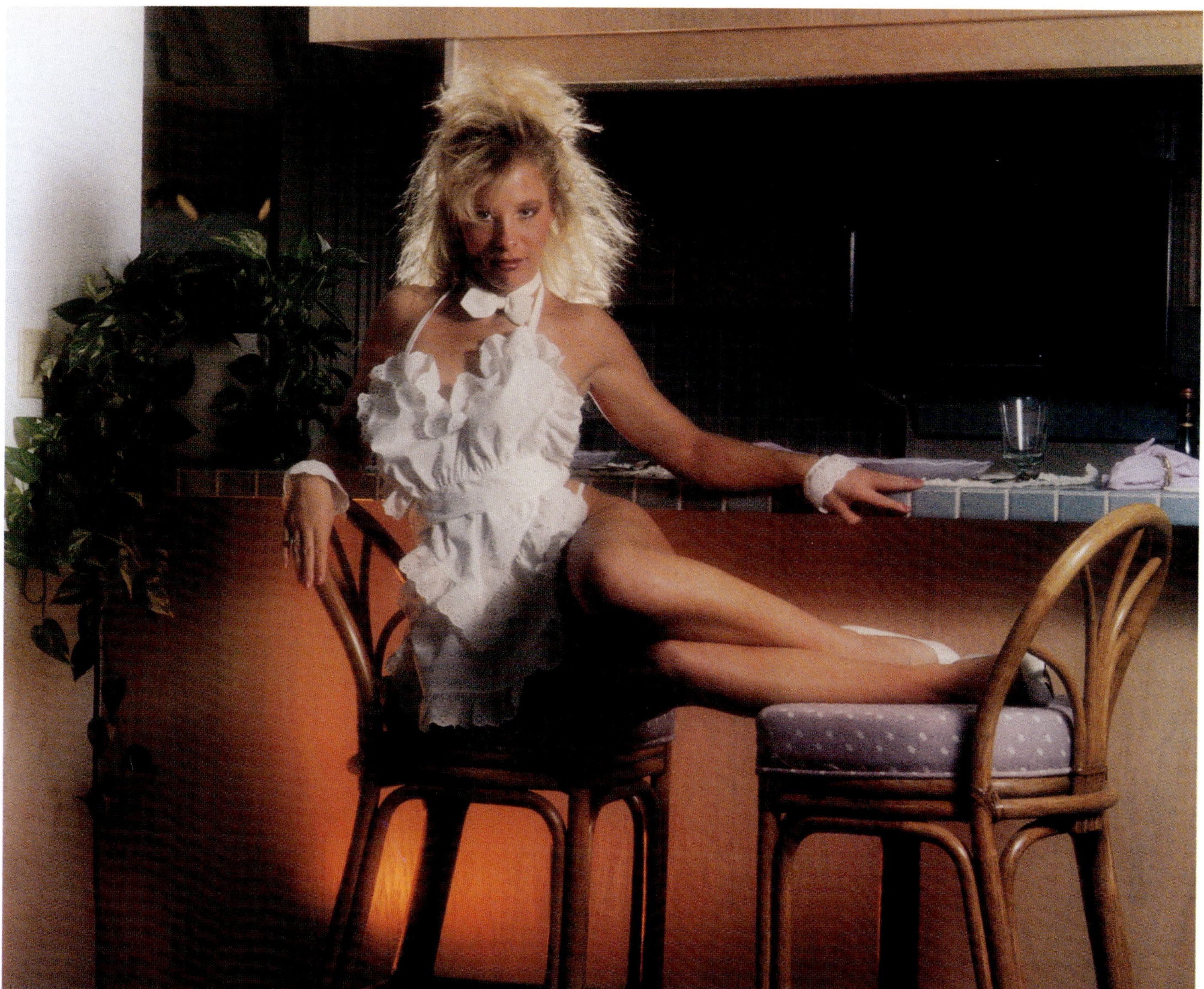

Once you have selected and placed a main light on a set for a subject, it becomes a simple matter to take a series of other shots that are slightly different by making minimal changes to the secondary sources of illumination.

For this photo, the same main light that was used to create Photo 33 was used. The only lighting difference between this image and the preceding one was in the two accent lights.

The floor light—in a 5-inch bowl reflector and covered with an amber gel—was moved and directed onto the wood paneling behind the subject. This gave good graphic separation. Its power was adjusted to one *f*-stop less light than the main light. The back light, also in a 5-inch bowl reflector, with barn doors, had its power adjusted to equal the output of the main light.

This pose is a modified reclining pose which works well for most subjects. By having the subject bend one of her legs slightly and placing it over the other, the lower portion of her body was thrown into deep shadow.

A medium telephoto lens was used, with a warming filter and a Softar 2. Exposure was at *f*-11.

35 PORTFOLIO

When planning a shoot in a subject's home, you must be aware of two major factors: the color of the walls in the shooting area and the size of the room.

The bathroom where this photo was created had colored walls and the room was very narrow. To get the viewpoint we wanted, we had to shoot from the hallway.

The main light was a light panel, backlit by a light in a 5-inch bowl reflector and powered by a 1000-watt-second power pack. It was positioned to the right of camera-subject axis. The close proximity of the bathroom's back and side walls generated ample fill-light reflection.

The colored bathroom walls created a distinct color cast in the final image. This could have been corrected, at least to some extent, through corrective filtration. However, we found the effect quite pleasing and decided to leave it.

A back light, in a 5-inch bowl reflector with barn doors, was put inside the tub and directed up onto the subject's back and hair. Its power was adjusted to one *f*-stop less than the main light. It was covered with an amber gel.

The subject was instructed to adopt a kneeling position. With her legs at different levels and somewhat separated, the upper portion of her body erect and arched, and her hands placed upon her thighs, the subject took on a very seductive appearance.

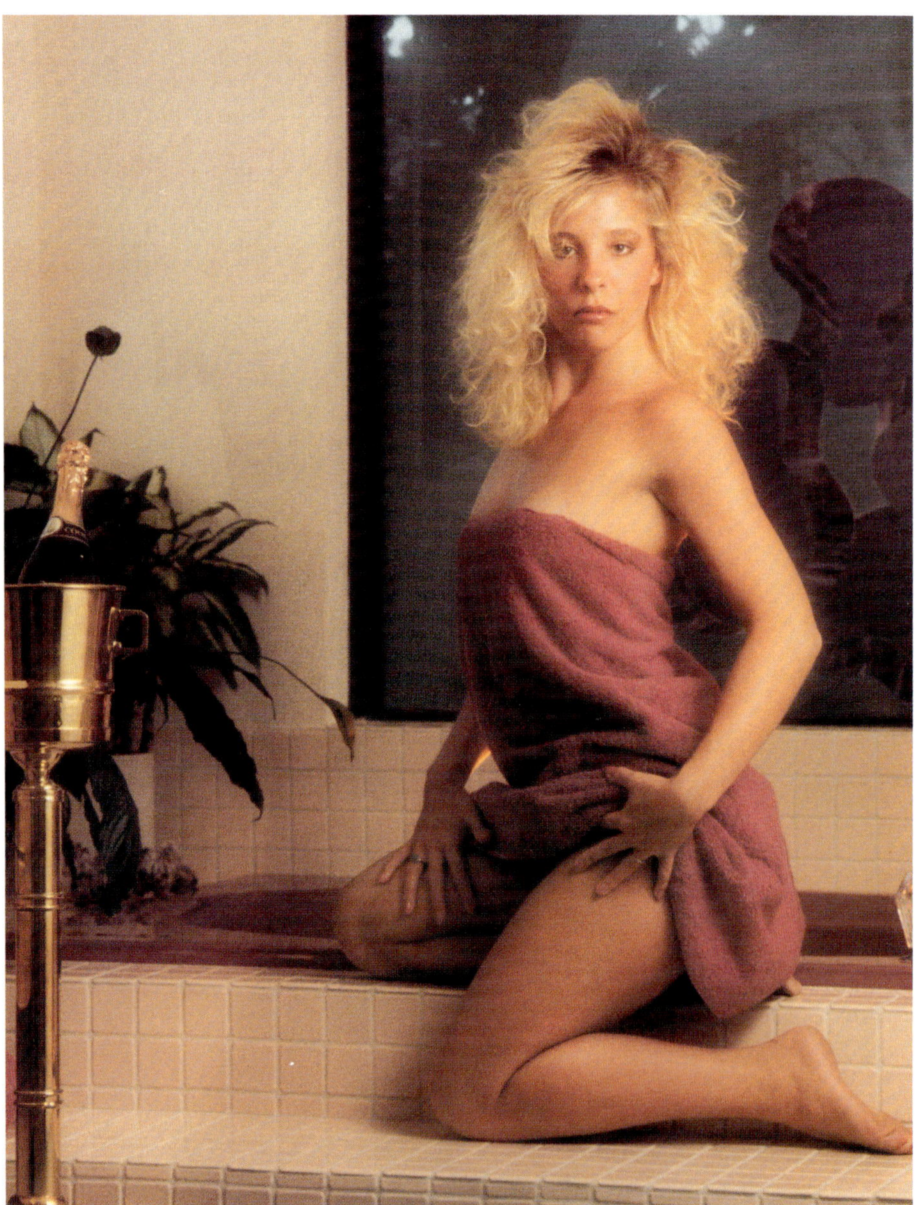

PORTFOLIO 36

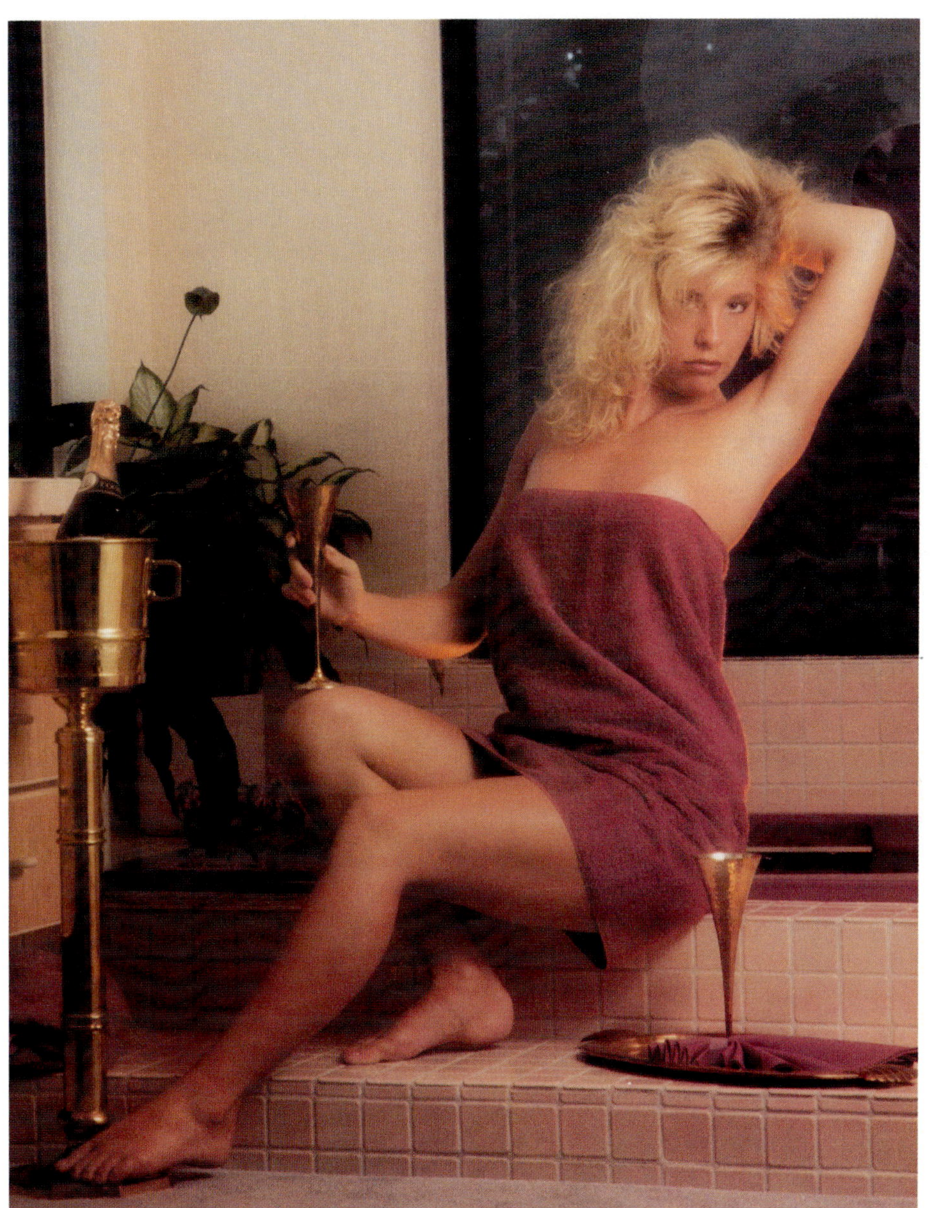

This photo is almost an exact duplication of Photo 35 in camera technique, lens employed and lighting used. The pose was slightly modified and some props were added to strengthen the design and viewer interest.

In this image, the subject was instructed to adopt a less aggressive pose. We sought more of a "come-hither" look. A leaning or stretching pose, such as this one, can often produce this result.

Once a subject is costumed and posed, she will often, on her own and quite naturally, display a facial expression consistent with both, as was the case here. If she does not, it will be your job to see that she does. After several minutes of trying, if she is still unable to obtain an appropriate facial expression, abandon the pose and go on to another. If all of the elements in a photo are perfect but the expression is not right, the image will not be a success.

There is no way of determining beforehand how long it might take a subject to adopt a suitable pose or facial expression. Some will need only a few seconds of practice before they exhibit the look you are after while others may take several minutes.

Look for obvious signs of frustration on the part of a subject. If possible, avoid a situation where the subject has to tell you that she cannot do a certain pose or adopt a certain look. If she finds it necessary to do this too often, she will lose confidence in herself, and your pictorial results will suffer.

PORTFOLIO 37

The home where this and the next three images were shot was lavish. The luxurious and spacious bathroom made an excellent setting. However, such a set can become intimidating and can cause uncertainty as to the "proper" lighting to be used.

When doing studio boudoir photography, you know from prior experimentation what lighting works best with each set that you have created. With the location session in a home, you don't have this luxury. You will not have photographed in that setting before. You must draw upon all of your past experiences and, for the most part, adopt a somewhat conservative approach with your lighting.

In the beginning, there might be a tendency to do an "overkill" and overlight every item that you see in the viewfinder. Don't do it! Keep the lighting simple. More images are ruined because of overlighting secondary elements than through underlighting. Choose your lights, their placement and their power output with care and thought.

In this image we used a light panel, backlit by a light in a 5-inch bowl reflector and connected to a 1000-watt-second power pack. It was placed to the left of camera-subject axis.

Three other lights, each in a 5-inch bowl reflector, were used as accent or kicker lights—see diagram. Each had its power adjusted to equal that of the main light. Two of these lights were covered with amber gels.

The biggest problem we faced when creating these bathroom images was unwanted reflections. Behind the subject and to the right of camera-subject axis were some gray, vertical blinds, dividing the bathroom from the bedroom area. Immediately in front of these blinds was an enormous glass plate, approximately 12 feet wide. No matter where the main light was placed, its reflection could be seen in the viewfinder when the standard lens was used. Accordingly, the lens was changed to a medium telephoto lens.

When executing boudoir images in a bathroom it's advisable to start with a conservative but slightly suggestive pose, such as is depicted here. As the subject's confidence builds, you can advance to more demonstrative and more suggestive poses.

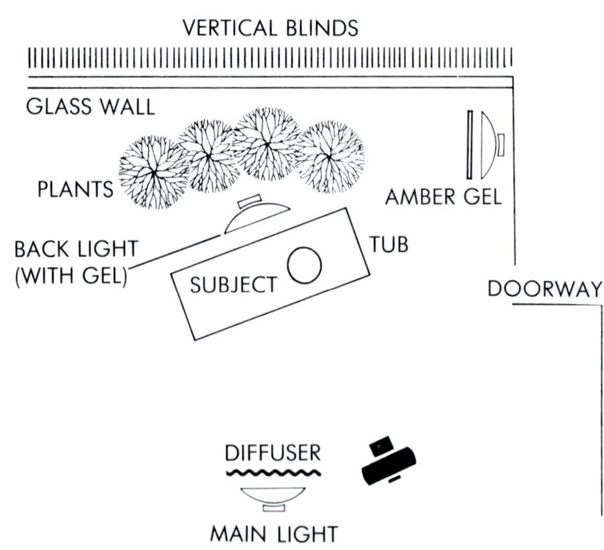

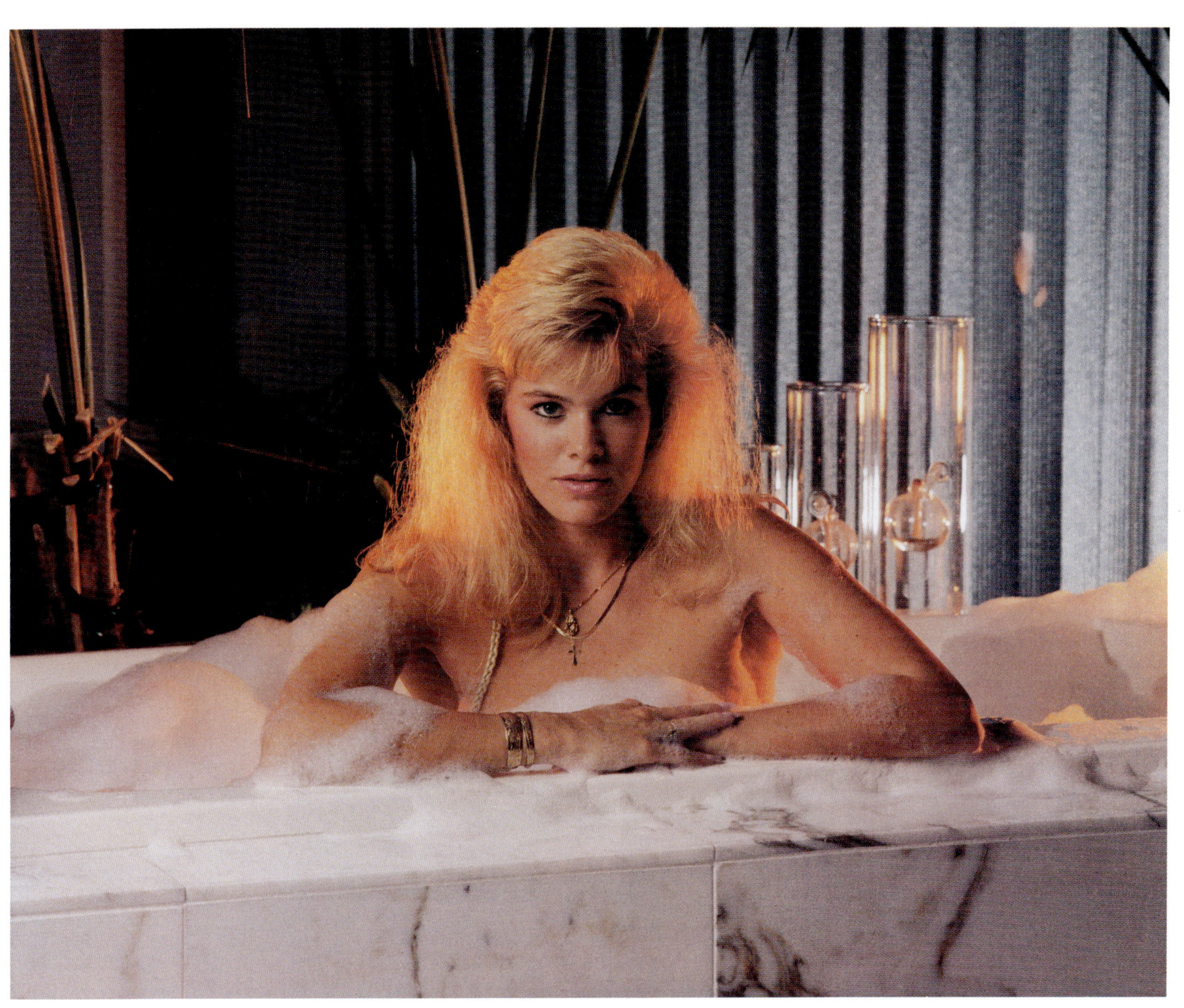

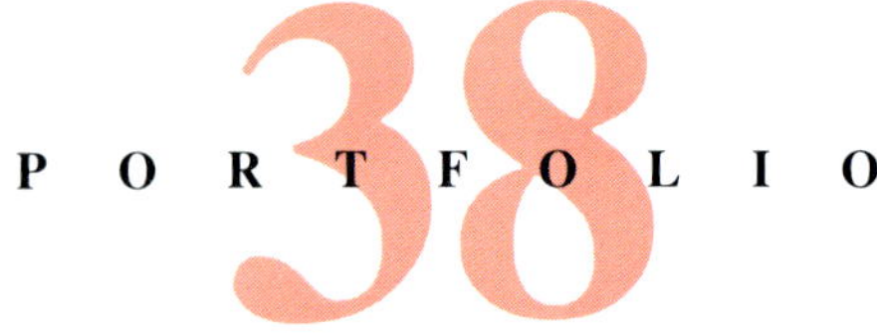

PORTFOLIO 38

The same lens and basic lighting were used for this photo as for Photo 37. Only the framing and the pose were modified.

When doing location photography of a subject in her home, it is necesssary to have most of the images show some part of the home. This is the reason the subject desires a home shoot: to display her home, with her in it. However, once you have satisfied this explict or implied request and have photographed the subject in a clearly discernible setting, don't pass up the opportunity to do some tighter shots. Do some head shots, head-and-shoulder shots, and three-quarter length shots to give added pictorial variety.

For this photo, we had the subject on her knees, with her back arched. The towel was carefully placed so that it would curve into her body. Even though little of her body can actually be seen, the tilt of the head, the look in her eye, and the pose all work together to create a very sensuous image.

To afford a different look from that of the preceding image, the camera was brought closer to the subject, giving a more intimate feeling to the scene.

A medium telephoto lens was used, and a warming filter and a Softar 1. Exposure was at *f*-11.

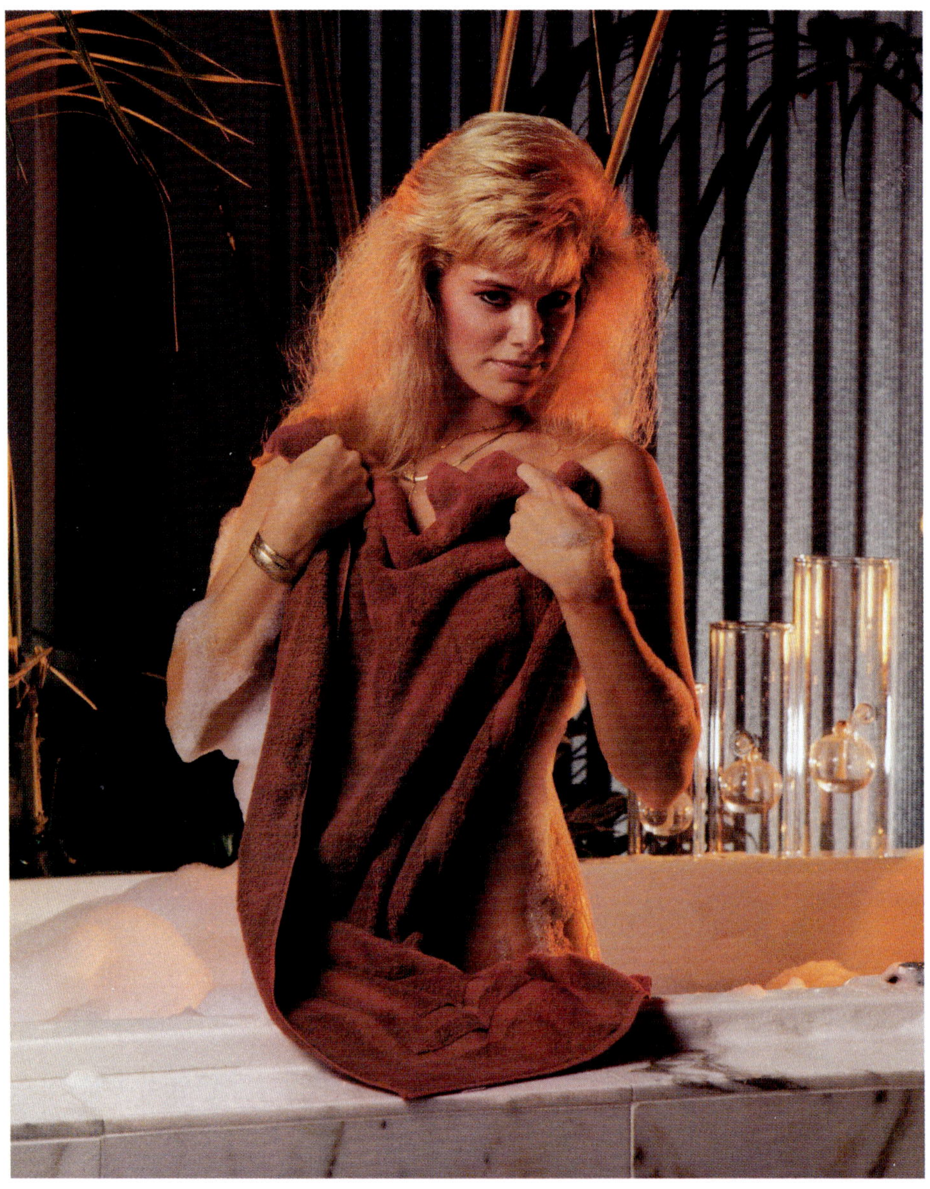

PORTFOLIO 39

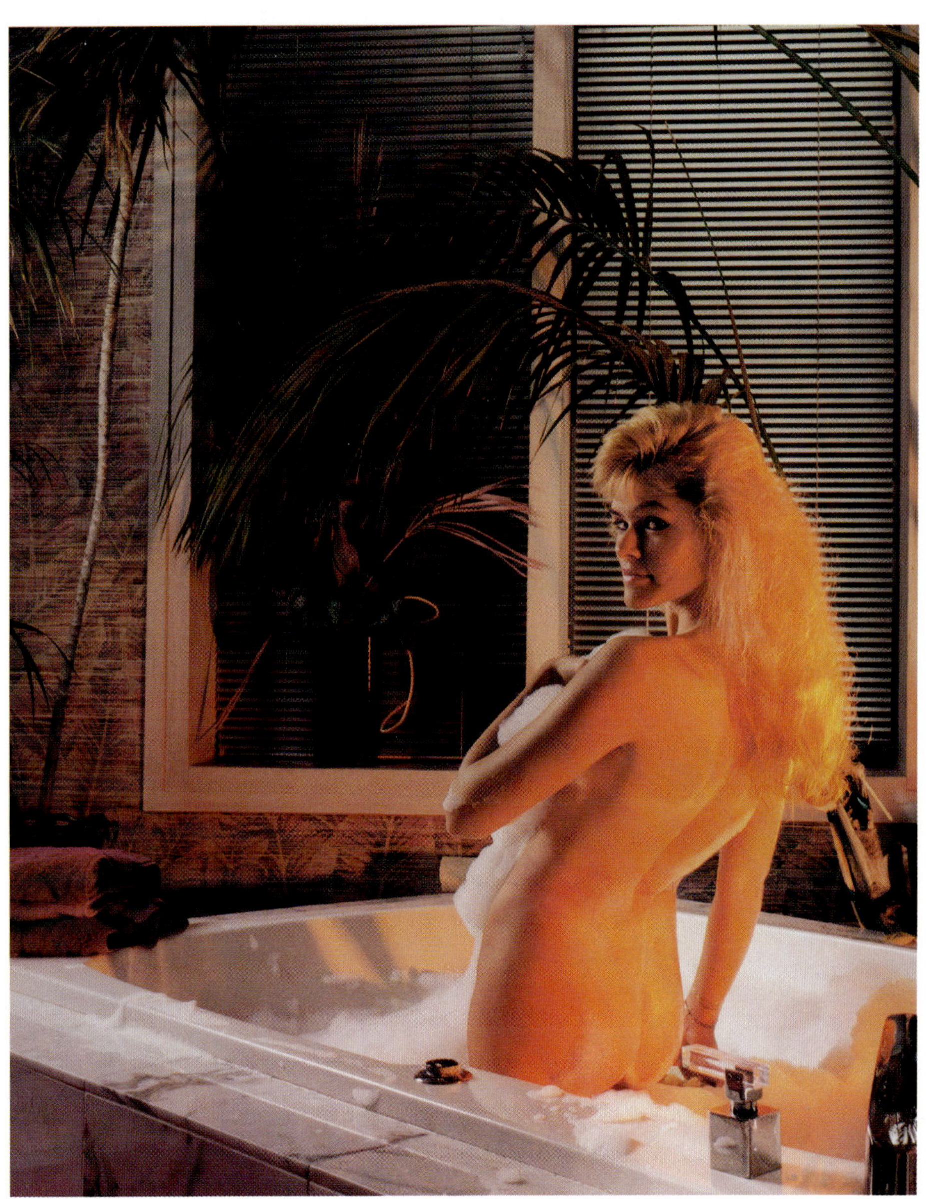

Once you have photographed your subject in the initially selected position, make changes in camera angle and camera position. This will give you additional, different looking images at the same location.

We had previously taken a series of images of this subject, including Photo 37 and Photo 38, and decided to change slightly the concept. Instead of a towel covering the subject, we decided on soap bubbles. In order to make the subject feel more comfortable, Robert left the room while Sheila and our two female assistants prepared the subject.

Upon returning to the shooting area, Robert caught a glimpse of the subject from the doorway. She looked just as you see her in this photo.

Even though we prefer not to use an amber-gelled light source as a main light for boudoir subjects, we were fearful that the subject would not be able to maintain the pose or expression while we adjusted the lighting. The camera and tripod were quickly moved into the hallway and this very provocative image was taken. The subject's expression says it all.

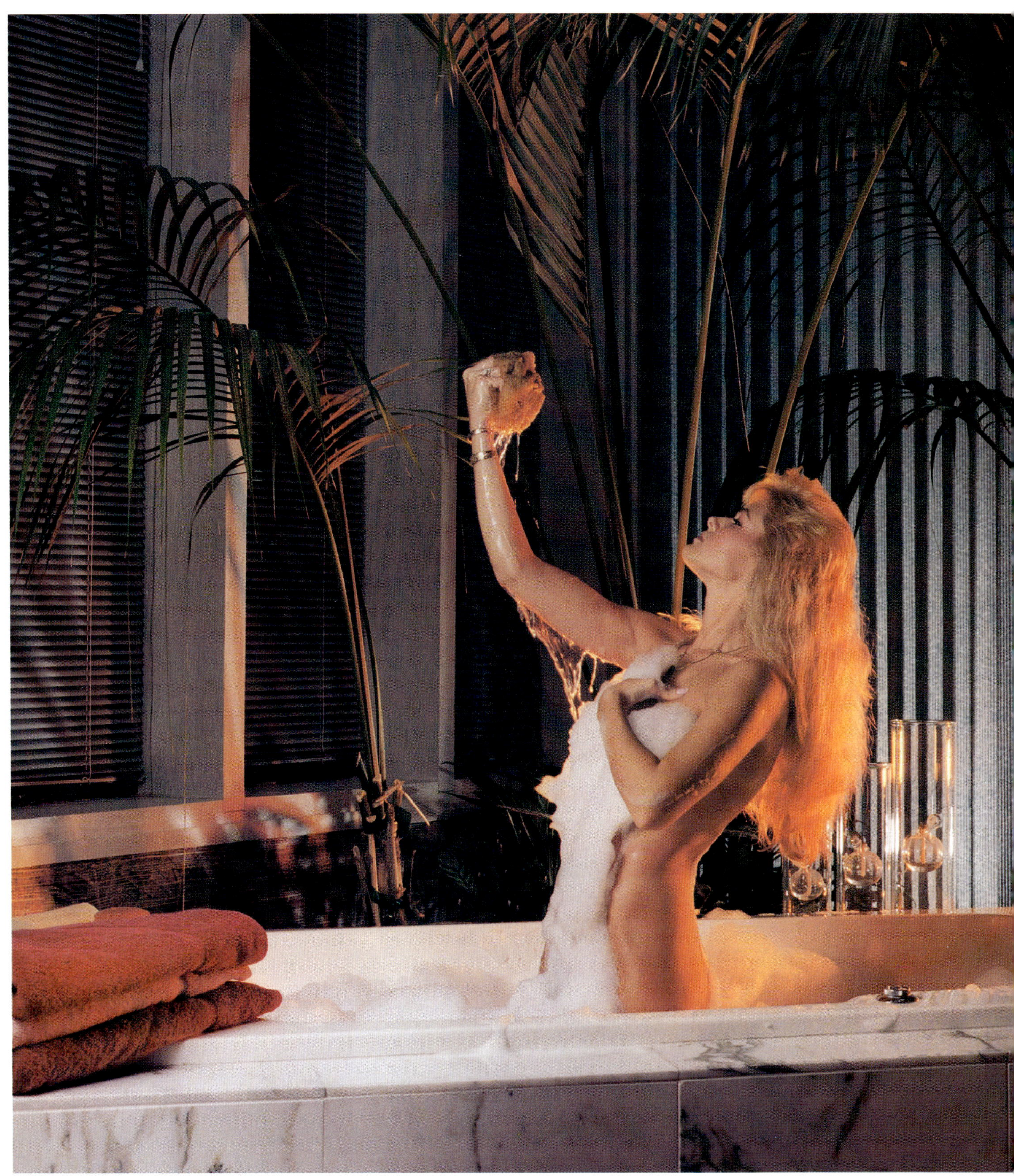

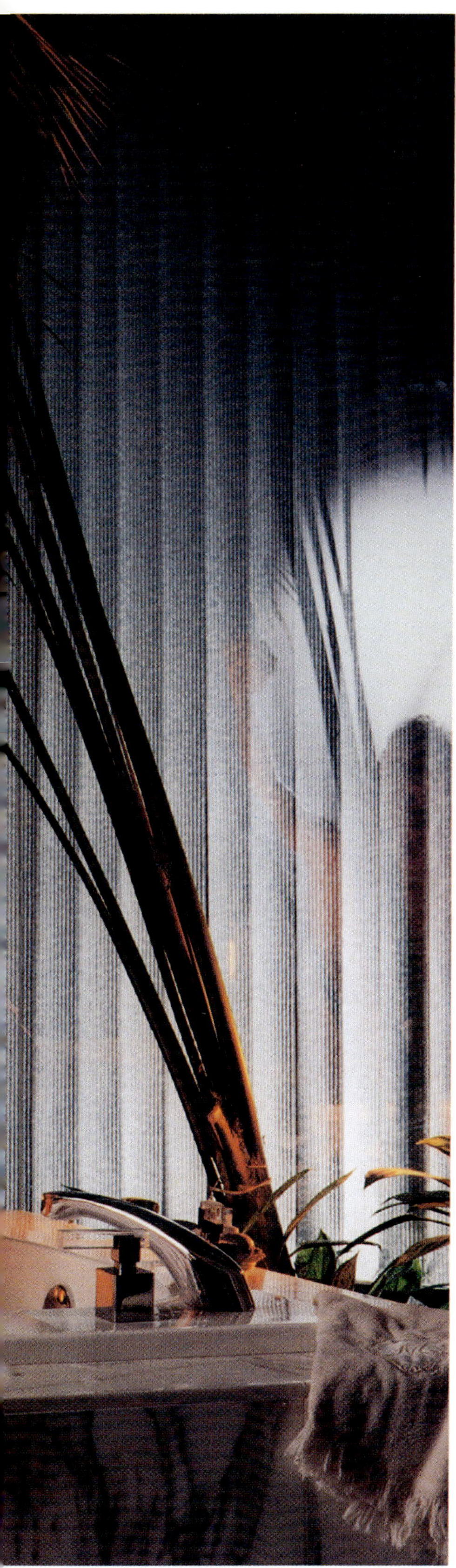

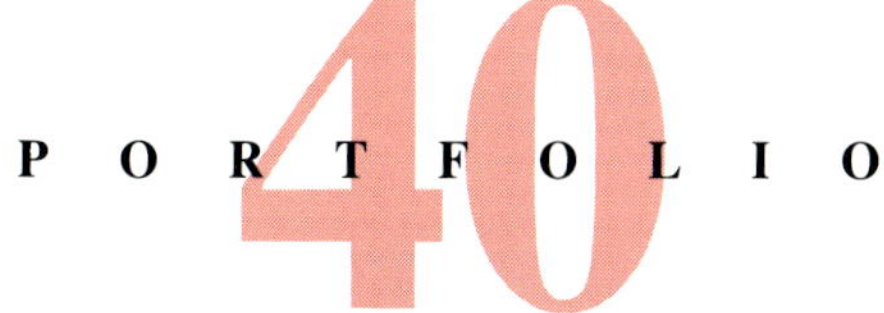

PORTFOLIO 40

Of all the shots taken of this subject in the bathroom, this is our favorite—and it took us the longest time to make. We had to expose 20 to 30 frames of film in order to capture this special image.

The subject's head and back had to have the correct amount of tilt and arch. Her right arm had to be just at the right height. The proper quantity of water had to run down her arm from the sponge. The soap suds had to be sparse enough to allow a portion of her body to be seen but thick enough to conceal other body parts from view.

After 45 minutes and a great deal of cooperation and patience on the part of the subject, this stunning image was created.

You can observe the reflection of the main-light source in the large glass panel to the right of camera-subject axis, and even a very faint reflection of the subject herself. In the prior photos, this reflection was not observed because a medium telephoto lens had been used.

For this photo, a standard lens was used, and a warming filter and a Softar 1. Exposure was at *f*-11.

BARN SETTING

Building an elaborate boudoir setting in a studio can be a costly and time consuming project and can take up a lot of valuable space.

Some settings, like the classic bedroom set, will automatically be received well by most boudoir subjects. They can relate to it and picture themselves being photographed in it. Other settings, such as a kitchen set, may be less successful.

If subjects relate well to a set and frequently ask to be photographed in it, the setting is a winner and should be made permanent. If it is not—no matter how great the setting might look or photograph—abandon it.

Not only does it take time and money to construct an elaborate set, but it takes time and money to light it. The more elaborate the setting, the more lights you will need.

We urge you to select the themes for your sets carefully. The following three images were made on our barn set. We were a little daring in constructing it, but it has proven very popular and successful.

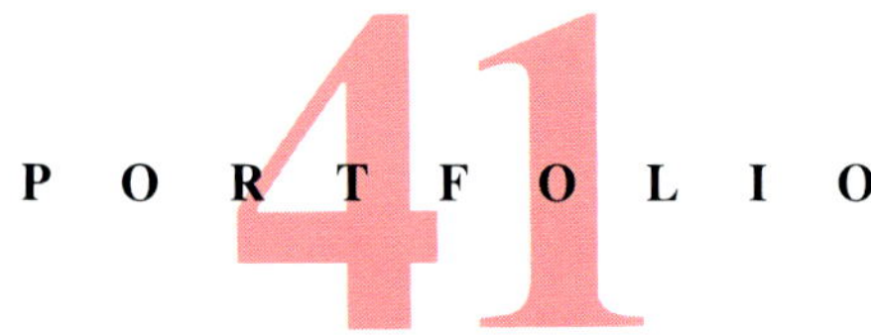

PORTFOLIO 41

This subject considered her legs her best features, so we chose all of the poses and the lighting to emphasize them.

To give motion to the body and draw attention to legs and buttocks, we had the subject lean over a bale of hay. She was instructed to stretch her left leg and bend the right one. This put tension on the front leg, making it more firm and exaggerating its length.

The legs and buttocks were further emphasized by the lighting. A light panel, placed about 40 degrees to the left of camera-subject axis and backlit by a flash in a 5-inch bowl reflector, was used as main light. It was connected to a 2400-watt-second power pack. A 3x4-foot softbox, placed about 20 degrees to the right of camera-subject axis, was used as fill light. Its power was adjusted to emit two *f*-stops less light than the main light.

Another light, in a 5-inch bowl reflector and snooted, was placed about 90 degrees to the right of camera-subject axis and directed onto the subject's legs and buttocks. The light was gelled with an amber gel and had its power adjusted to equal the main light.

Two additional lights were used. One, in a 5-inch bowl reflector, was placed slightly behind and above the subject and aimed at the subject. It was gelled with an amber gel and had its power adjusted to emit one *f*-stop less light than the main light. The final light was a background light. It was in a 6-inch bowl reflector and gelled with an amber gel. This light was placed on the floor and directly behind the bale of hay and directed at the background. Its power was adjusted to emit one *f*-stop less light than the main light.

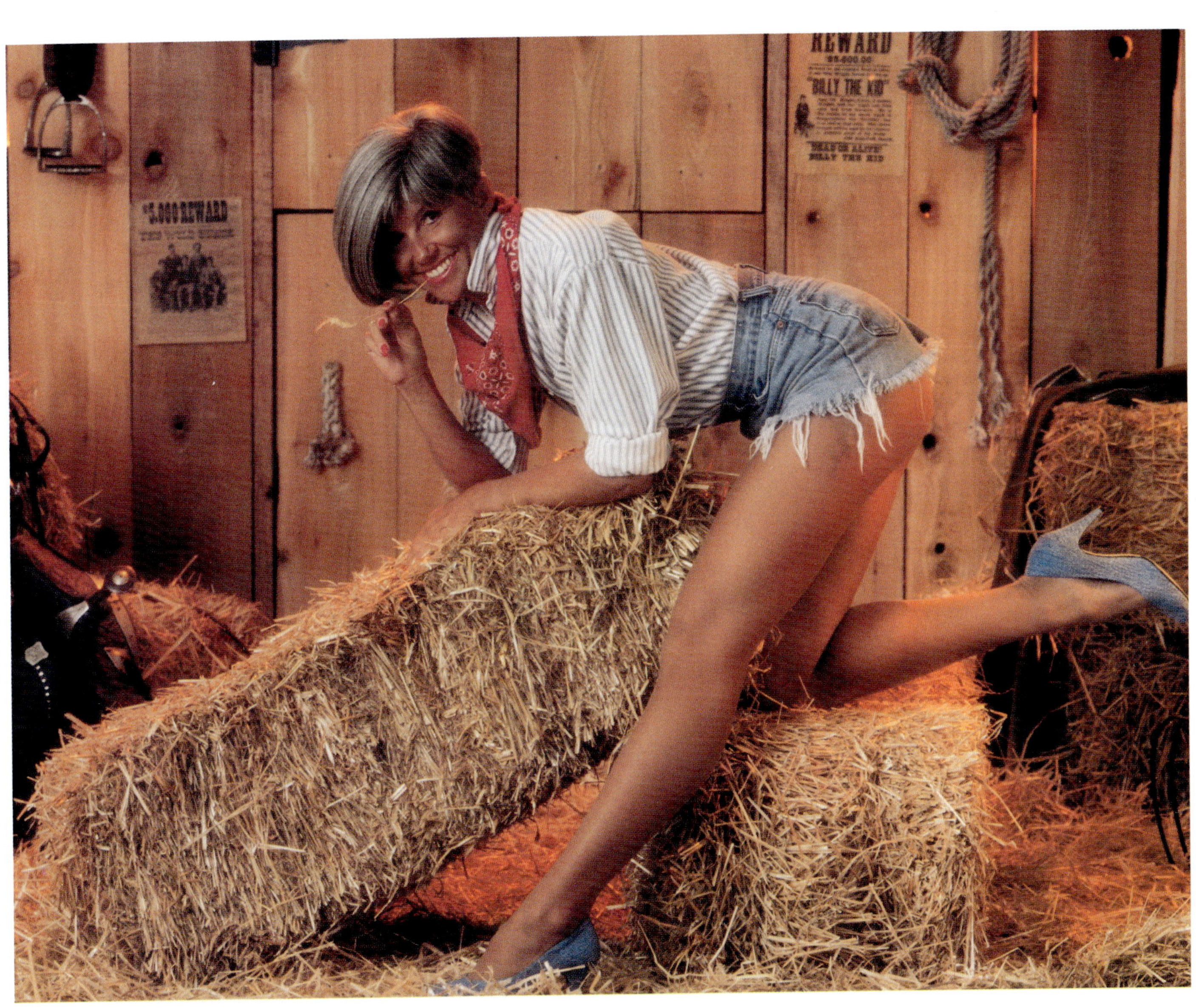
REWARD
"BILLY THE KID"
BILLY THE KID

PORTFOLIO 42

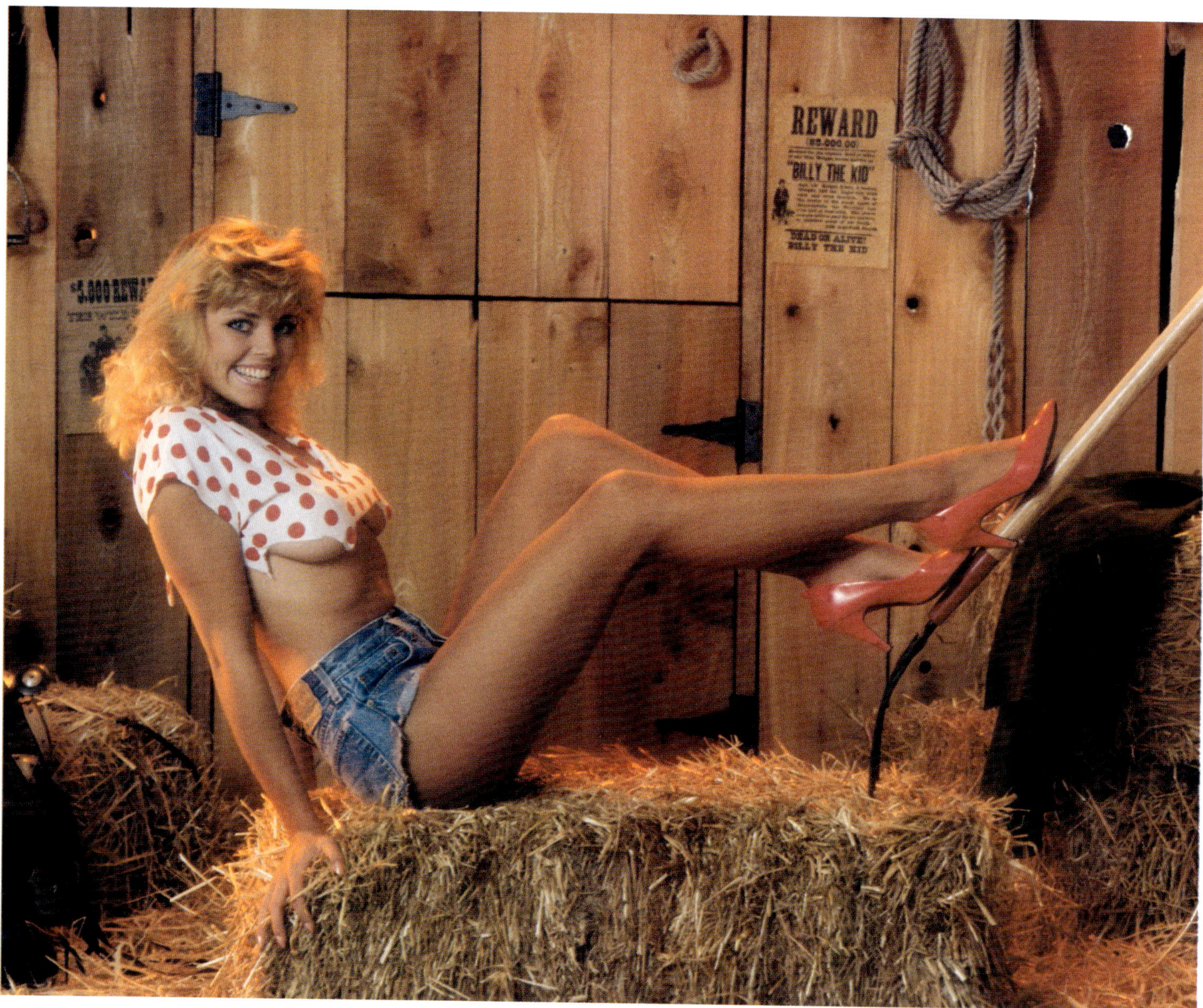

Our barn set is large and elaborate. The back wall is 14 feet wide and 7 feet high. Each of the two side walls measures 9x7 feet. Before we had made this setting and its lighting permanent, it took about 90 minutes to set it up and 45 minutes to tear it down. This is too much time for the assembly and removal of a standard and typical boudoir set. Once a setting of this size is in place, and the lighting basically arranged, a variety of different looks and lighting effects can be easily achieved.

For this photo, we wanted the emphasis placed on the subject's legs and bust. This pose accentuates both.

Not all subjects will be able to achieve this pose. It puts great strain on the upper arms and stomach muscles. The subject must lean backwards, arch her back, and stretch.

The subject maintained her balance partly with her arms, but put no appreciable weight on them. Placing too much weight on the arms can cause the upper arms to appear heavy and unflattering. If a subject has heavy upper arms to begin with, this pose should be avoided altogether.

PORTFOLIO 43

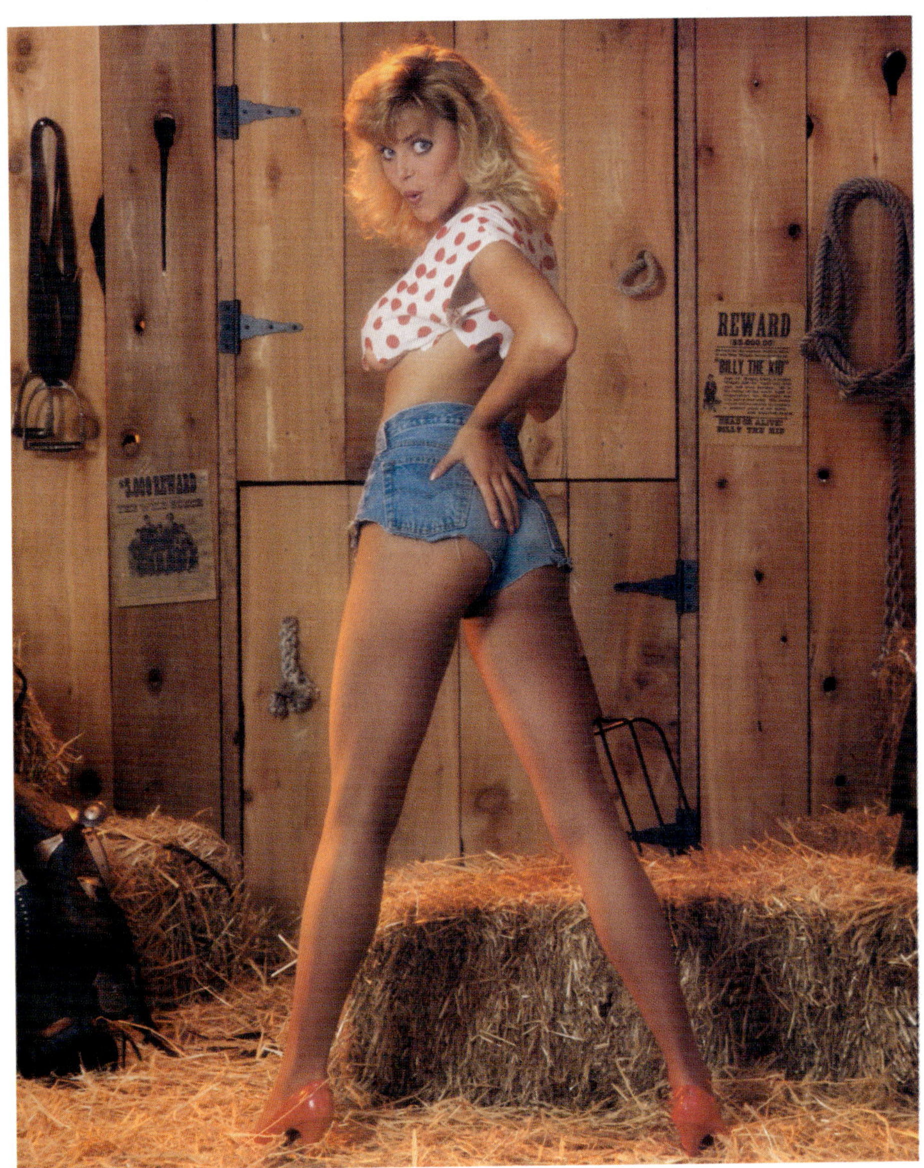

To justify the construction and permanent placement of an elaborate setting in your home or studio, it must be versatile. It must photograph well, be easy to work with, and flatter most subjects. An ideal set should be capable of yielding at least 12 different looking images without the need for major changes in lighting.

We chose this pose to accent three of the subject's features—her legs, bust and buttocks. Oblique lighting, and the turn in the pose, accomplished this result.

In addition to main light, fill-light reflector, hair light and background light, we placed an accent light at about 100 degrees to the left of camera-subject axis, adjusting its power to emit one *f*-stop more light than the main light. Notice how nicely it outlined the subject's shapely legs.

LOCKER ROOM SET

We like to offer a subject additional choices of set, besides the classic bedroom, bathroom and other domestic settings.

Today, many women are concerned about their figures and shapes and go to great lengths to keep fit. Many husbands and boyfriends find their mates very sensuous when attired in an aerobic costume. The photographic possibilities in a gym or locker-room setting are virtually limitless.

At our studio, we have created a very simple locker-room set. We purchased three used lockers from a second-hand store. Each locker is approximately 26 inches wide, 21 inches deep and 84 inches tall. We added an old bench, and use a towel or two as props. We keep the lighting simple.

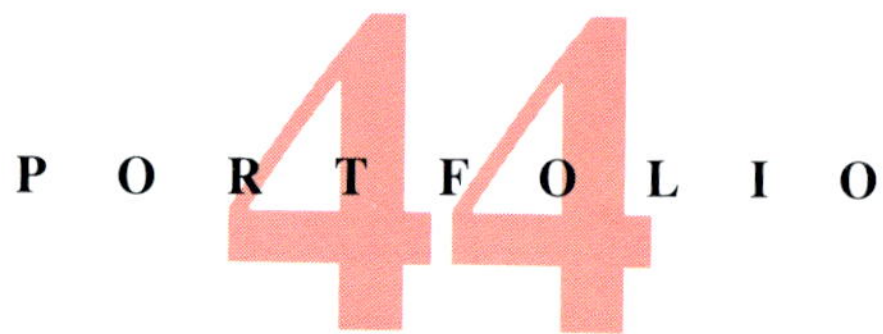

We like the effect provided by a blue background. The inherent mystique about a women's locker room is enhanced by allowing the background to be shrouded in deep-blue light. In this first locker-room image, we were not aiming for drama. We wanted the viewer to be able to see the subject clearly, so we followed a previously expounded rule: If you want to see something, light it; if you don't, don't! Because we chose to light the set as we did, we selected a pose that was somewhat guarded but yet had a suggestion of sensuality.

We used a medium telephoto lens with a Softar 1 filter. Exposure was at *f*-11. The main light was a 1200-watt-second Balcar Opalite, with a 20-degree grid spot and plastic diffuser cap. The fill light—a 3x4-foot softbox—was placed on the opposite side from the main light and its power was adjusted to emit one-half the power of the main light.

An accent light was placed high and behind the subject. This light was in a 6-inch bowl reflector and its power was adjusted to equal that of the main light. Another accent light, with a blue gel, was put low, behind the locker, and directed onto the white seamless background. This light was also in a 6-inch bowl reflector. Its power was adjusted to emit one full *f*-stop less light than the main light.

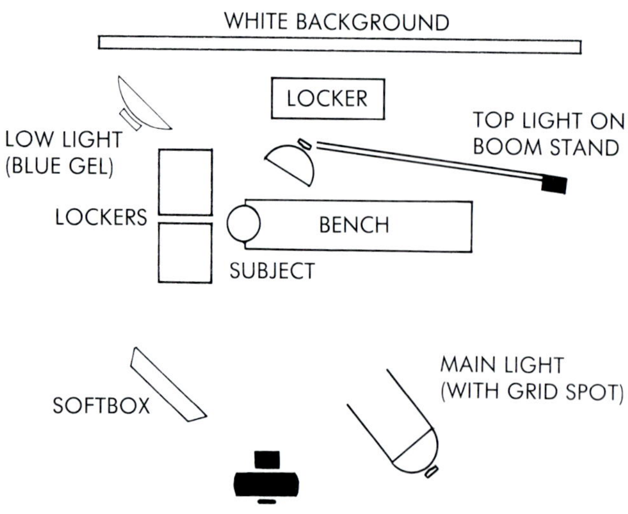

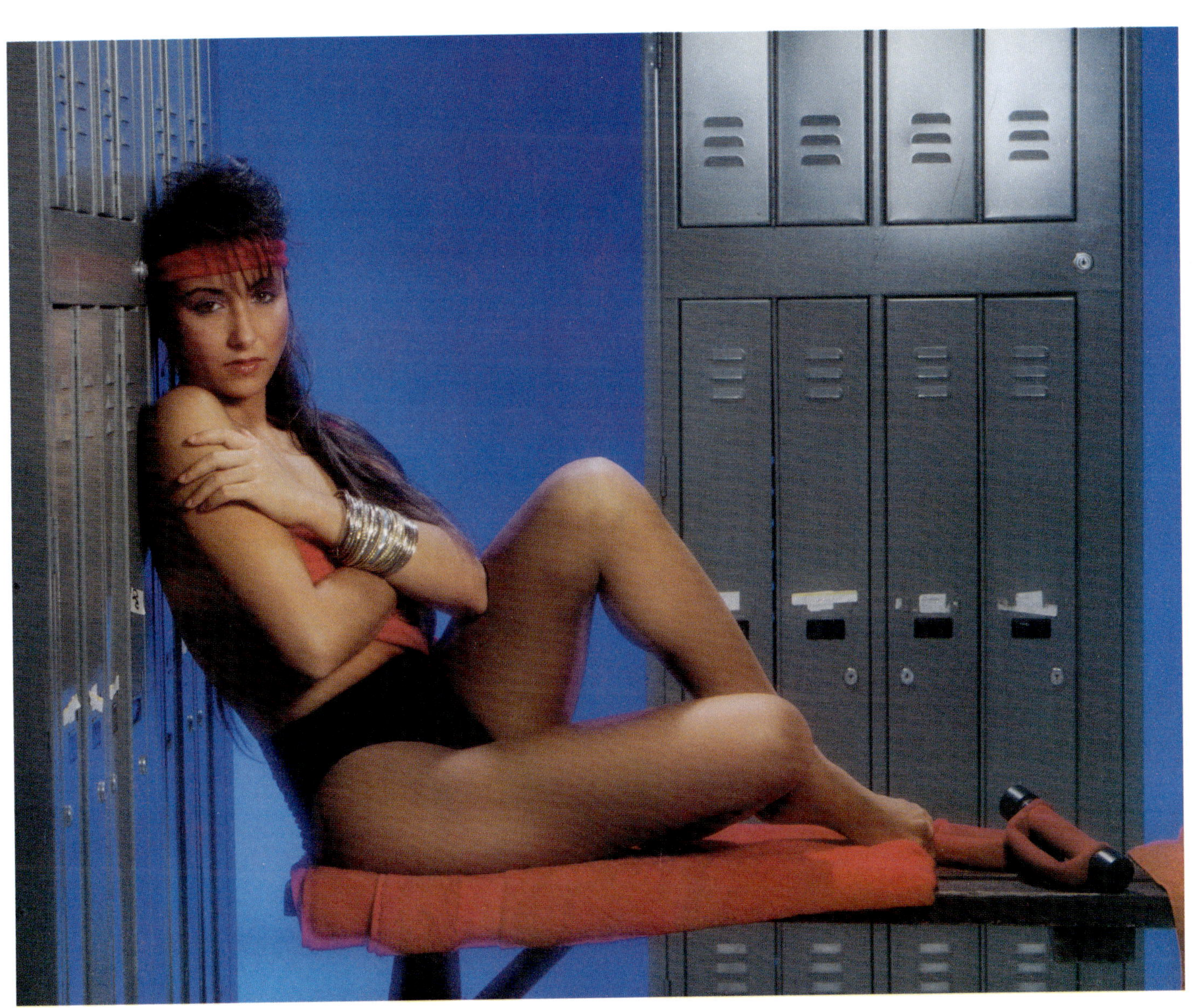

PORTFOLIO 45

Once the basic locker set is in place, it is a very simple proposition to create a different looking image, as this photo shows.

Instead of being lit by four lights, as in the preceding photo, this subject and set were illuminated by only two lights: A top light, above and slightly behind the subject—in a 6-inch bowl reflector and connected to a 1200-watt-second power pack—was the main light; an accent light—also in a 6-inch bowl reflector, connected to another 1200-watt-second power pack—was low and behind one of the lockers, gelled with a blue gel and directed onto the white seamless background. Its power was adjusted to one-half the power of the main light.

The lighting and pose enhanced the desired feeling of mystery and drama.

A medium telephoto lens was used, and a Softar 1 filter. Exposure was at *f*-8.

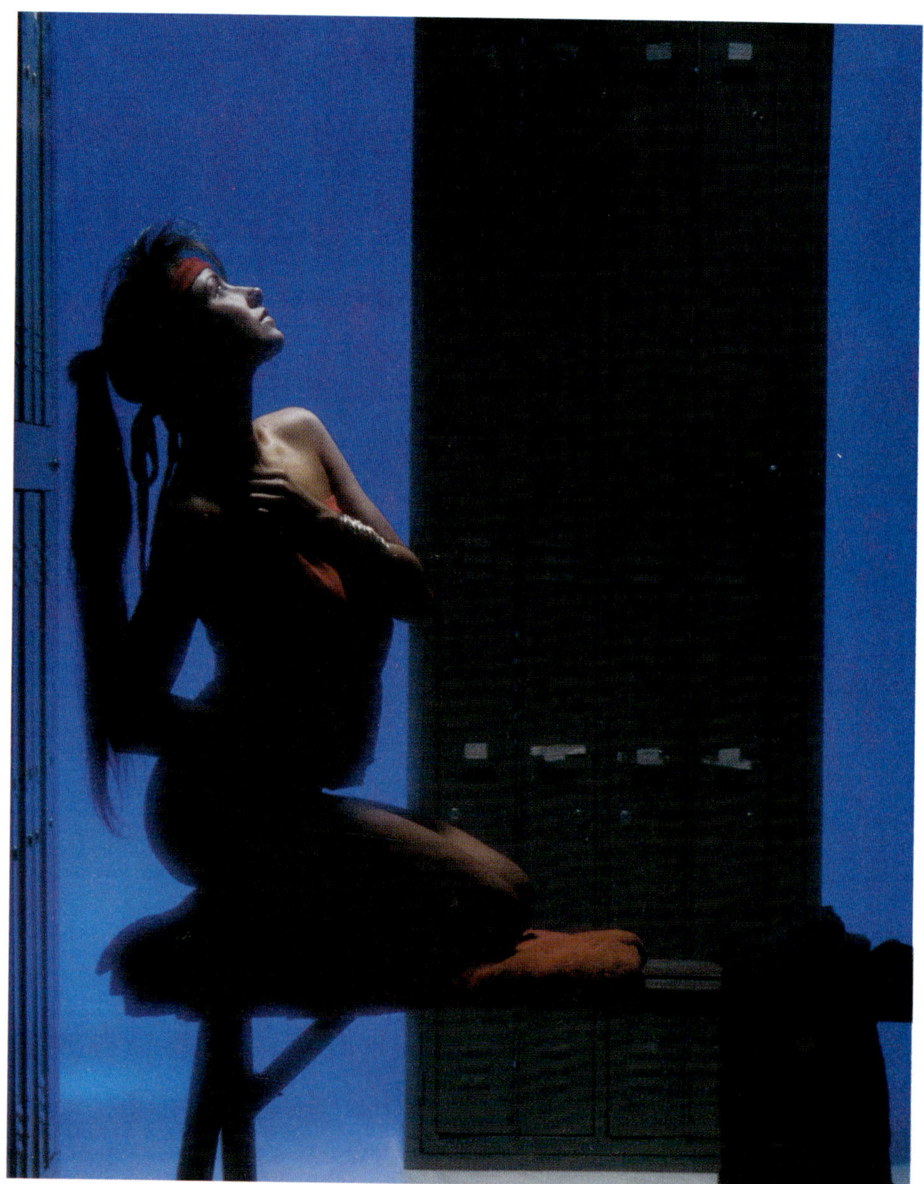

PORTFOLIO 46

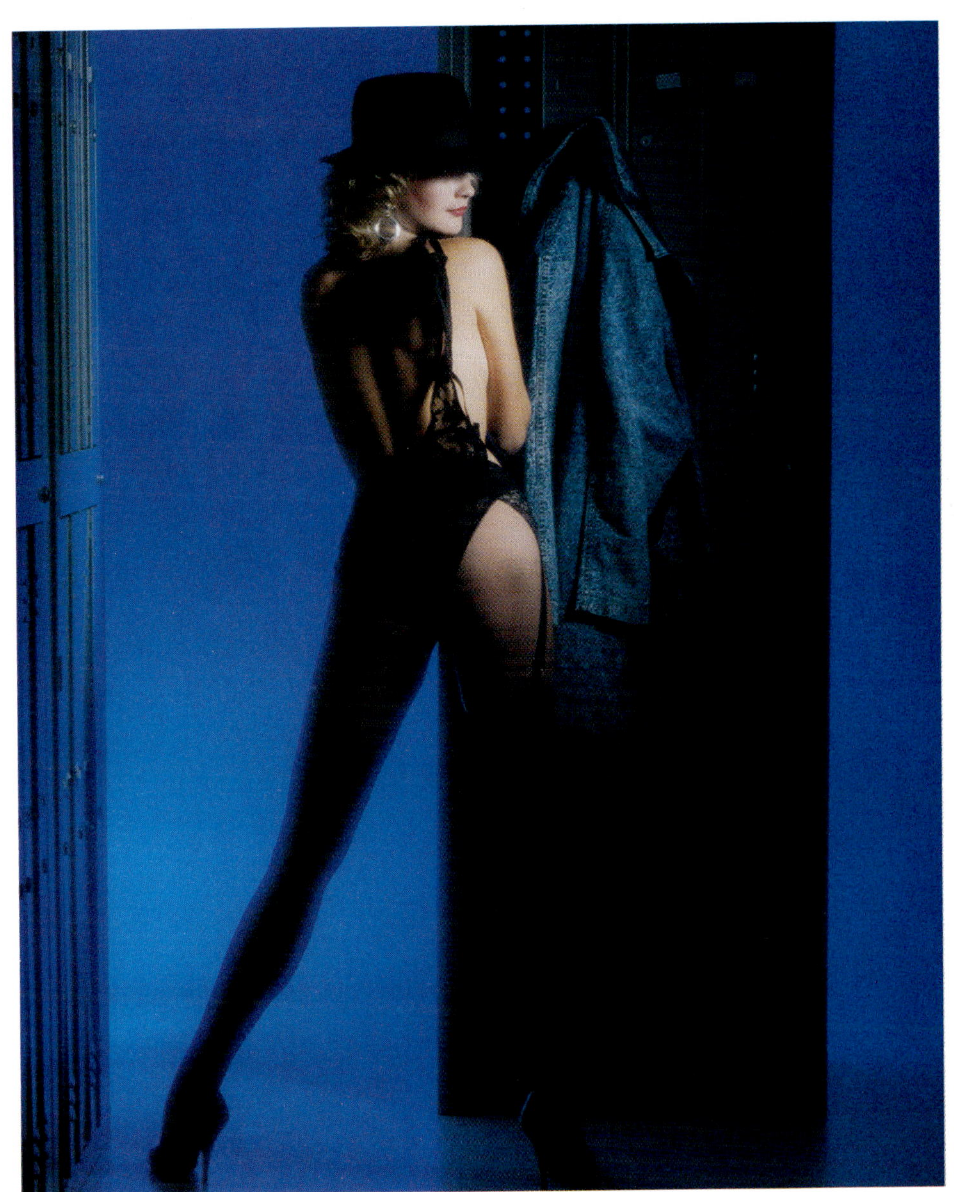

For this photo, too, only two lights were used. A Balcar Opalite, connected to a 1200-watt-second power pack, was used as main light. The other source was an accent light, in a 6-inch bowl reflector, illuminating the white seamless background. The accent light was connected to a second 1200-watt-second power pack and was placed low, behind one of the lockers, and gelled with a blue gel. Its power was adjusted to emit one-half the power of the main light.

In order to add to the sensuality of the image, the subject was costumed in panties and garter belt. Her bra was intentionally draped over her shoulder to heighten viewer interest. Although we shot several frames of this subject in this pose without the hat, we thought that the one with the hat worked best.

A medium telephoto lens was used, with a Softar 2 filter. Exposure was at *f*-11.

PORTFOLIO 47

In order to make this stunning image, we used our basic locker set, and three lights. The Balcar Opalite, connected to a 1200-watt-second power source, was the main light. Another flash, in a 6-inch bowl reflector, placed high and slightly behind the subject, acted as top light. This one had its power adjusted to equal that of the main light. An accent light, also in a 6-inch bowl reflector and covered with a blue gel, served as background light. The blue-gelled light was positioned low and behind the locker to give illumination to the background and additional separation to the subject. The background light had its power adjusted to one full *f*-stop less than the main light.

Most of the subject's face was intentionally hidden from view by her hat in order to concentrate viewer attention on her body. The main light was approximately 35 to 45 degrees to the right of camera-subject axis to enhance the lines of the subject's bust and other parts of her body.

A medium telephoto lens was used, and a Softar 1 filter. Exposure was at *f*-8.

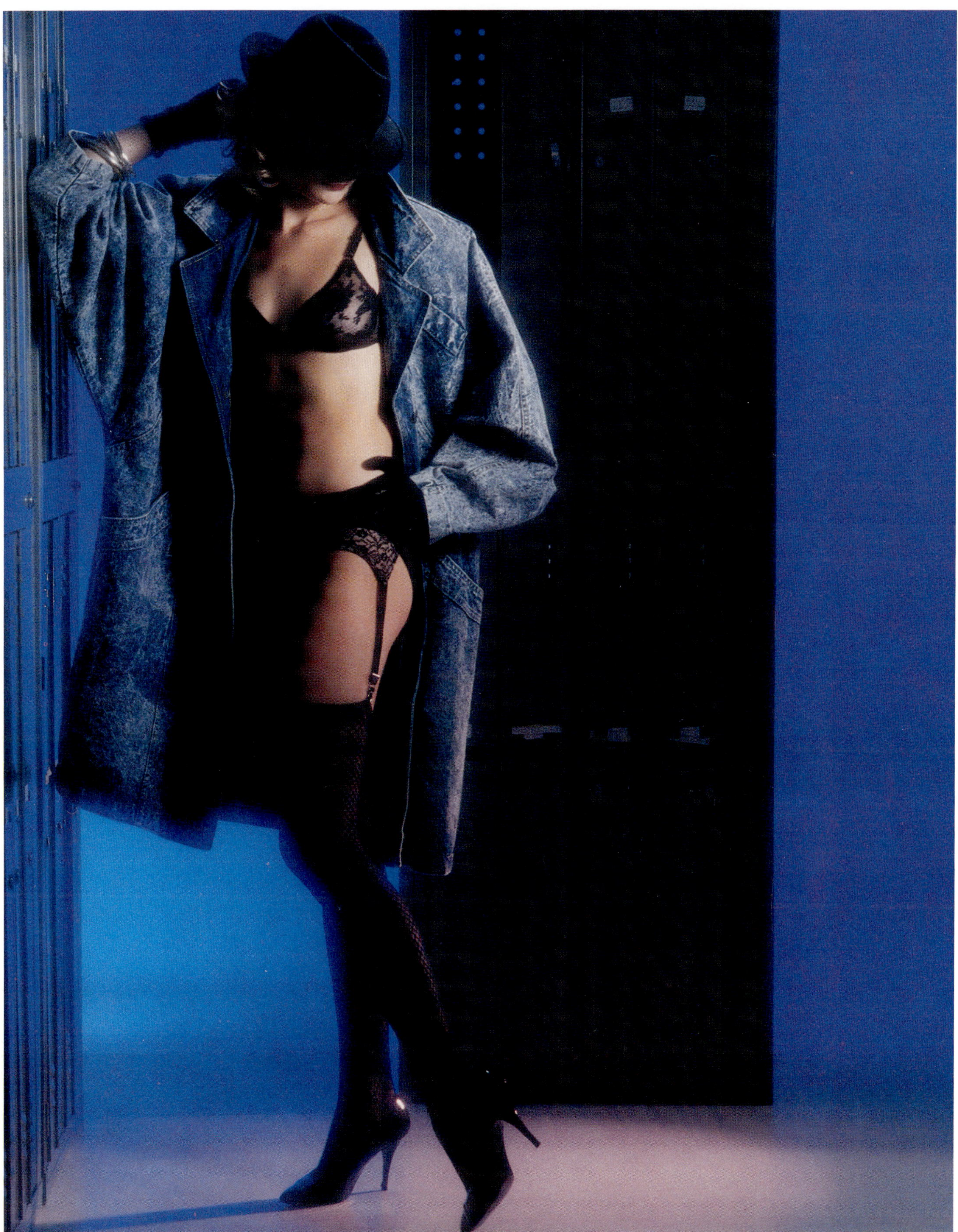

JAMES BOND SCENARIO

For years, men and women alike have admired the movie hero, James Bond. Not only have men related to the "Agent 007" image, but so have women. Women think of "007" as having encounters with sultry femmes fatales and, openly or secretly, desire to have their spouse or special someone think of them as such. With this thought in mind, we created a special "007" setting for our boudoir subjects.

The images that follow are but a few examples of the possibilities offered by the James Bond theme. With simple props, such as a trench coat, gun, red light and some fog, the pictorial possibilities are fabulous.

You may encounter some problems when you want to use fog. First, to rent a fog machine will cost about $50 to $60 per day plus the cost of the fog fluid. To help defray this cost, we suggest you schedule a number of boudoir sittings at which fog is to be used for the same date. If you're doing boudoir photography commercially, you may wish to charge extra for this service.

Our studio owns a fog machine. It is a Rosco Model 8211 and cost about $600.

A second problem with fog is its unpredictability. In each shot you'll get a different pictorial result. The fog will quickly wander and spread over the entire shooting area. To minimize this problem, turn off the air conditioner or fan while you're using the fog.

Because fog tends to produce a soft visual effect, you will generally not need to use a soft-focus filter when using a fog machine.

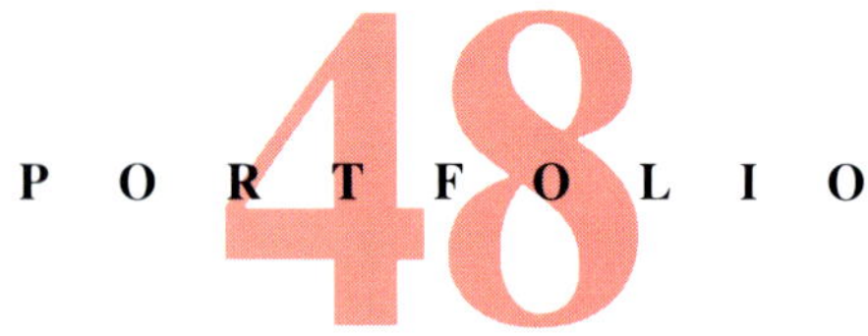

In this photo, the subject received most of her illumination from a top light, high and slightly behind her and in a 6-inch bowl reflector, connected to a 1200-watt-second power source. This was the main light. A Balcar Opalite, with its power adjusted to one full *f*-stop less than the main light, acted as fill light.

The background became pale in tone due to the fog invading that area. We feel that the pose, the gun, the trench coat, the red color on the background and the subject's costume all worked well together to make this a strong and sensuous image.

The background light, also in a 6-inch bowl reflector, was placed low and behind the subject. Its power was adjusted to emit one full *f*-stop less light than the main light. It was covered with a red gel.

A fourth light, with a 4-inch snoot, was placed low and about 90 degrees to the left of camera-subject axis. It was directed onto the fog. Its power was adjusted to equal that of the main light.

A 3x4-foot plastic mirror was placed to the left of camera-subject axis to get additional light on the subject and to add highlights to the gun.

A medium telephoto lens was used and exposure was at *f*-8.

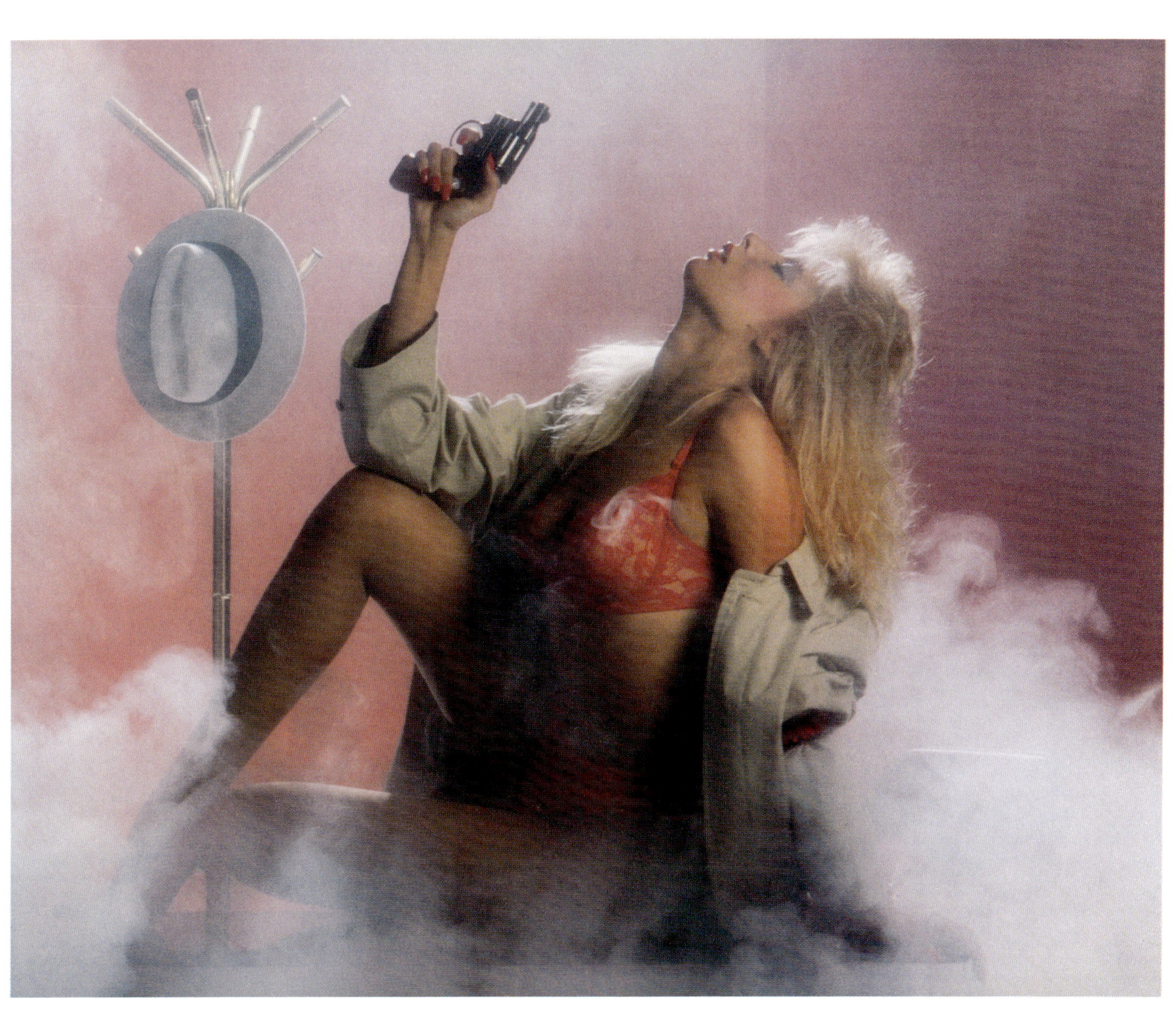

49 PORTFOLIO

With the basic James Bond set in place, we can take several very different shots while making only minor changes.

We used the same number of lights, in the same positions, as for the preceding photo. However, the Opalite's power was balanced to equal that of the top light. Because the subject was facing the camera, the Opalite now became the main light. Because its power had been increased, the Opalite gave more illumination to the subject's body. The top light now acted as a strong hair and rim light. The other two lights—the background light and accent light for the fog—remained at the same power setting as before.

Although the same background illumination was used as in the previous shot, the background appears to be a deeper tone. This is because less of the fog invaded that area.

A medium telephoto lens was used. Exposure was at *f*-8.

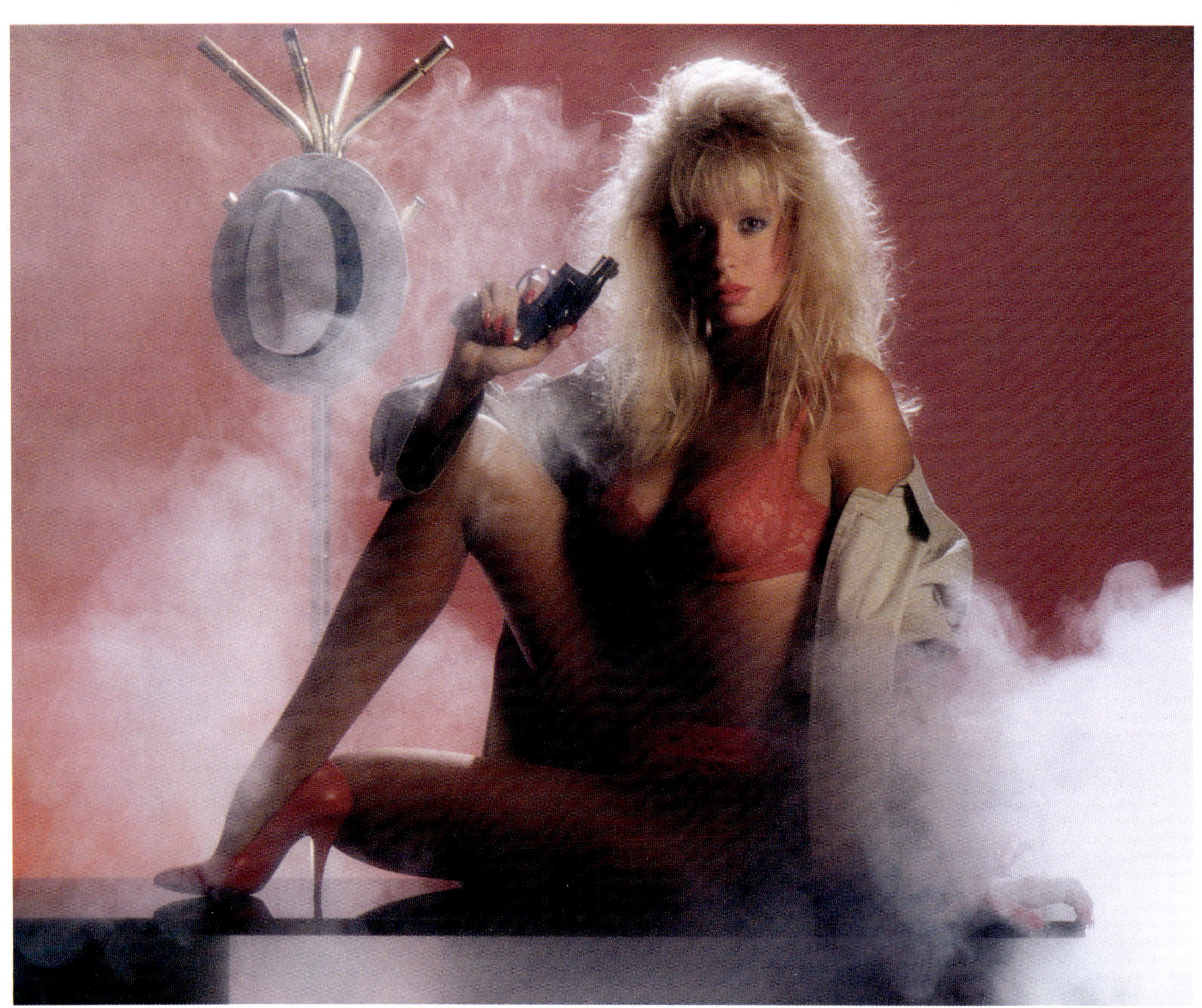

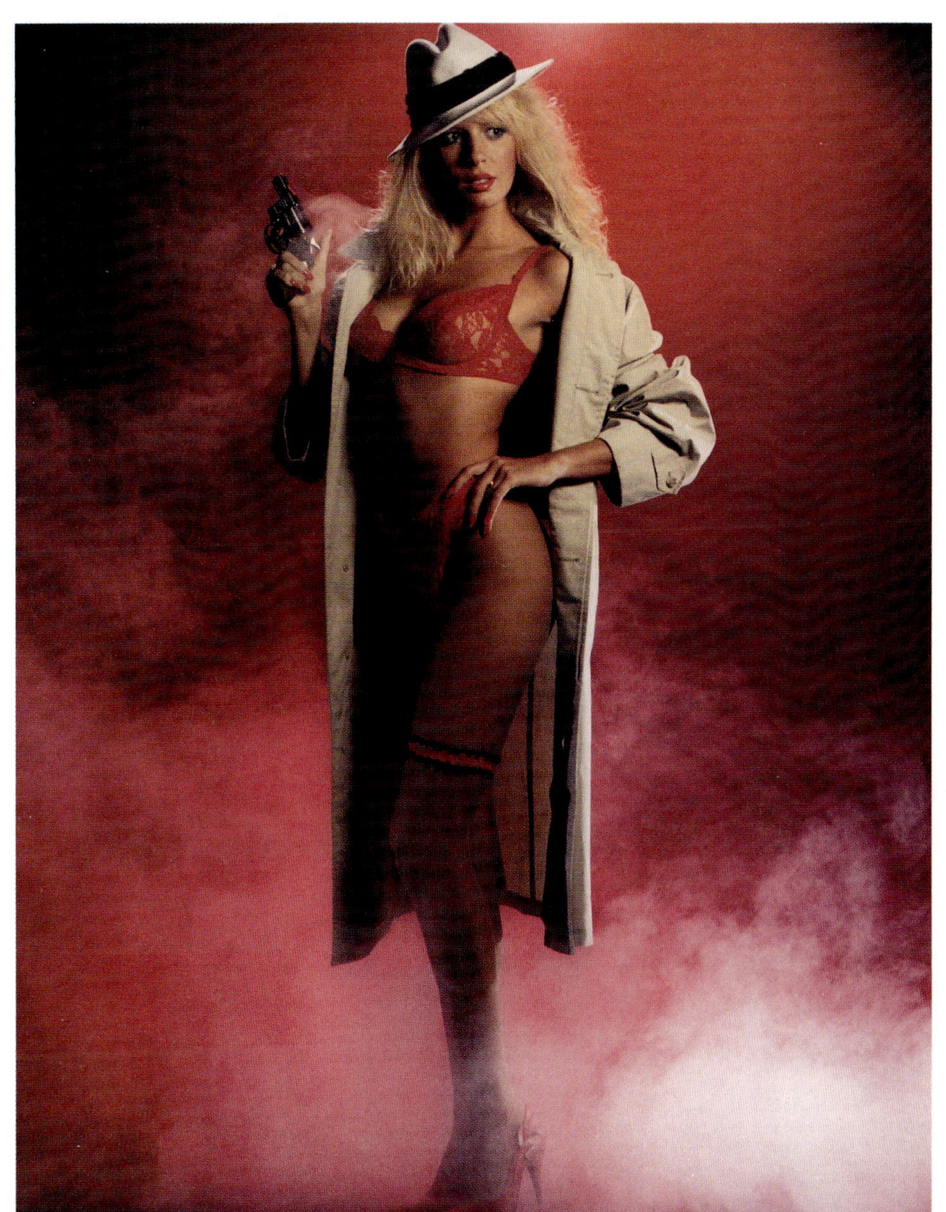

PORTFOLIO 50

This variation of the "007" theme required the use of only three lights. A Balcar Opalite, with a 20-degree grid spot and plastic diffuser cap, positioned at about 45 degrees to the right of camera-subject axis, acted as main light. It was connected to a 2400-watt-second power pack.

A second light, in a 6-inch bowl reflector, with a red gel on it, was placed low, behind and to the side of the subject and directed onto the plain background. Its power was adjusted to emit one full *f*-stop less light than the main light.

A third light, with a 4-inch snoot on it and connected to a 1200-watt-second power pack, was positioned low, slightly in front of the subject and approximately 90 degrees to the right of camera-subject axis. This light illuminated a portion of the fog. Its power was adjusted to equal that of the main light.

The setup and lighting for a photo such as this are simple to create. However, there are a number of variables that can affect a subject's look: the density of the fog surrounding her, the tilt of her head, the direction of her gaze and her leg position. To guarantee capturing the "right" look, several frames of film should be shot. To get this photo, we exposed more than 30 frames of film.

We used a medium telephoto lens. Exposure was at *f*-11.

PORTFOLIO 51

If the opportunity presents itself, involve a subject's husband or boyfriend in the boudoir session.

In this case, we had previously taken several boudoir images of the subject's wife. When the couple subsequently learned of our "007" concept, they both wanted to be photographed in this setting.

Although most of the shots taken for this couple depicted both of their faces, toward session's end we decided to become more bold. The result was this stunning and different image of the husband and his wife's beautiful legs. The couple loved it.

The Opalite was again used as main light, but with a 10-degree grid spot and a plastic diffuser cap. The light was connected to a 2400-watt-second power pack and placed to the right of camera-subject axis. A back light, in a 6-inch bowl reflector, was positioned high and slightly behind the subjects. Its power was adjusted to equal the main light. A third light, also in a 6-inch bowl reflector, was positioned low, behind the subjects, and covered with a blue gel. It was directed onto a white background. Its power was adjusted to emit one-half the power of the main light.

A medium telephoto lens was used and exposure was at *f*-8.

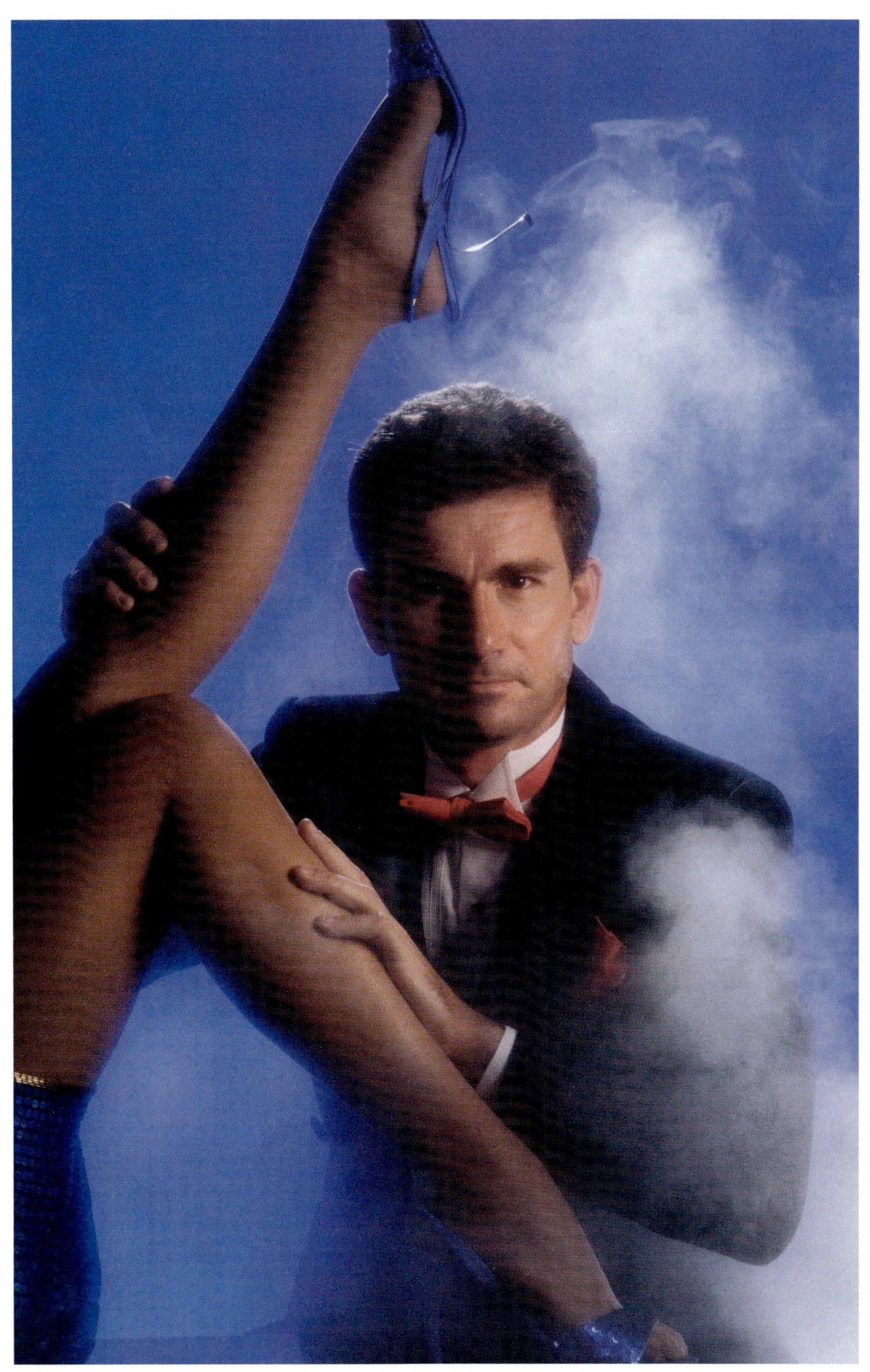

SILHOUETTES

The silhouette is one of our more popular studio boudoir techniques. It is simple to set up and tear down, flatters most subjects, and produces very dramatic images.

The following three images are but a few examples of how the silhouette or near-silhouette can be used. With experimentation, you can create many variations of these images, to suit your taste.

We used a white background on all three of the following images but you could use blue, red, amber or any other light color that might suit the subject. The main goal is to create a strong, dramatic, graphic image in which the subject's unlit or partially lit figure stands out against a bright background.

The amount of space you have available in your shooting area will dictate the lens focal length you use. If you have limited space to work in—if the distance from the background to your camera is approximately 20 feet or less—you'll have to use a standard lens.

Other equipment and props needed for silhouette shots are a set of venetian blinds, two stands to hold the blinds in position, a block for the subject to pose upon, and two lights—one for each side of the background.

Our blinds are black, approximately 7-1/2 feet in width and 8 feet in height. Our posing block, which is also black, is approximately 24 inches wide, 12 inches tall, and 12 inches deep. If the block were smaller than this, the subject could overpower the block and she might appear too large. If the block were too large, it could become too prominent and too much of an obstacle, dwarfing the subject and preventing her from executing some of the poses comfortably.

The two lights that we use are each powered by a 2000-watt-second power pack and each is housed in a 40-inch silvered umbrella. The lights should be placed so that the main thrust of each strikes the approximate center of the background, which should be at least 6 to 8 feet from the subject. If the background were any closer than this, you would stand a chance of having the background illumination radiate onto the subject, thus degrading the image.

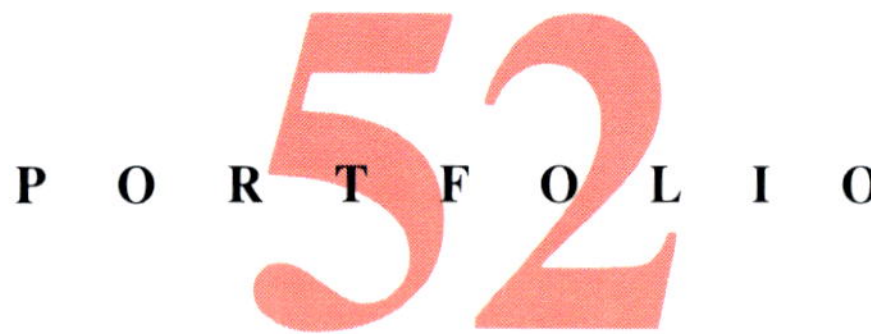

A standing silhouette can be a gorgeous image provided the subject's stomach, hip and thigh areas are not too heavy. If they are, they will often appear glaringly out of proportion in the final print.

When doing a standing shot, be certain that the subject's face and body are turned into a profile position in relationship to the camera-subject axis. If you don't do this, the final image will merely show a mass of black against a white background, with no discernible outline of the subject's body.

To prevent the standing pose from becoming a static image, have the subject bend at least one leg and one arm and have the subject wear a see-through garment. The garment can add some design to the image as well as giving the subject a prop to work with, giving her something to do with her hands.

When you shoot through blinds, they should be fully opened. The more the blinds are closed, the less light will be striking the film and the darker the background—and therefore the entire image—will appear.

For this photo, a medium telephoto lens was used. Exposure was at *f*-16.

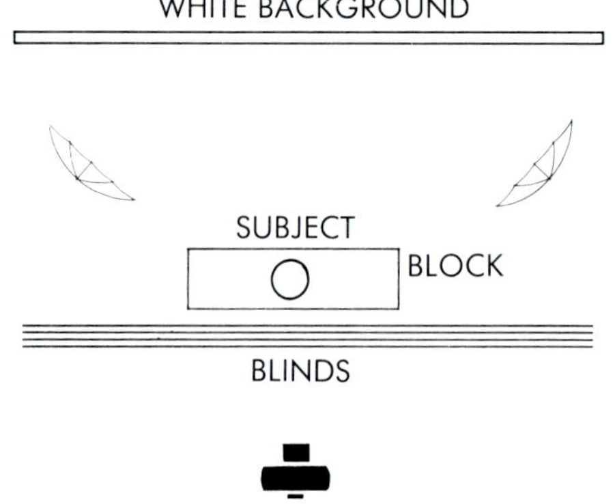

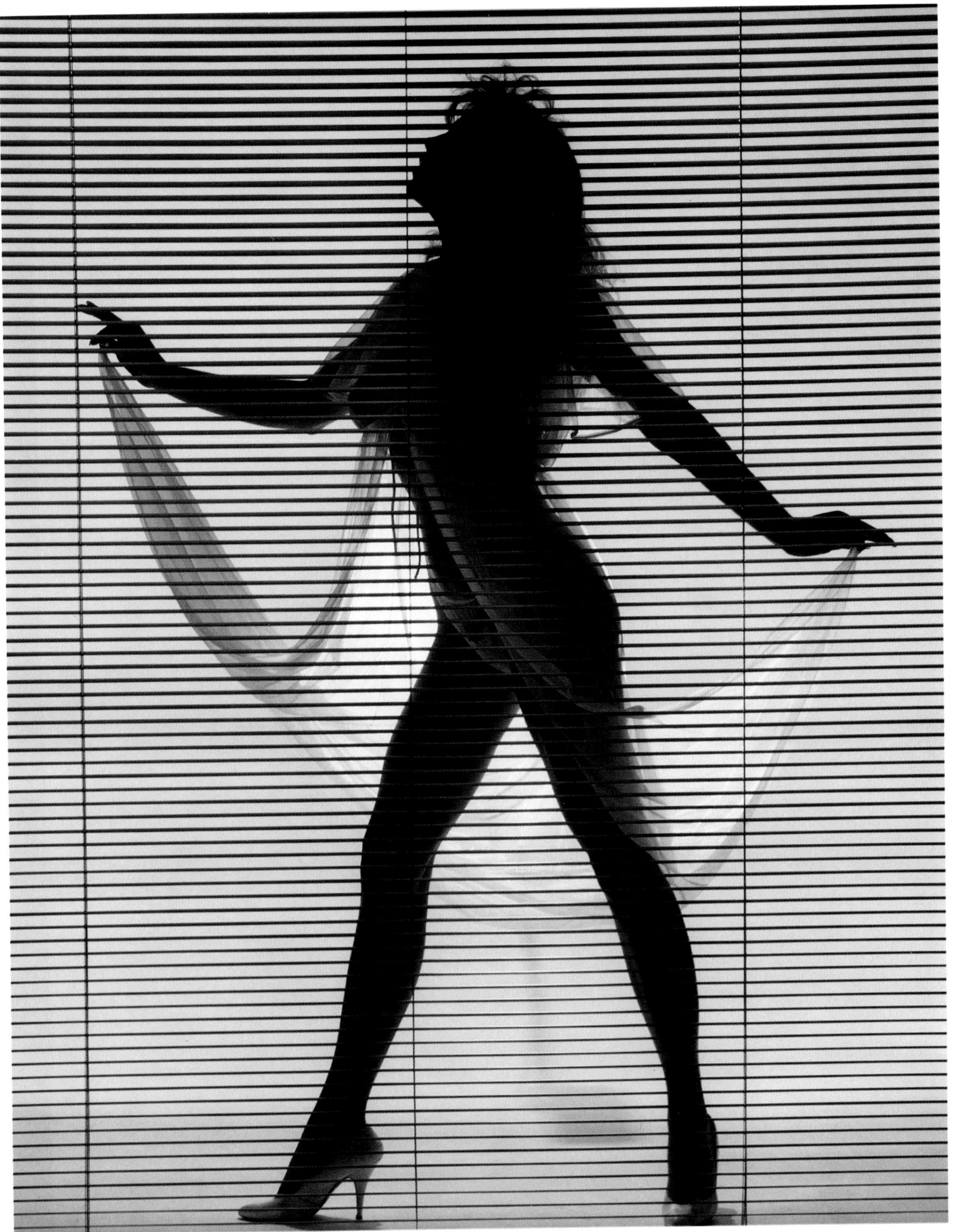

PORTFOLIO 53

When attempting to shoot a silhouette such as this one, you must consider two important factors: The subject's apparel and the pose. A subject really has only two choices, when it comes to what to wear: a full body stocking or nothing at all. If a subject were to wear something else, such as a standard leotard, bathing suit, shorts with halter top or similar outfit, you would see the outline of the garment and its tight fit around the upper thigh, the upper arm, and the chest area in the final print. It would not look or photograph well.

Since the object of the silhouette is to capture a graphic outline of the subject's body, you must have poses that will clearly outline the figure. A standing shot of a subject facing the camera head-on will not work. Too much information will be lost. There will be no bust or buttock outline and no facial features will be displayed. Turning the body and face to the side, into a profile or near-profile position, works best.

We call the pose in this photo the back-bend pose. It is a very flattering pose for most women, even those who may have a bit too much weight around their tummies. It is a stretching pose and thins out the body very effectively. Allowing the head to fall back also eliminates any problems a woman might have with a double chin. Although this pose has great advantages, not all women will be able to adopt it. It is a difficult pose, so be prepared with alternative poses.

We made this photo with a medium telephoto lens. Exposure was at *f*-16.

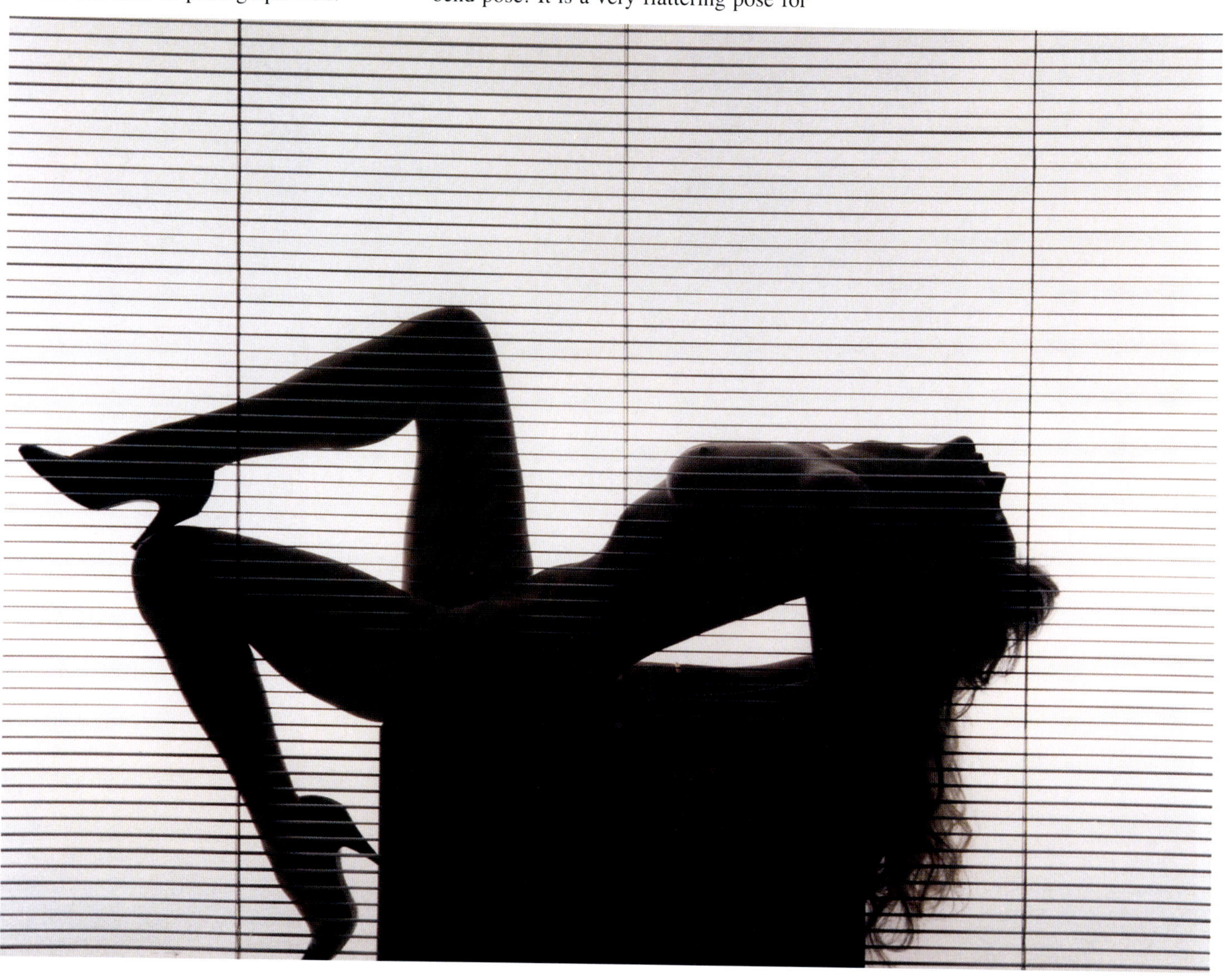

PORTFOLIO 54

This pose, which we call the cat pose, can be stunning. As with Photo 53, this is a difficult pose that will not work well with all women, especially those who might have a large stomach. Because it is such a difficult pose, it will require advance demonstration as well as assistance in getting a subject into the position.

The legs of the subject must be separated sufficiently for the viewer to distinctly see two legs. The chin of the subject should be raised to reduce or eliminate any possible problems a subject might have with a double chin. The subject's back should be arched in order to make the pose look feminine as well as a little animalistic.

For a silhouette shot, proper lighting is essential. With both of the background lights on, a meter reading should be taken of the light coming from the background. A second meter reading should be taken at the subject's position. For this second reading, the dome of the incident meter should be facing the camera and not the background.

There should be at least a five *f*-stop differential between these two light measurements to get an effective silhouette. The less differential you have between these two readings, the more detail you will see in the subject's body and the less of a silhouette you will have.

A medium telephoto lens was used, and exposure was at *f*-16.

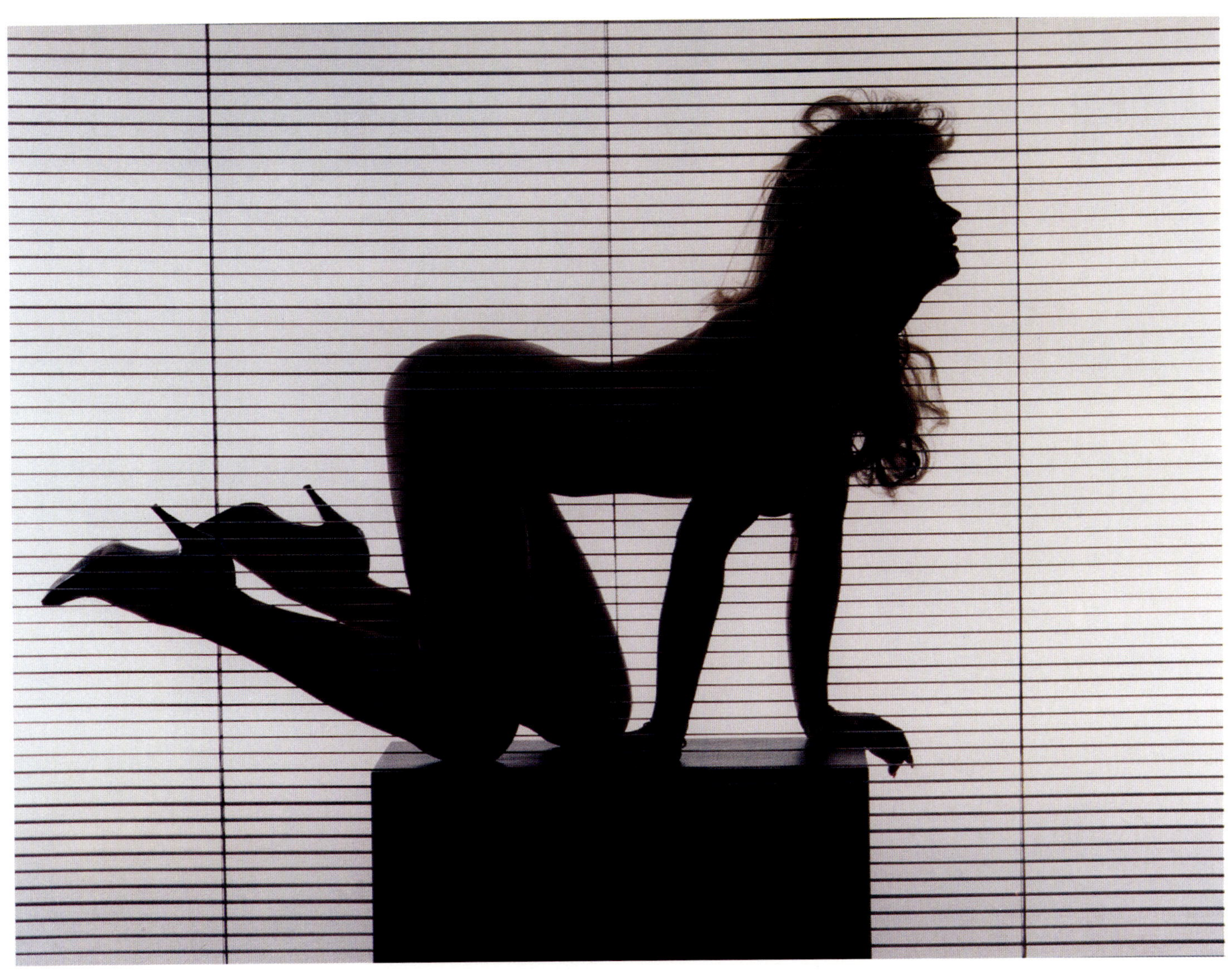

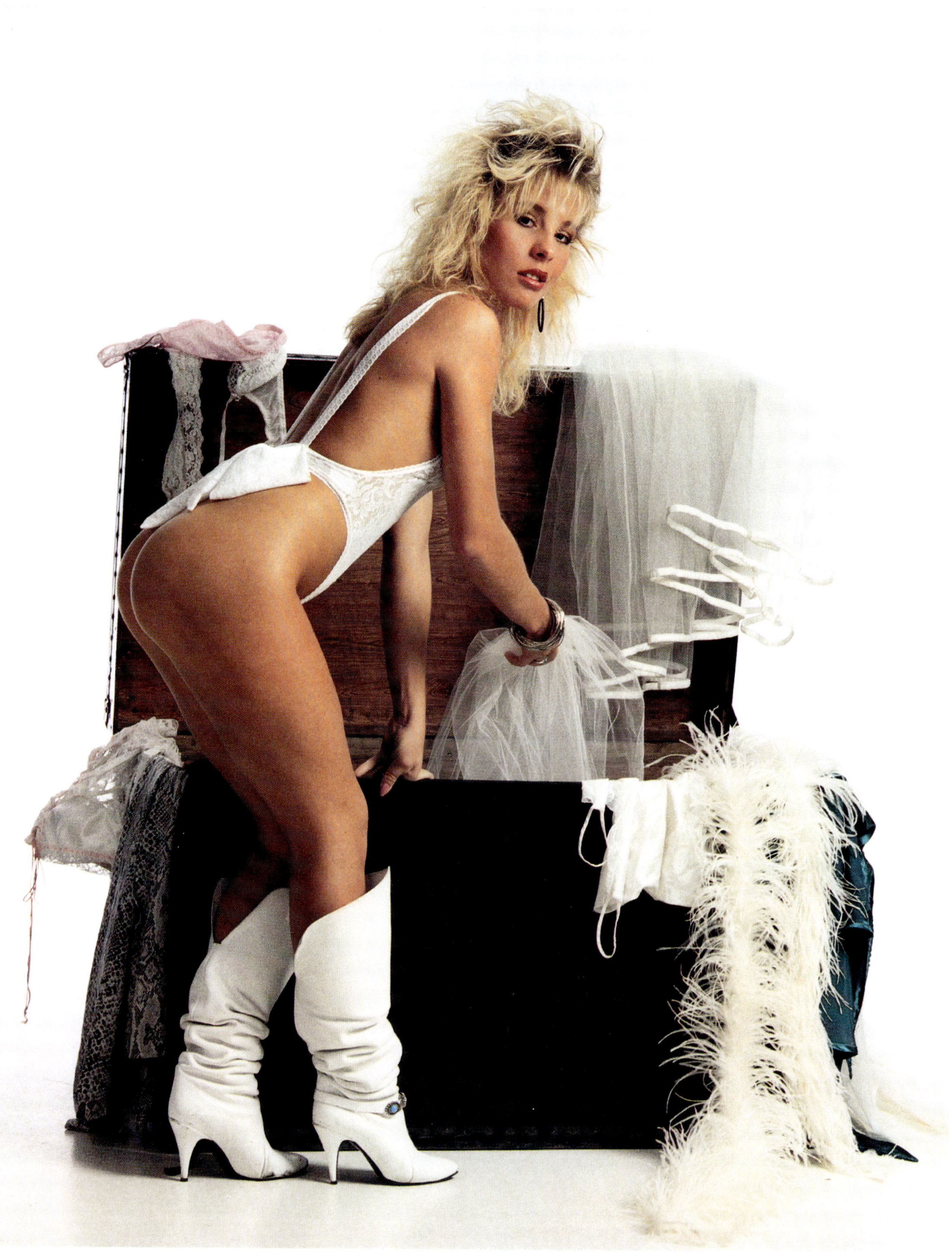

SIMPLE THEMES

There will be times and reasons when you will not use an elaborate setting for a boudoir subject. Some subjects may not identify with the sets that you have. Others may not like the idea of using an elaborate, full set and want to keep the session simple. They may want more photographic emphasis placed on their bodies.

Others may have a special idea that they wish to convey or a costume that they want to feature prominently. Some of these demands may not lend themselves to any set you may have.

You can have a very successful session with no set at all, using only simple props and a little imagination and creativity.

The next three photos answer very eloquently the simple question, "Can different looks be easily achieved with very simple propping?" The possibilities are almost limitless.

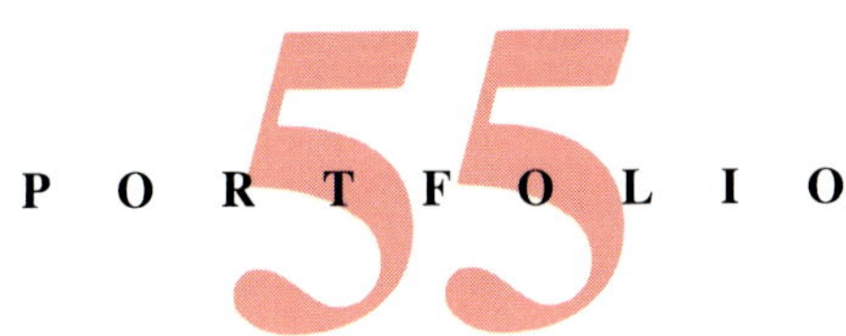

The boudoir photographer can achieve a lot with a simple prop such as a steamer trunk and a few frilly accessories. This photo and the two that follow are but a few examples.

You can arrange the lighting so that you can easily make changes in subject position without the need for major moves of the lights. You can also achieve more complex changes by adding or removing lights, changing from high-key to low-key, adding colored gels to lights, introducing a new prop, and so on. Even when drastic changes are sought, they can be accomplished with minimal effort and delay because the basic setting is so simple.

A 3-foot, silver-lined umbrella, connected to a 2400-watt-second power source, was used as main light. It was placed about 45 degrees to the right of camera-subject axis. A second light, in a 3x4-foot softbox, was placed about 20 degrees to the left of camera-subject axis. It was used as fill light, its power adjusted to emit two *f*-stops less light than the main light.

Two background lights were used—one on either side of the subject—each housed in a 3-foot, silver-lined umbrella. Their power was adjusted to emit two *f*-stops more light than the main light.

In this and the following two photos, lighting on the trunk was intentionally low-key. We wanted the emphasis on the subject.

The pose and outfit were selected to emphasize the subject's buttocks. We directed her to turn her face toward the camera. Eye contact with the camera—and viewer—keeps the image from having an undesirable "voyeuristic" quality.

PORTFOLIO 56

For this photo, only the pose was changed. In all other respects, the image is almost identical with the preceding one.

The subject was instructed to stand inside the trunk and turn so that her body would be in an approximate three-quarter position in relation to the camera-subject axis. With this pose, the illumination from the main light skimmed across the bustline, accentuating it and making it more full and sensuous in appearance.

To keep the waistline slim in appearance, we had the subject arch her back and, at the moment before exposure, tuck her tummy in.

Always select your lighting to suit the subject. High-key lighting is less forgiving than low-key lighting because it reveals everything that's visible at camera position. The shadows in low-key illumination can serve to hide undesirable areas. Don't allow a subject to persuade you to use lighting that you know will be less than flattering. You should be the expert in this area and you must convince your subject to trust you to do the most favorable thing.

In the case of this subject, overall illumination was fine because there was no need to hide parts that might appear less than flattering.

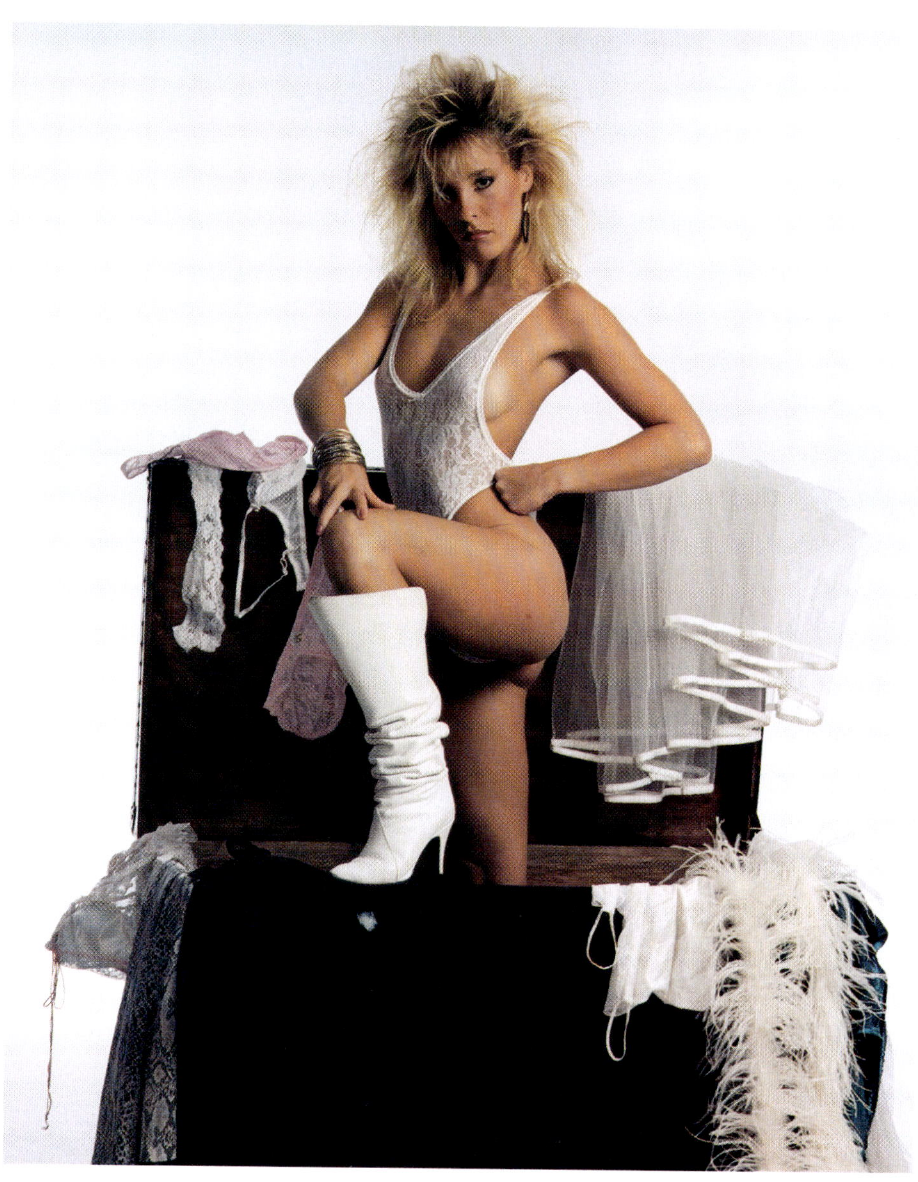

PORTFOLIO 57

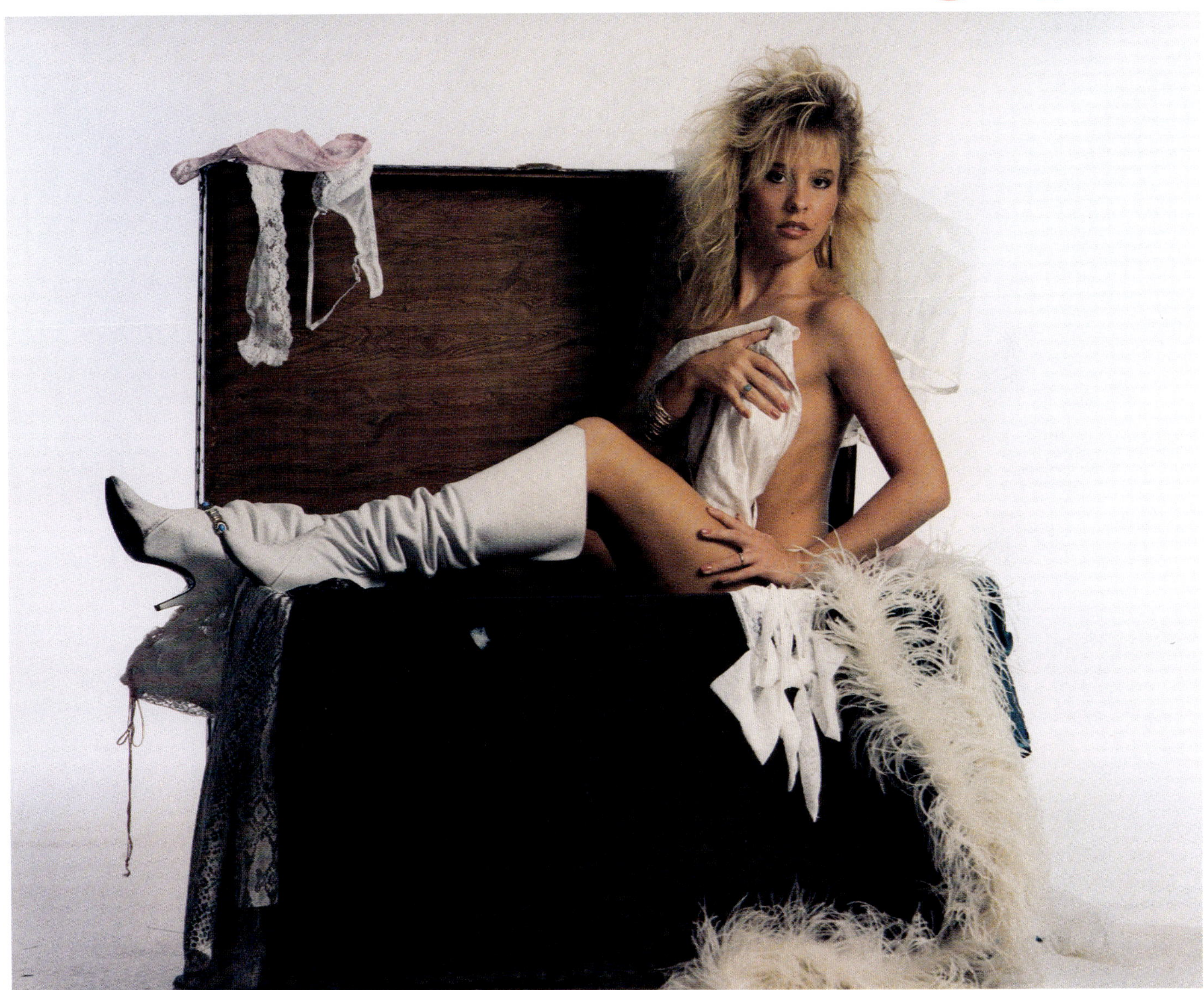

In this photo, again, only the pose was changed. The lighting remained the same as in the previous two photos.

To give emphasis to the subject's legs and to give a suggestion of nudity, the subject was seated inside the trunk. The trunk covered the lower portion of her body. To prevent her from being too deep inside the trunk, the subject was seated on several boxes. She was raised just to the point where the shorts she was wearing would not show.

When seated in this position, a small crease appeared around the waist area. To eliminate this problem and also put more emphasis on her chest, the subject was instructed to lean slightly backwards and then stretch.

When a subject is being photographed in an elaborate setting, she can often exhibit a less than perfect facial expression or body language and still have a beautiful photo result. The elaborate setting will offer a visual "crutch" and often compensate for what the subject may be lacking. However, when the setting is simple, as it is in this photo, this luxury is not usually afforded. The subject, and she alone, is responsible for making or breaking the photographic results.

PORTFOLIO 58

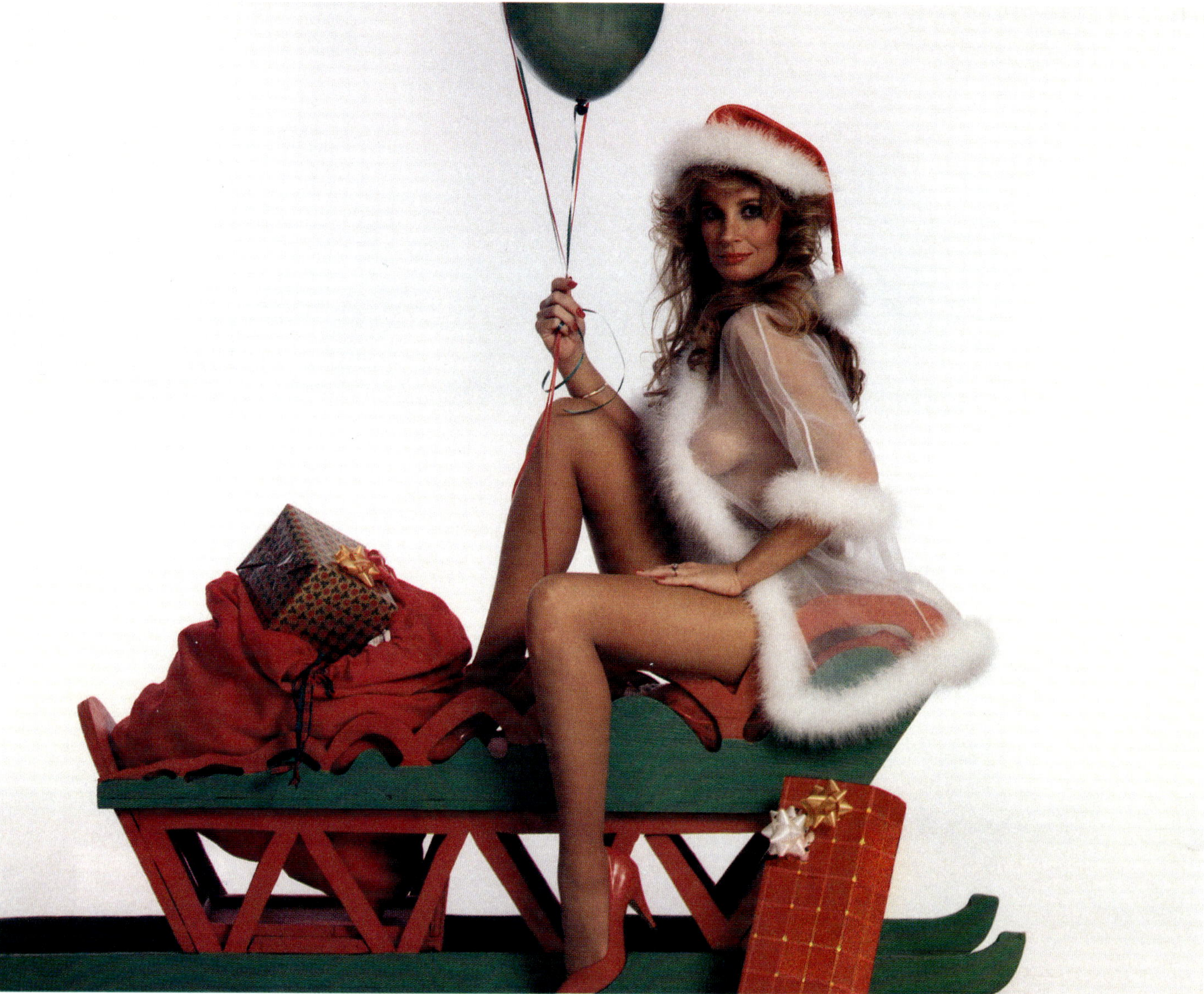

When a subject wants a photo created for a special day or season, such as Christmas, a simple setting often works best. A simple prop can be effectively symbolic and offer many varied photographic possibilities.

For this photo, we had the subject assume a pose that was somewhat guarded. Much of the subject's body was hidden from the camera's view, and yet there is still a strong suggestion of nudity and sensuality.

The subject was instructed to raise her left heel to make the leg look more shapely. Her left hand was carefully positioned to hide the pantyhose top and shorts she was wearing.

A flash in a 40-inch white-lined umbrella was used as main light. It was placed approximately 40 degrees to the right of camera-subject axis and connected to a 1200-watt-second power source. A 3x4-foot softbox was used as fill light, placed approximately 20 degrees to the left of camera-subject axis. Its power was adjusted to emit one *f*-stop less light than the main light.

Two additional lights were used as background lights, each housed in a 3-foot silver-lined umbrella. They were placed on either side of the white background material. Their power was adjusted to two *f*-stops more light than the main light.

PORTFOLIO 59

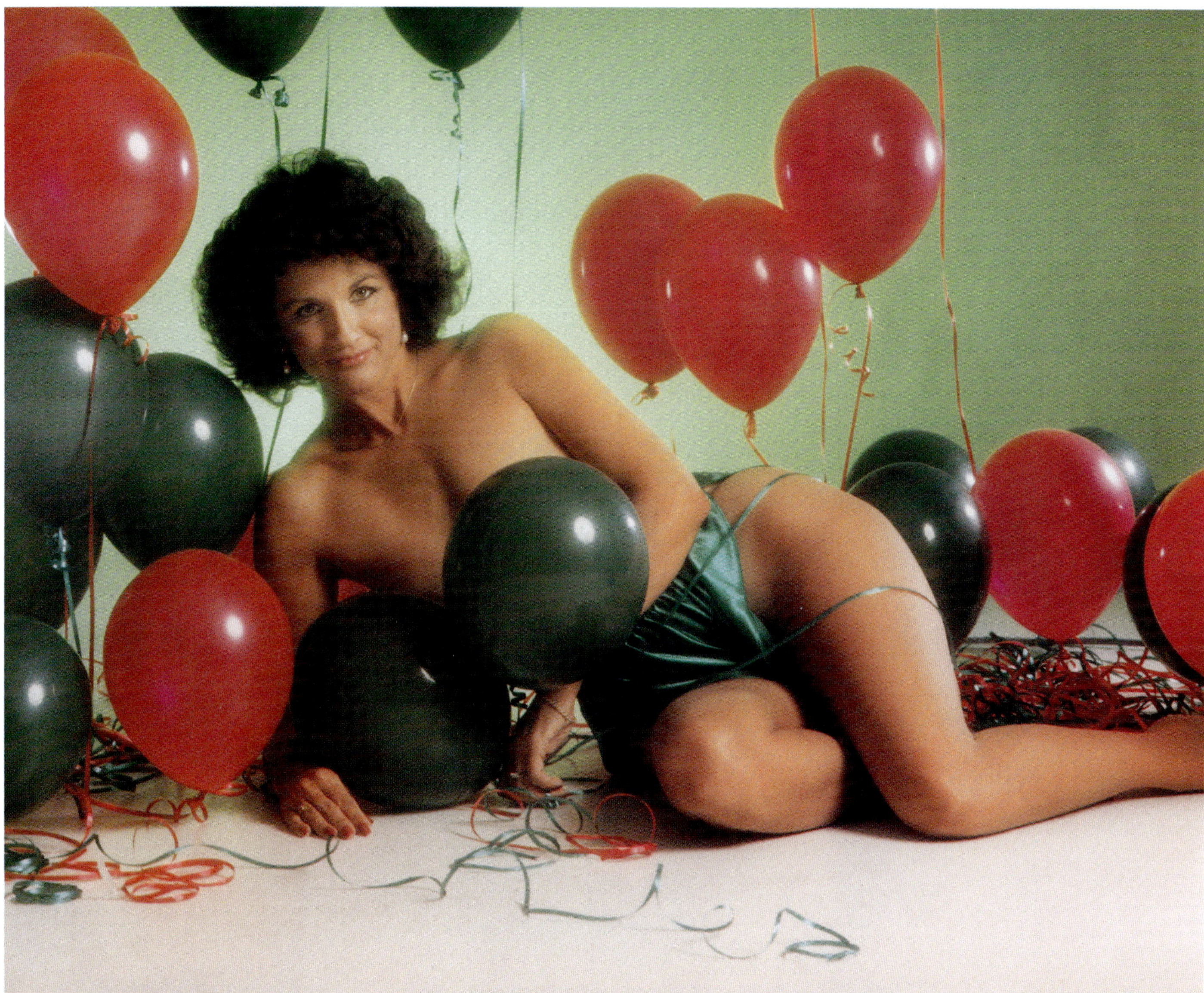

Competent photographers use equipment, accessories and props that they know will give consistent results again and again. However, there are times when an item will be used—such as fog—where the results will vary each time it is used. Working with balloons is similar.

A balloon from one manufacturer may not be the same as one from another. Not only can the colors vary, but the density or thickness of the material can vary as well.

When using balloons in a photo scene, they should all be of the same kind, from the same manufacturer. If they are not, you could end up with a photo where the lighting and color looks good for some of the balloons and not for others.

This subject wanted a fun, party-type theme but not an elaborate setting. The balloons were used to accomplish this result and the colors were chosen to complement the subject's costume.

The lighting was simple. A Balcar Opalite, with a 20-degree grid spot and plastic diffuser cap, was used as main light. It was 40 degrees to the right of camera-subject axis.

A plastic mirror was placed to the left of camera-subject axis. It acted as a fill reflector. A background light, in a 5-inch bowl reflector and with a green gel, was placed behind the subject and directed onto the white background.

AT THE BEACH

Doing boudoir photography at the beach can be a lot of fun, but there are several important things to remember.

First, a subject's makeup and hairstyle will not stay fresh for long. The wind, sand and sea spray will all take their toll. Makeup must be freshened frequently and hair styled back into place, perhaps a dozen or more times during a session.

Secondly, you will need to scout and select your shooting location well in advance of any session. On the day of an actual shoot, you cannot afford to waste time driving to some general area and looking around for the "just right" spot. By the time you find the ideal location, the light may have changed, the beach become crowded, or your subject may have become tired or disenchanted.

Beach shots should be done very early in the morning or late in the afternoon, when the sun is low over the horizon. This is the best time for the "sweet light": The sunlight is warm and golden in color and softer in quality than at any other time of the day. This type of lighting is present for only a few minutes around dawn, and again at the time of sunset.

When we do early-morning beach shots, we and our subject usually arrive at our pre-selected location 45 to 60 minutes before dawn. This gives us time to set up our equipment, talk with the subject about where exactly we will be shooting, the poses we want, the clothing she will wear, make last-minute adjustments to her makeup and hair, and otherwise prepare her and our equipment for the shooting. By the time dawn breaks, we are set and ready to shoot and can immediately take advantage of the special early-morning light.

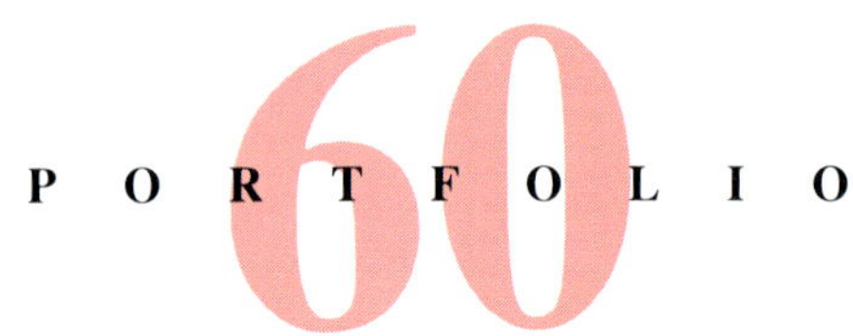

Although we prefer to do boudoir beach shots with a subject attired in a lacy, see-through dress or blouse, we have nothing against bathing suits, provided their design is sexy and they flatter a subject's figure.

In this and the following beach images, the sun was low, to the right of the camera-subject axis and to the far side of the subject.

When you do beach shots, you have several viable lighting options. We commonly use two techniques: shots where the daylight acts as main-light source and flash is used as a fill light, and shots where flash provides the main light and the ambient daylight is used as fill light.

This photo, and the beach shots that follow, demonstrate that dynamic location images can be taken using very little equipment and few props, provided the subject's costume, her pose and the lighting are strong enough to carry the image.

A battery-powered Multiblitz flash, with standard bowl reflector, was used as main light for this photo. It was placed to the right of camera-subject axis. A plastic, 2x4-foot mirror was put on the left of camera-subject axis to act as a weak fill light.

A medium telephoto lens was used, with a warming filter. Exposure was 1/15 second at *f*-8.

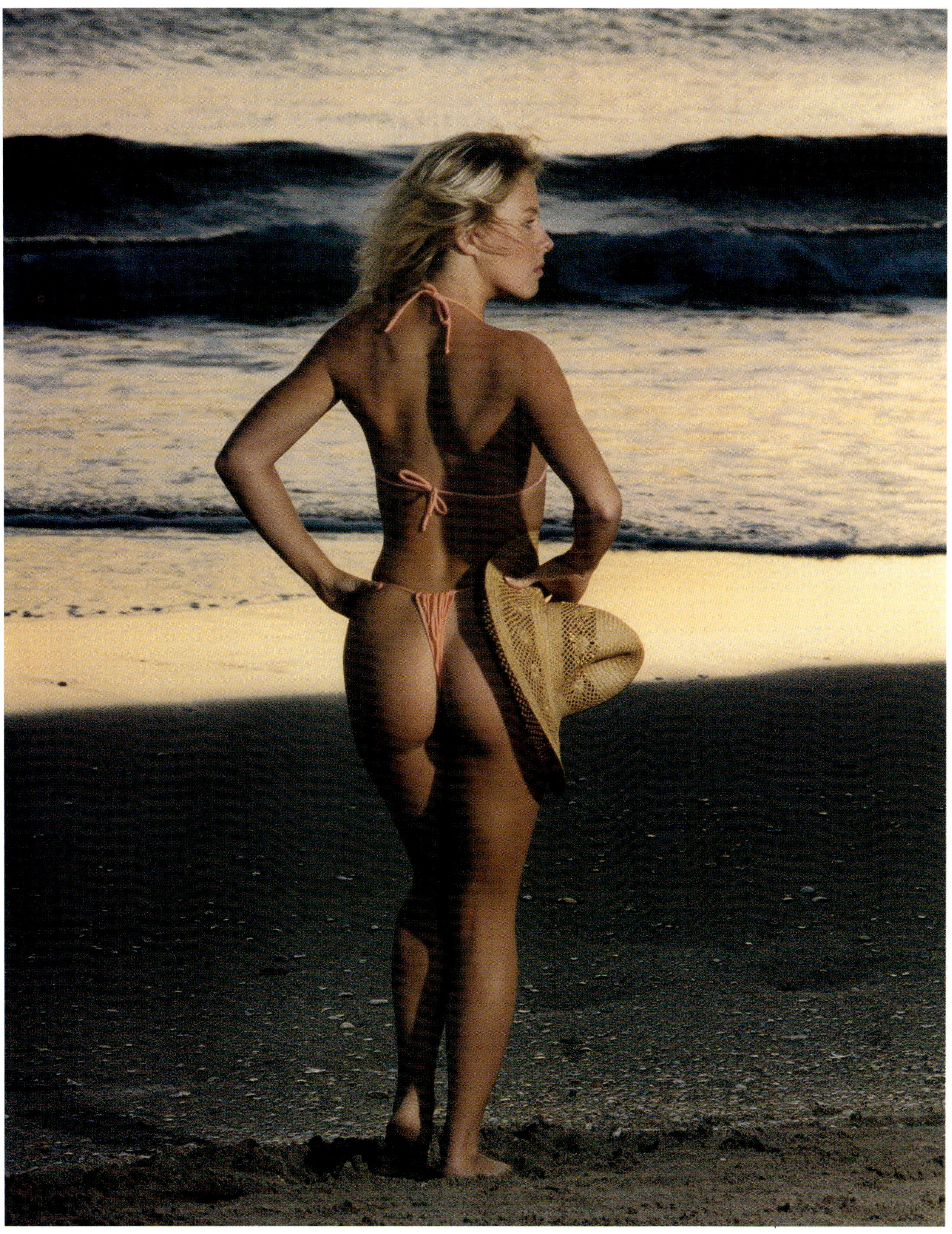

PORTFOLIO 61

Other than having the subject turn her body slightly, this photo is an exact duplication of Photo 60 in camera technique, lens employed and lighting.

We would have preferred a slightly different pose. Had the subject swiveled her upper torso more toward the camera and raised her more distant elbow, more of her chest area would have been shown. Also, some background would have been visible between the subject's right arm and her body—a compositional improvement. Although we attempted to accomplish this result, the subject "lost it" and we had to go on to other poses.

Never try to force a pose on a subject. Not all poses will work with all subjects. If you have made one or two attempts—especially when working with non-professional models—and a pose has not worked, abandon that pose and go on to others. This will help keep your subject's confidence and prevent her from becoming frustrated.

Several elements prevent this shot from being static: The subject's front leg is raised, giving some motion to the body. The placement of the hat on the ground, and the color of the light reflecting from sand and water, give "life" to the image.

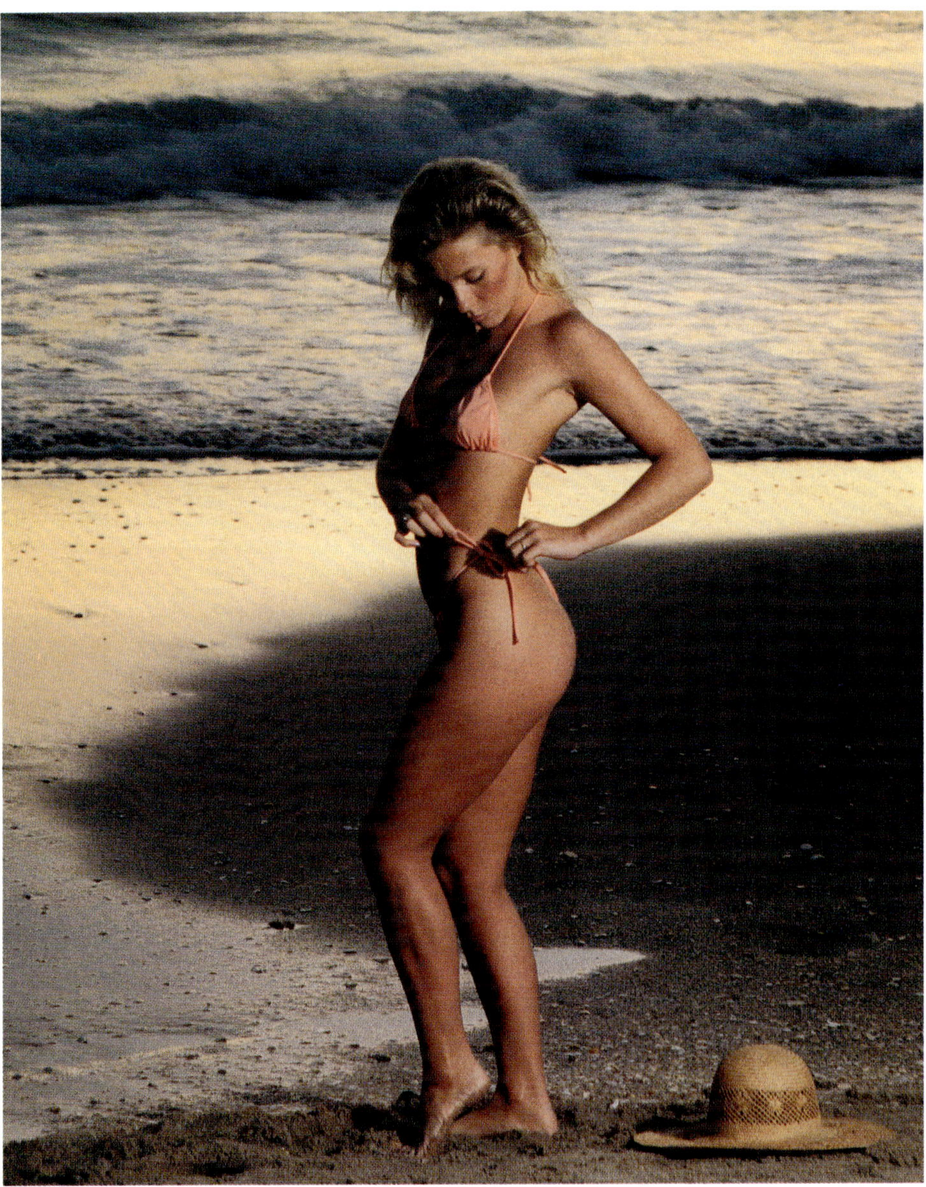

PORTFOLIO 62

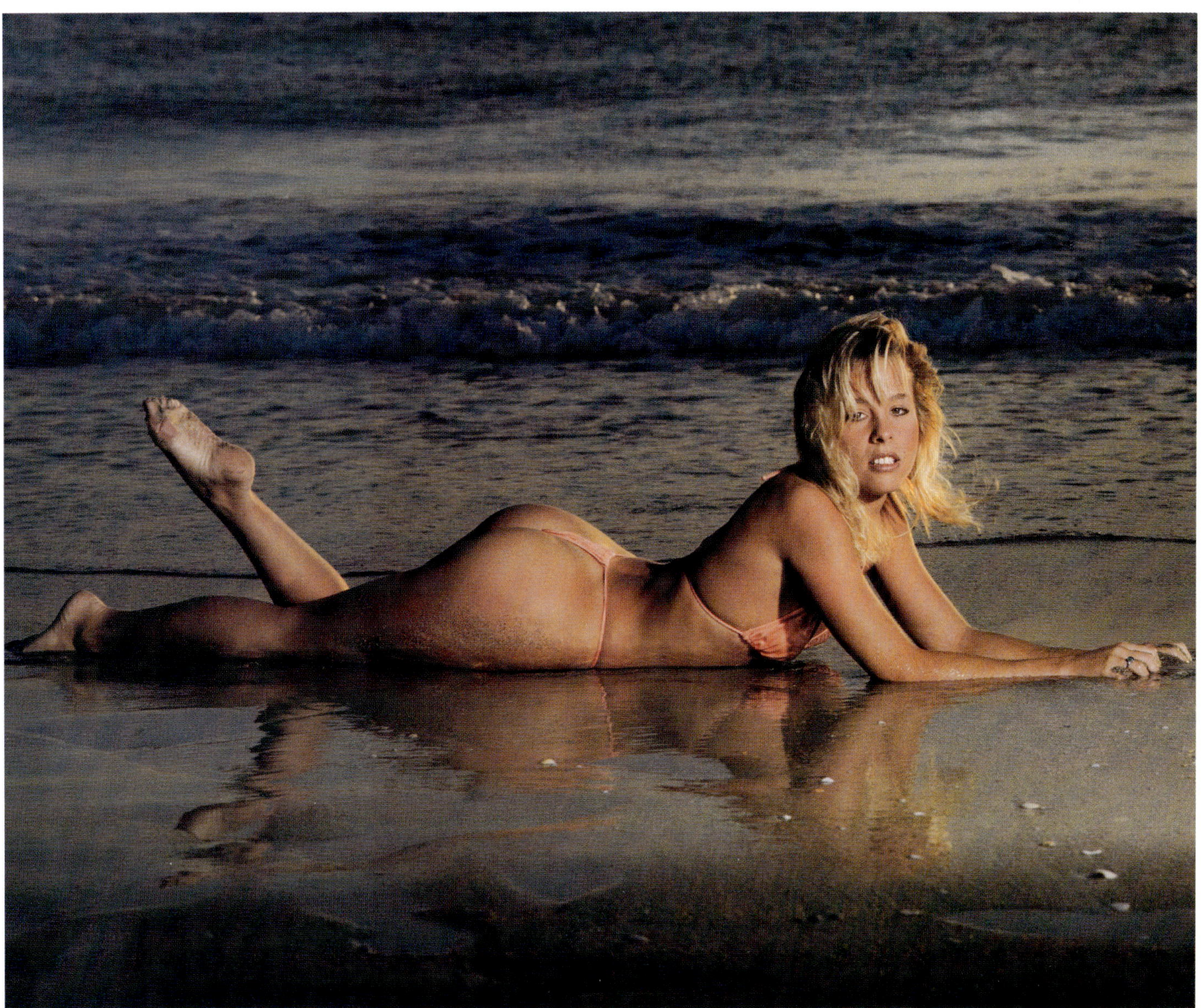

For this image, the battery-powered Multiblitz flash, with standard bowl reflector, acted as main-light source while the sunlight strongly rimmed the subject's body and hair from behind. Reflected light from the sand, and the skylight, provided fill lighting.

Timing for this photo was critical. In order to capture the reflection of the subject's body in the sand, we had to wait until the surf had rolled in and was just on its way back out before we took the shot. If we had waited too long, the sand would have absorbed the water and the reflection would have been lost. If we had acted too quickly, too much water would have covered the sand and the reflection would not have been as prominent and clearly defined.

Since there are only a few seconds within which to take such a shot, a subject must be placed into a basic pose in advance and then wait for the water to rise and fall. If you were to wait for the water to rise before posing the subject, the reflection would be lost before the subject was in the desired position.

A medium telephoto lens was used, with a warming filter. Exposure was 1/8 second at *f*-11.

PORTFOLIO 63

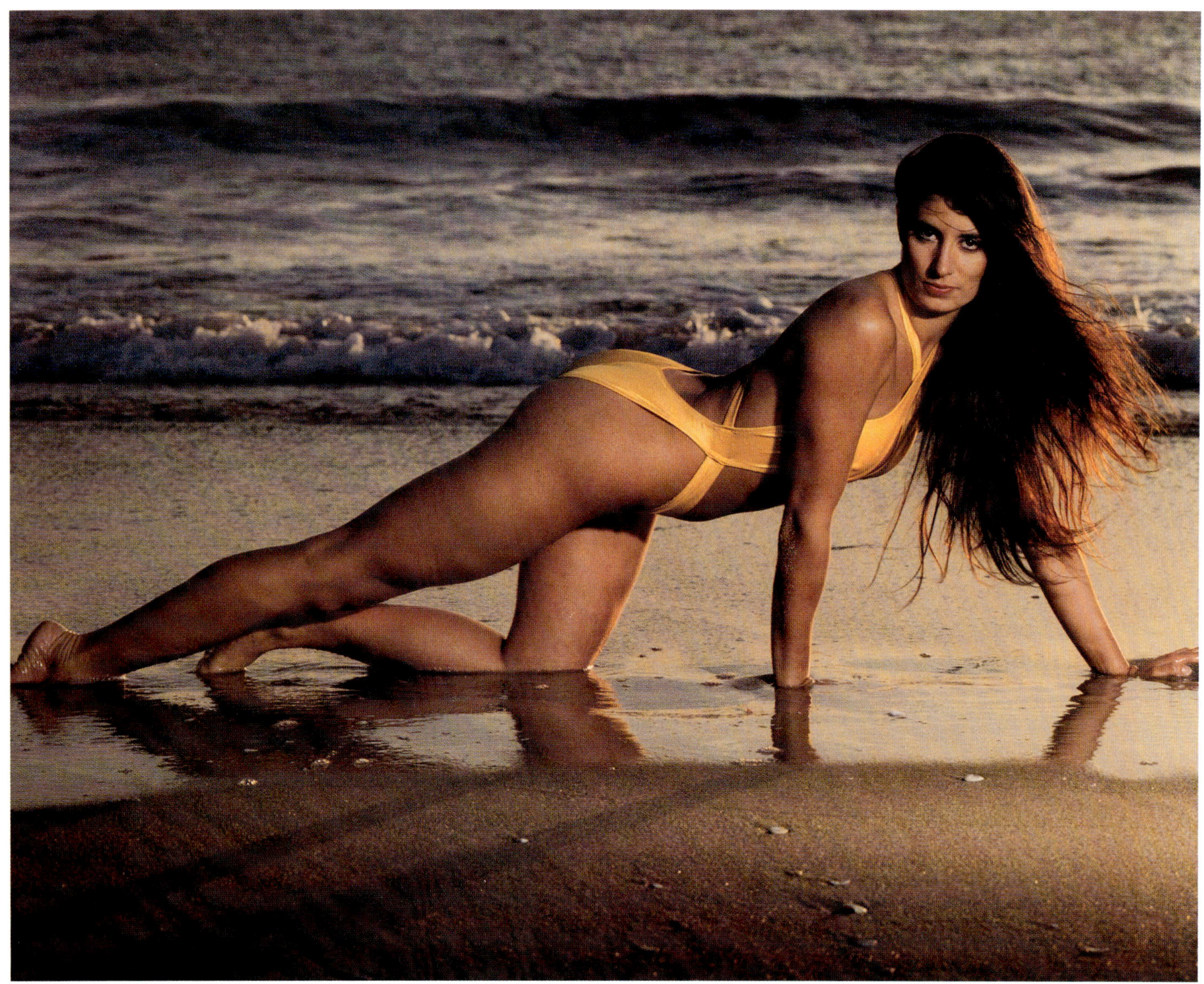

This is another example where the portable Multiblitz, with standard bowl reflector, was used as main light. The sunlight acted as rim light for the subject's body and hair. A plastic mirror was used to lighten some of the shadows on the subject's body.

Although subject and pose are both stunning, we would have liked to see a better reflection in the sand. In this case, the timing was just not right to record all elements perfectly. The subject was able to get into the pose we wanted, but not until after the sand had started to absorb most of the water and had dissipated most of the reflection. Notwithstanding, it's a lovely image.

When doing outdoor photography, especially at the beach, where there is nothing to shield your camera's lens from the sunlight, care must be exercised to avoid lens flare. Flare can seriously degrade an image through loss of color saturation and detail and a shift in the overall color balance. Always use a lens hood, or shield the camera lens effectively in some other way.

This photo was taken with a medium telephoto lens, and a warming filter. Exposure was 1/30 second at *f*-8.

PORTFOLIO 64

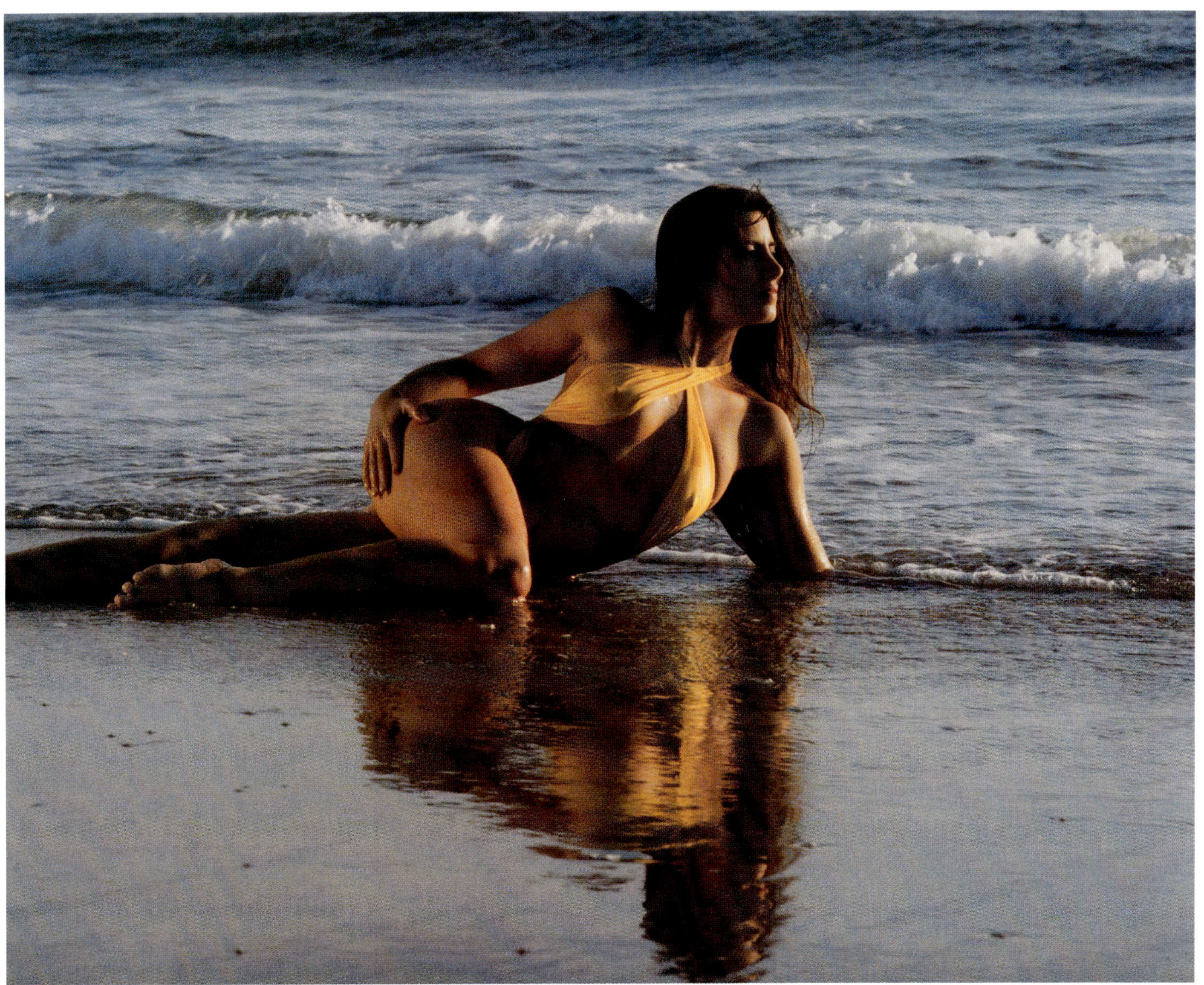

Unlike the previous beach shots, for which flash had been used, this one was executed solely by natural light. A 2x4-foot plastic mirror reflector was placed near the feet of the subject—to the left of camera-subject axis—to act as a fill light and to lower the contrast level of the image, in keeping with the latitude of the color-negative film we use. Exposure was based on the main light—the sunlight striking the subject.

We took meter readings of the highlight areas and shadow areas. With the use of fill light or reflectors, you can control these extremes to achieve the contrast level you desire.

The closer a reflector is moved toward a subject, the less contrast there will be between the highlight and shadow areas. The farther the reflector is moved from the subject, the more contrast there will be between these two areas and the more dramatic the image will appear. Which effect you choose will be based upon personal preference and style. You should experiment to see which effect you prefer.

PORTFOLIO 65

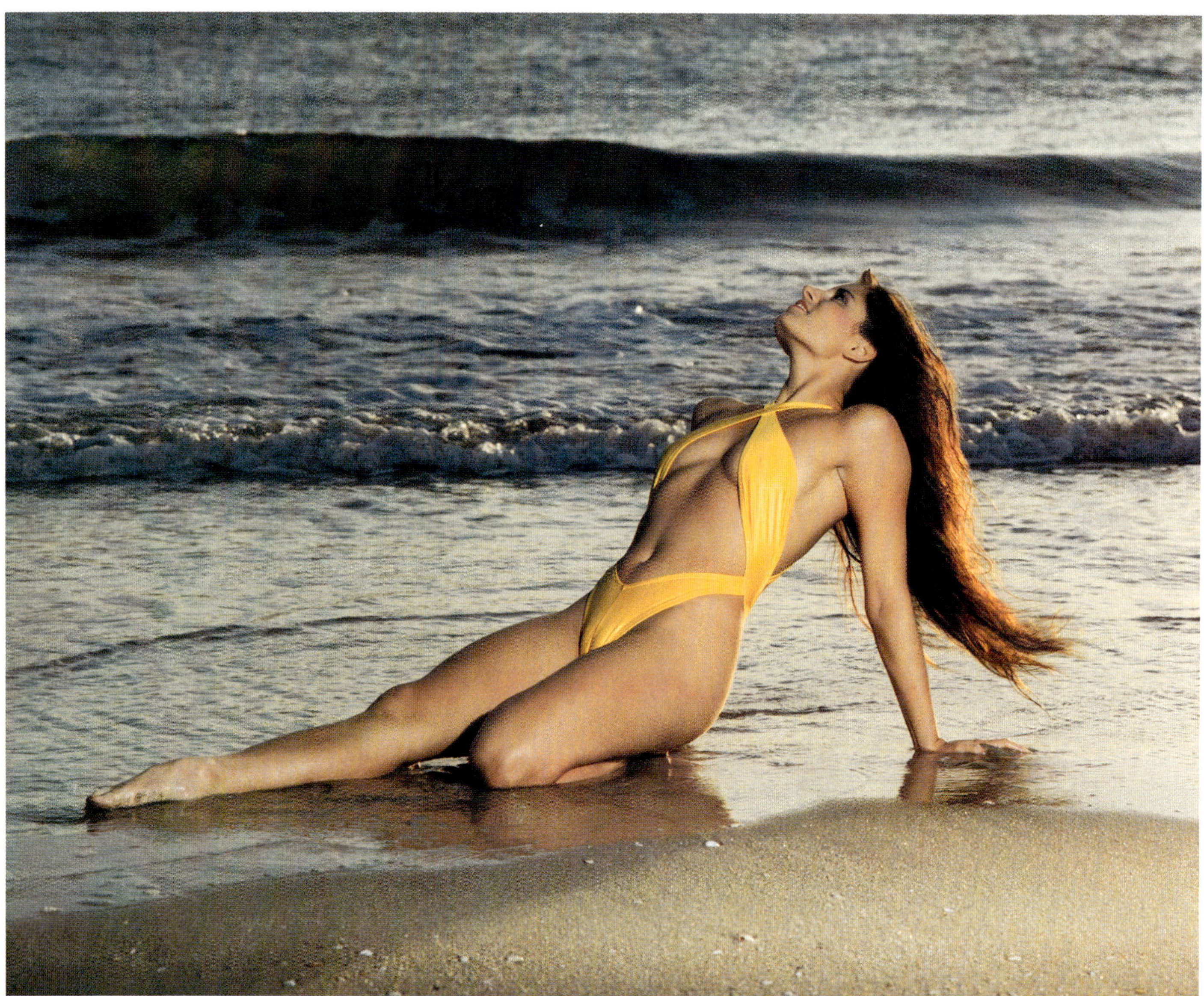

Totally natural light is great to work with provided it is not too flat. When the differential between highlight and shadow is one-half *f*-stop or less, we don't do natural light boudoir shots. We generally prefer higher contrast to our lighting.

At the time this photo was taken, the natural light was too flat for our taste, so the portable Multiblitz, with standard bowl reflector, was again used as main light source. It was placed to the right of camera-subject axis, with hazy sunlight providing the fill and rim light for the subject's hair and body.

Often a subject's costume can hide certain body imperfections—and most women have some—that show when you attempt certain boudoir poses. When a subject wears a tight-fitting bathing suit, you will not have the luxury of allowing the costume to hide certain body areas from view. Therefore, poses must be selected carefully so that both the subject and her outfit present well.

Placing a subject into a stretching pose, such as this one, elongates the body and reduces problems that might be present in a subject's waistline. The subject looks sensuous, and this is a pose most women will be able to execute easily.

A medium telephoto lens was used and exposure was 1/15 second at *f*-8.

PORTFOLIO 66

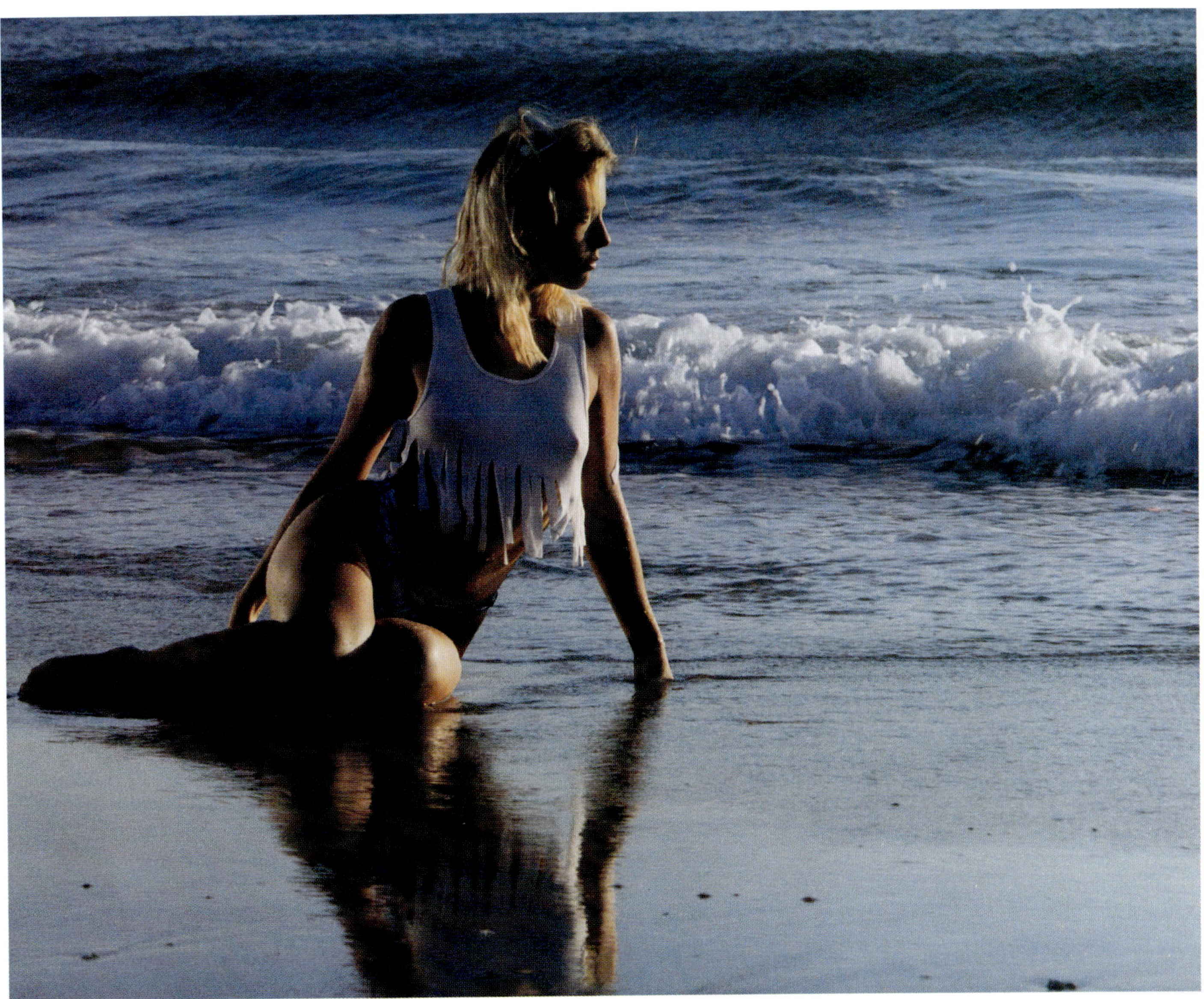

Natural light was the sole source of illumination for this photo. A 2x4-foot plastic mirror was used to reflect some of the daylight back into the shadow area and onto the back of the subject's head and buttocks.

When this shot was initially set up, the subject was wearing a very skimpy two-piece bathing suit. It did not look well enough on her to support the boudoir image we were trying to create. Accordingly, her costume had to be modified.

We took a man's undershirt, cut it down to shorten it, and frayed it. We then wet the undershirt and had her put it on. This yielded a much more appealing and sensuous image.

When going on location for a boudoir session, carry a few items of clothing with you just in case you need to draw upon them. We carry undershirts, T-shirts, and a man's dress shirt—made of very thin material—for just such situations as this one.

A medium telephoto lens was used, with a warming filter. Exposure was 1/15 second at *f*-11.

67 PORTFOLIO

This last image in our series of beach shots is one of our favorites, although it was very simple to execute.

Natural light was the main source of illumination. We used the 2x4-foot plastic mirror reflector—placed to the left of camera-subject axis—to rim and accent the subject's legs and midriff area.

Don't become discouraged if only a few of your subjects can adopt this pose. It is a very difficult one to do, requiring a lot of body flexibility and concentration on the part of the subject, especially when you are working with slow shutter speeds, as was the case with this shot, exposed at 1/15 second.

Not all subjects will be able to execute all the poses you suggest. When one pose does not work, quickly go on to others. This will help keep a subject's confidence level high.

The pose in this photo, the action of the waves, the subject's costume, the reflection of her in the sand, and the dramatic lighting all help to make this image an extremely sensuous one.

A medium telephoto lens was used, with a warming filter.

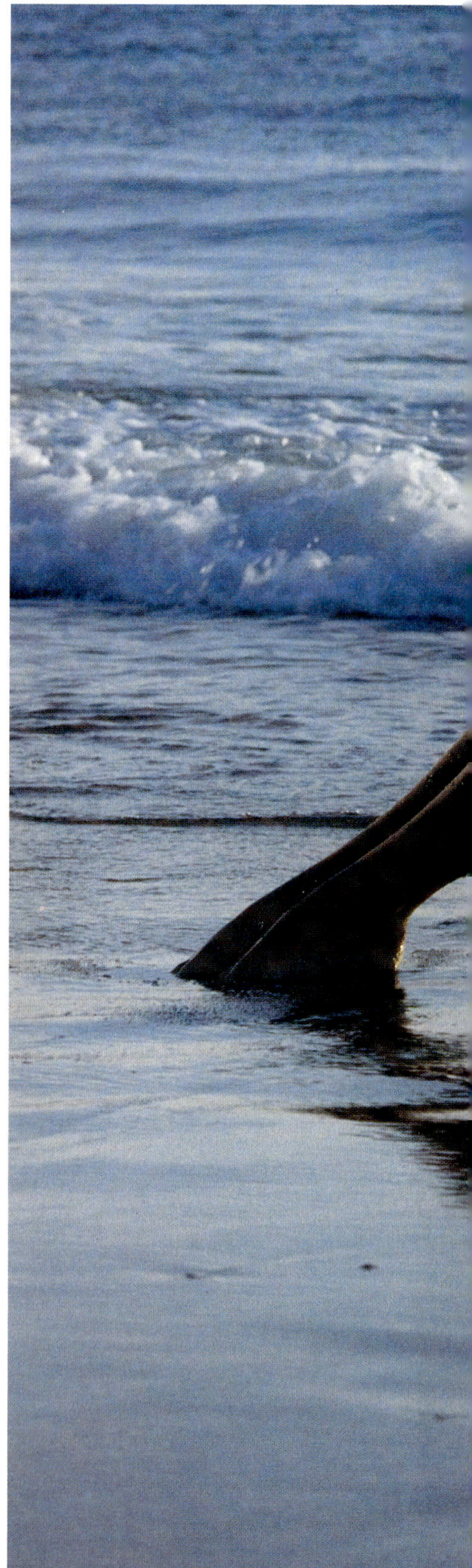

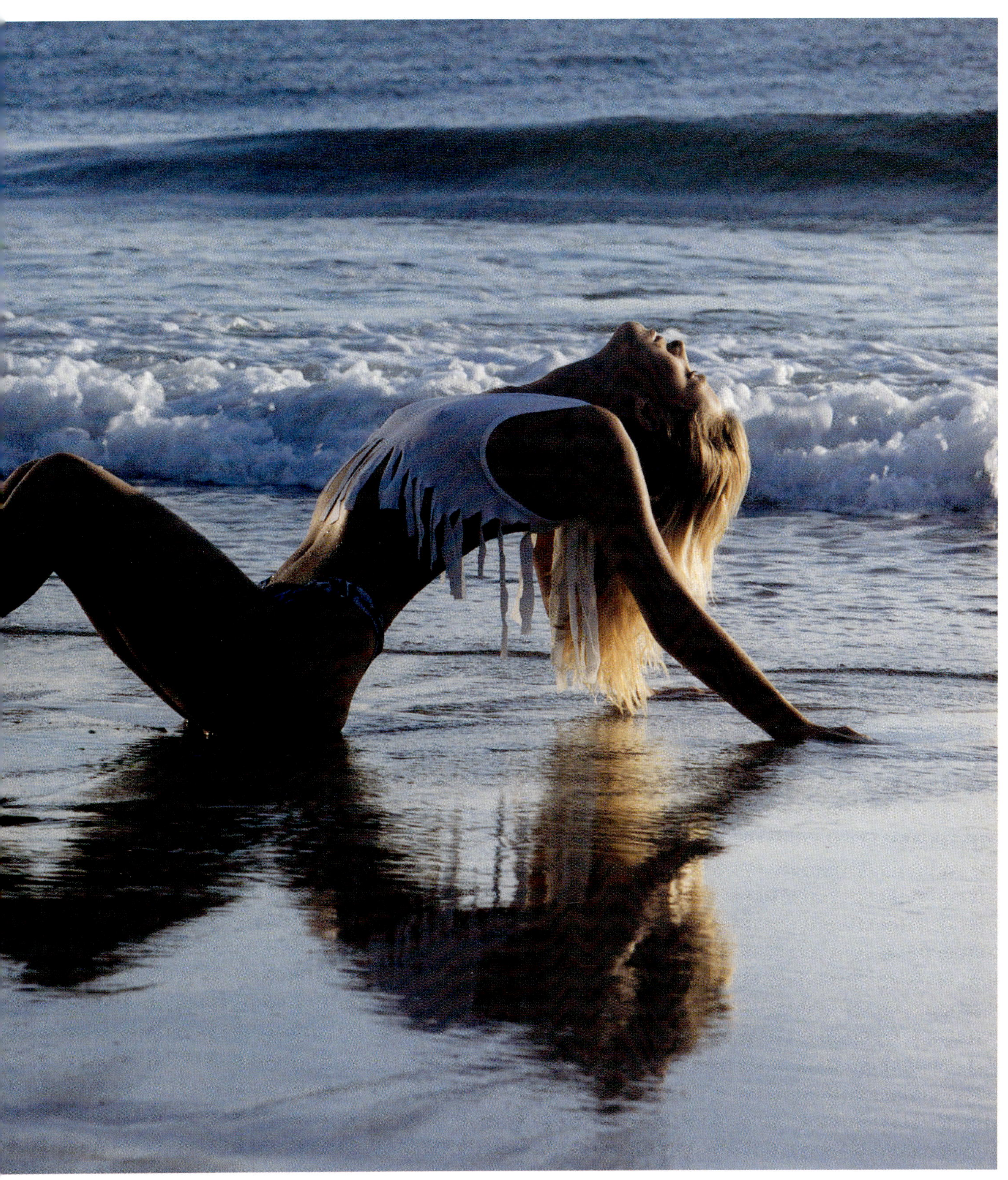

WATERFALL SCENE

All of photography involves a certain amount of problem solving. One of the major challenges in boudoir photography on location is finding a suitable shooting site. Scout likely areas well in advance of an actual shoot. On the day of the session, you cannot afford to waste time seeking out just the right place.

Here in southern Florida, we have numerous ideal locations for outdoor boudoir photography: the beach, parks, deeply wooded areas—and even some very attractive waterfalls. In addition to the beach, we often favor a waterfall, because water and the female form seem to complement each other well.

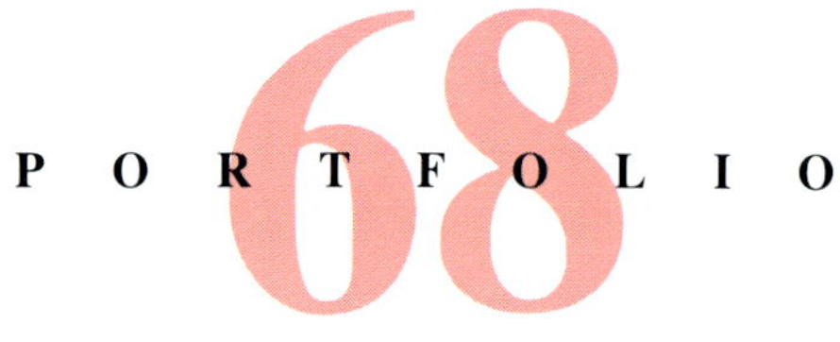

When photographing subjects who are not trained models, do not start with the most difficult or provocative pose you can think of or ask for scanty attire without first building up to this stage.

In the beginning of a session, a subject's body language or facial expression will often show anxiety and a lack of self-confidence. The early photos will generally not be the best.

When you're working with a nonprofessional subject, her photo session with you will often be her first experience with this form of photography. Most subjects require time to "warm up" to being good models and attaining the poses and looks you are after. Be patient and understanding and constantly express your approval of a subject's efforts.

For this photo, we had the subject wear one of her bathing suits. We posed her on the rocks and directed her into a simple, cat-like stretching pose. Several photos were taken in and around this location—to build the subject's self-confidence—before we moved on to other costumes and more demanding and provocative poses.

A single, portable 400-watt-second battery-powered flash, in a 6-inch bowl reflector, was used. It was about 10 degrees to the right of camera-subject axis and its power was adjusted for balance with the daylight falling on the scene.

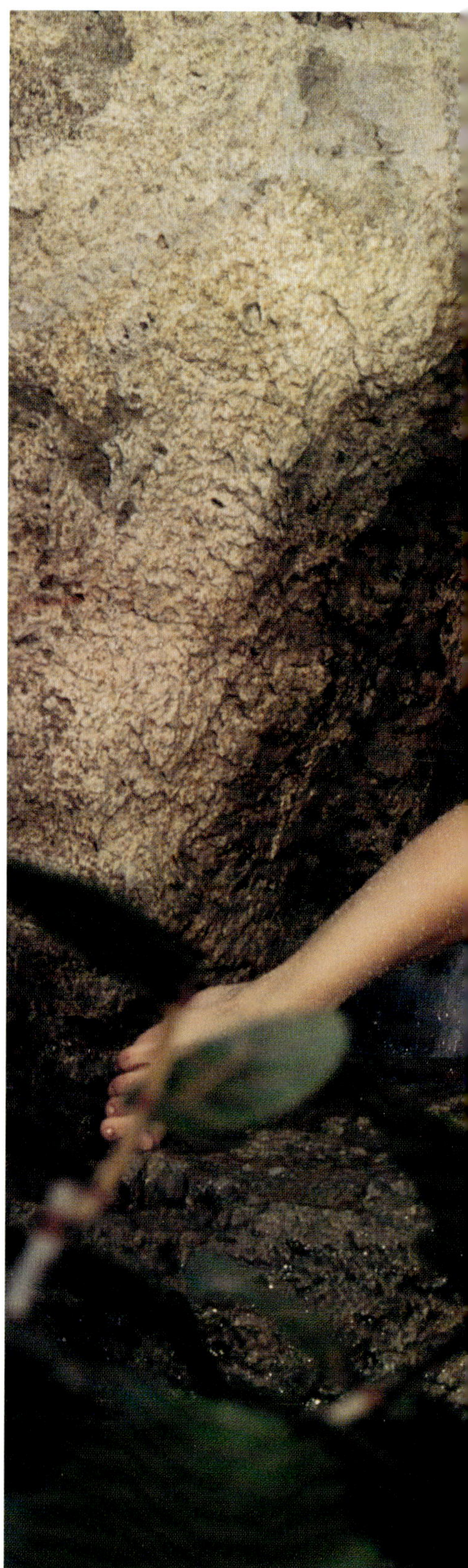

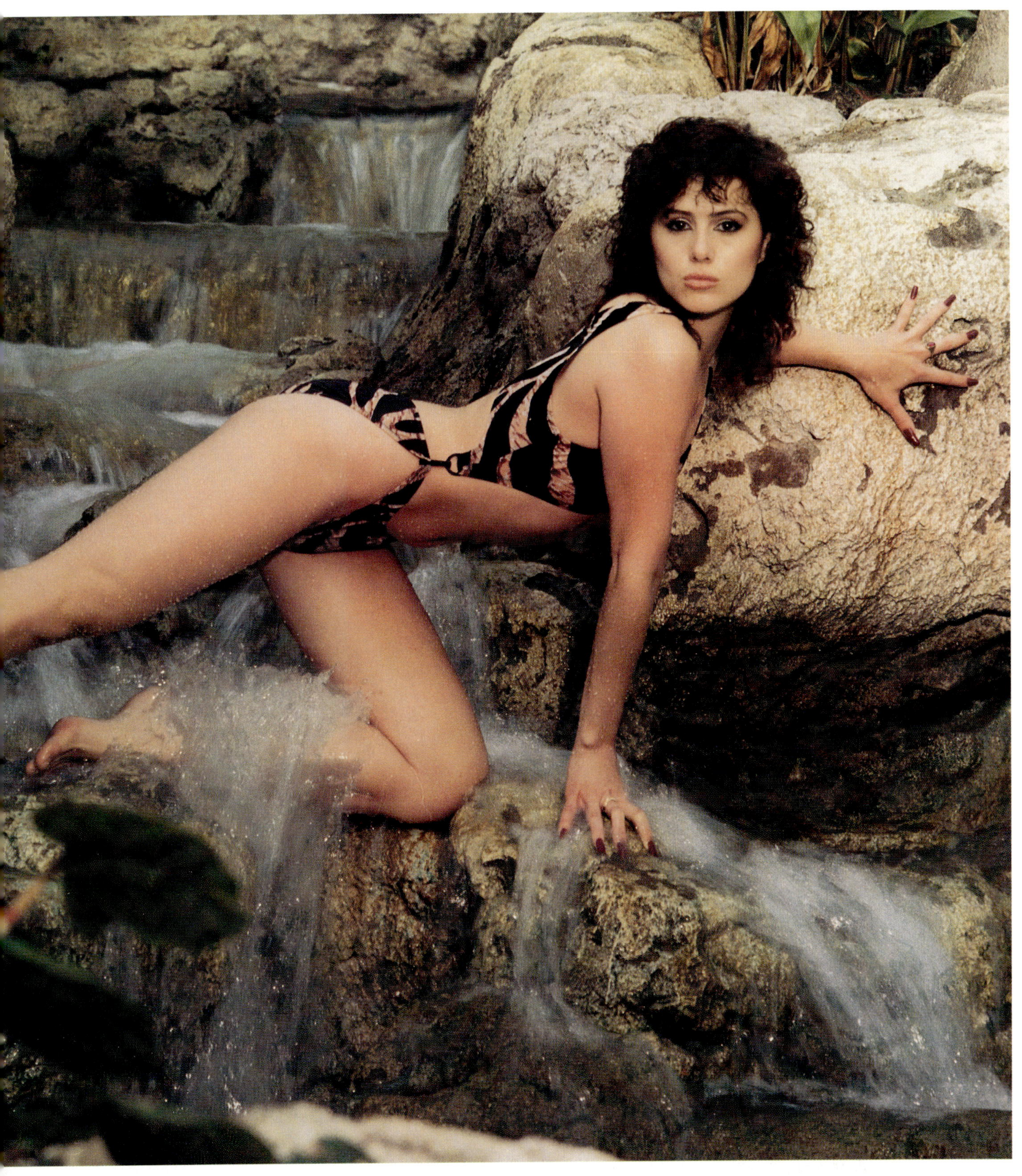

PORTFOLIO 69

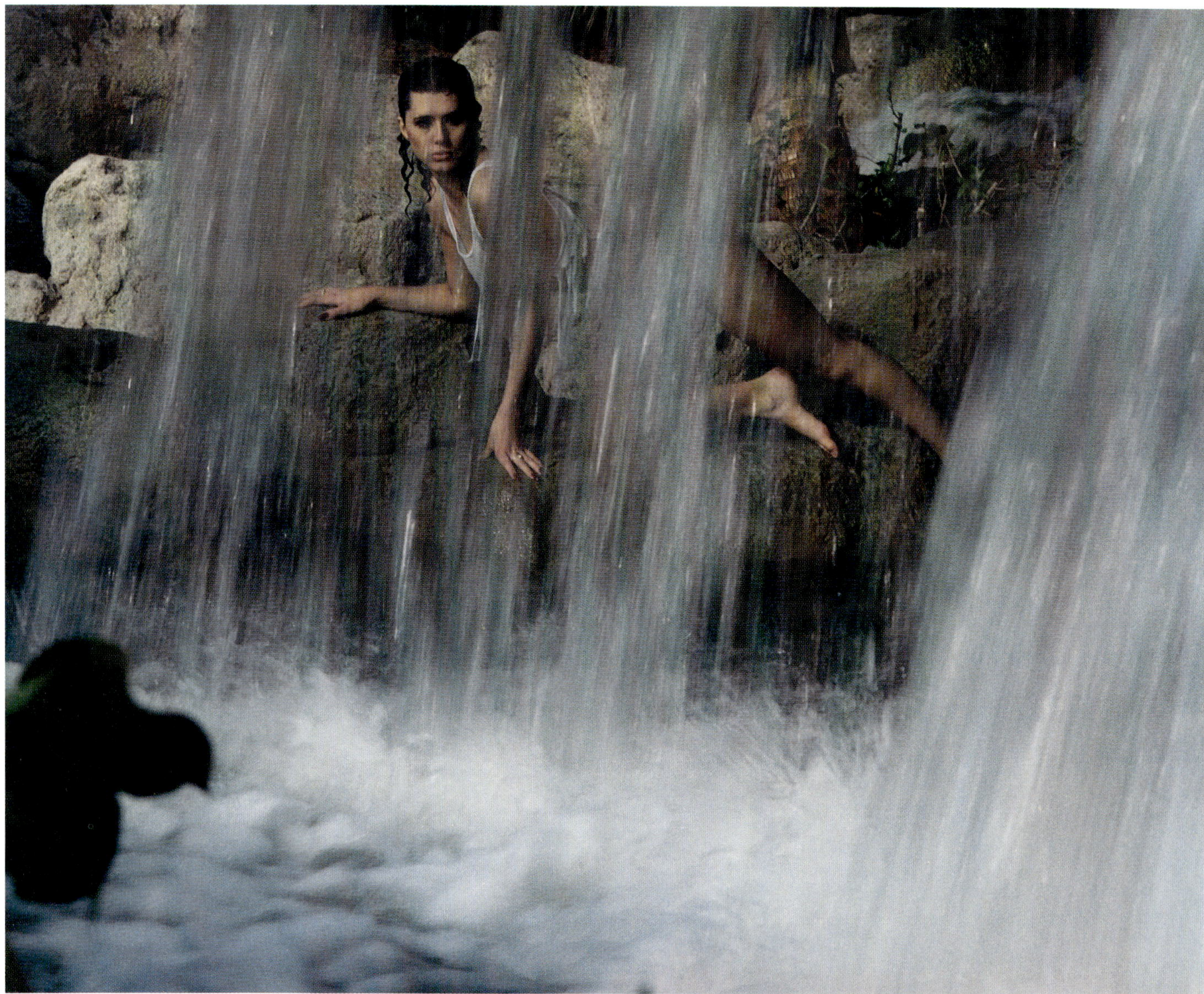

We always discuss required clothing with a subject prior to a shooting session. However, this is no guarantee that she will bring the best items. Be prepared to improvise on the day of the actual shoot.

Nothing brought by the subject in this photo seemed to work very well.

We took an old undershirt, cut some of it off and shredded the remainder. We then had the subject exchange her bathing-suit top for the torn shirt. She was instructed to assume a cat-like pose at the far end of the waterfall. Although not much of the subject's body can be seen, the image is suggestive and enticing.

Due to the erratic falling of the water, a number of images had to be taken to guarantee that the subject's face and parts of her body could be seen through the cascading water.

To get the nearby waterfall and the more distant subject in proportion, the camera was moved some distance from the waterfall and a telephoto lens was used. We did not want the natural environment to overpower the subject in the photo.

A warming filter was used, and an exposure of 1/15 second at *f*-8 was given. Daylight was the only source of illumination.

PORTFOLIO 70

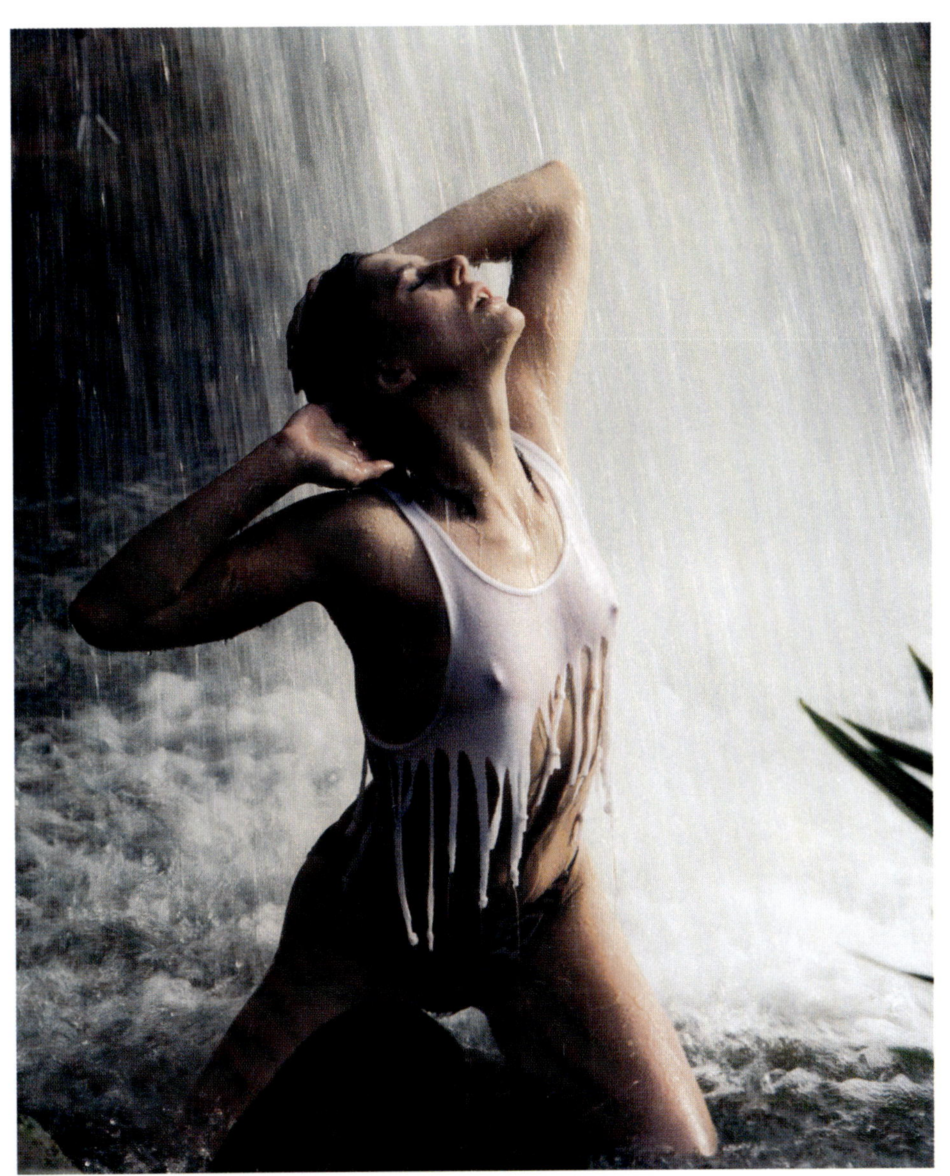

On the morning we photographed this subject, the temperature was a cool 50 degrees and the water temperature wasn't much higher. Nonetheless, the subject was very cooperative, agreeing to remain in the water for more than 30 minutes while we shot this and several other photos.

Always consider the comfort of the subject, even when she is prepared to suffer considerable discomfort for the sake of worthwhile photographs. Two of our assistants stood by, just out of camera view, with hot coffee, dry towels and blankets. The assistants were also watchful at all times for the subject's safety.

For this photo, the subject was instructed to assume an open stance, place her arms behind her head, bring her elbows back, close her eyes, open her mouth—and playact. We wanted her to act as though, at that moment, nothing in the world mattered except the feel of the water on her face and body.

Although many frames had to be taken in order to capture this particularly stunning photo, the subject followed our directions perfectly.

Daylight was the main light source and a 3x4-foot plastic mirror, placed to the left of camera-subject axis, acted as a reflector fill light. A medium telephoto lens was used, and a warming filter. Exposure was 1/15 second at *f*-5.6.

71 PORTFOLIO

Outdoor locations for boudoir photography should be as secluded as possible. Inquisitive strangers tend to distract subjects and make them feel extremely self-conscious and nervous.

To avoid a crowd at this waterfall, we arrived before dawn and started shooting with the first light of day. The entire session was concluded before any onlookers appeared.

This is basically a duplication of the preceding photo in camera technique, lens employed and lighting used. Only the pose was changed.

The pose in Photo 70 suggests comfort and pleasure in the water. In this photo, by contrast, there is a more challenging, defiant attitude of the subject toward the waterfall.

Having her arms thrust back, her back arched, and her head tossed back, the subject generates an animalistic pose, with a feeling of power and strength. In spite of this—or perhaps because of it—the pose is a very sensual one.

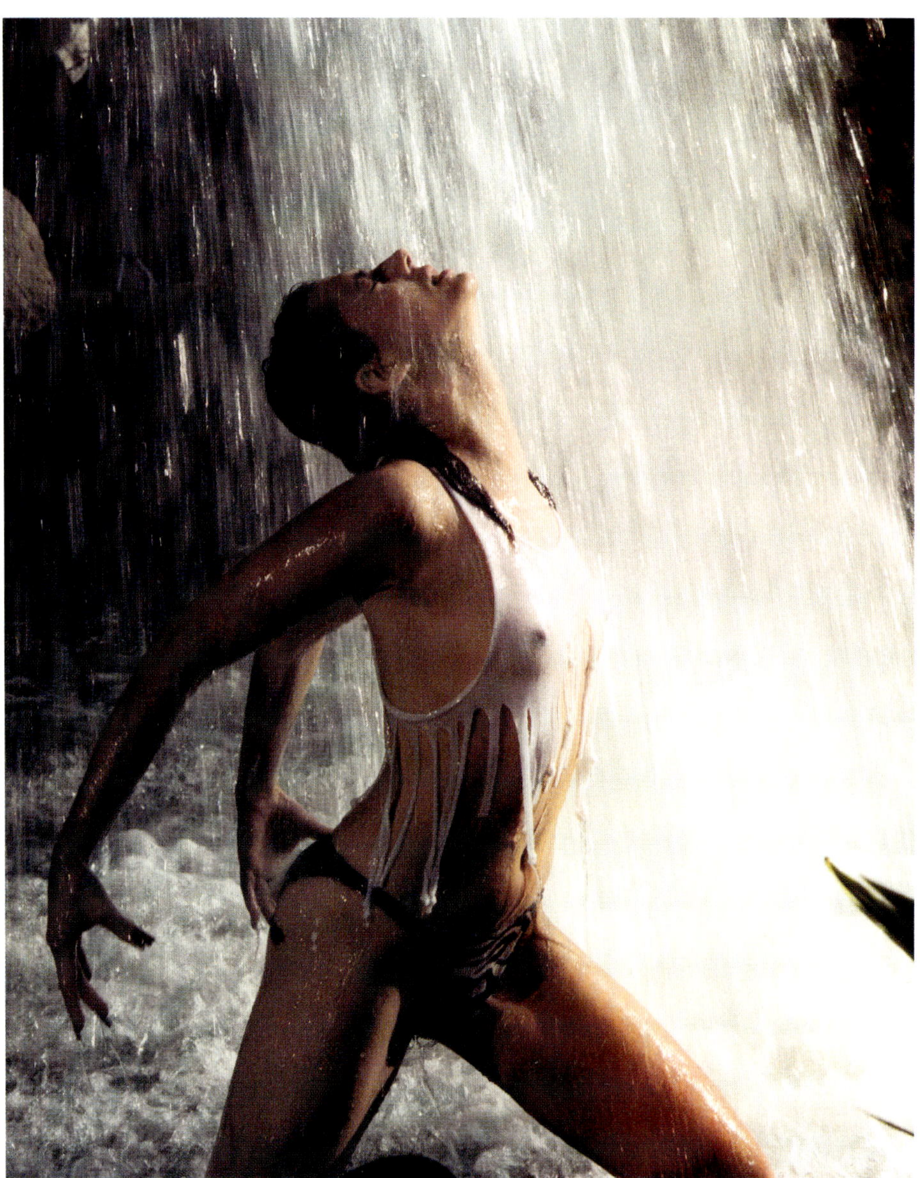

PORTFOLIO 72

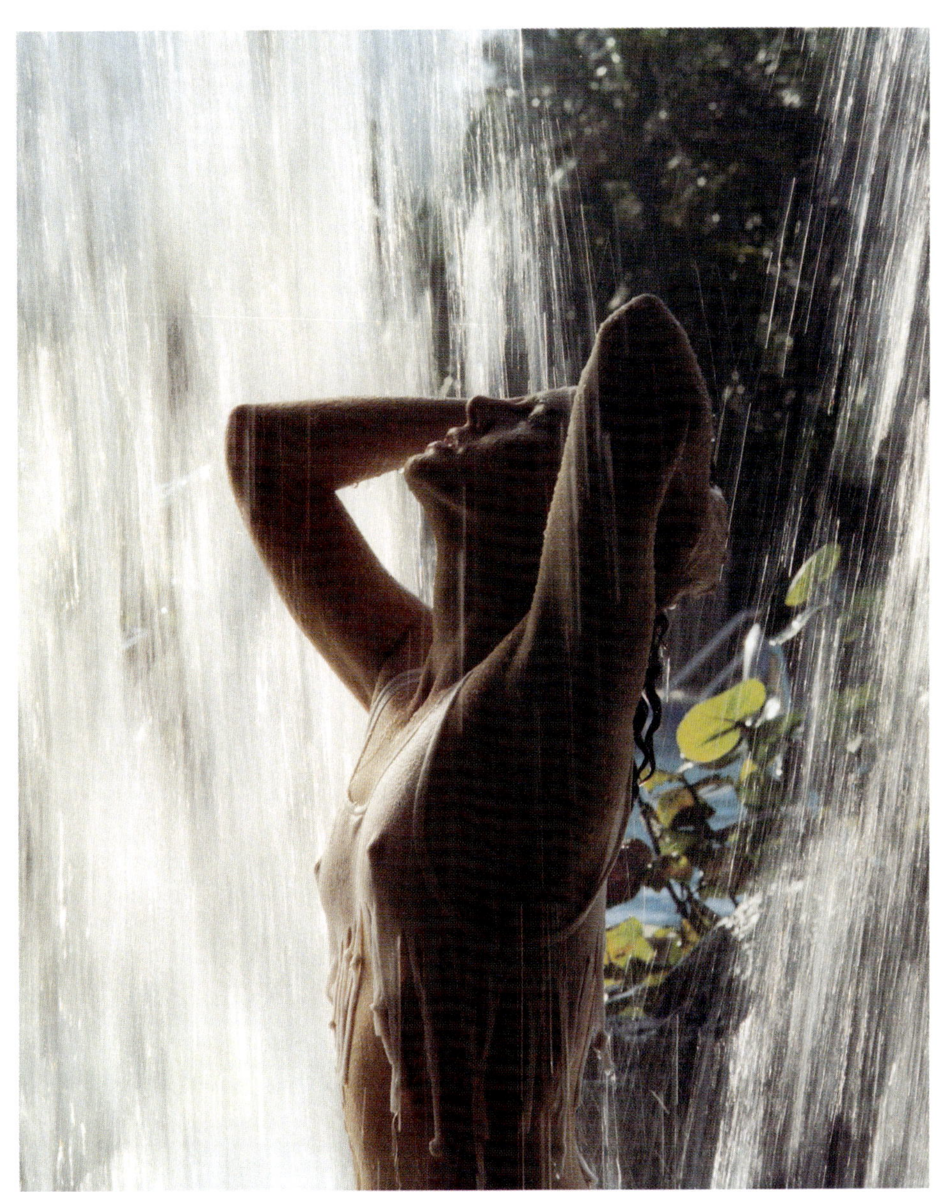

For boudoir photography to be successful, it's essential for the subject to have and display a very positive attitude. She must think of herself as attractive, if not beautiful. She must also have a positive attitude toward you, your assistants, the environment she is in, and the setting and poses you have chosen for her. Without such an attitude, you will get less-than-perfect pictorial results.

The subject was moved right into the center of the waterfall, giving her a wonderful opportunity to interact with the water.

With her arms up, back arched, and the sun backlighting her face, arms and body, the viewer can almost sense the subject's total enjoyment and involvement.

Daylight was the sole source of illumination. A medium telephoto lens was used, and a warming filter. Exposure was 1/15 second at *f*-11.

PORTFOLIO 73

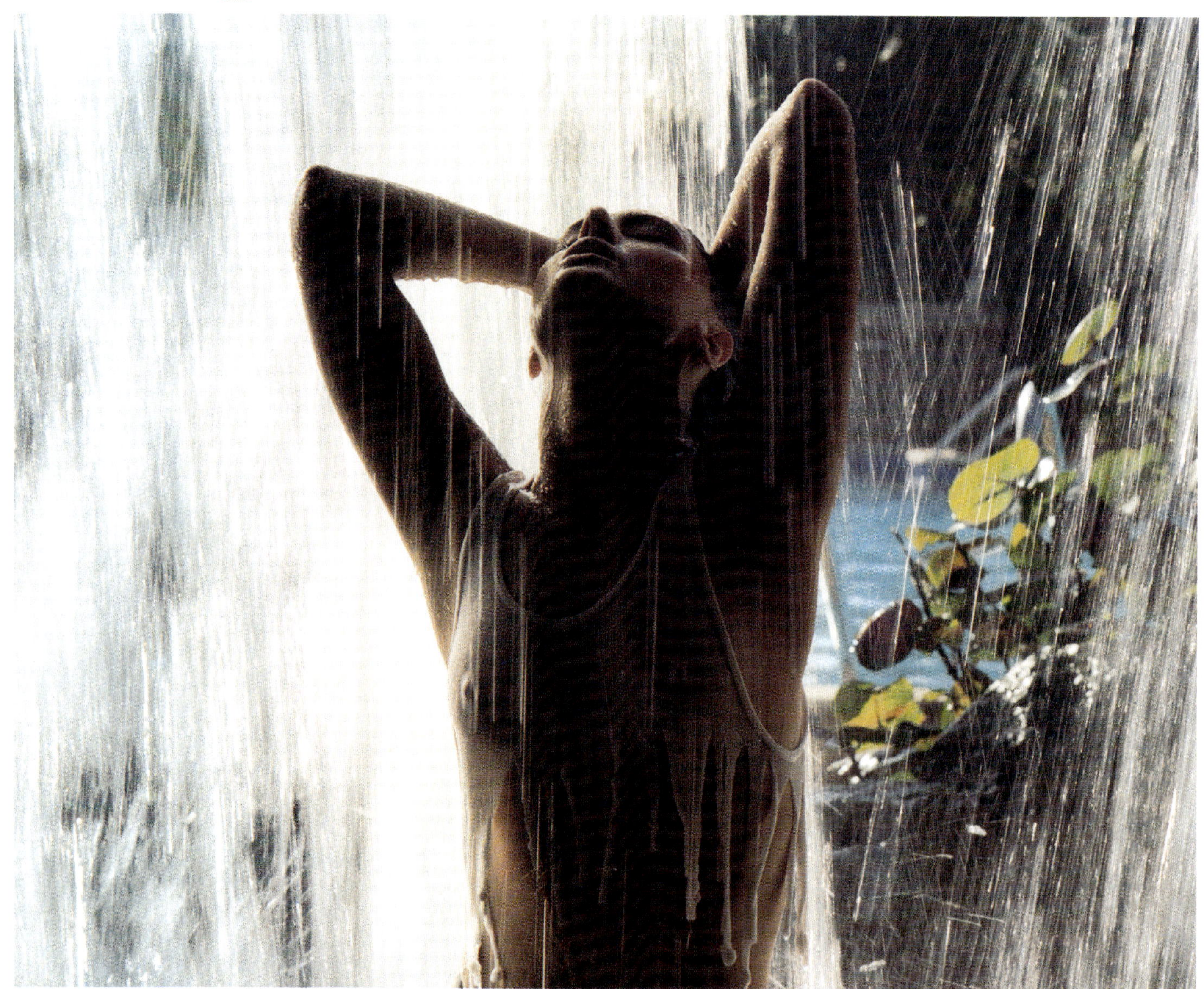

This photo is similar to the previous one in camera technique, lens used and lighting. Only the pose was modified.

By instructing the subject to turn her body almost directly toward the camera, we were able to photograph most of her body in shadow, with only a portion of one breast highlighted. The image conveys the subject's total involvement with the water and with her own body.

Your first impression of a location, a camera angle, or even of a subject, can often be wrong. When we first met this subject, she gave the impression of being totally uninterested in this form of photography, withdrawn, and unwilling or unable to relate to us, the camera, or the poses. As you can see, we were very wrong! Once on location, she followed instructions to the letter. She was cooperative beyond belief and put her heart and soul into every shot we took. She was just fabulous—and the pictorial results bespeak her efforts.

74 PORTFOLIO

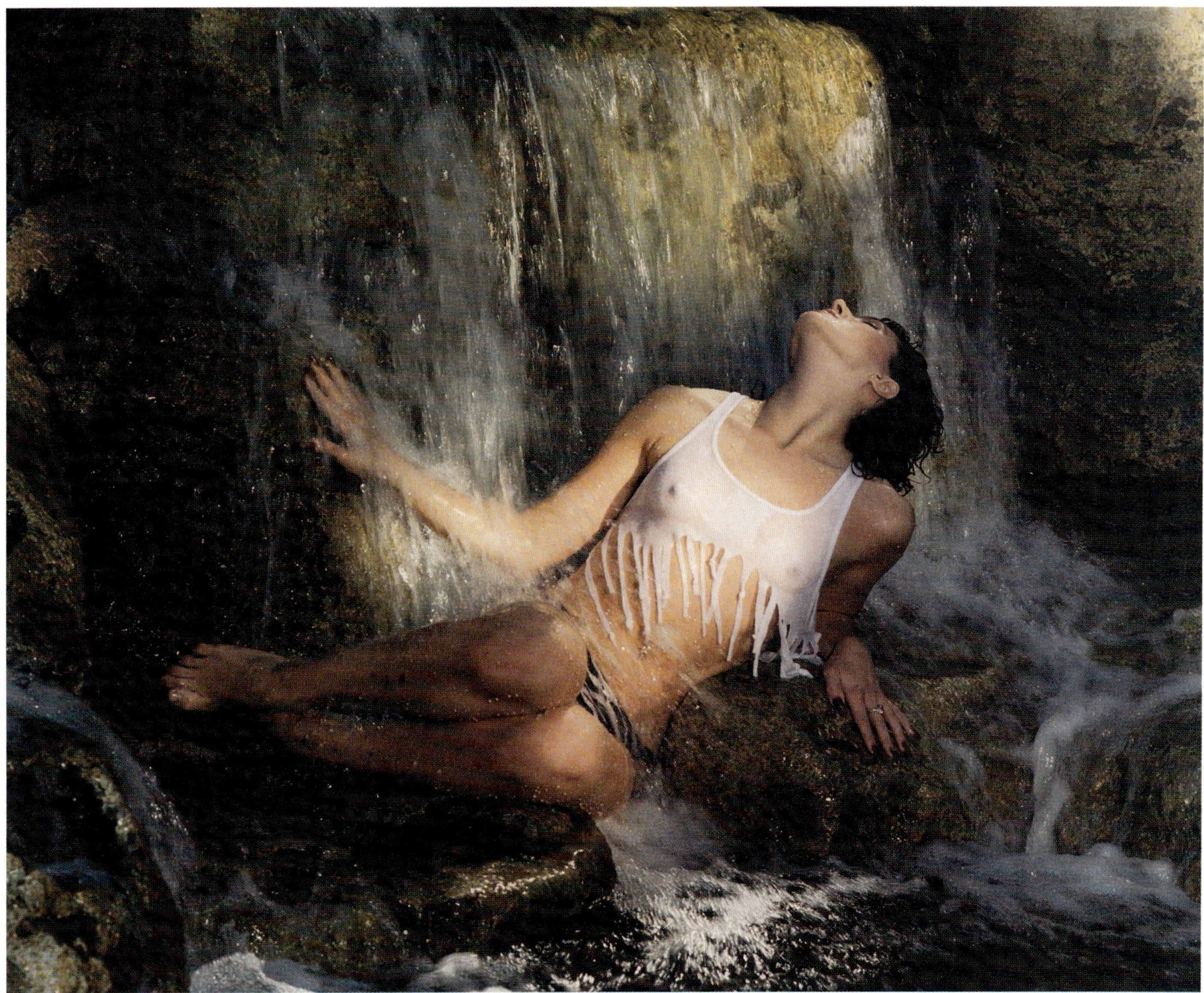

For this photo, we moved to a smaller waterfall. By this time, the sun was bright and warmer. The sunlight was filtering through the trees, causing patchy, lighting.

We normally dislike working in such lighting conditions because they are often unflattering to a subject's face and body and create a great contrast range between highlights and shadows. However, as with all rules, this one should not be adhered to so steadfastly that it cannot be broken to achieve a different pictorial result.

Since there was a stretch of 20 feet of water between the camera and the subject, we gave directions and took meter readings from that distance.

We directed the subject into this general pose and then asked her to turn her head away from the camera. This placed more emphasis on her body. We asked her to keep her legs close together and position them as shown. This put her legs more in shadow, adding emphasis to the upper part of her body.

Daylight was the main light source. One portable, 400-watt-second, battery-powered electronic flash, in a 6-inch bowl reflector, placed 10 degrees to the right of camera-subject axis, was used as fill light. Its power was adjusted to emit one *f*-stop less light than the metered daylight. A medium telephoto lens was used, and a warming filter.

75 PORTFOLIO

This is one of our favorite photos from the waterfall session. The pose, body language and facial expression add up to a very sensuous image.

Although the subject is wearing the bottom to her bathing suit, she could just as easily have been nude from the waist down. The rushing water has all but concealed the garment from view.

Images such as this are not merely "taken" but are "created." Creating a stunning image often involves a lot of time, effort, patience, and film, as well as the cooperation of all involved.

Rushing water can produce unpredictable pictorial results. Even with the same subject, pose and angle of view, six different photos taken in cascading water will each create a different pictorial impression. The water will interact with the subject differently in each case.

This photo was lit by available daylight only. Any additional lighting would have been superfluous. A fill light or other additional illumination would only have served to weaken the dramatic impact of the image.

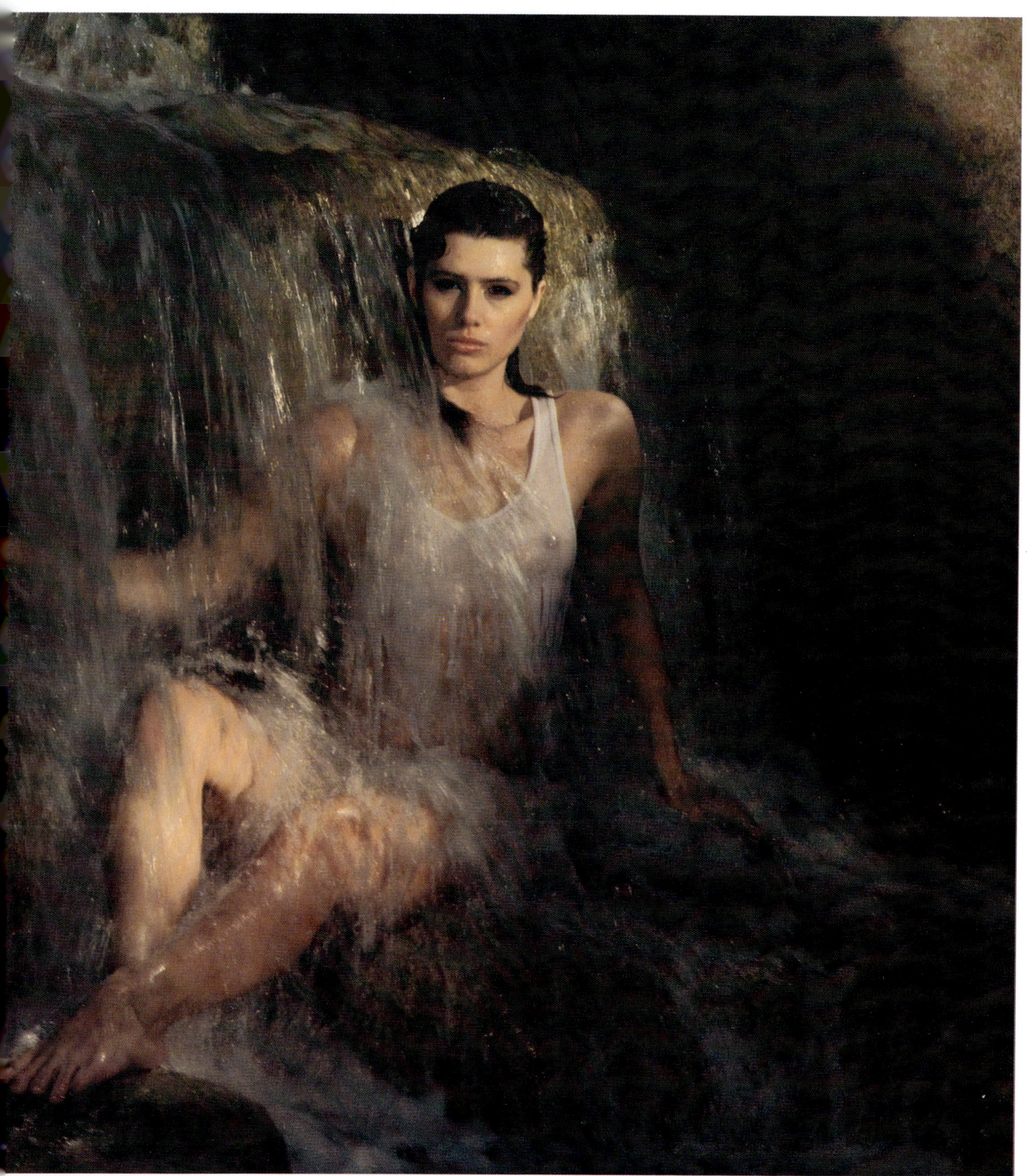

DETAIL SHOTS

For subjects who have especially attractive features or attributes, we offer additional pictorial variety by photographing those specific features in detail.

Many subjects have outstanding eyes, gorgeous, flowing hair, beautiful legs, voluptuous breasts, and so on. Capitalize on these features by taking photos that present them in a new, different, detailed and exciting way. Be creative. The more imagination you show, the more your reputation will grow as a creative photographer.

Because of time limitations, you will often have to limit this close-up photography to one or two features during any one session. Work with care, to present a specific feature of a subject's body with the same sensuality and good taste you used in photographing her total person.

Even though a close-up of a specific feature will not necessarily reveal a subject's identity, such an image can still be very meaningful to the subject and her "special someone."

The following three photos are a few examples of what you can do. Use them as a guide to help you create your own images. Base your selection of subject matter on the subject's preference as well as your own observation.

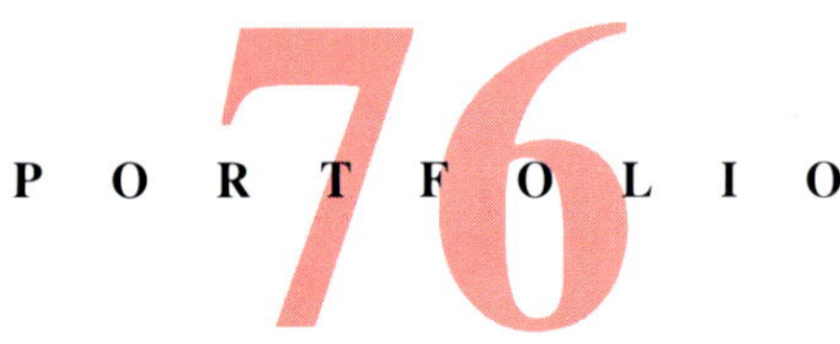

If you have the opportunity to bring a favorite possession of a subject's, such as a bracelet or necklace, into a photo, do so. It will add a personal touch, making the image easier for the subject or her "special someone" to relate to.

To heighten the sensuality of this image, we applied body makeup to the subject and added a spray of water.

A word of caution: If you want to use color makeup but are inexperienced in its use, or unfamiliar with the materials, let a professional makeup artist, who has expertise in this specific area of makeup, do the job. You should be aware that some body-makeup materials can have toxic effects when not used properly or, at the very least, they can be irritating to some sensitive subjects.

Some body makeup can be removed easily with plain soap and water while some takes a considerable time to remove, even with the help of special cleansers.

Inform your subject of the potential problems before you start. Then, let her decide whether to go ahead with the body makeup or not.

The main light for this photo was a flash in a 6-foot Larson Starfish umbrella. It was connected to a 1250-watt-second power source and placed about 40 degrees to the left of camera-subject axis. The fill light, a 3x4-foot softbox, was placed about 10 degrees to the right of camera-subject axis. Its power was adjusted to two *f*-stops less light than the main light.

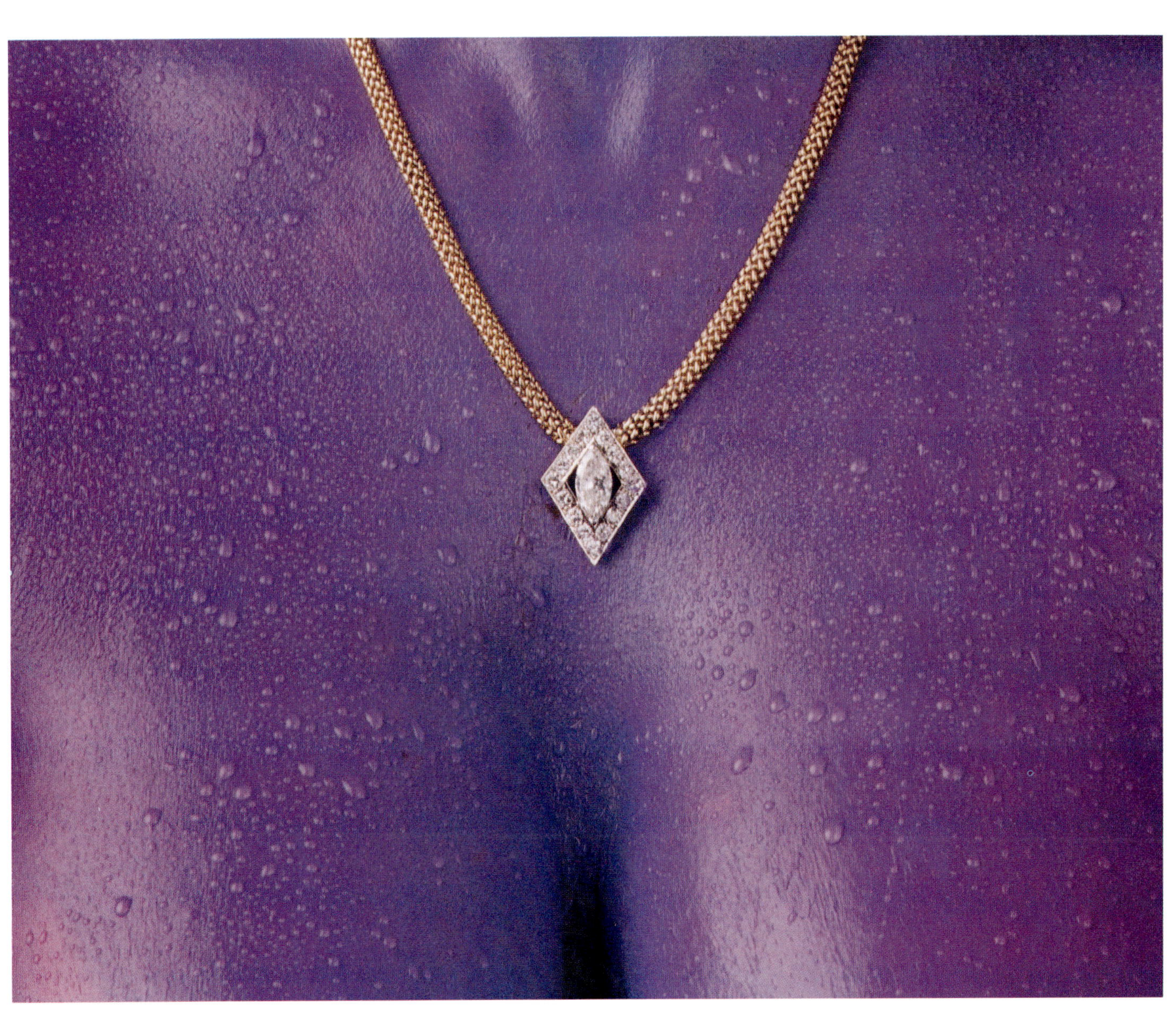

77 PORTFOLIO

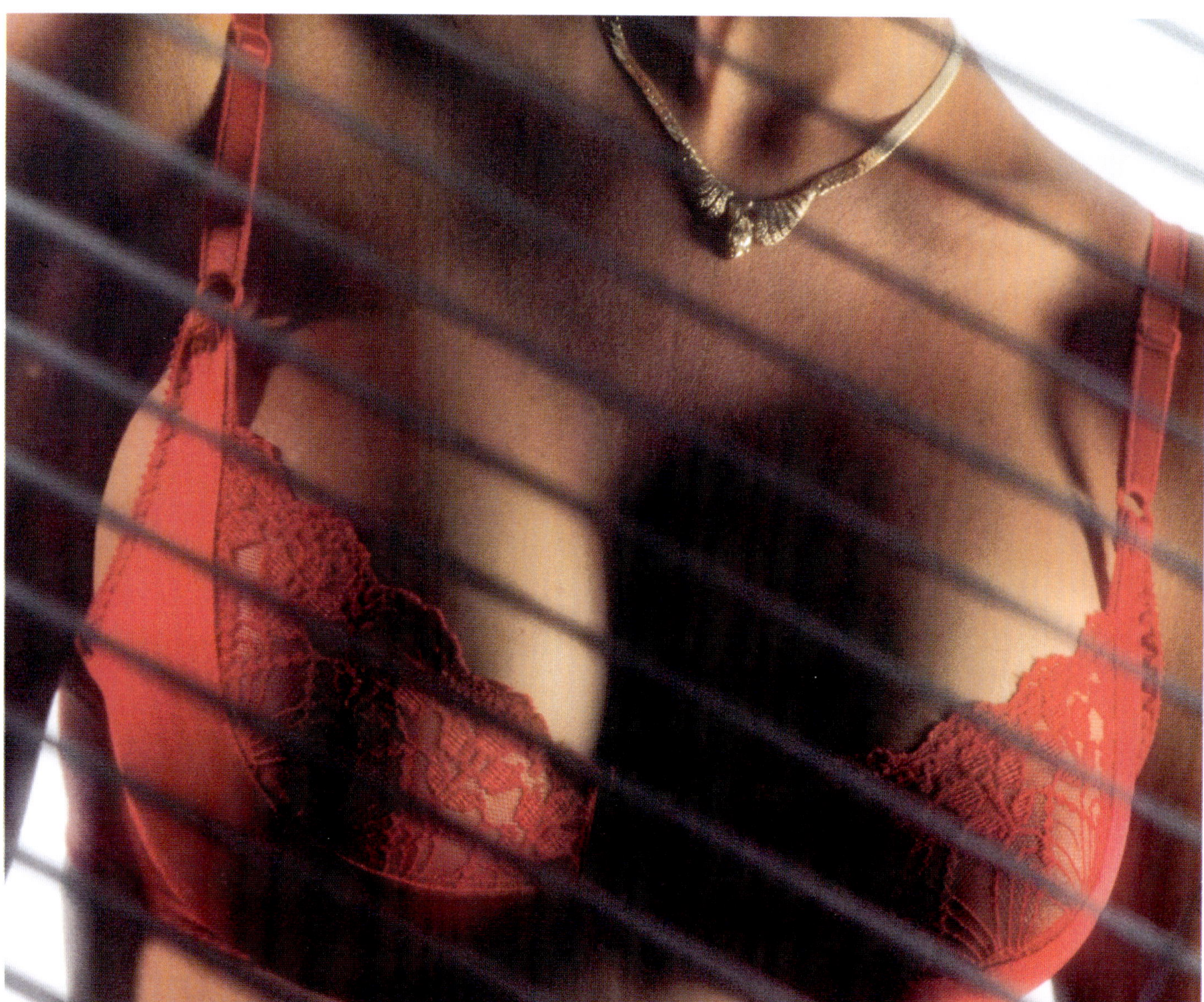

We took this special photo for a subject who was in her last month of pregnancy. She was clearly not prepared for full-length photography but did want us to create a sensitive image of her bust.

We suspended a black venetian blind in front of the subject. By focusing on the subject's necklace and using limited depth of field, we were able to record the slats of the blind somewhat softly.

A Balcar Opalite, connected to a 2400-watt-second power pack, was used as main light. It was placed almost 90 degrees to the right of camera-subject axis. A 3x4-foot plastic mirror was placed about 80 degrees to the left of this axis to serve as a reflector fill light. A background light, in a 5-inch bowl reflector, was placed directly behind the subject and directed onto white background material. Its power was adjusted to emit one *f*-stop more light than the main light.

Although the shot was taken with the camera level and the slats in the blind perfectly horizontal, we angled the enlarging easel when making the print to give the image added impact.

A medium telephoto lens was used, and a Softar 1 filter. Exposure was at *f*-11.

PORTFOLIO 78

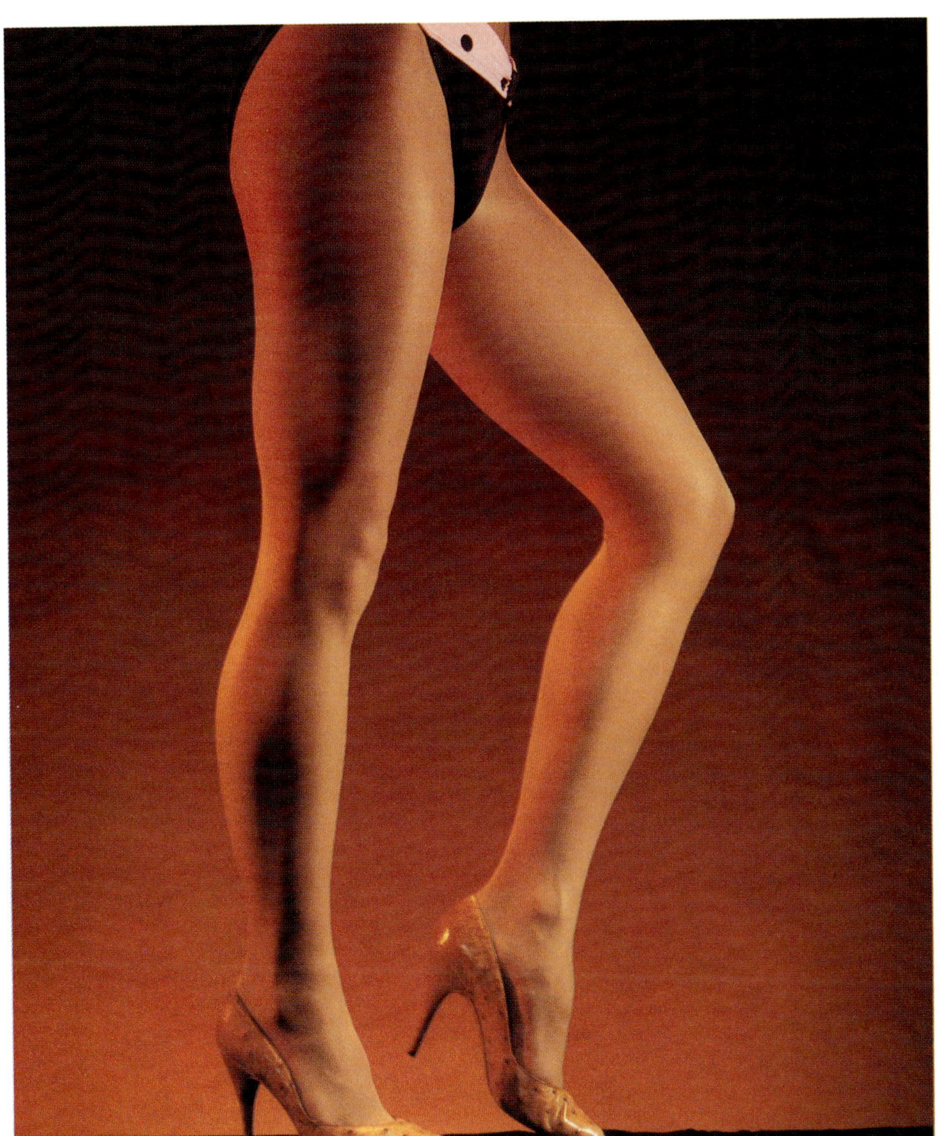

The feature most frequently requested in close-up is the legs. A wide variety of different images can be created with minimal effort and delay, and without major lighting changes. One leg can be draped with a prop, such as pearls or a feather boa. The color of the lights can be varied. The subject can wear a very short, tight-fitting skirt or she can wear a full skirt and have it blow upwards—using an electric fan beneath her feet, out of camera view.

For a shot such as the one reproduced here, a subject should wear pantyhose and high-heeled shoes. This ensures a firm and shapely appearance of the legs.

For this photo, a Balcar Opalite was used as main light, with a 20-degree grid spot and plastic diffuser cap. The light was connected to a 2400-watt-second power source and was placed approximately 90 degrees to the right of camera-subject axis.

A kicker light, housed in a snooted 5-inch bowl reflector, was placed approximately 90 degrees to the left of camera-subject axis. It was covered with an orange gel and directed onto the back part of the subject's legs. The power of this light was adjusted to emit one *f*-stop less light than the main light.

A background light, in a 5-inch bowl reflector, was hidden on the floor below the subject, who was standing on a platform. This light was directed onto the black background. The light was covered with an orange gel and its power was adjusted to emit one *f*-stop less light than the main light.

A medium telephoto lens was used and exposure was at *f*-11.

LIGHT BACKGROUND

A clean, white background is appropriate for much boudoir photography. The background can be white, seamless paper, a white wall, or even a large light bank.

To ensure a truly white background, exposure for it should be about two *f*-stops more than subject exposure. For example, if a meter reading of the light falling onto a subject indicates *f*-8, a reading from the background should indicate about *f*-16. If the lighting differential between subject and background is much less than two *f*-stops, the background may record as a tone of gray.

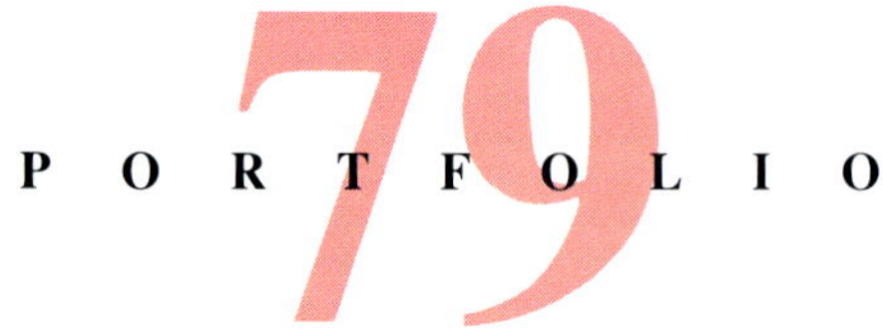

This subject had lost a great deal of weight prior to being photographed. At the time of the session, she was still on her diet and had reservations about engaging in this form of photography. There were areas of her body that she was still less than proud of and that she wanted hidden.

A full-figured woman can be made to appear very alluring by careful choice of props, costumes and poses. For this image, the small pillow and man's pajama top helped conceal just enough of the subject's body to make her feel comfortable and confident, while giving her the sensuous image she sought.

The main light was in a 40-inch, white-lined diffused umbrella. It was connected to a 1200-watt-second power pack. The light was placed approximately 45 degrees to the right of camera-subject axis. A 3x4-foot softbox was used as fill light, placed about 20 degrees to the left of the camera-subject axis. Its power was adjusted to emit two *f*-stops less light than the main light.

Two background lights were used, one on either side of white background material. Each was housed in a 3-foot silver-lined umbrella. The background lights had their power adjusted to emit two *f*-stops more light than the main light.

A medium telephoto lens was used, and a Softar 1 filter. Exposure was at *f*-11.

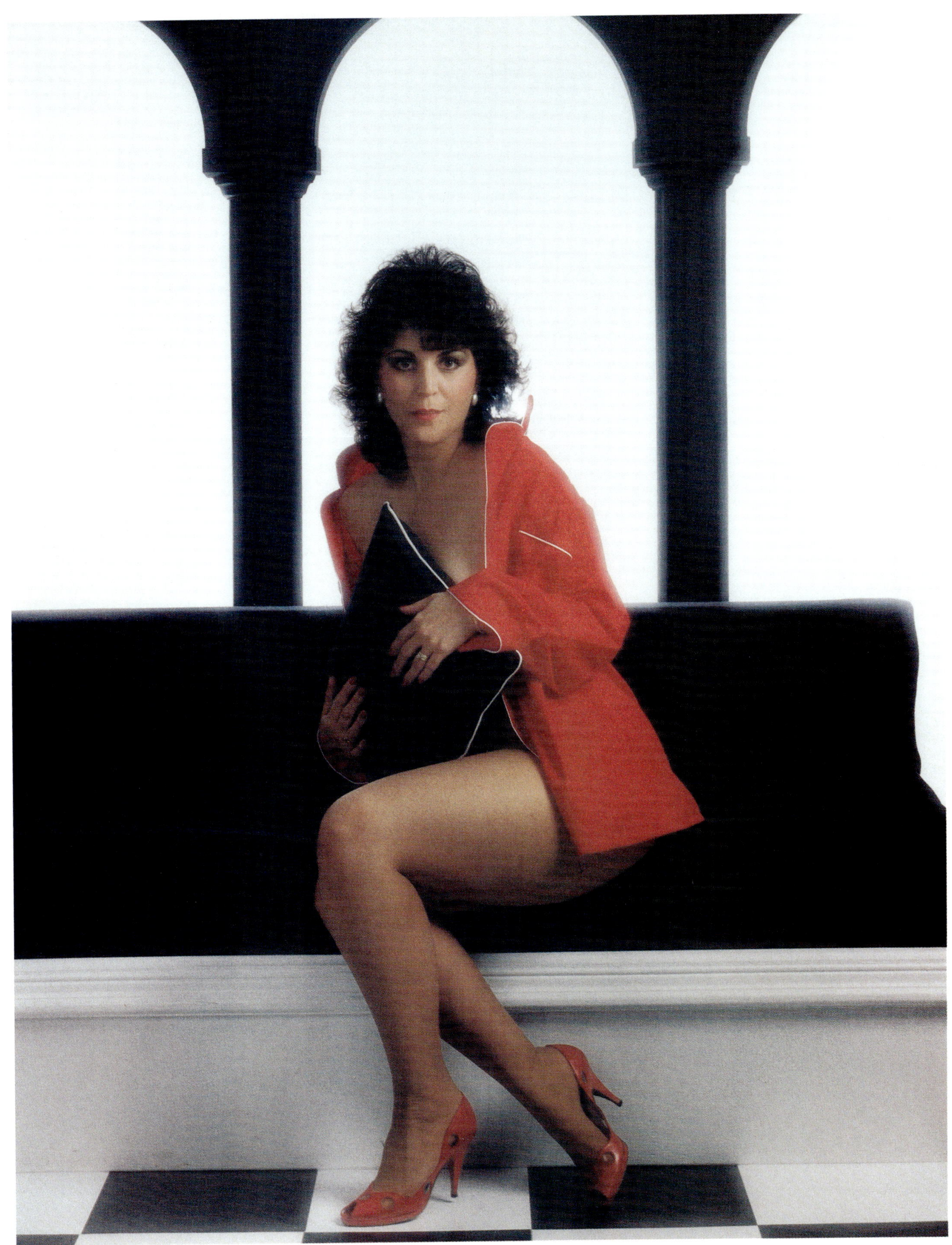

PORTFOLIO 80

There are several ways to light a white background. Some photographers use a single light, placed behind the subject and above her head. Some will use two lights, one on either side of the background and each aimed toward the center of the background. Still others will use four lights, placing one high and one low on each side of the white background material.

Whichever way you choose, the goal is to achieve even illumination over the entire portion of the white background that will be seen in the final photos. To ensure uniform illumination, meter readings taken from all parts of the background should be the same.

For this photo, the same camera technique, lens and lighting were used as for the preceding photo.

We instructed the subject to be seated and put her legs into the position depicted. We then told her to arch her back. This positioning gave emphasis to her chest and legs. This is a flattering pose for most women.

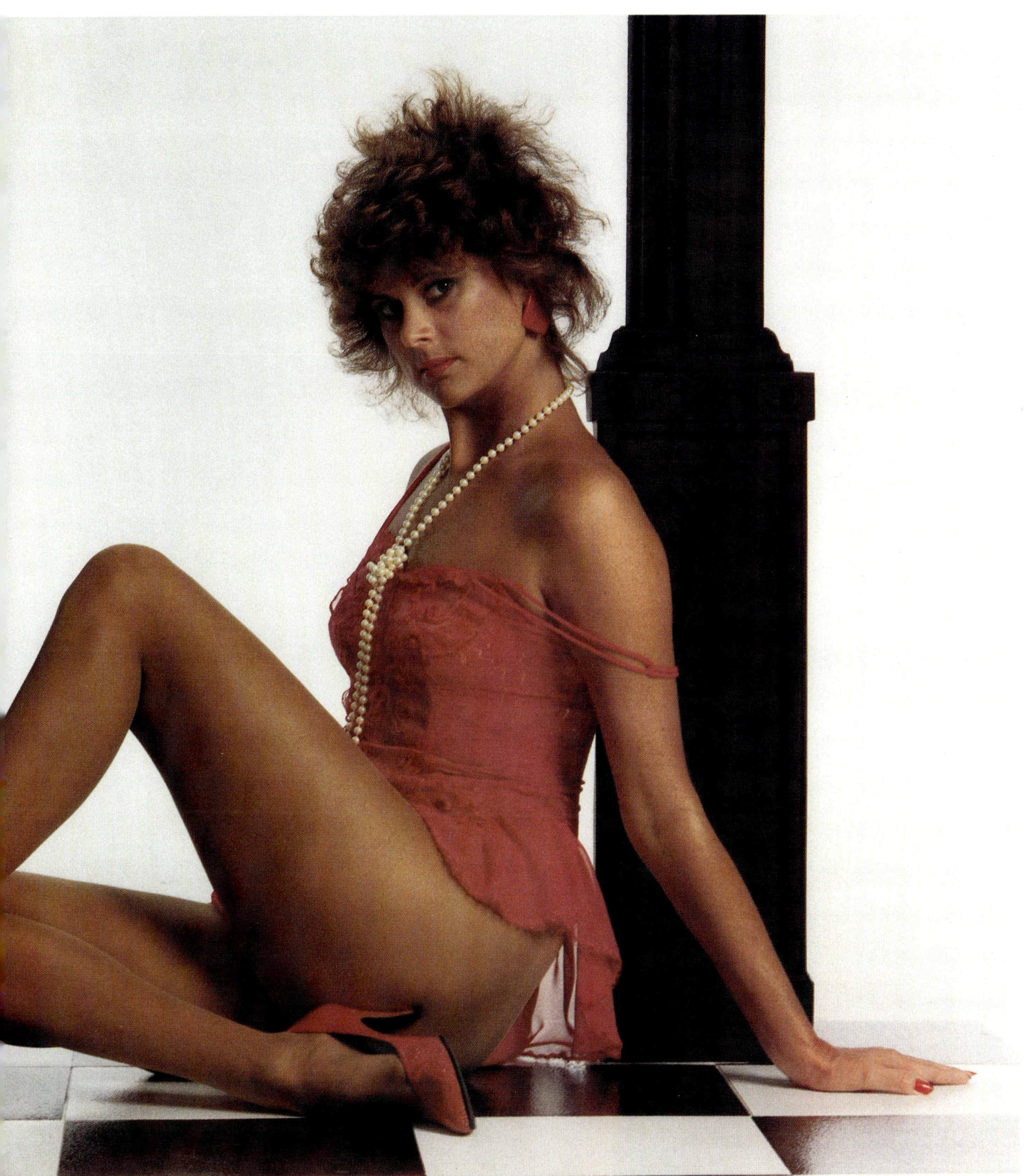

81 PORTFOLIO

If a subject is posed too close to a bright, white background, the light from the background can cause a halation around the subject. This can destroy clear, decisive outlines around a body. Unless you are aiming for a specific, dreamlike effect, this is an unacceptable result.

To ensure against such halation, place a subject at least 9 feet from a white background. Also, be sure that the light from the background isn't more than two *f*-stops brighter than the main light from the subject.

For example, if the main light on the subject metered *f*-8 and your background lights metered *f*-45, a difference of five *f*-stops would exist. In this situation, even if you placed your subject 9 feet from the background, you would still experience halation around the subject.

For this photo, we chose a low camera angle, to emphasize the subject's statuesque beauty. Posing the subject sideways gave emphasis to her legs and buttocks.

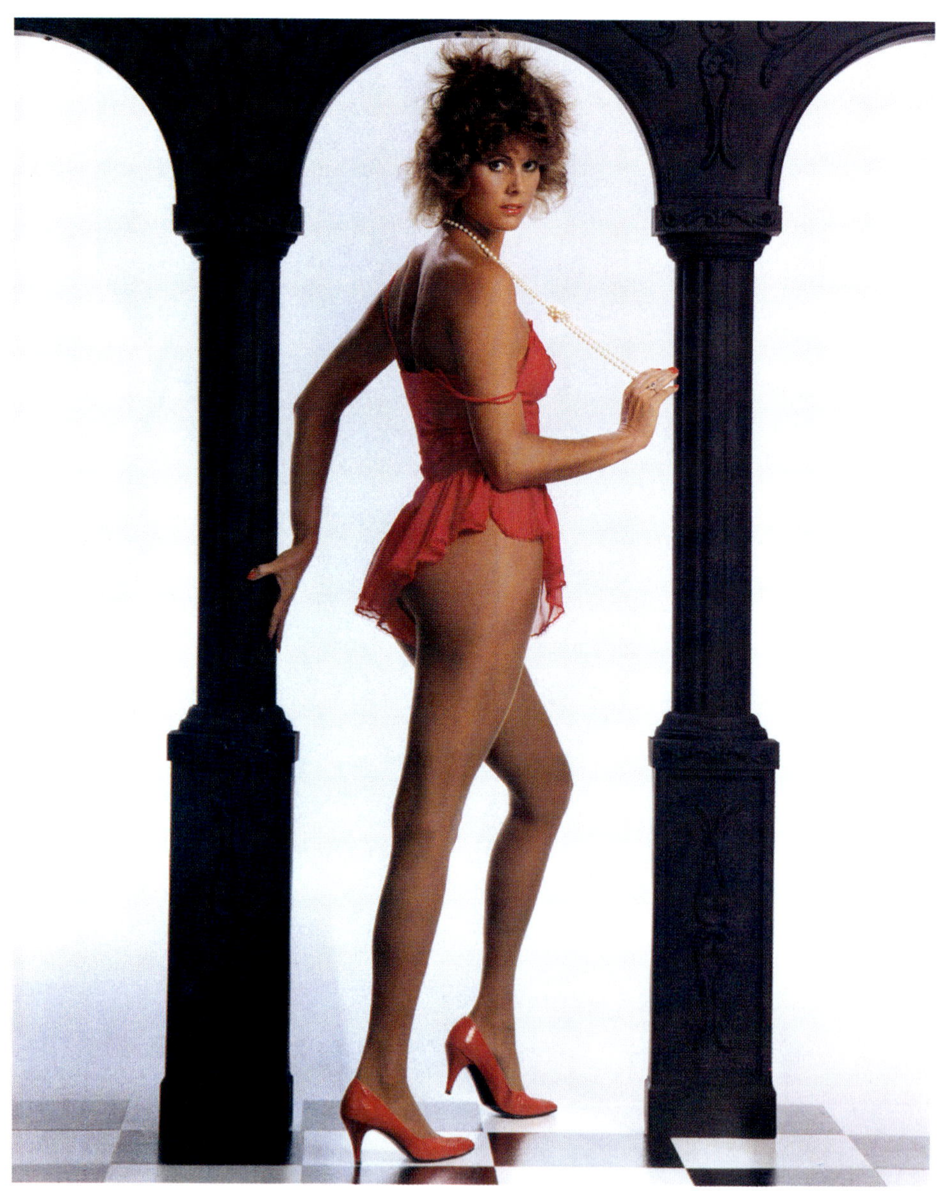

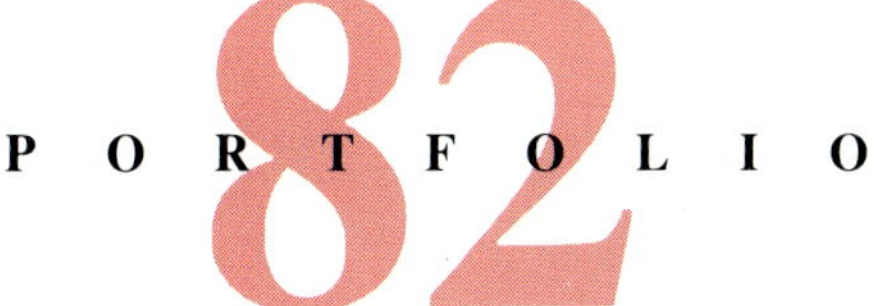

PORTFOLIO 82

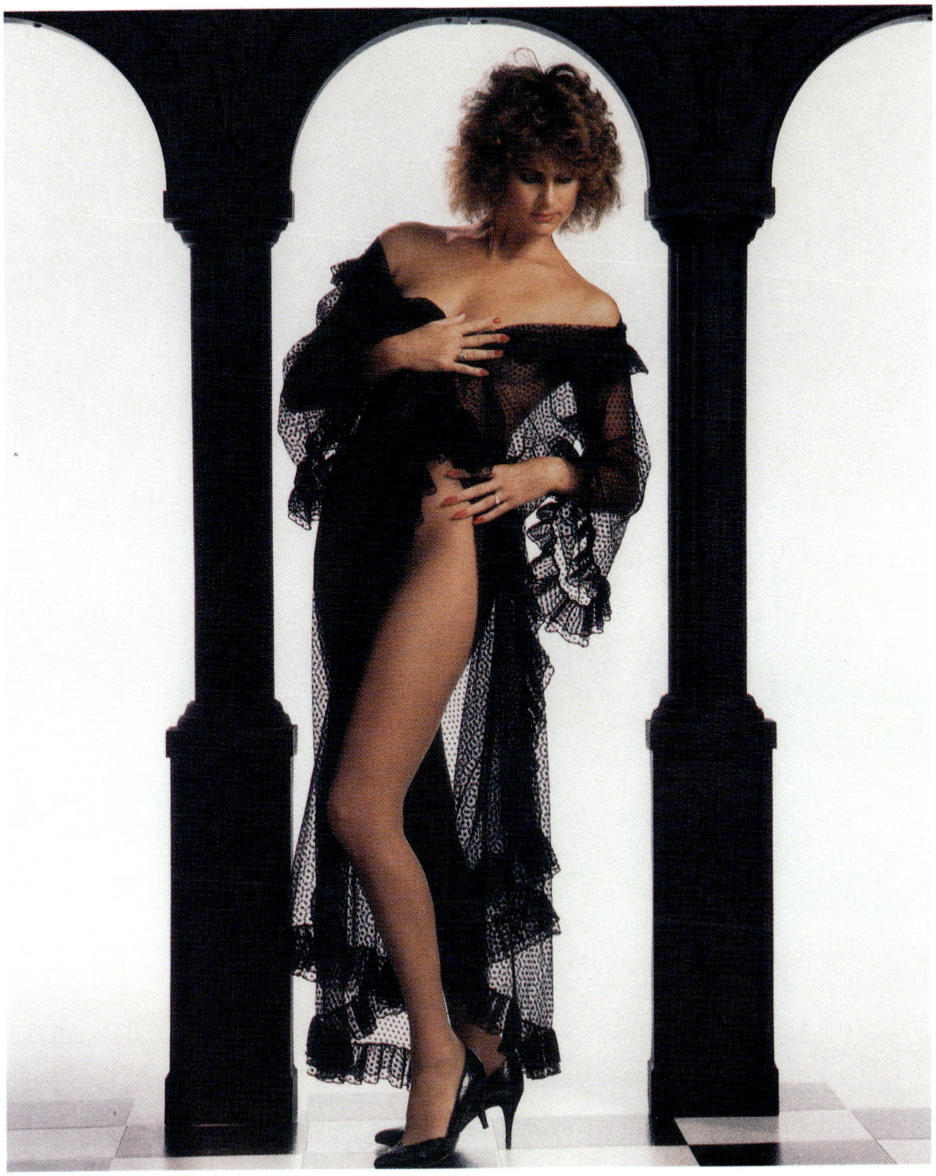

A set such as this takes only minutes to erect. We used 12x12-inch black and white stick-on tiles and carefully placed them on the floor. The arches, which we purchased from a second-hand store, had once been part of a local department-store display.

To add an ethereal look to the image, we deliberately placed the white background close to the tiled floor. The effect of the bright background on the tiles has caused almost a fog effect.

A see-through robe was carefully draped about the subject's body so that just the right amount of her was revealed—and concealed. The image was made more sensuous by the pose itself, which included a leaning, twisting and arching motion of the subject's body.

PORTFOLIO 83

Boudoir photography is an art of illusion and fantasy. This subject was not interested in an elaborate setting. She was primarily interested in being portrayed in the maid's costume in which she appears in this image.

Some men like to fantasize about being catered to by a beautiful attendant. This subject thought that it would be a cute idea to give her boyfriend some special photos of herself, attired as a seductive maid.

In this pose, little is concealed, so it is suitable only for subjects with a really good figure.

When shooting a side view of a "walking" pose, such as the one depicted here, the subject must bend one leg to simulate the motion of walking. The pose places great emphasis on the subject's legs, waist and bustline.

The main light was in a 40-inch white-lined umbrella with a plastic diffuser cap. It was positioned about 50 degrees to the right of camera-subject axis and connected to a 1200-watt-second power pack. A 3x4-foot softbox was used as fill light, placed about 10 degrees to the left of camera-subject axis. Its power was adjusted to emit two *f*-stops less light than the main light.

Two background lights, each in a silver-lined umbrella, were used, one directed on each side of the white background material. The background lights had their power adjusted to emit two *f*-stops more light than the main light.

A medium telephoto lens was used, and a Softar 1 filter. Exposure was at *f*-16.

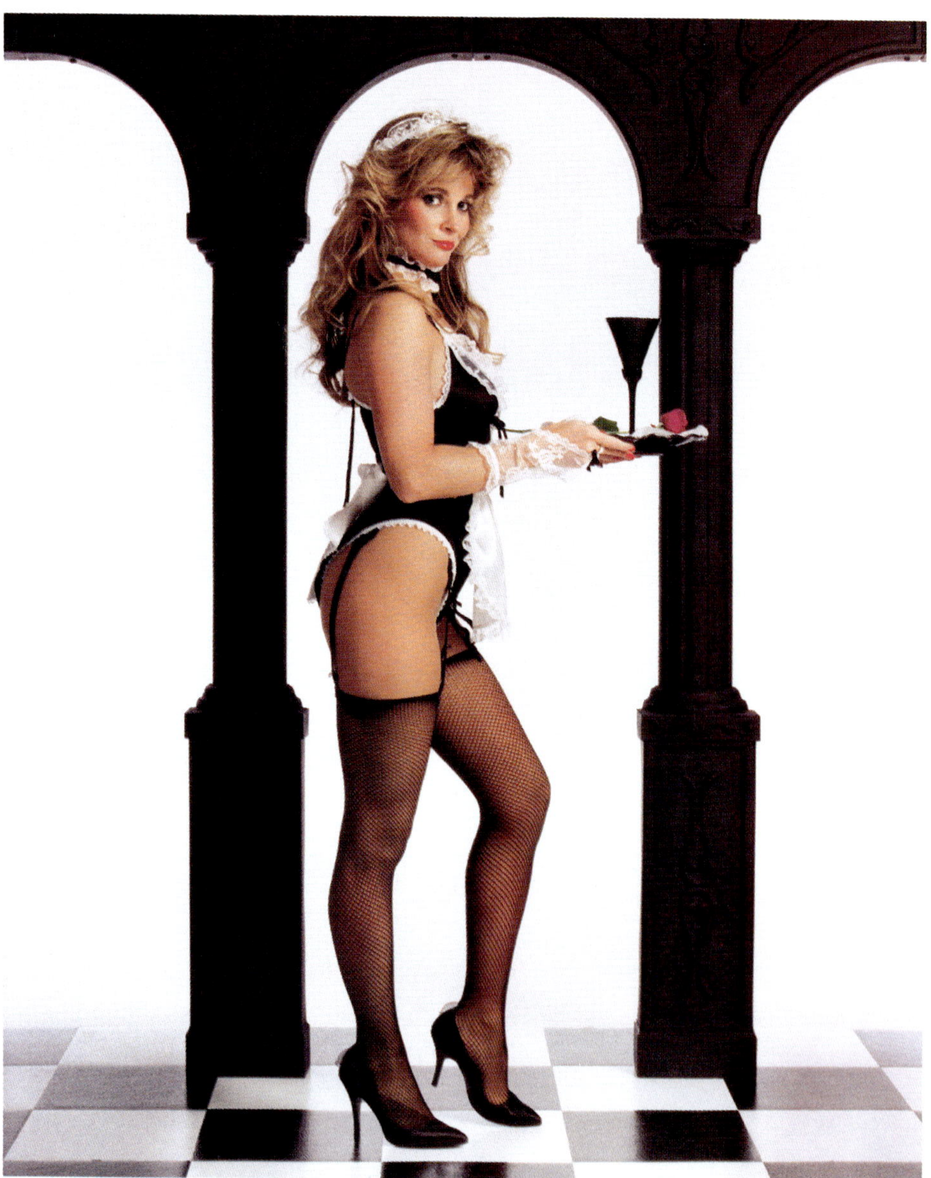

PORTFOLIO 84

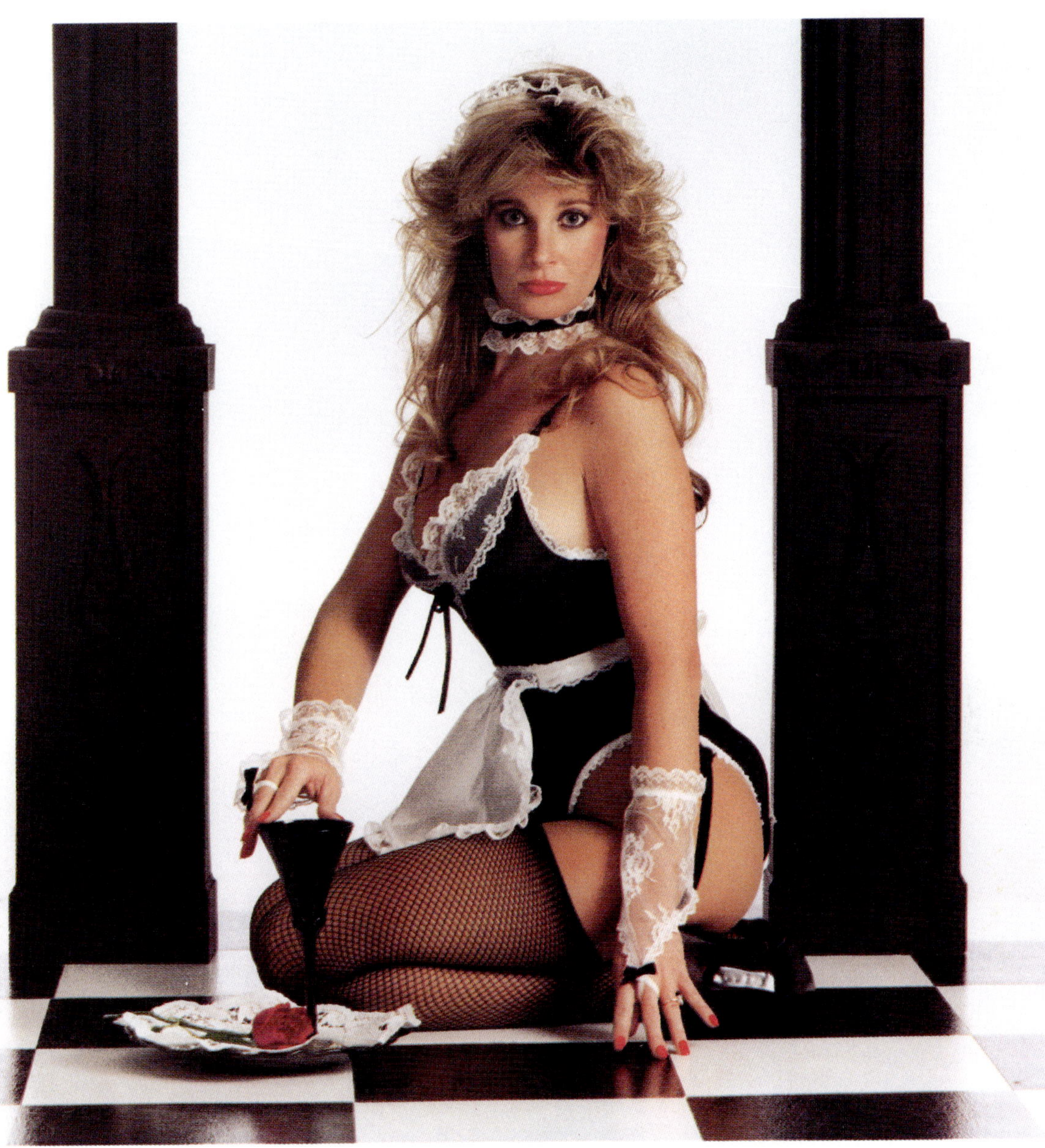

The basic technique for this photo was identical with that used for the preceding image. Only the pose was changed.

To justify a set's existence, and to produce an ample selection of images, you should shoot several poses, sometimes in different costumes, on each set.

Poses and facial expressions that you may think look great may not be thought of so highly by the subject when she sees the resulting prints. The more you vary subject attitudes, expressions and poses, the more likely you are to totally satisfy your subject.

Your aim should be to produce a dozen or more images on no more than three sets. If you were to spend a lot of time merely changing sets, your subject might leave your studio thinking of you more as a "stagehand" than a photographer!

No matter what the setting, if you find that it does not work for a specific subject, abandon it and move on to another setting that may be more pictorially productive.

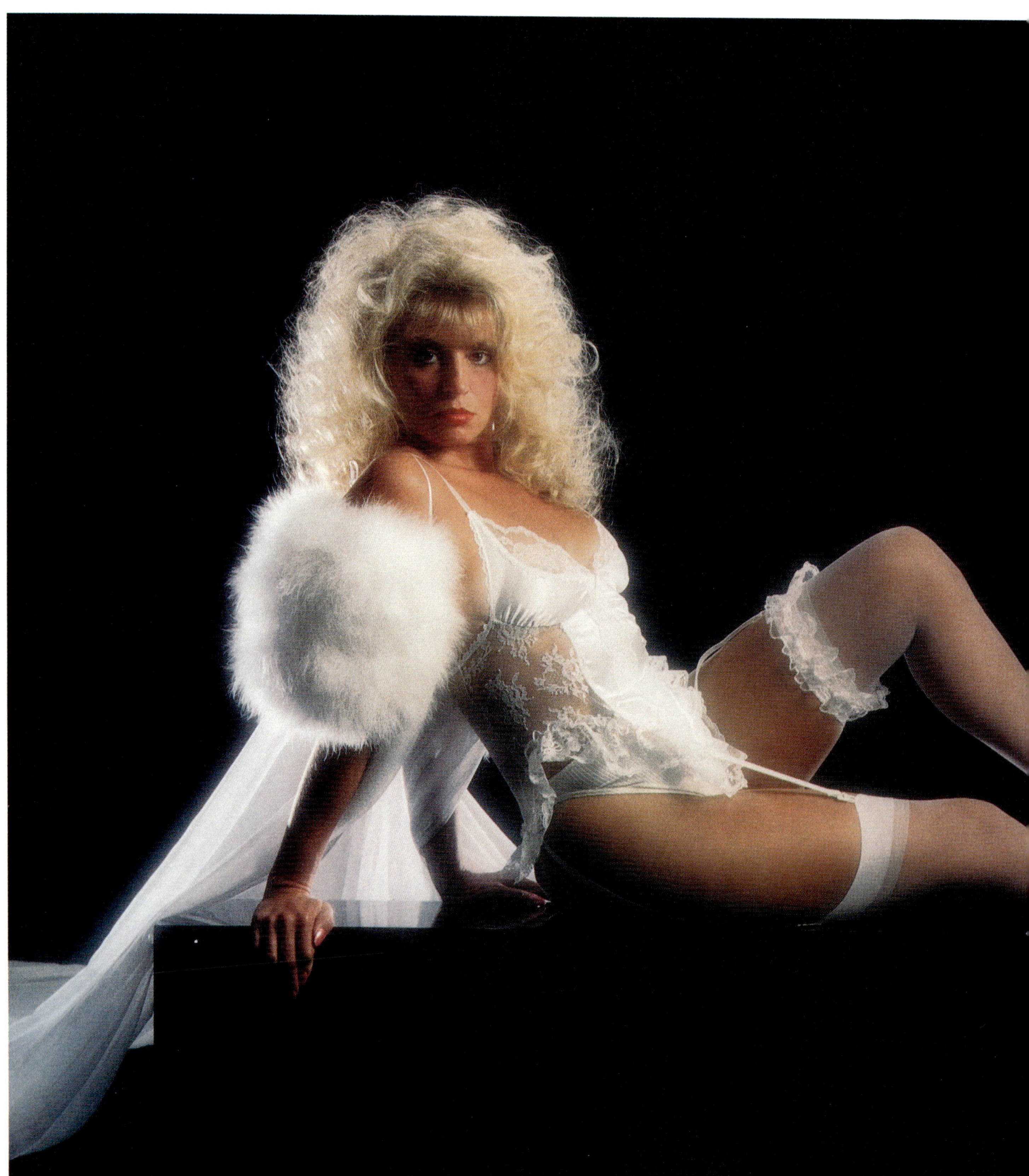

DARK BACKGROUND

Boudoir photos can look stunning and dramatic against a dark background. It is usually very easy to create since elaborate settings are generally not needed.

There are no hard and fast rules when it comes to choosing a background for a boudoir subject. Experience will be your best guide, tempered by your own style and taste, as well as a subject's wishes.

Some subjects may request that you take some photos with a light background and others with a dark background. It's up to you to advise a subject regarding what you think will, or won't, work.

Generally, heavy women should not be photographed in front of a bright background and very slim women should not be photographed against a dark background. But there are exceptions and, as a creative photographer, you should do whatever you feel looks good with any subject.

In the following photos, we show you how easy it is to create a new and different look for a subject against a dark background, with the aid of some simple props and accessories.

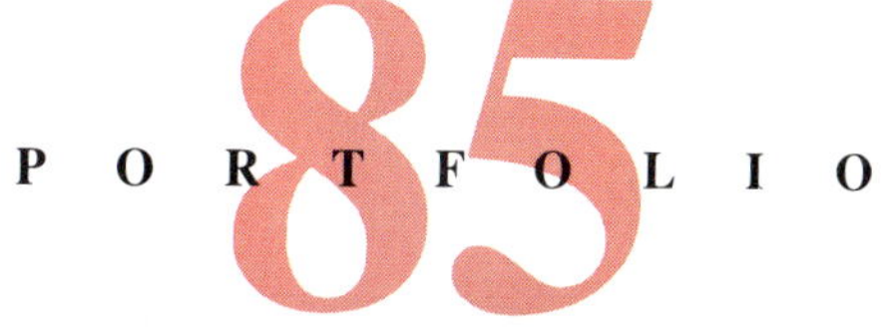

Subject, pose, costume and lighting all work together to make this a strong image. An actual set might have detracted attention from the subject.

The subject was directed into this relaxed, seated pose on two black blocks. With arms to the rear and one leg stretched out, the body becomes thinner in appearance. Accent is placed upon the bust and the appearance is one of sensuousness.

Main light was a flash in a 5-inch bowl reflector, directed through a queen-size bedsheet stretched between two stands. This light was placed approximately 70 degrees to the right of camera-subject axis and was connected to a 1000-watt-second power pack. A 4x8-foot white, foamcore board was used as a reflector fill light. It was placed approximately 90 degrees to the left of camera-subject axis.

Three additional lights were used. One, in a 5-inch bowl reflector, was placed slightly behind and above the subject and directed onto her hair. A second light, also in a 5-inch bowl reflector but with barn doors, was placed on the floor behind the subject and about 130 degrees to the left of camera-subject axis. It was directed onto the subject's gown and back. The final light, also in a 5-inch bowl reflector with barn doors, was placed on the floor and immediately behind the subject's left leg. It served to outline both legs.

All three of these lights were connected to 1000-watt-second power packs and each had its power adjusted to emit one *f*-stop more light than the main light.

PORTFOLIO 86

This photo depicts the same subject and, believe it or not, the same costume as the preceding photo. A completely different look is achieved.

The subject was instructed to stand and turn her body slightly sideways. This allowed the main light to skim across her bust and accentuate it.

The gown, designed and made by us, was stretched to its full limits and pinned to the floor. Compositionally, this placement of the gown, along with the telephone on the floor, helped to create a solid, triangular base for the subject, so that she does not appear to be "floating" in black space.

The main light was the same as in the previous photo. It was placed 45 degrees to the right of camera-subject axis and connected to a 1000-watt-second power pack.

Only two other lights were used. One, in a 5-inch bowl reflector, was placed a little way behind the subject and above her and directed onto her hair and gown. The other light, also in a 5-inch bowl reflector, was placed on the floor and directly behind the subject. It was directed at the lower portion of the gown. Each of these two accent lights was connected to 1000-watt-second power pack and covered with a magenta gel. Each had its power adjusted to emit one *f*-stop more light than the main light.

A medium telephoto lens was used, and a Softar 1 filter. Exposure was at *f*-8.

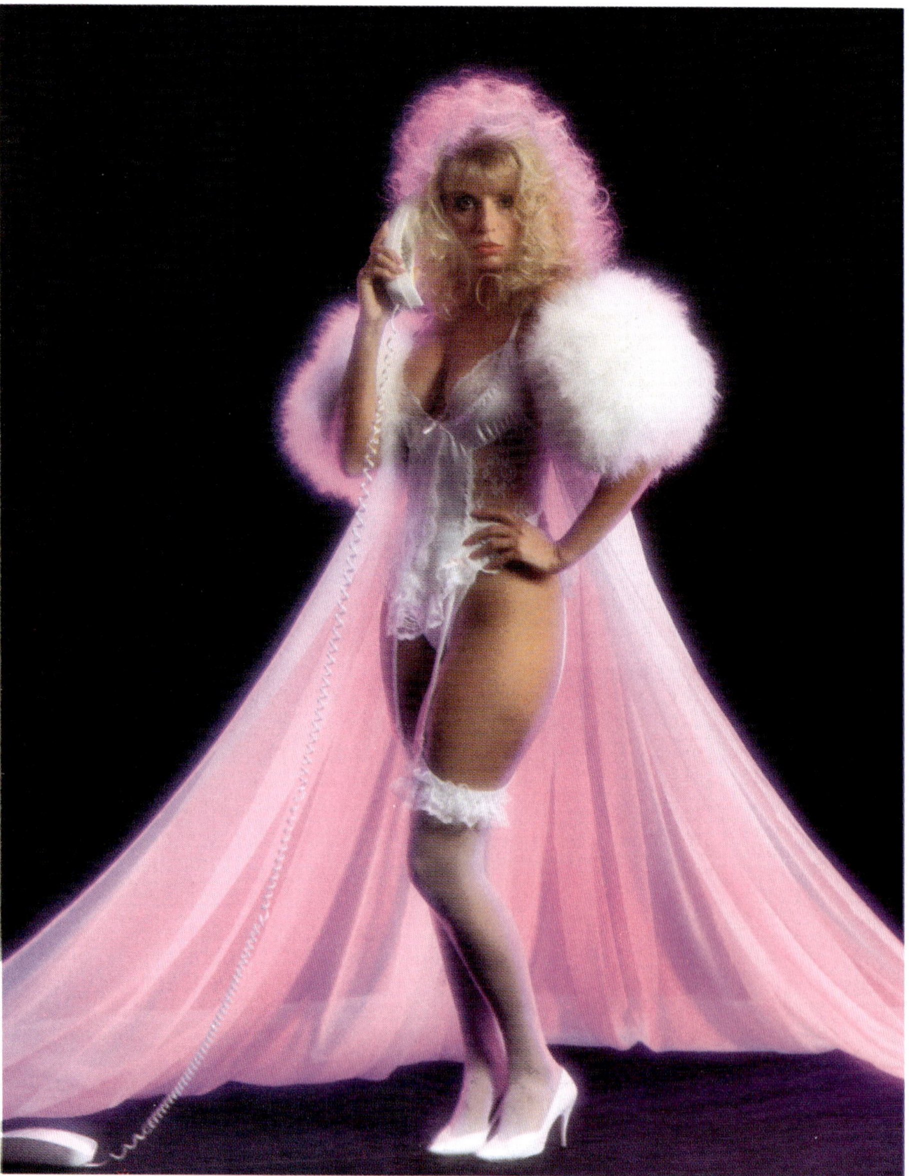

PORTFOLIO 87

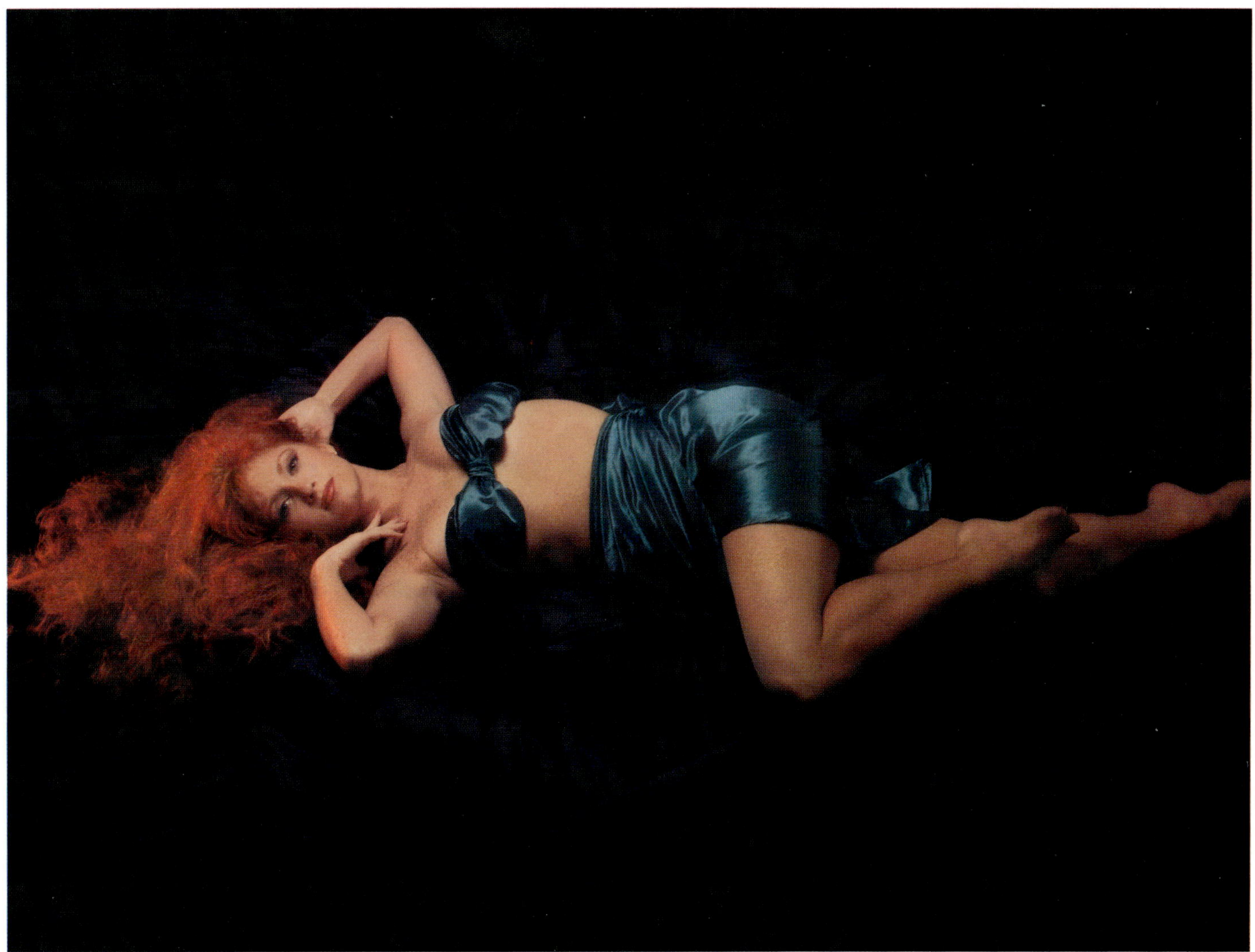

This is one of our favorite images. The pose is very popular with many of our subjects. It was inspired by an old Rita Hayworth photo that appeared in a national magazine many years ago.

The pose is not as easy as it looks and, therefore, is not suitable for all subjects. You should be prepared to spend several minutes with a subject, demonstrating and assisting her into this pose.

A 4x4-foot cushion, covered with black, satin-like material, was placed on the black floor. The subject was directed to lie on her back on the cushion and our assistants then helped her into the pose depicted.

A 2x2-foot piece of architectural vellum was secured to a lightweight wooden frame and then suspended about three feet above and slightly behind the subject. It was transilluminated by a flash in a 5-inch bowl reflector, connected to a 2000-watt-second power pack. This main light was directed onto the subject's body.

The vellum diffused the light, giving it a very soft quality. This yielded a gentle, gradual transition from highlights to shadows.

Another light, in a 4x10-inch snooted reflector, was placed on the floor, about 90 degrees to the left of camera-subject axis. It was covered with an amber gel and directed onto the subject's hair. Its power was adjusted to equal that of the main light.

To achieve the look we were after, we shot down at the subject from a height of about 8 feet. A standard lens was used, and a Softar 1 filter. Exposure was at *f*-11.

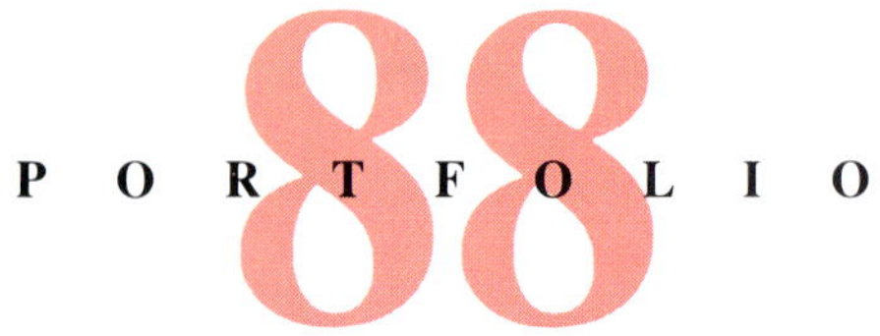

PORTFOLIO 88

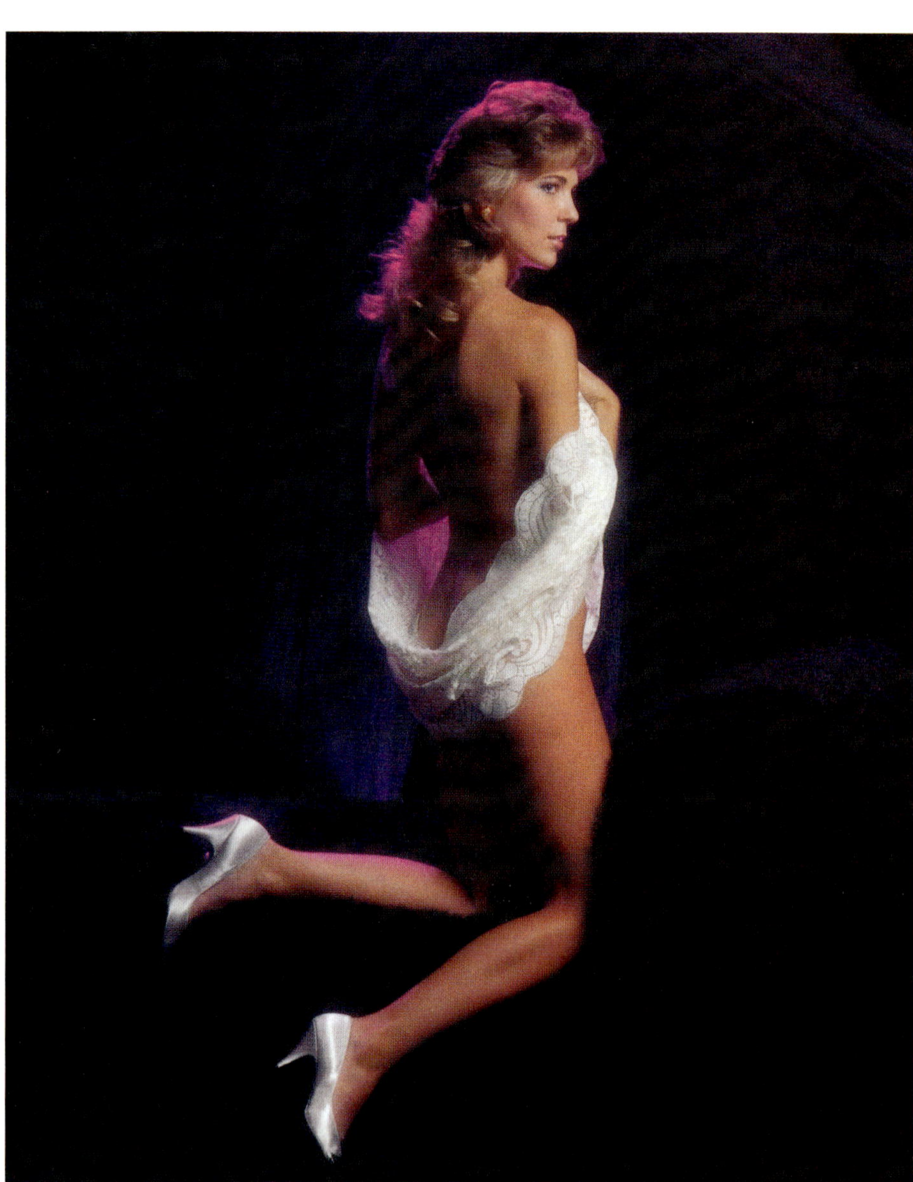

This is a lovely pose and an easy one, that most subjects are able to assume. The pose is very popular, flattering a subject's body. This image gives a strong suggestion of nudity without being too revealing.

Subjects are often concerned about their stomach or buttocks appearing too large and less than flattering. The use of a drape helps to eliminate or minimize this concern.

The subject was kneeling on a small couch, covered with a black synthetic fur. Directly above and behind her was a large piece of black netting. The netting was added to give further dimension and interest to the photo. It was intentionally underlit to keep its statement subtle.

A 6-foot Larson Starfish, placed approximately 45 degrees to the right of camera-subject axis, was used as main light. It was powered by a 1250-watt-second power pack.

Another light, in a 5-inch bowl reflector, was placed above and slightly behind the subject and covered with a magenta gel. Its power was adjusted to emit one *f*-stop less light than the main light. This second light was directed onto the back of the subject's head.

A third light, also in a 5-inch bowl reflector and covered with a magenta gel, was placed directly behind the couch, on the floor. It was directed onto the subject's midsection and the drape. Its power was adjusted to emit two *f*-stops less light than the main light.

The final light, in a 4-inch bowl reflector with barn doors and covered with a magenta gel, was also placed behind the couch, on the floor. It was directed solely onto the black netting. Its power was adjusted to emit three *f*-stops less light than the main light.

89 PORTFOLIO

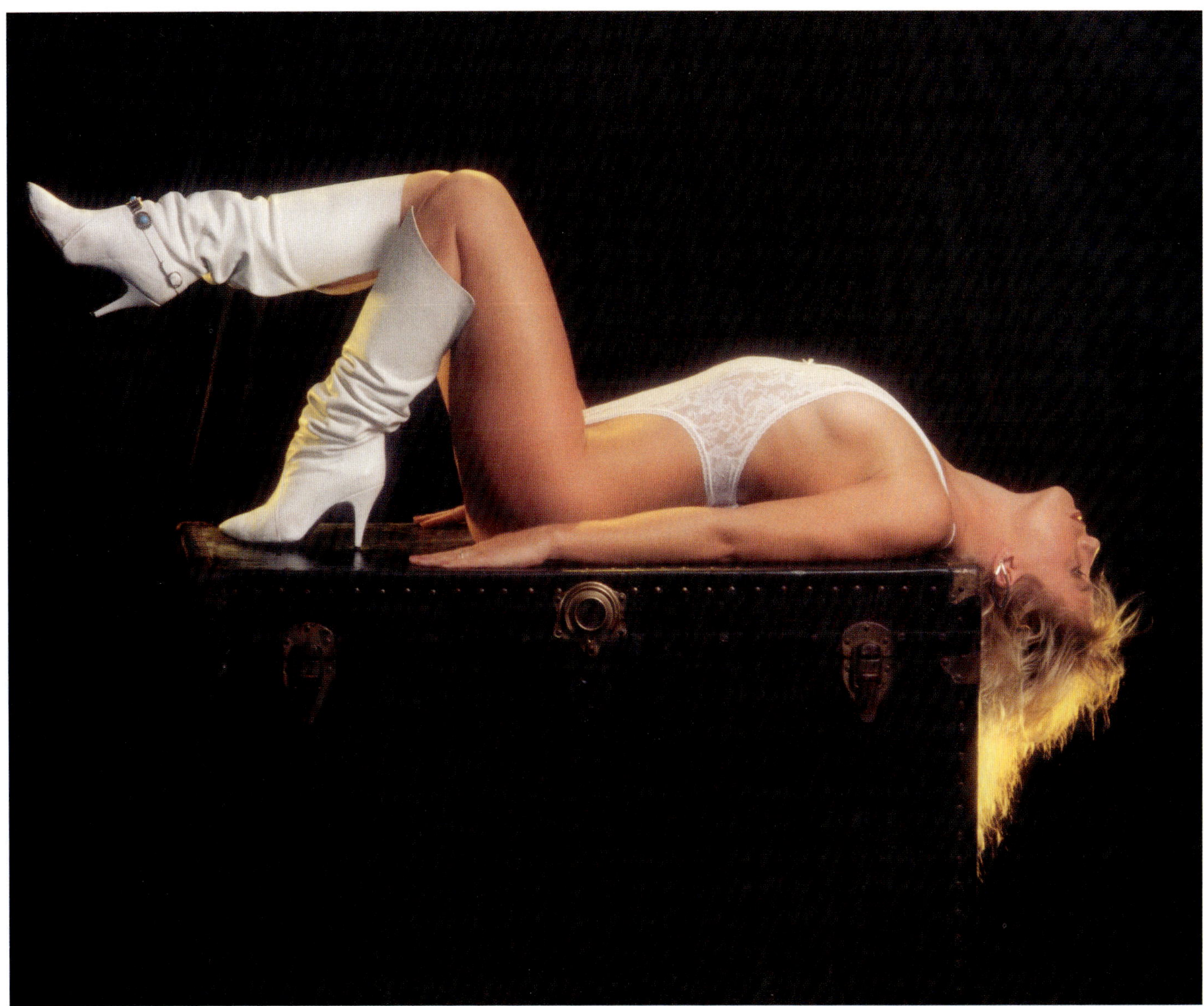

The main light for this image was a 6-foot Larson Starfish, placed above and slightly behind the subject and directed down onto her body. The light was connected to a 1250-watt-second power pack.

A light in a 4-inch bowl reflector with barn doors was placed on the floor behind the trunk, near the subject's head. This light, covered with a yellow gel, was directed onto the subject's hair. Its power was adjusted to one *f*-stop more light than the main light, thus emphasizing the hair.

Another light, in a 4-inch bowl reflector with barn doors, was placed on the floor on the far side of the subject's legs and directed onto her legs and buttocks. It was covered with a yellow gel and had its power adjusted to one *f*-stop less light than the main light.

A large piece of black netting was placed behind the subject to add further dimension to the image. Both of the gelled floor lights were allowed to spill some of their light onto the netting, so that the netting could be subtly perceived.

A medium telephoto lens was used, and a Softar 1 filter. Exposure was at *f*-8.

PORTFOLIO 90

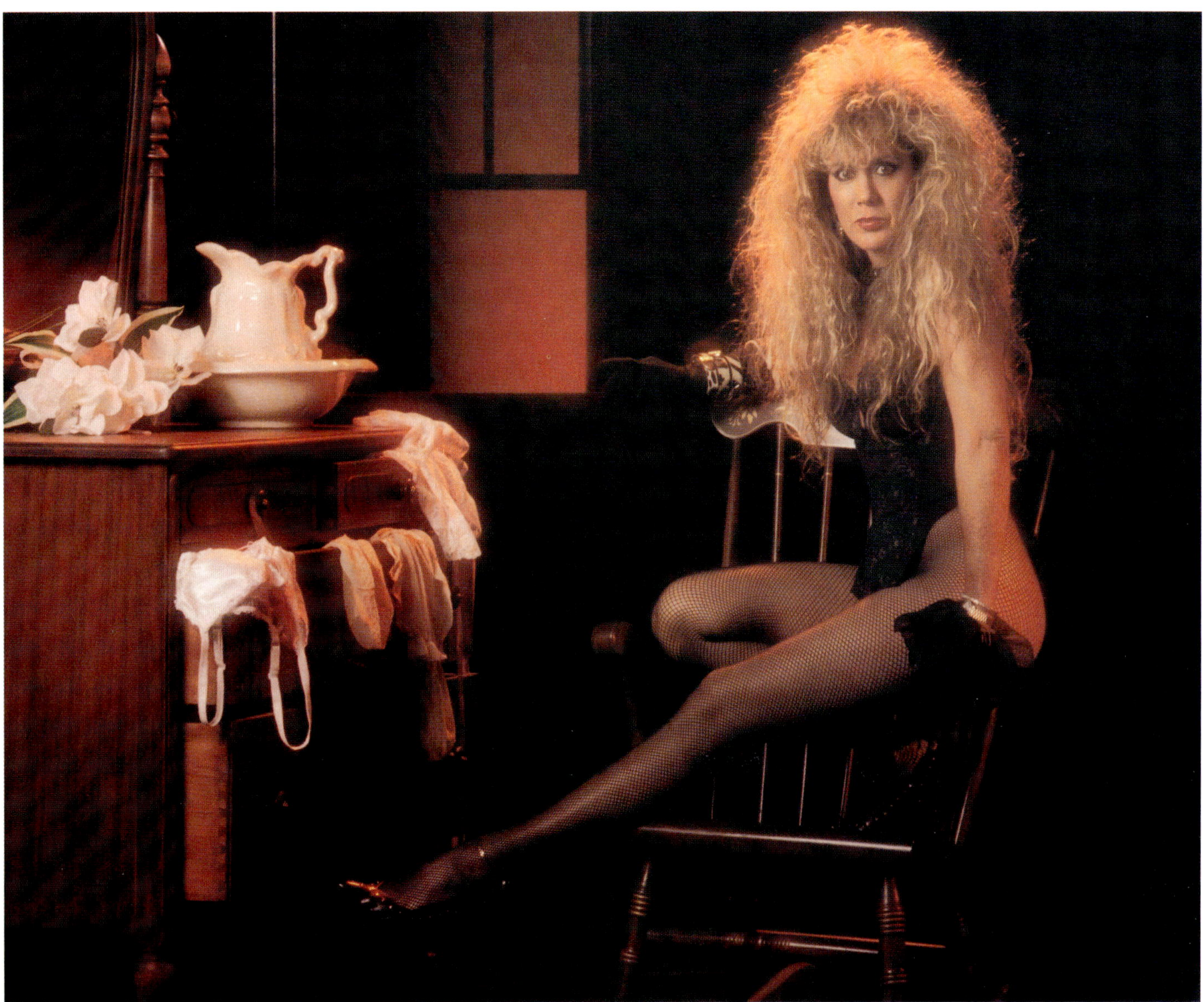

The dresser was first moved into position and angled for best visibility of the drawers. To bring the scene to life, clothing was hung from the drawers. The bowl, pitcher and flowers were placed on top of the dresser to add interest and atmosphere.

The mirror on the dresser had to be angled so that it could reflect some background color.

An 8x9-foot window-wall, made of foamcore board, was placed about 6 feet behind the dresser and covered with black velvet. The wall was positioned so that the window would not invade the space of the subject's body nor compete with it.

Black background paper was put approximately 3 feet behind the window. It was illuminated by a light with a red gel, to provide the warm, "outdoor" glow.

The rocking chair was put in place and the subject instructed into her pose.

A 6-foot Larson Starfish was used as main light. It was positioned about 30 degrees to the left of camera-subject axis.

A light in a 5-inch bowl reflector was placed above and slightly behind the subject and covered with an amber gel. It was directed onto the hair of the subject.

Another light, in a 4x10-inch snooted reflector, was placed 90 degrees to the right of camera-subject axis. It was covered with an amber gel and directed onto the subject's back and buttocks.

PORTFOLIO 91

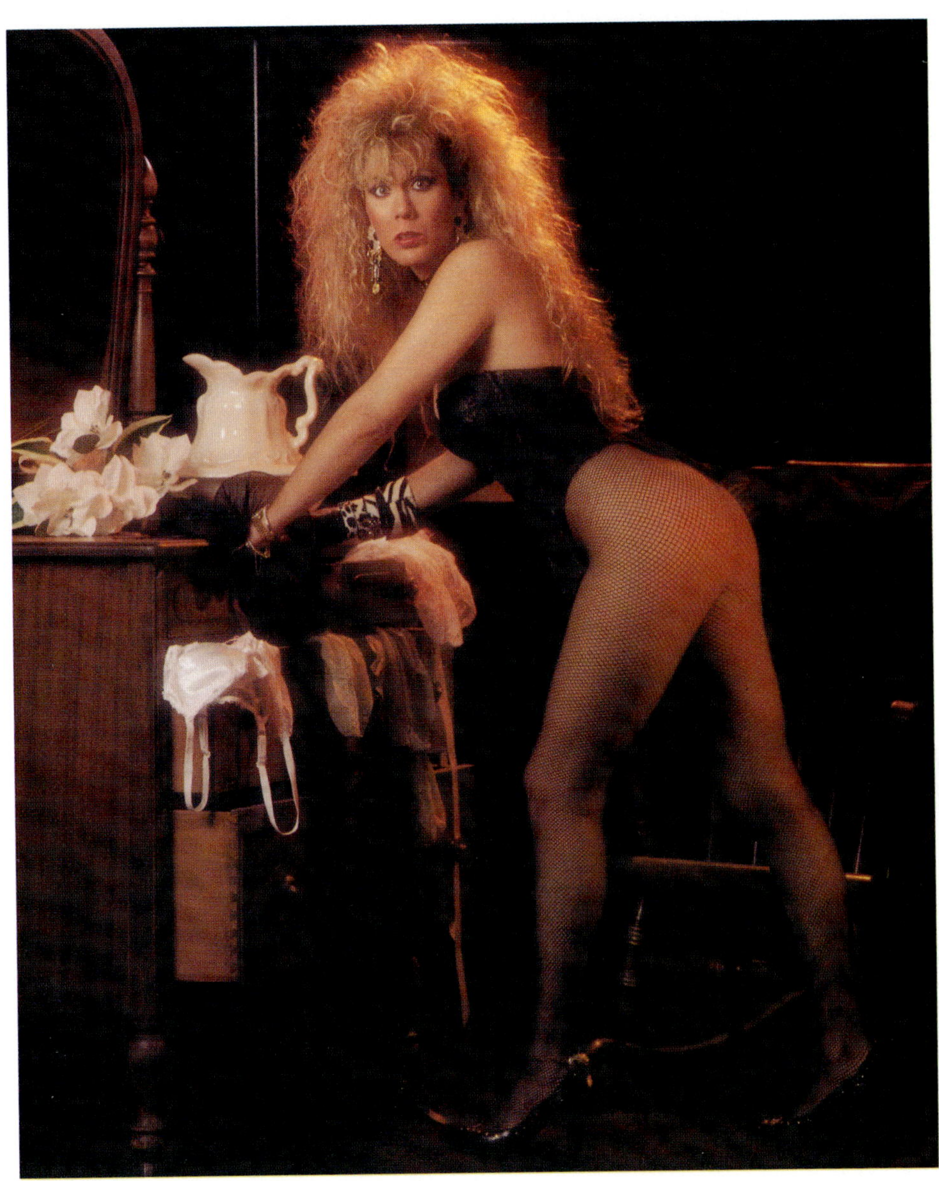

The only major difference between this photo and the previous one is the pose.

You must be able to control your lighting. Precise light control is particularly difficult in a low-key situation where there are extensive dark areas. In a high-key photo, a misguided or misplaced light or two may never be noticed. However, in a low-key photo such as this one, badly placed lighting would be very obvious.

To control a light's direction and keep it from striking unwanted parts of the subject or set, numerous photographic tools are available. They include snoots, barndoors, flags and gobos. Having these tools readily available during a photo session is important.

To make this image, and place light exactly where we wanted it, we needed one snoot, one barndoor, two black flags and one gobo.

PORTFOLIO 92

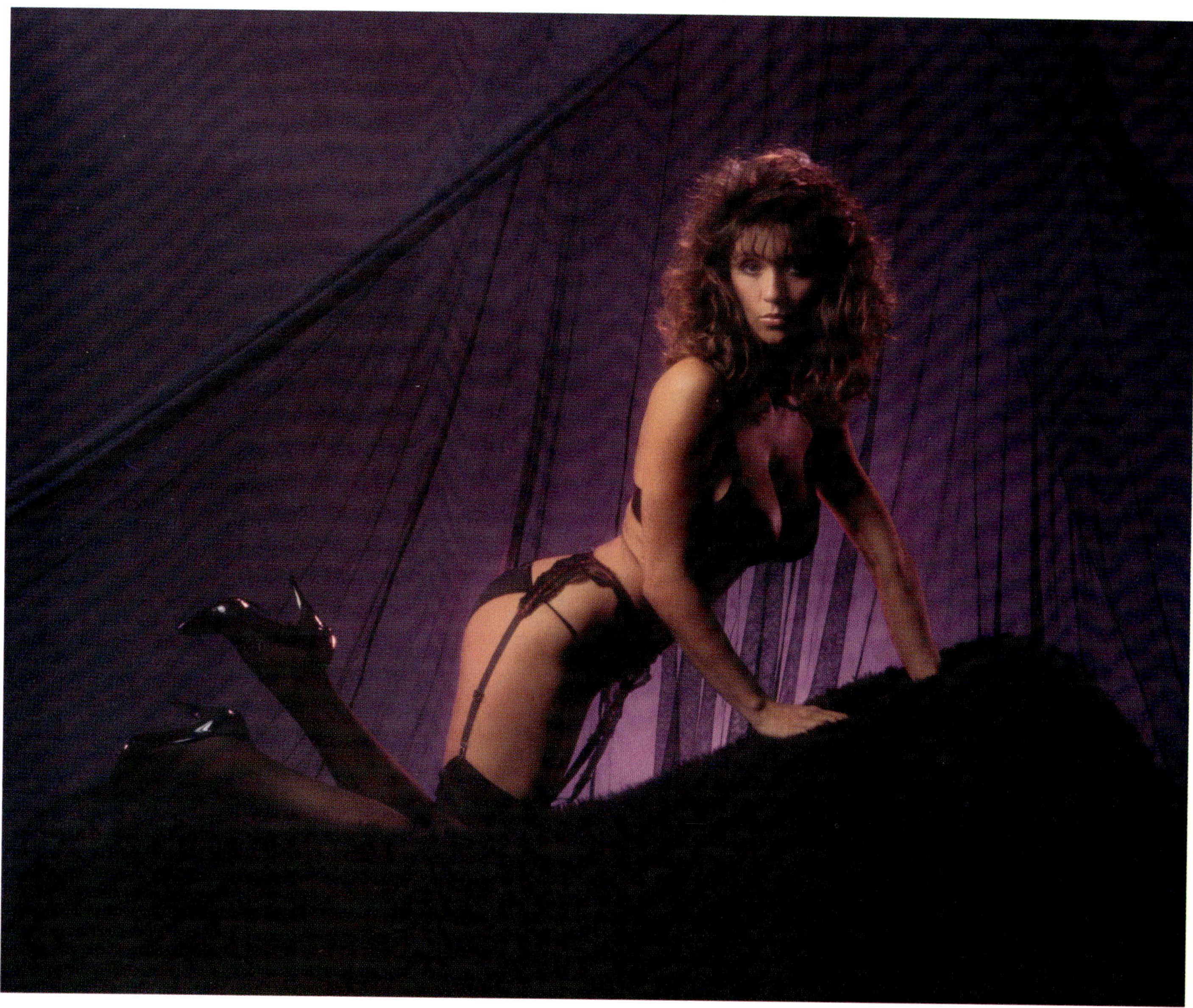

For this photo we used a couch, covered with black synthetic fur. A queen-size bedsheet, supported by two stands and backlit by a flash in a 4-inch bowl reflector, was used as main-light source. It was positioned about 45 degrees to the left of camera-subject axis and powered by a 1000-watt-second power pack.

Another light, in a 5-inch bowl reflector, was placed above and slightly behind the subject and covered with a magenta gel. Its power was adjusted to emit one *f*-stop less light than the main light.

Two other lights, each in a 5-inch bowl reflector with barndoors, were placed on the floor to the far side of the subject and covered with magenta gels. One light was directed onto the back of the subject and the other onto the black netting in the background. The black netting was lit sufficiently to become a prominent part of the composition and overall design.

We wanted the subject's breasts to be lit subtly but decisively. This was accomplished by having the main light skim across her bust. To provide further accent, the top light—equipped with a set of barndoors—was adjusted to spill a slight amount of its magenta light onto the subject's bust.

PORTFOLIO 93

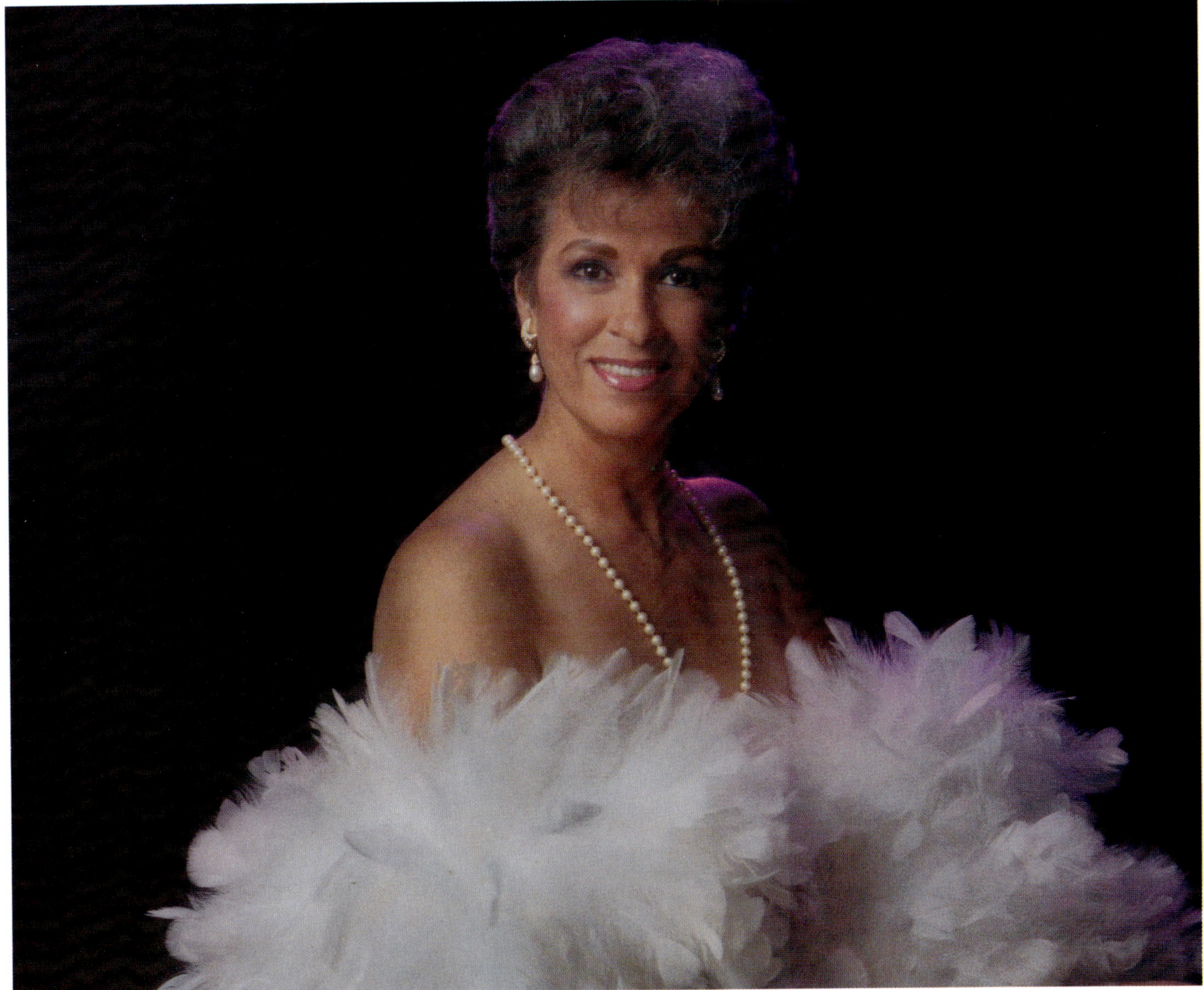

Generally, a boudoir photo session should start out simply. A subject needs time to gain confidence in herself, in you, and in your assistants.

We often begin a session—as we did here—with tight head-and-shoulder shots, employing guarded poses and concealing costumes. After several frames of film have been shot and a few minutes have elapsed, the subject will begin to feel more at ease and confident. At this point, you can use more revealing costumes and more daring poses.

This subject, who is in her 50s, was very apprehensive and skeptical about engaging in this form of photography. The first few shots of her were less than great. However, as the session progressed, we were able to capture some truly outstanding images of her.

A 3-foot Larson Starfish was used as main light. It was placed about 45 degrees to the left of camera-subject axis and its flash was connected to a 1000-watt-second power pack. A light in a 5-inch bowl reflector was placed above and slightly behind the subject and covered with a magenta gel.

PORTFOLIO 94

Like the woman in the previous image, this subject was also in her 50s and very apprehensive about engaging in this form of photography. However, after a few simple head-and-shoulders shots had been taken we felt the subject was ready. The camera was moved farther back and this stunning seated, full-length image was created. A study of the subject's facial expression clearly indicates that all of her initial anxieties had disappeared. Her face is free of tension and concern and, like the pose, appears very natural and relaxed.

There are two primary goals in boudoir photography: The subject should thoroughly enjoy the experience and have fun and beautiful images should result. Neither of these goals can be achieved until the subject gains confidence in you and in herself.

A 6-foot Larson Starfish, placed about 45 degrees to the left of camera-subject axis, was used as main light. Its flash was connected to a 1000-watt-second power pack.

Another light, in a 5-inch bowl reflector, was placed above and slightly behind the subject and covered with a magenta gel. Its light was directed onto the shoulders of the subject and her head. Its power was adjusted to emit one *f*-stop less light than the main light.

Black netting was placed behind the subject to add interest and dimension to the photo. Another light, in a 5-inch bowl reflector and covered with a magenta gel, was placed on the floor directly behind the subject. It was aimed at the black netting and its power was adjusted to emit two *f*-stops less light than the main light.

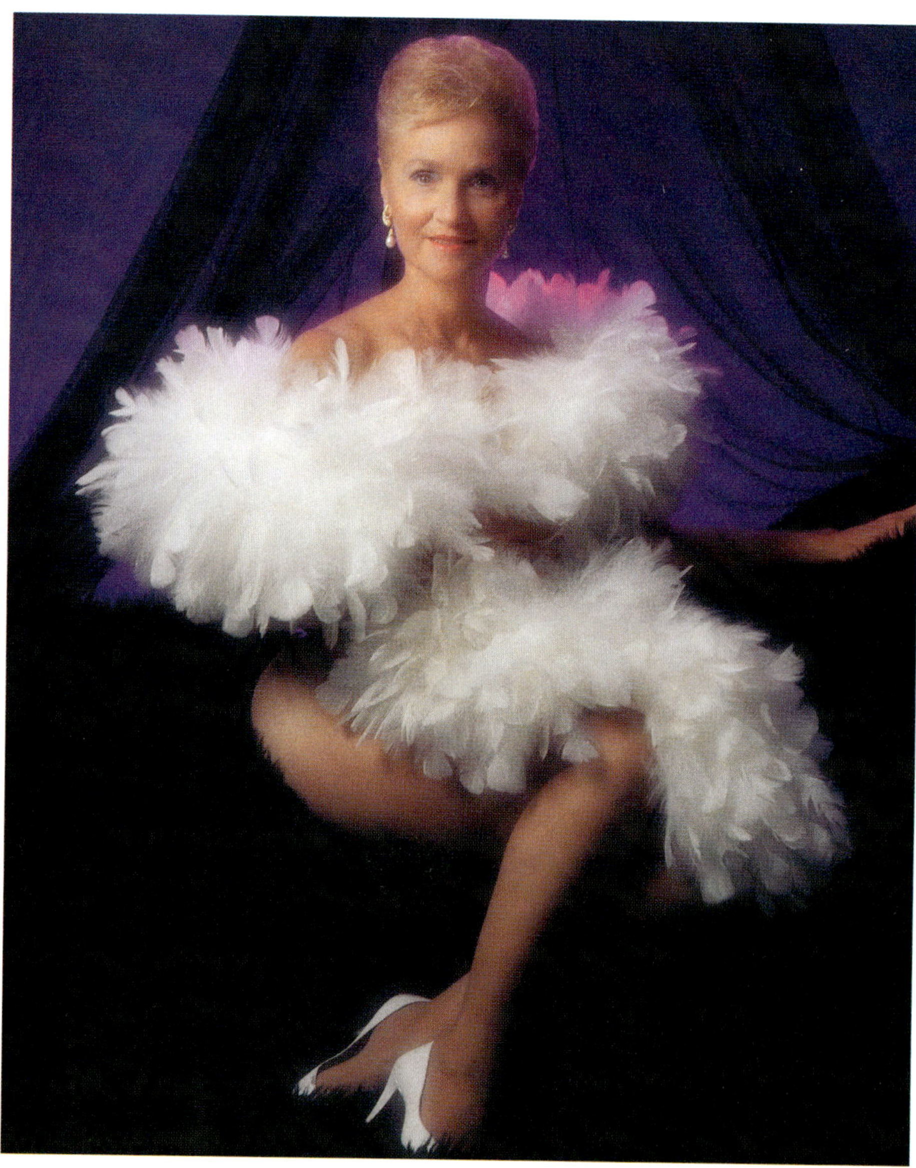

PORTFOLIO 95

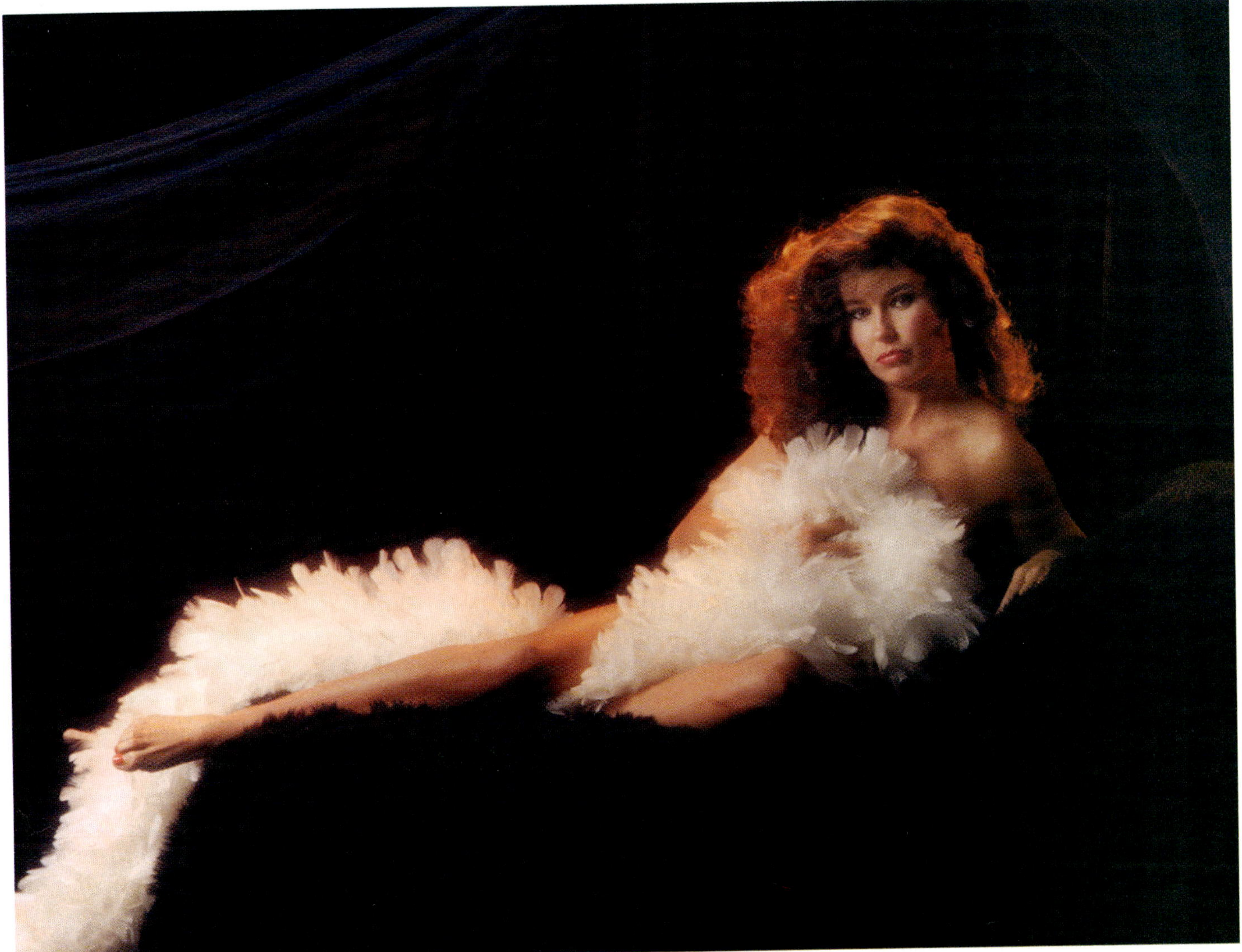

This lovely and sensuous pose is easy to adopt and flatters most women.

The boa not only adds to the overall design of the image but also affords the subject a feeling of security by allowing body parts which she may consider to be less than flattering to be concealed.

The couch, which was covered with a black synthetic fur, served two purposes: It afforded the subject a comfortable location and also helped to conceal. Because the pile of the fur is deep, when a subject sits or lies on it, portions of the body become slightly hidden from view. This can have a thinning effect on a subject.

A 6-foot Larson Starfish was used as main light. It was placed about 60 degrees to the left of camera-subject axis and its flash was connected to a 1000-watt-second power pack. A white, 4x7-foot foamcore reflector was placed to the right of camera-subject axis, close to the subject's face and just out of camera view.

A light in a 5-inch bowl reflector was placed above and slightly behind the subject and covered with an amber gel. Its light was directed onto the back of the subject, to rim light her body and hair.

Another light, in a 6-inch bowl reflector, was placed directly behind the subject's hair. It, too, was covered with an amber gel. It added the distinct rim light to the hair.

A final light, in a 5-inch bowl reflector and covered with an amber gel, was placed directly behind the subject and directed onto the black background netting. Its power was adjusted to emit just enough light to make the netting discernible.

WITH CARS

Beautiful women and beautiful cars always seem to go well together. A photograph of a subject posed with a gorgeous car—especially a car that has special meaning for her and her "special someone"—will always be a winner.

We shoot most of our boudoir car photos on location, at the subject's home. A novice boudoir photographer can easily be tempted to place too much emphasis on home and possessions, and not enough on the subject, especially at a lavish home. It's easy to become so involved with the grandeur of the home and all of its appointments that the real purpose of the shoot—capturing dynamic images of the subject—is forgotten.

If you are going to do location boudoir photography involving a car, confine your main points of interest to subject and car. Of course, you should select the most attractive possible background, too. This can often be the subject's home.

At the other extreme, beware of showing too little. The car is an important integral part of the composition. Show enough of the car to make it a key part of your pictorial story. Depict both subject and car in an attractive, flattering way.

Don't plan to shoot too many poses, at too many locations. Remember, a nonprofessional model will tire after a relatively short time and you must shoot fast to capture all your images while she is still fresh and enthusiastic. Four good images, made at two locations or angles, are better than 20 unattractive shots, made over a tedious three-hour period.

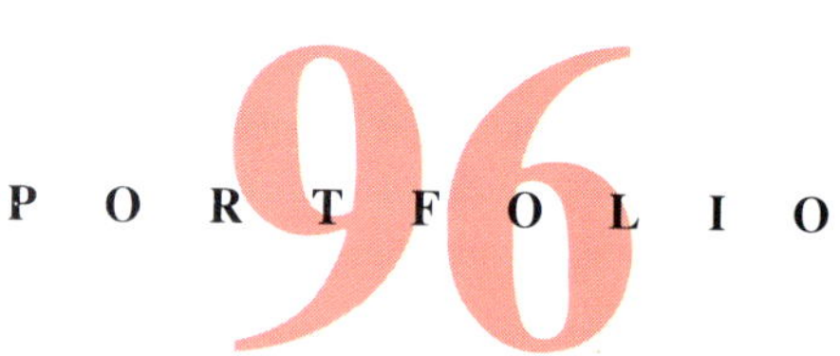

P O R T F O L I O 96

A beautiful car is a very versatile posing prop. You can photograph your subject outside the car or in it. She can be in front of the car, behind it, beside it, or even on top of it. At each location, as many as half a dozen different poses can easily be photographed. This offers great pictorial variety.

When the natural daylight is overcast, dull and lifeless—as it was when this photo was taken—we augment the lighting with flash.

For this photo, flash was used as main-light source and the ambient light was used as fill light. The flash illumination came from a 4x7-foot light panel. It was placed about 60 degrees to the left of camera-subject axis.

A 3x4-foot plastic mirror was placed about 60 degrees to the right of camera-subject axis. It was used as an additional reflector fill light.

Based upon an incident-light meter reading, the shutter speed was adjusted so that the ambient light would be underexposed by one *f*-stop.

A standard lens was used, and a warming filter. Exposure was 1/30 second at *f*-11.

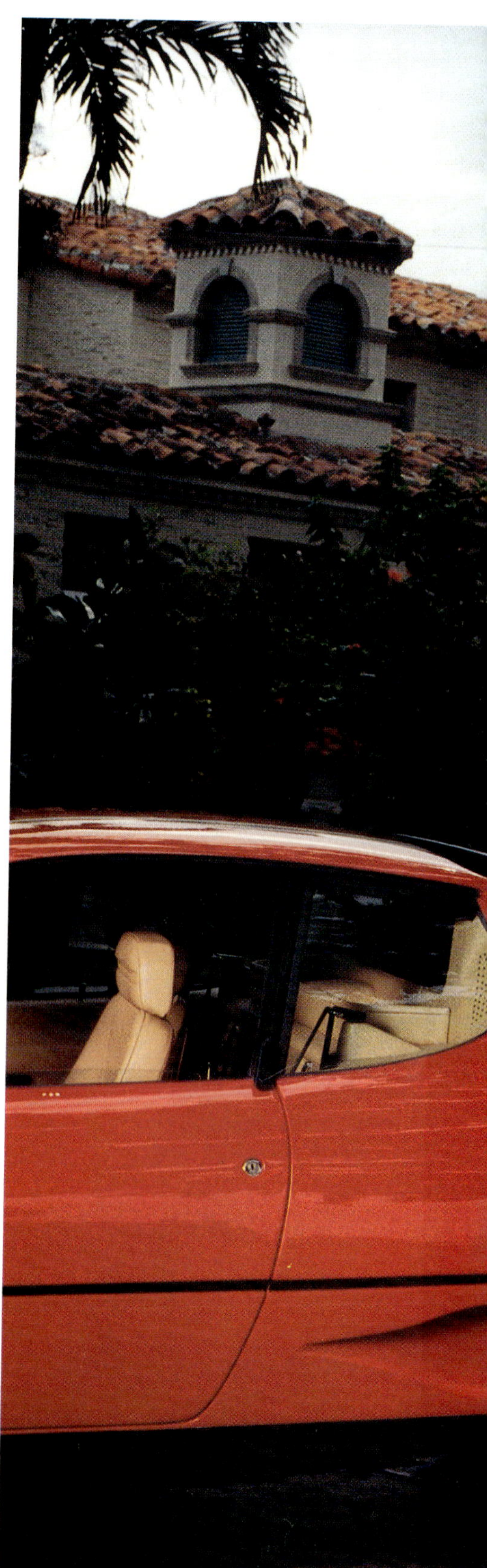

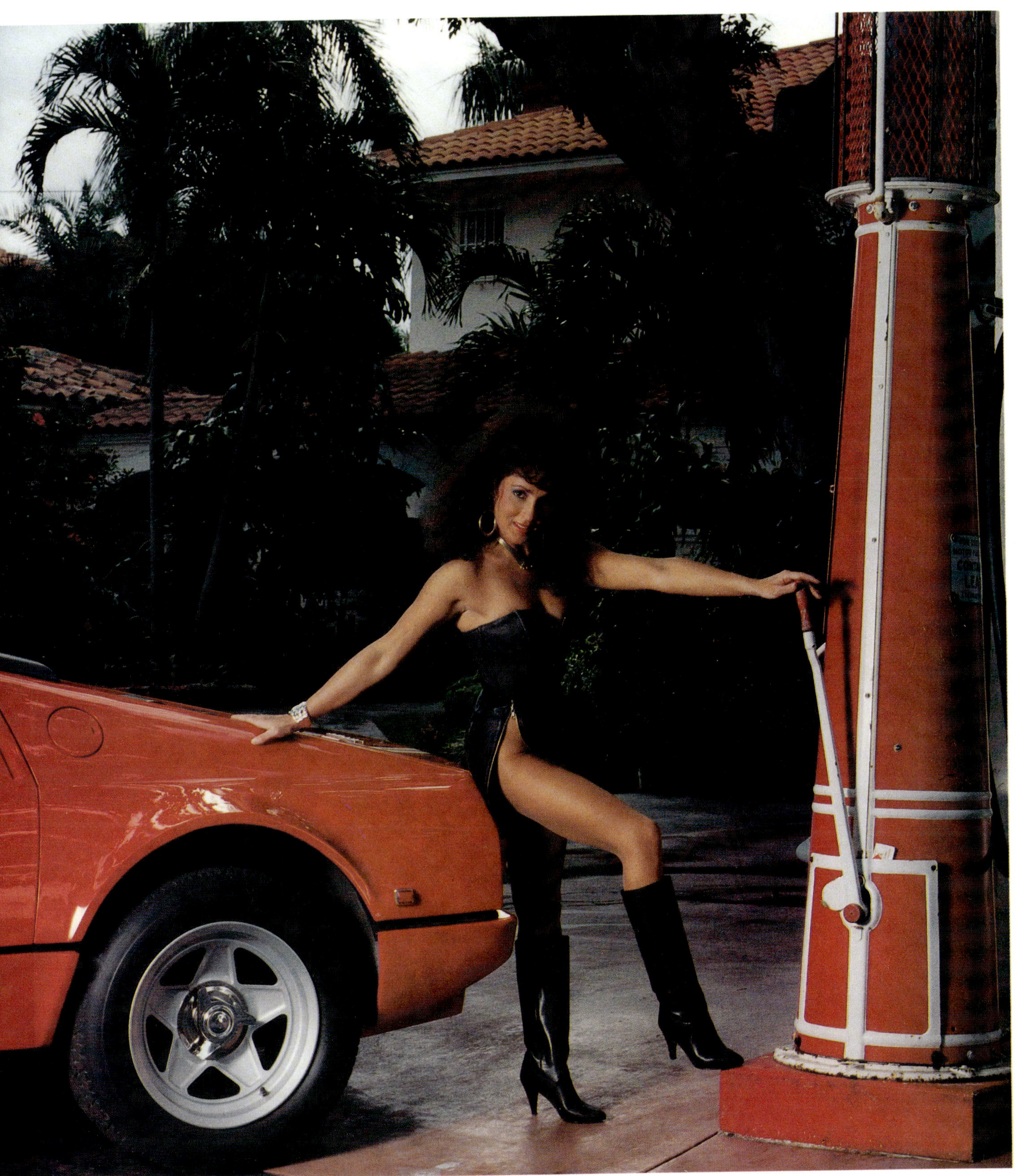

97 PORTFOLIO

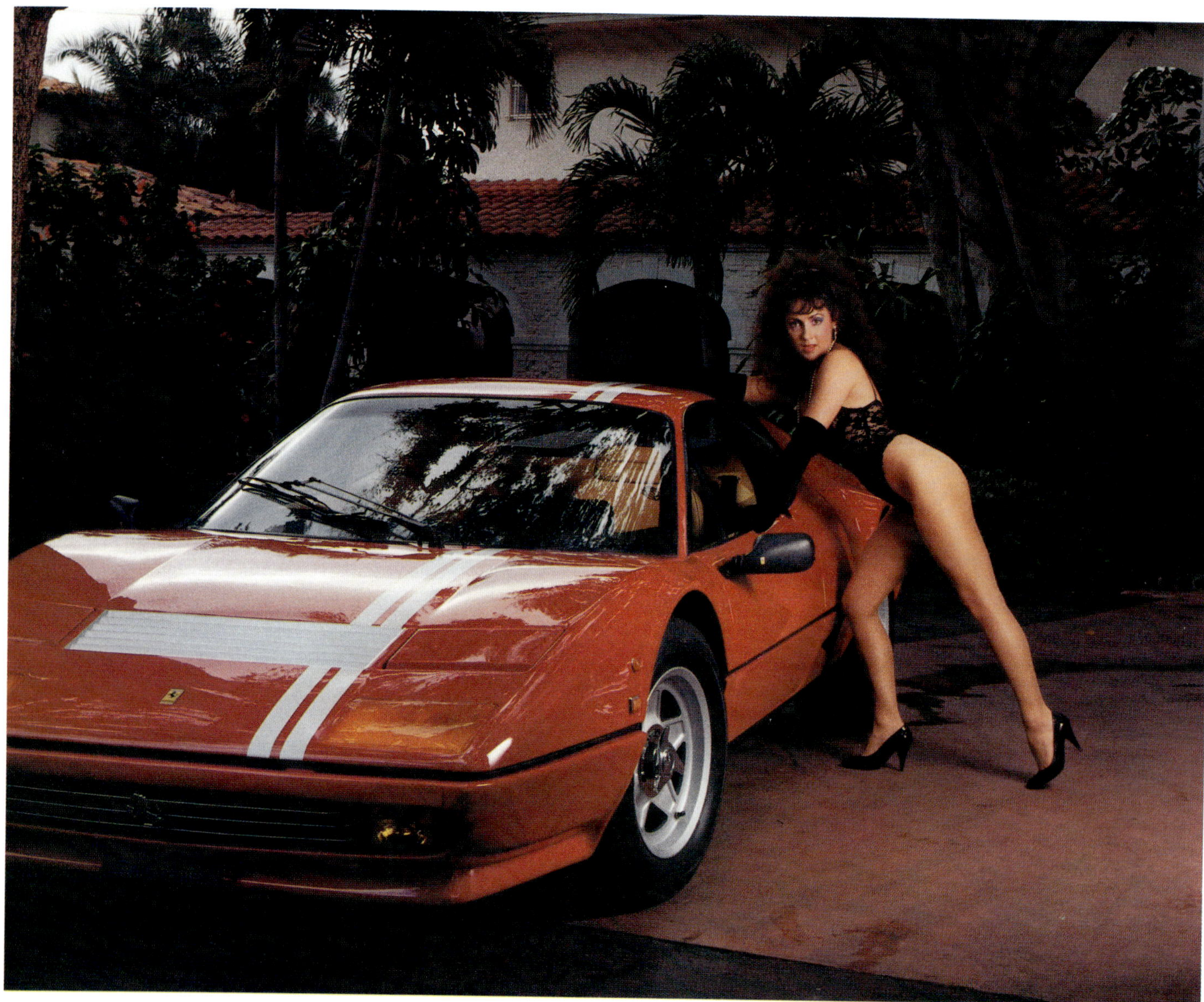

If you feel it will help an image, you can use any number of lights. For this photo, for example, we could have placed a light under the car and another inside the car. In addition, the car's headlights and parking lights could have been turned on. Other lights could have backlit the car. However, you should remember that the main point of interest must always be the subject. The car should not upstage her.

Main light of 1000-watt-seconds power, was a backlit 4x7-foot light panel, placed approximately 45 degrees to the right of camera-subject axis.

A 3x4-foot plastic mirror, placed about 100 degrees to the right of the camera-subject axis, was used as an accent light. It reflected some of the daylight and light from the flash onto the back of the subject and the side of the car.

The ambient light, used as fill light, was intentionally underexposed by one *f*-stop from the indicated meter reading. Exposure was 1/30 second at *f*-11.

When photographing shiny cars, always be on the lookout for unwanted reflections. You can avoid or minimize such relfections by selecting car and camera positions carefully, as well as by using a polarizing filter. However, don't be tempted to try and remove all reflections. This could lead to a dull, lifeless image.

PORTFOLIO 98

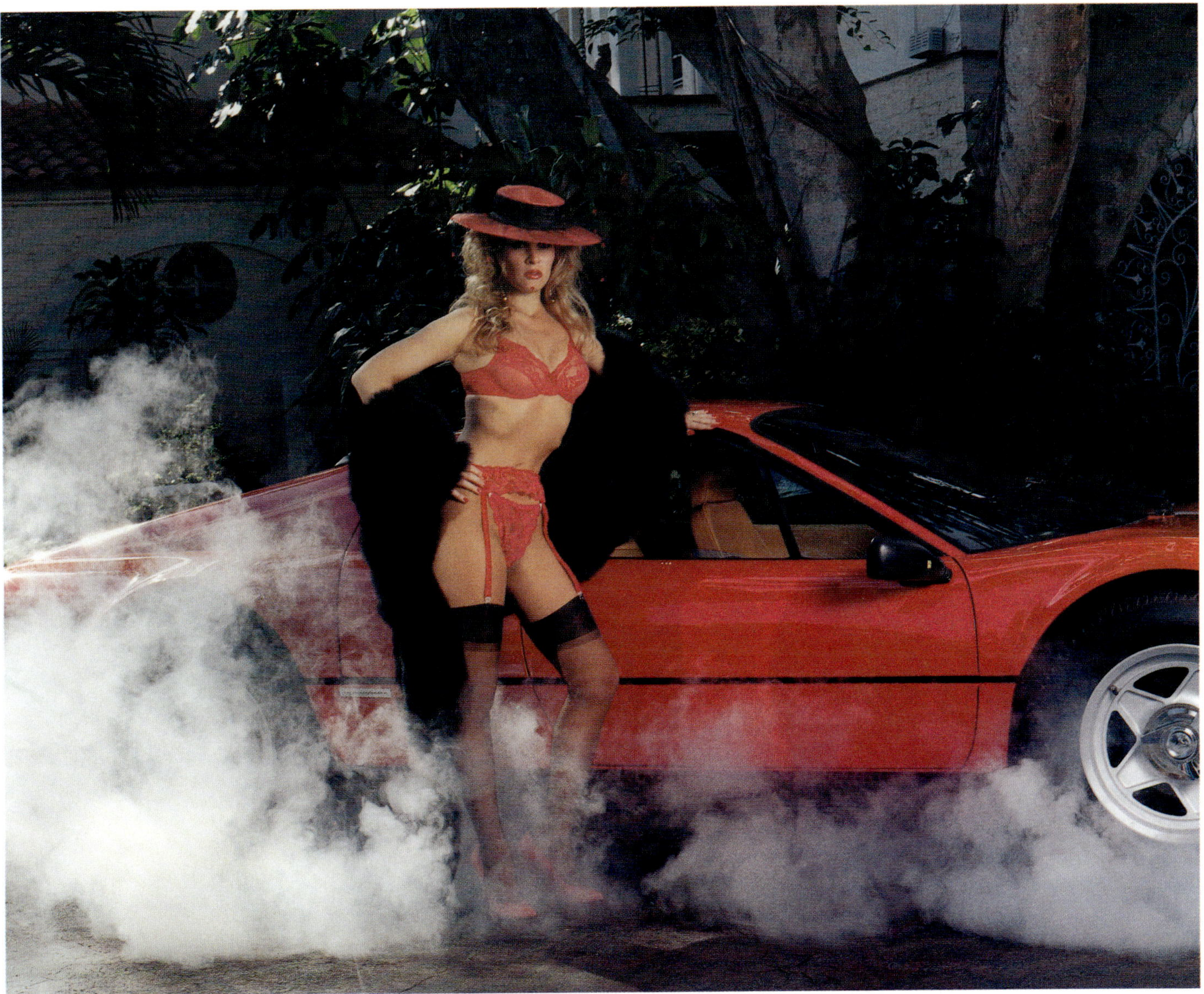

In a studio, the effect provided by a fog or smoke machine is unpredictable. Outdoors, if there is any appreciable wind present, it can be totally uncontrollable. Often, the fog or "smoke" will not localize for a long enough time to allow you to take even one photograph.

Indoors, you can generally take at least two or three shots before the vapor rises to a height where it begins to block too much of the subject from view. Outdoors, you'll be lucky to get one shot before the vapor either invades too much of the subject or dissipates. To get the image reproduced here, we had to shoot 28 frames of film.

Main light was a 4x7-foot light panel, backlit by a flash in a 4-inch bowl reflector and placed about 30 degrees to the right of camera-subject axis. A 3x4-foot plastic mirror was placed about 50 degrees to the left of camera-subject axis and used to accent the subject's body. The daylight was used as fill light, being deliberately underexposed by one *f*-stop.

A standard lens was used, and a warming filter. Exposure was 1/30 second at *f*-8.

99 PORTFOLIO

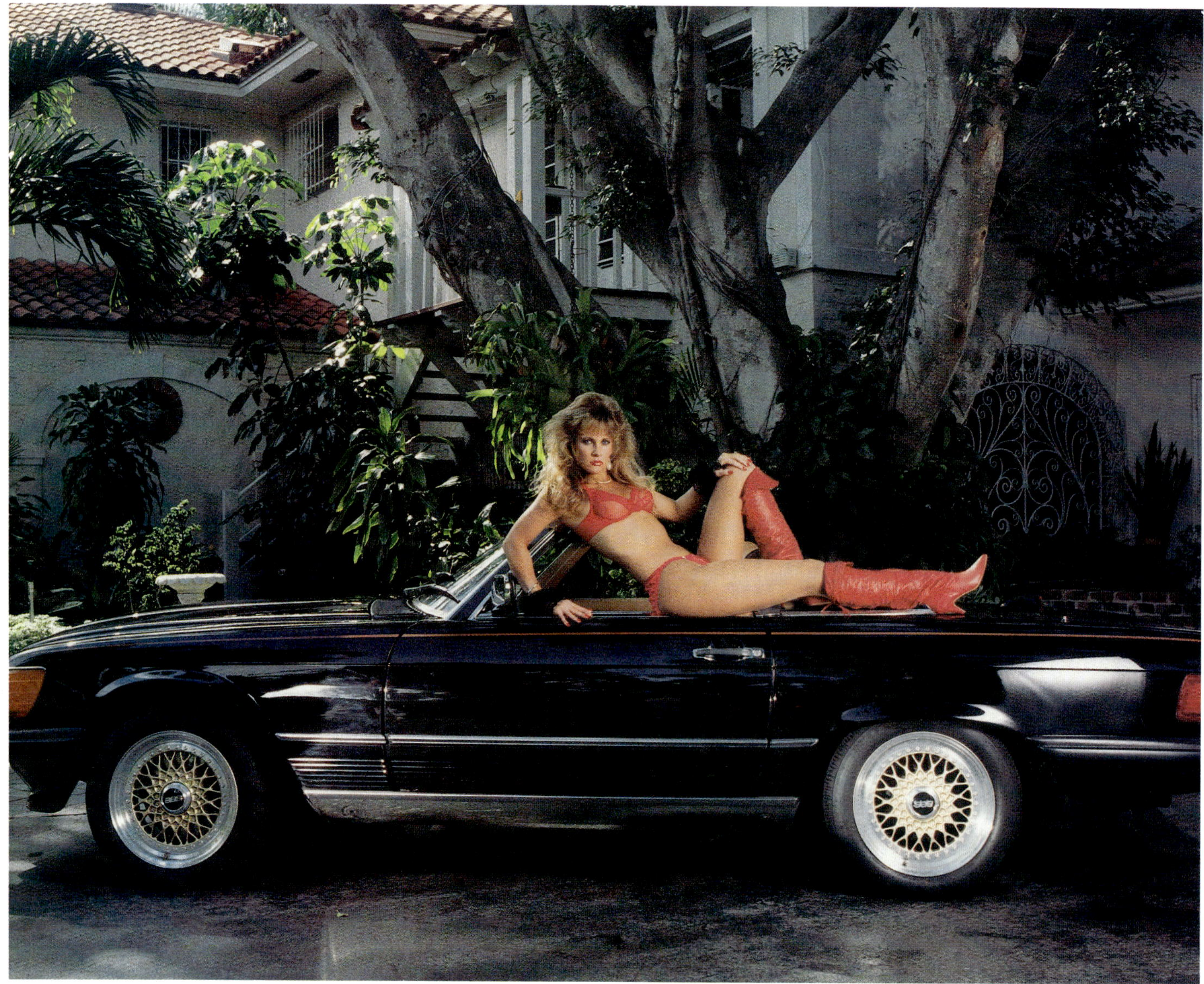

Although flash was the primary source of illumination for this photo, the background was allowed to be recorded somewhat lighter than in previous photos. We wanted more of the background to be visible in this shot.

The camera's *f*-stop was adjusted based upon a meter reading taken solely of the illumination coming from the flash. An incident-light meter reading was also taken of the ambient light. Our Hasselblad shutter was set to twice the speed indicated by the meter. The end result was a fairly accurate flash exposure and a slightly underexposed background.

If we had wanted the background even darker, we would have increased the shutter speed while leaving the *f*-stop setting unchanged. If we had wanted the background lighter, the *f*-stop would again not be changed and we would have decreased the shutter speed.

Exercising such control over a situation can give you a variety of results.

Main light was a 4x7-foot light panel, backlit by a flash in a 4-inch bowl reflector. It was placed to the right of camera-subject axis. A 3x4-foot plastic mirror was used to the left of the camera to add some specular reflections at the front end of the car. The daylight acted as both a fill light and a rim light for the subject. Exposure was 1/15 second at *f*-11.

PORTFOLIO 100

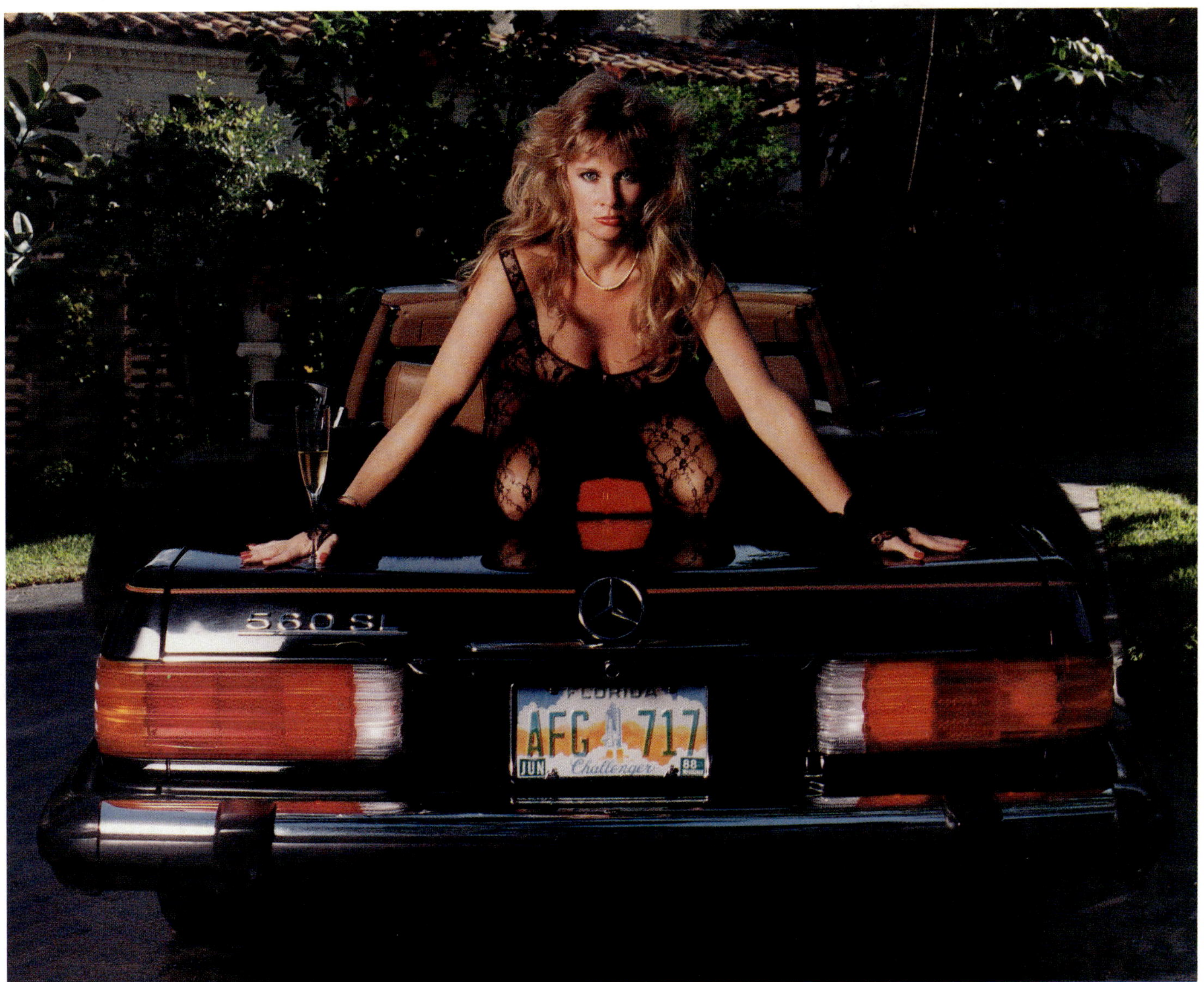

Photographing a subject on a black car can present some problems. Often there is a tendency to overlight the scene. Don't do it! To bring some life to a shiny, black object, lots of light is not the answer. Rather, you should concentrate on the careful placement of reflections. Large areas of soft reflection are best. Avoid small specular reflections.

In this image, the subject is well lit and the car has just enough reflections to give it life and shape. To further define the vehicle and add more color to the image, we turned on the car's brake lights and tail lights. Exposure for the subject was based on an incident-light flash-meter reading and exposure for the car's lights was based on a separate meter reading, taken only of these lights.

Main light for the subject was a 4x7-foot light panel, backlit by a flash in a 4-inch bowl reflector. It was placed about 45 degrees to the left of camera-subject axis. The flash head was connected to a 1000-watt-second power pack. A 3x4-foot plastic mirror was used as fill light to the right of camera-subject axis. Daylight added more fill light, as well as some well placed reflections on the car.

A medium telephoto lens was used, and a warming filter. Exposure was 1/15 second at *f*-11.